CORE ISSUES IN POLICING

PEARSON
Education

We work with leading authors to develop the
strongest educational materials in law, sociology and
psychology, bringing cutting-edge thinking and best
learning practice to a global market.

Under a range of well-known imprints, including
Longman, we craft high quality print and electronic
publications which help readers to understand and
apply their content, whether studying or at work.

To find out more about the complete range of our
publishing please visit us on the World Wide Web at:
www.pearsoneduc.com

CORE ISSUES IN POLICING

Second Edition

Edited by

FRANK LEISHMAN

BARRY LOVEDAY

STEPHEN P. SAVAGE

PEARSON

Longman

Harlow, England • London • New York • Boston • San Francisco • Toronto • Sydney • Singapore • Hong Kong
Tokyo • Seoul • Taipei • New Delhi • Cape Town • Madrid • Mexico City • Amsterdam • Munich • Paris • Milan

Pearson Education Limited

Edinburgh Gate
Harlow
Essex CM20 2JE
England

and Associated Companies througout the world

Visit us on the World Wide Web at
www.pearsoned.co.uk

First published in Great Britain in 1996
Second edition published in 2000

© Pearson Education Limited, 1996, 2000

The rights of Frank Leishman, Barry Loveday and Stephen Savage to be
identified as authors of this work have been asserted by them in accordance
with the Copyright, Designs and Patents Act 1988.

ISBN 0 582 36986 X

British Library Cataloguing-in-Publication Data
A CIP catalogue record for this book can be obtained from the British Library

Library of Congress Cataloging-in-Publication Data
A catalog record for this book can be obtained from the Library of Congress

Transferred to digital print on demand, 2007
Typeset by 7 in 10/12pt New Baskerville
Printed and bound by CPI Antony Rowe, Eastbourne

Contents

PART III ACCOUNTABILITY, ORGANISATION AND MANAGEMENT

Contributors

Jennifer Brown is currently Director of the Forensic Psychology Masters Programme at the University of Surrey. Previously the research manager at Hampshire Constabulary and a Principal Lecturer at the University of Portsmouth, she has published widely on gendered aspects of occupational culture and occupational stress within the police service.

Ray Bull is Professor of Psychology at the University of Portsmouth. An acknowledged international expert on witness testimony, he (along with Horncastle) was the author of a major study of the effectiveness of the Metropolitan Police's 'Skills Training' programme in the 1980s. He is founder co-editor of the international journal *Expert Evidence*.

Tony Butler is Chief Constable of Gloucestershire and a frequent contributor to policing and public sector management journals. His book, *Police Management*, appeared in its second edition in 1993.

Sarah Charman is a Lecturer in Criminology at the Institute of Criminal Justice Studies at the University of Portsmouth. She took her Masters degree in Social Research at the University of Bangor in 1994. She has published a variety of articles and chapters on the politics of policy-making and Chief Police Officers.

Julie Cherryman is a Senior Lecturer at the University of Portsmouth, working mainly as a Course Tutor on the MSc course 'Child Forensic Studies: Psychology and Law'. She is currently researching investigative interviewing.

Stephen Cope is Principal Lecturer in Public Policy at the University of Portsmouth. He has authored a variety of articles on policy-making and has a specialist interest in local authority finances, on which he took his doctorate. He is currently researching governance in the public sector.

Daniel Gilling is Senior Lecturer in Criminology at the University of Plymouth. He has published variously in the areas of crime prevention, multi-agency policing and social policy. He is author of *Crime Prevention: Theory, Policy and Politics* (1997, UCL Press).

Les Johnston is Professor of Criminology and Director of Research at the Institute of Criminal Justice Studies, University of Portsmouth. He has research and teaching interests in public, commercial and civil policing, the politics of law and order, criminal justice policy and social theory and the state. His publications include *The Rebirth of Private Policing* (1992, Routledge), *Policing Britain: Risk Security and Governance* (2000, Longman) and (with Clifford Shearing and Philip Stenning) *Governing Diversity: Explorations in Policing* (forthcoming, Routledge).

Frank Leishman, formerly a Senior Lecturer at the (then) Institute of Police and Criminological Studies at the University of Portsmouth, is Principal Lecturer in Criminology at the Southampton Institute. A former police officer, he has published widely on Anglo-Japanese policing issues.

Barry Loveday is Principal Lecturer and a Deputy Director at the Institute of Criminal Justice Studies, University of Portsmouth. He has published extensively on policing issues and is a specialist on police accountability.

Ian McKenzie is Principal Lecturer in Police Studies and a Deputy Director at the Institute of Criminal Justice Studies, University of Portsmouth. A former Metropolitan Police Superintendent, he served for two years as force psychologist with the Fort Worth Police, Texas. He is co-author (with Pat Gallagher) of *Behind the Uniform* (1989) and is a frequent contributor to a range of academic journals. He is also co-editor of the *International Journal of Police Science and Management.*

Rob Mawby is Professor of Criminology and Criminal Justice at the University of Plymouth. A noted scholar of comparative criminal justice studies, he is author (with Sandra Walklate) of *Critical Victimology* (Sage) and Editor of *Policing across the world: issues for the 21st Century* (1999, UCL Press).

Robert Reiner is Professor of Criminology in the Law Department, London School of Economics. He is co-author of *The Blue-Coated Worker* (Cambridge University Press), *Politics of the Police* (Wheatsheaf, 1985: 2nd edition, 1992; 3rd edition, 2000), *Chief Constables* (Oxford University Press, 1991), and editor (with M. Cross) of *Law and Order* (Macmillan, 1991); (with S. Spencer) *Accountable Effectiveness, Empowerment and Equity* (IPPR, 1993); (with M. Maguire and R. Morgan) *The Oxford Book of Criminology* (Oxford University Press, 1994, 1997).

Stephen P. Savage is Professor of Criminology and Director of the Institute of Criminal Justice Studies. University of Portsmouth. He has published widely on policing and criminal justice policy. His publications include *The Theories of Talcott Parsons* (1981, Macmillan) and, as co-editor, *Public Policy under Blair* (2000, Macmillan). He is co-editor of the *International Journal of the Sociology of Law.*

P.A.J. Waddington is Professor of Political Sociology at the University of Reading. He has published extensively on all aspects of policing and especially on armed and public order policing. He is the author of *The Strong Arm of the Law* (1991, Clarendon), *Calling the Police* (1993, Avebury), *Liberty and Order: Public Order Policing in a Capital City* (1994, UCL Press) and *Policing Citizens: Authority and Rights* (1999, UCL Press). In 1992 he conducted an official inquiry into the policing of the Boipatong massacre in South Africa, under the auspices of the Goldstone Commission.

Neil Walker has been Professor of Legal and Constitutional Theory at the University of Aberdeen since 1996. His main interests lie in the relationship between state and non-state policing and in the constitutional dimension of multi-level governance in Britain and the European Union.

Sandra Walklate is Professor of Criminology at Manchester Metropolitan University and was formerly Reader in Criminology at Keele University. She co-authored (with Mike Brogden and Tony Jefferson) *Introducing Policework* (1988) and is the author of *Victimology* (1989). She wrote *Gender and Crime* (1995, Harvester Wheatsheaf) and *Understanding Criminology* (1998, Open University).

Ian Waters was until recently a senior lecturer in criminology at Nottingham Trent University. Prior to that he occupied the position of senior research officer in Hampshire Constabulary, where he first began his research into quality of service and police performance. His other academic interests include police complaints and discipline, and war crimes. He has written articles for journals such as the *International Journal of Police Science and Management* and the *British Journal of Criminology*. He has recently returned to working for the police service in the area of performance management.

Tom Williamson is Deputy Chief Constable of Nottinghamshire and Visiting Professor at the Institute of Criminal Justice Studies, University of Portsmouth. A chartered psychologist, he has published a number of papers on the right to silence and police interrogation practice.

Tom Wood is Deputy Chief Constable of Lothian and Borders Police, with responsibility for crime policy. He is a member of the Crime Committee of the Association of Chief Police Officers in Scotland and a frequent contributor to drugs debates in Scotland.

Alan Wright is a Senior Lecturer in Police Studies at the Institute of Criminal Justice Studies, University of Portsmouth. He has published a variety of papers on police governance, human rights and organised crime and has been advisor on integrity in policing to police forces in Central and Eastern Europe.

List of figures and tables

Acknowledgements

The editors would like to thank our publishers for their support and encouragement throughout this project. We would also like to thank all of the contributors for the quality of their chapters. We would reserve, however, our special thanks for Kellie Diggins, for her outstanding commitment (and patience) throughout the preparation of this second edition.

Crown copyright is reproduced with the permission of the Controller of HMSO.

AC	Audit Commission
ACC	Assistant Chief Constable
ACMD	Advisory Council on the Misuse of Drugs
ACPO	Association of Chief Police Officers
ACPOS	Association of Chief Police Officers in Scotland
APA	Association of Police Authorities
BCS	British Crime Survey
BV	best value
CDA	Crime and Disorder Act
CI	cognitive interview
CI	constabulary independence
CJPOA	Criminal Justice and Public Order Act
CM	conversation management
CPD	crime prevention departments
CPO	crime prevention officers
CPOSA	Chief Police Officers' Staff Association
CSR	Comprehensive Spending Review
DAT	drug action team
DPPB	District Policing Partnership Board
DTOA	Drug Trafficking Offences Act
DTTO	Drug Treatment and Testing Order
EDU	European Drugs Unit
EFQM	European Foundation for Quality Management
EU	European Union
GTR	Getting Things Right
HMCIC	Her Majesty's Chief Inspector of Constabulary
HMIC	Her Majesty's Inspectorate of Constabulary
JHA	Justice and Home Affairs
KO	key objective
KPI	key performance indicator
LLDE	low level drug enforcement
LPA	local police authority
MDA	Misuse of Drugs Act
MPS	Metropolitan Police Service
NCIS	National Criminal Intelligence Service
NCS	National Crime Squad
NPM	new public management
NPT	National Police Training

NVQ	National Vocational Qualification
OPR	Operational Policing Review
PA	police authority
PACE	Police and Criminal Evidence Act
PBR	plastic baton round
PCCG	Police Community Consultative Group
PI	performance indicator
PMC	Performance Management Committee
PMCA	Police and Magistrates' Courts Act
PRU	Police Resources Unit
PSRCP	Public Safety Radio Communication Project
PTSD	post-traumatic stress disorder
QOS	quality of service
SCPV	statement of common purpose and values
SPD	strategic policy document
VFM	value for money
ZTP	zero tolerance policing

Chapter 1

Introduction: core issues in policing revisited

FRANK LEISHMAN, BARRY LOVEDAY AND STEPHEN P. SAVAGE

In the Introduction to the first edition of this book, completed in 1995, we stated that the publication of a text on core issues in policing, in the climate that then prevailed, could hardly have been more appropriately timed. Indeed, from the standpoint of the mid-1990s, there was much evidence of an emerging or immanent 'watershed' in the history of British policing. A service that had survived remarkably intact for many decades, still bearing many of the distinctive features of its nineteenth-century origins, was very much under siege. Challenges to the status quo of policing at that time came from a myriad of quarters and threatened to transform fundamentally the ethos of the 'British way' of policing, from the way the police organisation was structured and governed, to the working conditions of police officers and the very definition of what those officers were there to *do*. As the earlier edition documented, there were various initiatives and developments which had placed the police service if not on a 'war footing' then at least on the defensive. The Conservative government's pursuit of *value for money* (VFM), evident throughout the 1980s in other areas of public policy (Savage *et al.* 1994), was beginning to impact seriously on the police organisation for the first time. In a phrase used at the time (*ibid.*), the 'party was over' for the police service, in the sense that the message went out from government that they could no longer expect privileged treatment in comparison with other parts of the public sector in relation to demonstrating 'Economy, Efficiency and Effectiveness'. The major thrust of VFM was to energise the principles of 'New Public Management' and institutionalise the *performance culture* within the police service. Alongside VFM, and fully consistent with its ethos, came two Home-Office initiated 'root and branch' reviews of the police service, the *Sheehy Inquiry* into police roles and responsibilities and what was known as the *Posen Review* of police functions. The former recommended wholesale reform of the conditions of employment and rank structure of the service, whilst the latter sought to make a distinction within policework between 'core police functions', which only police officers could undertake, and 'ancillary tasks', which could potentially be delivered by non-police bodies. Though, as Mawby argues in Chapter 7 of this volume, this may have been exposed as a 'seductive myth', nevertheless, taken together, these reviews posed a number of threats to established arrangements. Amongst these were the spectre of *privatisation* of police functions and the introduction of schemes such as performance-related pay, viewed widely as totally inappropriate to policing.

Even more controversial than VFM, *Sheehy* and *Posen*, however, was the passage through Parliament of the Police and Magistrates' Courts Act 1994 (PMCA). What this legislation introduced was a fundamental reform of *police governance* and, above all, a restructuring of the relationship between the police service and central and local government. It introduced radical changes to the role and constitution of the local police authorities and gave the Home Secretary new powers to set national priorities for police forces. Although its final draft involved some significant concessions (for example, over the Home Secretary's powers to appoint chairs of police authorities) – after a partially successful campaign launched out of an alliance of police chiefs, the local authorities and senior parliamentarians – the PMCA nevertheless entailed some quite radical departures, even if much lay in the *potential* they offered for radical change. A central initiative was the establishment of 'local policing plans': the police authorities were to have a formal responsibility in the process of setting local policing priorities, even if the scope for that involvement has been very much the subject of debate (Loveday, Chapter 13 in this volume; Jones and Newburn, 1994). Whichever way, there is little doubt that the PMCA opened up new chapters in the agenda of police governance and signalled that things would never be the same again. Together with the other developments mentioned, it appeared that we were on the verge of a 'new policing paradigm'.

Half a decade onwards, however, we are confronted with challenges to British policing which are, in many ways, even more radical. It is arguably the case that, taken together, they present an even more challenging environment for British policing than did the reform agenda of the mid-1990s. The arrival of the Labour government in 1997, despite the close relationship which had formed between Labour in opposition and the police associations throughout the early- to mid-1990s (Savage and Charman, 2000), has not led to any reduction of pressure on the police service. What distinguishes the present scenario from that prevailing in the 1990s is the sheer *scope* of the challenges to the status quo of policing in Britain as we enter the new millennium. This has come about through a combination of government initiatives (no less cost-inspired than under the Conservatives) aimed either directly or indirectly at the police, changes in the policing environment, including economic and social change, transnational and international developments and a series of specific and controversial events which have impacted heavily on the standing of the police and on police organisations themselves. The chapters contained in this book map out in a variety of ways the range of challenges which together constitute the current catalogue of *core issues in policing*. By way of an introduction, we shall highlight just some of these.

A development which has sent and will continue to send shock waves across the police service is the legislation which stands as the hallmark of New Labour's crime strategy, the Crime and Disorder Act 1998 (CDA). This comprehensive and far-reaching Act has within its sights a range of bodies in addition to the police – above all, the local authorities – and their role in crime reduction, but in many respects it is the police service which is most affected by the measures contained in the legislation. As Chapter 8, by Daniel Gilling, makes clear, this is not least because the police have to an extent been relegated in the government's mind from being *the primary* agency in the fight against crime to becoming just *one* agency amongst many. The message contained in the CDA is that, if anything, it is the local authorities which have primary responsibility for crime strategy and local community safety policy. A related challenge to and for the police service is that, as never before, the police are being required to work in *partnership* with other agencies in tackling crime and disorder. This will inevitably entail a degree of *power sharing* and loss of control and autonomy over many areas of decision making (such as cautioning policy), areas which have to date been monopolised or at least dominated by the police and their chief officers. As we shall see at a number of stages in this book, the CDA presents some major dilemmas and raises some fundamental questions about the role of the police as a crime control agency and enforcer of public order, questions which promise to have a long-lasting impact on the future shape of policing.

A second source of challenge to policing in the new millennium is 'best value'. As Ian Waters makes clear in Chapter 16, the *best value* agenda is in many ways a far more radical framework for decision making in the public sector than VFM, and is to that extent likely to have a deeper impact on the working of the public services than VFM has done, particularly on those services allied to local government. Any ideas that Labour were going to 'ease off the brakes' on public spending and reduce the pressures on the public sector to operate according to the 'performance culture' have been roundly refuted. *Best value* stands as a monument to New Labour's firm commitment to place the public sector under continuing and intensifying scrutiny and the police have been no less exposed to this agenda than the rest of the public services. From the standpoint of policing, *best value* presents many fundamental challenges, but perhaps the biggest threat to the status quo lies with the philosophy of 'what matters is what works'. This apparently simple dictum contains within it a quite radical agenda for service providers in that it allows, even encourages, budget holders at whatever level to focus less on *who* delivers than *what and how* it is delivered. Potential rests in this, for example, for local authorities to purchase some of their 'policing services' from bodies other than the 'public police' if it can be demonstrated that those other bodies offer 'best value' in terms of cost and quality of service. The implications of *best value* are still unfolding, but one clear outcome of this agenda as it takes hold will be the (further) *privatisation* of policing, perhaps to an extent never dared in this area by the Conservatives (see Les Johnston, Chapter 5). Police managers are now on warning that 'if they don't do it, others will'! This is setting in motion a complete rethinking of the way the police service positions itself as a service provider (one reason why virtually every police force in England and Wales has a dedicated 'best value officer'); central to this is a refocusing of performance measurement and performance management. The earlier emphasis on the measurement of resource *inputs* and employee performance *outputs*, is now giving way to a greater attention to the measurement of *outcomes*, the environmental impact of policing on crime reduction, public order, fear of crime, and so on. This reflects that other mantra of New Labour: *evidence-based policy* – policy must increasingly be justified in terms of identifiable and desirable effects, the 'what works' principle in action. What has been taking place as a result has been a 'paradigm shift' in the performance culture, which is posing a huge challenge for police managers and police policy making more generally. Another feature of the best value agenda worthy of mention at this stage is the requirement placed formally on policy makers at local level to engage in processes of *consultation* with consumers of public services in the determination of priorities and the design of service provision. In the policing context, as is made clear in Chapters 3 and 13 in this volume, this has the real potential of again shifting some power of discretion away from chief officers and to bodies *outside* the police service and of challenging the apparently established convention of *constabulary independence* in some interesting ways. In Chapter 4, Robert Reiner suggests that even the media image of policing has shifted to one more appropriate to the 'age of the Audit Commission'!

Another wider policy initiative which is presenting new types of challenges to the police service is the *human rights agenda*. Labour's manifesto for the 1997 General Election committed a Labour government to the full inclusion of the European Convention on Human Rights into UK domestic law. The Human Rights Act 1998 places public authorities under a statutory obligation to respect and abide by the diktats of the Convention. For the police service this can be expected to present new types of problems for operatives, supervisors and managers, especially in the more 'morally ambiguous' areas of policework such as drugs, public order and police use of force (see respectively Leishman and Wood – Chapter 9, Waddington – Chapter 10, and McKenzie – Chapter 11). The exercise of police powers will now come under even closer scrutiny and the potential for legal action on the grounds of abuse of powers under the Human Rights Act is immense. This will have an impact at every level of the police organisation and will need to be reflected in the way officers are *trained, supervised* and *managed*. What makes the human rights question even more telling is that its introduction into British law comes at a time when issues of police *integrity* have been placed firmly back on the policing agenda. When the then Metropolitan Police Commissioner, Sir Paul Condon, announced in 1998 that he was aware of a 'hard core' of over 200 officers who could be labelled as *corrupt*, this was formal acknowledgment that *police corruption*, not a cause of major concern since the mid-1970s, was back with us as a systemic problem within British policing. As Chapter 2, by Tom Williamson, shows, the re-emergence of the issue of police integrity, generated at least in part by the threat of police corruption, is posing a wide range of challenges to contemporary police management.

What police corruption and the challenge of police integrity really expose, however, are fundamental questions over *police culture*. It is the debate over police culture which is particularly acute as we set out the policing agenda for the new millennium. In Chapter 15, Jennifer Brown examines the problems of stress and gender relating to police culture. Very much to the fore in the 1980s in relation to the abuse of police power, police racism is also back with a vengeance as an issue of public concern and political attention. As Sandra Walklate discusses in Chapter 14, the legacy of the *Stephen Lawrence* case has brought central concerns about police culture very much to the surface. The *Macpherson Report* into the events and process surrounding the police investigation into the racially motivated murder of Stephen Lawrence, a young black man killed in London in 1993, undoubtedly stands as one of the most challenging statements on the question of police culture to emerge since the publication of the *Scarman Report* in the early 1980s. On the one hand, *Macpherson* raises the whole question of the extent and depth of *police racism* within the British police service and exposes problems in the *policing of diversity*, issues around which there had grown a degree of complacency in previous years, almost as if they could be catalogued as 'yesterday's problem'. On the other hand, the Report raises some fundamental and disturbingly basic questions about the levels of *competence* of police officers, in this case in the area of investigative skills. As Cherryman and Bull (Chapter 12), Williamson (Chapter 2) and Wright (Chapter 17) argue, criminal investigation remains a 'core' area of policing activity, though still very much open to examination and debate. At root, the problems of policing diversity and of police competence are about the *quality* of policing – an area which, as Chapter 16, by Ian Waters, also makes clear – the performance culture all too often understates or undermines.

A final set of challenges rests with what might be called the *changing geography of police governance*. Labour came into power committed to a programme of *devolution* and *regionalisation*. The former is definitely with us in the shape of the Scottish Parliament and Welsh and Northern Ireland Assemblies, while the latter is emergent and will arrive in full, subject to electoral politics, in the not too distant future. The implications of these developments for British policing are many and complex – not least the question of whether we can continue to use the term *British* policing in the same way ever again. However, it seems clear that police *governance* and *policing structures* will be transformed in a variety of ways as the devolution and regionalisation agendas take shape. On the one hand there will (or at least should) be a degree of *decentralisation* of power from Whitehall to the devolved assemblies and regions. This must involve a continuing readjustment of the role of central government in the 'tripartite' framework of British policing, perhaps in the direction of 'more steering, less rowing' (see Chapter 5 in this volume). On the other hand, perhaps more likely, there will be a process of diminution of the capacity for individual police forces to operate in relative autonomy from one another. Regionalisation will involve the *de facto* creation of *super-forces* with regional level resource allocation and regional level decision making. As the chapters by Butler (Chapter 18), Savage *et al.* (Chapter 3) and Loveday (Chapter 13) make clear, this will create new structures of police governance, presenting a range of new threats and opportunities to future generations of police managers. Neil Walker's extended essay (Chapter 6) raises similar issues in relation to the developing transnational dimension to policing structures.

With all of these challenges to contemporary policing, and others documented in this book, it is difficult to disagree with those who insist that what is now required is a *Royal Commission on the Police*. Policing functions, police governance, police culture and all other core issues in policing should all come under examination in a comprehensive review of the current and future state of British policing. Over the past two decades the two Royal Commissions relating to the police (*Phillips* in 1981 and *Runciman* in 1993) dealt only with specific aspects of policing, given their wider concern with the criminal justice process. Other reviews have been similarly focused and restricted. The closest we have come to a commission of inquiry of the type required, interestingly, is the *Patten Commission* on policing in Northern Ireland. Despite the unique circumstances of the policing of Northern Ireland, the Patten Commission, as Loveday demonstrates (Chapter 13), has shown how it is possible to draw together key challenges and core issues of policing – including governance, integrity, culture, diversity and so on – within a comprehensive framework of analysis and policy formation. The central message of *Patten* was that none of these issues should be taken in isolation and that they should be approached and tackled as interwoven processes. *Core Issues in Policing* and the chapters within it should be seen in the same light.

References

Jones, T. and Newburn, T. (1994) *Democracy in Policing*. London: Policy Studies Institute.

Ryan, M., Savage, S. and Wall, D. (eds) (2000) *Policy Networks in Criminal Justice*. Basingstoke: Macmillan.

Savage, S., Atkinson, R. and Robins, L. (eds) (1994) *Public Policy in Britain*. Basingstoke: Macmillan.

Savage, S. and Charman, S. (2000) 'The Bobby Lobby' in Ryan *et al., op. cit.*

Part I
CONTEXTS

Policing: the changing criminal justice context – twenty-five years of missed opportunities

TOM WILLIAMSON

Introduction: safer criminal justice?

The 1993 Royal Commission on Criminal Justice reached the remarkable conclusion that criminal justice was in good shape. It then made a total of 352 separate recommendations, including changes to the law relating to the right of silence, but, in the main, these recommendations amounted to tinkering. The extant system remained intact.

The superficial manner in which many issues of substance were dismissed was a disappointment to many practitioners and observers of the criminal justice system. In particular, the Report failed to identify that the present system places inadequate emphasis on the needs of the victim and communities. The Royal Commission's report was a defence of the indefensible.

In contrast to the Royal Commission, a journalist, David Rose, reached the conclusion that the criminal justice system was in a state of collapse (Rose, 1996). He investigated miscarriages of justice and went on to conduct a penetrating analysis of the criminal justice system showing not only that there are cases where the innocent have been condemned, but that the most serious offenders are unlikely to be convicted under our present system. In an indication of things to come, he described the national debate on criminal justice as becoming more shrill and mired in archaic cliché. He questioned the traditional views of the liberal left and revenge justice of the right, identifying the need for a new way forward.

The essence of this new way was captured in a soundbite used by the then Shadow Home Secretary, Tony Blair, (*Independent*, 4 December 1993) and then by his successor, Jack Straw, in the successful New Labour campaign during the 1997 general election: 'Tough on crime, tough on the causes of crime.'

Once in government, New Labour quickly set about creating a statutory framework through the Crime and Disorder Act 1998 for their 'third way' approach to law and order (see also Wright, Chapter 17 in this volume).

Is 'tough on crime, tough on the causes of crime' just a soundbite, a cynical political statement designed to appeal simultaneously to liberals and conservatives or does it and the Crime and Disorder Act represent a paradigm shift? If so, to what extent are the changes to criminal justice being led by government or simply reactive and event-driven?

We will address these questions by considering:

(i)   evidence-based policy making as seen in the research basis for the new philosophies in the Act;
(ii) new strategies for the criminal justice system and policing, in particular indicating that it is adapting to the need to provide safer justice in which the public can have greater confidence;
(iii) the ethical, economic, political and scientific pressures which will be the drivers for further change.

Is New Labour's crime policy evidence-based?

Professor Geoffrey Stephenson, an informed observer of the psychology of criminal justice (Stephenson, 1992), discussing the trend or development in forensic psychology which has given him the least satisfaction recently said:

> The way in which the Home Office repeatedly kowtows to political pressures, blithely disregarding, even discarding, the academic findings, frequently sponsored by themselves, is thoroughly depressing. Could psychologists have done more to advertise the evidence which should inform policy? It is difficult to say, but informed sentencing and penal policy has certainly taken a hammering over the past 15 years or so, and to be sure, we could have been more vocal ourselves.
>
> (Stephenson, 1999: 6)

A similar point has been made by David Faulkner, a retired senior Home Office official, who pointed to the wide fluctuations in policy between Home Secretaries, including those of the same party. 'Within a period of less than 12 months much of the programme had been politically discredited and seems to have been largely abandoned' (*Guardian*, 16 April 1994).

Farrington (1998) traces the antecedents of the new philosophies reflected in the Crime and Disorder Act. He classifies major methods of crime prevention into four categories with reference to recent papers which best describe a particular approach:

- developmental prevention which is designed to inhibit criminal potential, targeting risk and using protective factors discovered in studies of human development (Tremblay and Craig, 1995);
- community prevention which is designed to change the social conditions such as families, peers, social norms and organisations that influence offending in communities (Hope, 1995);
- situational prevention which targets the physical environment in order to reduce opportunities for crime (Clarke, 1995);
- criminal justice prevention refers to traditional deterrence, incapacitation and rehabilitation strategies operated by criminal justice agencies (Tonry and Farrington, 1995a).

Farrington argues that over the last 25 years successive Home Secretaries have emphasised situational and criminal justice prevention rather than tackling the root causes of crime addressed in developmental and community prevention approaches.

The dismal criminological discourse

In order to understand why developmental and community prevention was so widely ignored, one has to turn for a partial explanation to the dismal science of criminology which has until recently deliberately ignored the role of the individual, family and community in effective crime prevention. Although some criminologists have long argued that crime policies focused on reducing opportunities for crime, such as target hardening, would reap more rewards in cost-benefit terms than offender-based measures, generally speaking, criminology had not been 'for' anything. In its prevailing discourse, it was anti-everything and most courses in criminology finished by concluding that nothing worked (Charman and Savage, 1999; Bean, 1998). This discourse may have been intellectually stimulating but from a policy-formulation perspective was totally sterile. Fortunately, this has begun to change recently. Charman and Savage (1999) describe a heated debate within left-wing criminology over the issue of how to approach crime which has laid some of the foundations of Labour's new discourse. The radical-left paradigm for crime analysis tended to see the crime control industry, of which the police were a significant part, as being more of a problem than crime itself (Young, 1997: 475, quoted in Charman and Savage, 1999). This was reflected in their view of the police. They were more concerned about whether the police were accountable than whether they were effective.

The change came about with a group of criminologists known as 'Left Realists' who argued that crime really was a problem and that it disproportionately harmed the weakest and most vulnerable in the community. This kind of debate began to influence the thinking of New Labour but was also evident in consultation papers emanating from the Home Office which began to reflect a change of mind-set.

In March 1997 a Home Office Green Paper, *Preventing Children Offending* (Home Office, 1997a), was published which proposed identifying children at risk of offending at an early age and referring them to programmes designed to help them stay clear of crime. The new strategy would be delivered by local agencies working together in partnership in Child Crime Teams. The Green Paper also proposed giving courts a new power to make a Parental Control Order requiring parents to exercise care and control over their children. Would this new emphasis on developmental and community prevention succeed?

The British Psychological Society responded to the consultative document by endorsing initiatives for early prevention as being the most cost-effective method of crime prevention and pointed to later interventions, such as social skills training in prison, as also being effective (see Loeber and Farrington, 1998). The Society also pointed out that individual difference factors are important in youth offending and account should be taken of low intelligence, impulsiveness and daring or risk-taking. These characteristics have been recognised by the new government in a paper published by the Prime Minister based on a report by his Social Exclusion Unit on how to:

> develop integrated and sustainable approaches to the problems of the worst housing estates, including crime, drugs, unemployment, community breakdown, and bad schools etc. (Blair, 1998)

The British Psychological Society has argued that an up-to-date knowledge base that should underpin developmental crime preventive measures which would address these issues was sadly lacking and little fundamental research on the causes of delinquency had been funded in the United Kingdom for many years.

The Labour government published its own White Paper, *No More Excuses – A New Approach to Tackling Youth Crime in England and Wales* (Home Office, 1997b). Despite the change in government, the proposals were similar in certain key respects. First, to stop children at risk from getting involved in crime and to prevent early criminal behaviour from escalating into persistent or serious offending. Second, Youth Offending Teams of social workers, probation officers, police officers, education and health authority staff would engage in prevention, assessment and supervision work. There would be Child Safety Orders and a Child Curfew Scheme.

The Crime and Disorder Act 1998

The Crime and Disorder Act has been described in Whitehall as a 'Christmas Tree' Bill. Anything could be hung on it (Travis, 1998). It is, therefore, difficult to present a total or logical description of the Act, but those parts of the Act which address the social exclusion issues which have been mentioned so far in this chapter are reflected in the measures to:

- tackle youth crime and nip youth offending in the bud;
- place joint responsibility for cutting crime and disorder on the police and local authorities;
- prevent anti-social behaviour that causes alarm, distress and harassment;
- protect the public from sex offenders;
- reduce delays in the criminal justice system.

The then Home Office Minister, Alun Michael, said that £250 million had been allocated under the government's Comprehensive Spending Review to be targeted on the underlying causes of crime: 'Social exclusion, under performance at school, peer pressure, family breakdown are all contributory factors' (Michael, 1998a).

New targets have also been provided to tackle delays in youth justice. The average time taken to deal with persistent young offenders was 142 days from arrest to sentence. The new targets include two days from arrest to charge, seven days from charge to first appearance, 14 days from verdict to sentence, and are intended to halve the time it takes from arrest to sentence. This was one of five key pledges which the government set for this Parliament. They also produced a ten-point contract which referred to being tough on crime and appointing a 'Drug Czar' to co-ordinate the fight against drugs (Government's Annual Report, 1998).

Under the Crime and Disorder Act 1998, local authorities and the police together with other 'responsible authorities' have a joint requirement to consult and publish a Crime and Disorder Strategy based on a local crime audit which must be closely focused on the needs of individual communities, e.g. individual town centres or estates, rural areas, etc. The intention is to empower local communities to identify and tackle problems of concern to them. The published document would include details of:

- co-operating persons and bodies;
- the crime and disorder audit and analysis;
- the strategy with its objectives, including short and long-term performance targets.

Progress would be monitored and a fresh audit conducted and new strategy published at the end of each three-year period.

It was intended that there would be a role for Her Majesty's Inspectors of Constabulary, other inspectorates and the Audit Commission in evaluating the new arrangements.

The new arrangements have given rise to concern about sharing information between agencies but the Act removes any doubt about the power of agencies to disclose relevant data, providing the data have been dealt with in ways which are consistent with European data protection legislation. The government published Guidance on the new Act. The new local strategies are now in place. The Guidance underlines the need for sustainable partnerships and emphasises a commitment to working together.

This flagship legislation is having the effect of forcing chief constables who see enforcement as their core business to rethink crime-reduction strategies. Community safety is being pulled in from the margins of policing to take a more central role in a multi-agency context, where crime reduction is the core business of all the agencies and not just that of the police working alone. This should pave the way for more robust targets for crime-reduction outcomes which would be shared between agencies, instead of narrow and easily manipulated output measures for one agency, such as crime clear-up rates, as an indicator of police effectiveness.

Safer and more responsive criminal justice?

Miscarriages of justice led to the the Royal Commission on Criminal Justice 1993 which recommended, *inter alia,* that the power of the Home Secretary to refer cases to the Court of Appeal under section 17 of the Criminal Appeal Act 1968 should be removed and a new body should be created. The role of the new body would be:

- to consider allegations put to it that a miscarriage of justice may have occurred;
- to ensure that any further investigation called for is launched;
- to supervise that investigation if conducted by the police; and
- where there are reasons for supposing that a miscarriage of justice might have occurred, to refer the case to the Court of Appeal.

It was intended that the new body should be independent of the court structure. The Criminal Cases Review Commission was set up under the Criminal Appeal Act 1995. It currently has 14 members from a wide variety of backgrounds who consider whether or not there is a real possibility that the conviction, finding, verdict or sentence would not be upheld if a referral back to the Court of Appeal were made. To establish that there is a real possibility of an appeal succeeding regarding a conviction there has to be:

- an argument or evidence which has not been raised during the trial or at appeal, or
- exceptional circumstances.

To establish that there is a real possibility of an appeal succeeding against a sentence there has to be:

- a legal argument or information about the individual, or the offence, which was not raised in court during the trial or at appeal.

The Commission can only consider, other than in exceptional circumstances, cases in which an appeal through the ordinary judicial appeal process has failed. Once a decision is taken to refer a case to the relevant court of appeal, the Commission has no further involvement.

· The Commission began handling casework in March 1997. By March the following year the Commission had received nearly 1,400 cases. Over 300 had been reviewed and of those 12 had been referred to the relevant courts of appeal, and of those, two appeals were heard and were successful. The new arrangements appear to be making a positive and independent contribution to safer justice representing an improvement on the politically controlled process which preceded it when the work was conducted by Home Office officials.

New aims and objectives for the criminal justice system

As part of the government's Comprehensive Spending Review, new overarching aims and objectives that will shape policing in the next millennium were drafted by Home Office and Treasury Officials and announced by the then Home Office Minister, Alun Michael (1998b), after very limited consultation with the service. This could have been problematic had it not been for the fact that there is considerable support for the new aims.

The new overarching aims and objectives include four elements:

- a statement of purpose;

- a set of guiding principles;
- three specific aims;
- detailed objectives to meet those aims.

The statement of purpose is:

- to help secure a safe and just society in which the rights and responsibilities of individuals, families and communities are properly balanced.

There are seven guiding principles outlining the way in which the police should carry out their functions. These include acting:

- with integrity;
- through partnership;
- in ways which reflect local priorities and are acceptable to local communities;
- efficiently and effectively.

The aims are to:

- promote safety and reduce disorder;
- reduce crime and the fear of crime;
- contribute to delivering justice in a way which secures and maintains public confidence in the rule of law.

In a joint statement by the Home Secretary, Lord Chancellor and Attorney General on 21 July 1998, the government announced its intention to provide a clear strategic direction to the criminal justice system in England and Wales. The statement pointed out that the system accounts for about £11 billion of public expenditure annually. The overarching aims for the system as a whole are:

- to reduce crime and the fear of crime, and their social and economic costs; and
- to dispense justice fairly and efficiently, and to promote confidence in the rule of law.

Whilst recognising that the attempt to ensure coherent direction must not interfere with the independence of those areas in which it would be improper to exert government control, it is intended that the government will publish for the criminal justice system as a whole:

- a three-year strategic plan;
- an annual forward business plan;
- an annual report of performance against objectives.

The government commissioned a review of the Crown Prosecution Service which examined, *inter alia*, what was meant by the 'Criminal Justice System'. The report argued:

'If the word "system" is used in its proper meaning of a complex whole, an organised body of connected parts, there is as yet no such entity as a "criminal justice

system" in England and Wales. There are separate bodies or agencies which all contribute to the aim of bringing to justice those who have committed offences against
the criminal law and which work together, to a greater or lesser extent ... These
bodies or agencies are the product of their different histories and thus, while they
contribute to that common aim, have different purposes of their own to achieve.'
This reiterates a statement made in the mid-1980s by Home Office researchers.

(Moxon, 1995)

The Glidewell report conceded: 'Whether or not there is a criminal justice
system there is undoubtedly a criminal justice process' (Glidewell, 1998: 121).

The Crown Prosecution System has since undergone a reorganisation,
local boundaries are now co-terminous with police boundaries in an attempt
to provide a more responsive prosecution service.

Developments in restorative justice

Williamson (1996) argued for new paradigms of justice 'where retribution is
replaced by an emphasis on restoration'. Former Home Office Minister Alun
Michael desired a youth justice system which promoted the 'three Rs' with
young offenders:

- restoration and apology to the victim;
- reintegration into the law-abiding community;
- responsibility on the part of offenders and parents.

Some police forces are now developing approaches to youth offending
based on concepts of 'restorative justice'. The Royal Commission on Criminal
Justice failed to identify that the present system places inadequate emphasis
on the needs of the victim and communities. It is focused almost entirely on
the offender. The offence is against the state and not against the victim. It is
an entirely adversarial arrangement, based on the premise of punishment and
blame, not on restoration. By design it encourages denial and deceit by
offenders instead of accepting responsibility for what they have done. It is also
both slow and expensive. Williamson (1996) has argued: 'The high level of
recidivism generated by the present system is ample evidence of its manifest
failure and the imperative for finding an alternative which works better.'

Restorative justice is an attempt to ameliorate some of the inadequacies of
the current criminal justice system. There is a shared understanding among
those working within the restorative justice framework that crime cannot be
solved by the police alone and that agencies and communities must work in
partnership. The processes which have been developed require all parties
with a stake in the offence to come together to resolve collectively how to
deal with the aftermath of the offence, and the implications for the future. In
contrast to an adversarial system of justice, there is far greater victim and
community consideration and it fully engages the offender.

One of the key aspects of restorative justice is the conference, and it is at
the conference that the offender is confronted with the harm he or she has
caused. It requires the victim and the community as well as the offender to

meet in a safe environment. The offender is given the opportunity to accept responsibility for the harm done as the conference examines the real causes and seeks practical solutions.

In examining the restorative justice model, it is important to ask what victims want from a system of justice. What victims really want are the things which are denied them in the adversarial system of justice. Williamson (1998) considers, on the basis of experiments in restorative justice being conducted in Nottinghamshire, that what victims appear to want is:

● support;
● to know what's happening;
● to be heard and taken seriously;
● to know 'why me?';
● was it random or was I targeted?;
● a quick resolution;
● to know it won't happen again;
● a closure to the episode.

Williamson considers that communities want similar things; they want:

● support when they feel their communities have been 'ravaged' by crime;
● to know what is happening;
● to know why their community is subject to crime;
● a quick resolution;
● reassurance that it will not happen again;
● to reduce the level of fear of crime and encourage a sense of safety.

Perhaps the most important thing is what restorative justice offers to offenders. They want many of the same things: support, to know what is happening, and to be heard and taken seriously. They want to be treated fairly and with respect. They want a quick resolution and sense of closure. They also want the opportunity to regain the trust of their parents, family and community.

Restorative justice principles have been applied to the police activity of cautioning. This closely fits the new overarching aim for the service in that it seeks to establish a balanced approach between the victim, community and offender by providing the opportunity for them all to become involved in finding solutions to the issue that brought them together. It is intended that all the participants should gain tangible benefits from their involvement in this form of justice.

Victims are empowered through the process as they become active participants and not passive observers. Every effort should be made by the offender to repair the harm suffered by victims. Communities are empowered to play a more positive role and become more resilient to crime.

Restorative justice also gets closer to the aims of International Human Rights (Williamson, 1998). There are clearly many issues which will have to be explored as more experience of restorative justice is gained. Can this form of mediation be an alternative to criminal justice? A number of special-interest groups in England and Wales have come together to agree fundamental principles which will provide useful guidelines for practitioners. The international evidence is that restorative justice is effective (Galaway and Hudson, 1996). Getting involved in a crime is an emotional experience for all concerned. The way in which shame and pride can be manipulated positively has been described by Nathanson (1992). Some police forces have also experimented with restorative justice as a way of resolving internal grievance issues with good success.

Restorative justice is a psychological model of justice based on sound research which appears to meet the needs of the victim, the community and the offender far better than the current 'legal' criminal justice system. This approach also embodies elements of an emerging socio-criminological framework to be found in Braithwaite's notion of 'reintegrative shaming' which extends social control theory into the realms of restorative and restitutive justice by placing emphasis on *positive* rather than *negative* shaming and *inclusion* of the offender rather than *exclusion* (Braithwaite, 1989). These new ideas are now starting to compete with traditional approaches to policing for acceptance within a service which is still in need of substantial change due to its inability to deal more effectively with old problems such as recidivism.

Pressures for further change

Ethics versus a culture of unprincipled policing

Cases of police corruption cases were a feature of policing in the 1960s and 1970s, but there was a widespread belief in the service that this issue had been 'managed out'. In 1990 the Association of Chief Police Officers (ACPO) adopted a Statement of Common Purpose and Values, but the actions taken by forces to implement the Statement varied greatly and for too many it consisted of no more than having copies of the Statement hanging on office walls. By the mid-1990s, corruption had once more been identified as an issue in the service, with the Metropolitan Police, in particular, identifying that they were taking action against approximately 200 corrupt officers, mainly detectives employed in élite specialist departments dealing with the most serious offenders. A review of integrity in police forces was conducted by a member of Her Majesty's Inspectorate of Constabulary (HMIC, 1999) with a view to establishing practical ways in which the concept of integrity could be enhanced and producing a model which would test organisational integrity and maintain standards. Forces, particularly those in urban areas with high levels of drug abuse, have begun to develop anti-corruption strategies and integrity testing based on undercover techniques and technology pioneered by the New York Police Department and the Metropolitan Police.

It is ironic that police forces around the world admire the standards of integrity set by British officers, whereas the issue of corruption continues to beset the service and clearly has not been managed out. The nature of the corruption is changing. It does not fit into the pattern of 'noble cause' corruption, an expression used by a previous Chief Inspector of Constabulary (Woodcock, 1992) to explain the pressure on officers to secure convictions by unlawful means. There is never anything noble in corruption and there is certainly nothing noble in taking money from a drug dealer. Corruption in the police service now has no defenders, in itself a reflection of the growth in professional ethics which has been encouraged by the use of technology in gathering evidence against officers who are corrupt or have been corrupted.

Ethics: racially sensitive policing

An important ethical dimension to policing relates to how people from the visible ethnic minorities and other vulnerable groups are treated. The Crime and Disorder Act contains important provisions on racially aggravated crime and racial violence. A thematic inspection by Her Majesty's Chief Inspector of Constabulary in 1997, 'Winning the Race', identified a number of ways in which forces needed to improve the delivery of their service to minority ethnic groups. Contemporaneously with that report an inquiry into the death in London of a black teenager, Stephen Lawrence, was held which also led to recommendations for future action.

The inquiry was conducted in two parts. Part 1, under the chairmanship of a High Court judge, Sir William Macpherson of Cluny, examined the investigation into the murder of Stephen Lawrence. Part 2 enquired into wider issues of race relations.

The family and its legal advisers believed that not only were the police corrupt and incompetent but that they were also racist. A debate similar to that over 'noble cause corruption' took place with regard to the expression 'institutionalised racism'. In its evidence to the inquiry, the Association of Chief Police Officers maintained that there may be individual officers who were racist but that they were dealt with robustly. There was no institutionalised racism in the police. This line was maintained until the inquiry visited Manchester where David Wilmot, Chief Constable of Greater Manchester Police, said that in his force there was institutionalised racism. Further debate amongst chief police officers found agreement around a definition of institutionalised racism which amounted to prejudice at a subconscious or subliminal level.

One way around the impasse of definitions of institutionalised racism might be to consider the nature of *responses* to racism. If, as with Scarman (1981), it is a question of urgent *institutional solutions* to racism, there is clearly an institutional problem to address. If there are admitted institutional problems which have a racial outcome, that is institutionalised racism, in effect, and it is irrelevant whether it is indirect or non-intentional racism, witting or unwitting.

The inquiry found that '*racism*' in general terms consists of conduct or words or practices which advantage or disadvantage people because of their colour, culture or ethnic origin. In its more subtle form it is as damaging as in its overt form (paragraph 6.4).

The inquiry considered that '*institutionalised racism*' consists of the collective failure of an organisation to provide an appropriate and professional service to people because of their colour, culture or ethnic origin. It can be seen or detected in processes, attitudes and behaviour which amount to discrimination through unwitting prejudice, ignorance, thoughtlessness and racist stereotyping which disadvantage minority ethnic people (paragraph 6.34).

There seems little doubt that members of the inquiry believe that the police service is a racist institution. They consider that the acknowledgement of its existence is to be seen as the first critical step to tackling it. It is recognised that this is not only a problem for the police as it is prevalent throughout society; however, the police occupy a special position and have discretionary powers and so it is incumbent upon them to tackle the problems of race with more sensitivity. The inquiry made a total of 70 recommendations aimed at establishing openness, accountability and the restoration of confidence. Its first recommendation has been accepted by the Home Secretary, namely that there should be a Ministerial Priority for the police service: 'to increase trust and confidence in policing amongst minority ethnic communities'.

Economics: the influence of the Comprehensive Spending Review

It is interesting to see how economic pressures influenced the development of the new aims and objectives for the criminal justice system. Former Home Office Minister Alun Michael said:

> The Comprehensive Spending Review showed our clear commitment to efficiency and better use of existing resources across the criminal justice system. These new aims and objectives reinforce that commitment. The new aims reinforce those for the criminal justice system as a whole. (Michael, 1998a)

This was an indication that the burgeoning public expenditure on a demand-led criminal justice system was to be checked. With 65 per cent of the expenditure on criminal justice going on policing, the police are clearly the biggest target. Forces are to be required to deliver 2 per cent efficiency savings each year against a commitment to increase expenditure by £1.25 billion over three years. The government's 'best value' regime will apply to forces. Policing will no longer be a special case meriting above-average funding.

Political expediency in proposals for reforming the criminal justice system

The Glidewell Report (Glidewell, 1998) is an example of policy making which is not evidenced-based. The report makes a number of recommendations for major reforms that may have been entirely appropriate but did so without the benefit of good quality research and instead appears to have relied on anecdote to inform these recommendations. The parties most affected by these recommendations, for example the Crown Prosecution Service, were justifiably concerned at the way in which these proposals were arrived at.

The Narey Review made a series of recommendations which were given effect in the Crime and Disorder Act to reduce delay in the adult and youth courts so that cases could be heard more quickly. Schemes which commenced in September 1998 would pilot the new arrangements and include:

- Crown Prosecutors and case workers in police stations;
- out-of-hours advice by Crown Prosecutors;
- early first hearings to be dealt with by a lay presenter for straightforward guilty pleas;
- early administrative hearings and pre-trial reviews in not-guilty or complex cases.

There would be youth justice schemes dealing with:

- parenting orders;
- youth offending teams;
- final caution or warning;
- reparation orders;
- action plan orders.

The new arrangements would be subject to strict time limits.

With the Crime and Disorder Act in place, the government started turning its attention to a new Criminal Justice Bill which would address a number of issues left over from the Royal Commission; for example, a defendant's right to opt for a jury trial in 'either way' cases would be the subject of a consultation paper with a view to removing the right.

A consultation paper has been published, 'Speaking up for Justice', which contains 78 recommendations designed to identify those who are vulnerable in the criminal justice system and how they can be helped to give their best evidence to the court. There are proposals to protect those who face intimidation because they are prepared to give evidence.

The Lord Chancellor is undertaking a further review of the criminal justice system.

Information technology to replace the quill pen

It is remarkable that there is still no joined-up computerisation of the criminal justice system, though there are a number of indications that this is beginning to happen. The criminal justice system would certainly benefit from a whole-system approach to information technology and this is being addressed as part of the cross-departmental review of the criminal justice system which is currently taking place and will map out improvements for the next ten years. Some work has already been conducted on common data standards to facilitate the exchange of information between different parts of the system, such as standard offence codes. Pilot projects have been illustrating significant savings which can come from sharing information through linked technology. When magistrates' courts were linked to the licensing agency, the DVLA, it significantly reduced the number of adjournments in motoring cases caused by the non-availability of a driver's previous convictions.

Each of the sectors has in progress a new generation of systems, the National Strategy for Police Information Systems, the Libra project in magistrates' courts and the Quantum project in the prison service. The new systems will give users throughout the criminal justice system instant access to all the information they need to make decisions. For example, access to the criminal records computer, PHOENIX, by prison and probation staff means that they can make risk-assessment decisions and prepare pre-sentence reports in a shorter timescale. At some point in the future the convergence of these mega systems means that they could be attractive as an outsourced Private Finance Initiative. From a police perspective, the switch from analogue to digital technology through the Public Safety Radio Communication Project (PSRCP) early in the new millennium means that access to many of these information systems will be available to officers on patrol through mobile data terminals.

The same technology that will enable for the first time a true 'command and control' approach to the deployment of police resources, will also mean that prolific offenders can be bailed and 'tagged' electronically creating incarceration without bars, a 'virtual prison' which is likely to be less expensive than the real thing (Hutton, 1998).

Scientific contributions towards safer criminal justice

A National Crime Faculty has been created at Bramshill. Its origins go back to the consequences of the inquiry by the then Chief Inspector of Constabulary into the Yorkshire Ripper case. His report (Byford, 1982) recommended that:

- senior investigating officers be trained in dealing with a series of major crimes;
- there should be an identified system which enables the collection of data, for inquiries to be merged, and the management of those inquiries to be electronically linked;
- there should be a facility which enables police forces to identify that more than one offence had been committed by the same person.

Although courses have been run at Bramshill since the early 1980s, the faculty was not established until 1995. It has four key functions:

- to provide senior investigating officers with support and a help desk facility;
- to maintain a database of serious crime and providing crime analysis;
- to maintain a programme of scientific research into serious crimes;
- to undertake training and development.

The faculty draws its members from within the police service, Forensic Science Service and Home Office Research and Crime Reduction Unit.

Despite the existence of the faculty with facilities which provide the basic requirements for a very professional approach to serious crime investigation, it is still possible for a murder to be investigated by an officer who is put into this position by his or her force without having had adequate training or relevant prior experience. The product of that investigation may be the subject of only a superficial review. New guidelines, the 'Murder Manual', have been produced by the Association of Chief Police Officers, which may help to alleviate these problems. What has not yet been embarked upon is the development of a science of investigation. Many investigators have no understanding of scientific theory, which can contribute to blinkered approaches to an investigation by, for example, concentrating on one suspect to the exclusion of others. Scientific theory would help inform investigators of the risk in adopting this approach by referring them to the null-hypothesis approach adopted in scientific investigations.

Investigative interviewing standards have also improved considerably as a result of a concerted training programme. The development of the concept of the investigative interview was possible because of the existence of sound psychological research (see, for example, Williamson, 1994; Williamson, 1996; and Bull and Cherryman in Chapter 12 of this book.)

Greater use is being made of forensic science. The Forensic Science Service dealt with 40,000 cases in 1991 and 90,000 by 1996/7; some of this rise is because of DNA. The national DNA database, set up by the Forensic Science Service, now holds over 230,000 DNA samples from suspects charged, reported, cautioned or convicted for a recordable offence. The database also holds 27,000 DNA profiles from stains found at scenes of crime. Over 50 per cent of these stains match suspect samples already on the database or match crime scene stains to other crime scene stains (Thompson, 1998). In one provincial force, two murders with no identifiable suspect were each solved within six days through DNA. However, the forensic science budget in forces is increasing exponentially. The appliance of science does not come cheaply.

Quicker and more effective ways for dealing with organised crime

Major crime units within forces are becoming more proactive in their targeting of those perceived to be the 'Mr Bigs' in their areas who are getting rich quickly through large-scale drug dealing. There have been successes but they come at a considerable cost. It is difficult to get the organisers, the drugs, the purchasers and the money in one place. Surveillance, like forensic science, is very expensive and organised criminals are extremely surveillance conscious. There is a constant drip feed of covert techniques into the underworld through corrupt police officers and unwise disclosure through fly-on-the-wall-type documentaries and dramatised television programmes.

A different approach has been developed in other countries such as the United States and the Republic of Ireland where the civil law is used to get at the assets held by organised criminals, instead of relying on the criminal law, which is ineffective. Under existing criminal law, which only allows assets to be seized from convicted criminals, about £10 million is confiscated each year. It is estimated that £10 billion is generated through illegal drugs alone each year with probably as much again through 'white collar' crime. The new system would work by relying on civil forfeiture for seizing both the assets and profit deriving from all serious crime, the rationale being that:

- civil forfeiture is demonstrably more effective;
- the organisers of crime would become uniquely vulnerable in a way they are not and never will be in the criminal process;
- the respondent in civil proceedings cannot adopt a benign position once the civil process commences. The absence of a credible defence leads to the court ordering forfeiture;
- the civil standard of proof presents opportunities to adduce evidence of criminal lifestyle, which by itself is insufficient to secure convictions in the criminal process.

Experience in other countries shows that to be properly effective, civil-forfeiture activity requires some form of new funding because if it were launched from existing resources:

- there would be an inevitable adverse impact on the ability of forces to meet their existing performance targets;
- this reflects the fact that part of the current problem is that existing seizure and confiscation work is not sufficiently resourced (nor likely to be) because of competing priorities;
- civil-forfeiture activity could be self-financing, provided that the issue of where the value of assets seized ends up is addressed. The present Treasury doctrine of 'hypothecation' means that the Treasury is the recipient.

Moreover,

- if the hypothecation issue is resolved or new money provided, the new processes could be cost neutral to government;
- if civil-forfeiture activity were self-financing, it would have the twin effect of tackling major criminality in a more effective way without diverting resources which would otherwise be used for the general prevention and detection of crime.

The then Home Office Minister, Lord Williams of Mostyn, in a Commons written reply announced plans to create a National Confiscation Agency with the power to seize assets generated by crime. A working group is examining measures to strengthen the legislation on confiscation and money laundering and its practical operation. It intends extending powers for the forfeiture of criminal assets in civil proceedings. It is intended that the new agency will be staffed by senior police and custom officers, Crown Prosecution staff and officials from the Serious Fraud Office. There will clearly be a backlash by civil rights groups who will see the new proposals as undermining the principle that a defendant is innocent until proved guilty (Williams, 1998).

The proposals are another illustration of the ineffectiveness of the current criminal justice system and the fragmentation that is beginning to happen. More cost-effective processes are being developed which allow people to be dealt with outside of the existing arrangements, such as restorative justice schemes for young offenders and proposals for recovering the proceeds of crime from the organisers of serious crime.

Conclusions

The criminal justice system in England and Wales has entered the millennium fragmenting, but set to remain adversarial. Treasury-driven aims and objectives will seek to ensure the various components behave more like a 'system' and become more cost effective, which may encourage greater recourse to restorative justice approaches for young offenders and the civil law for asset confiscation from those involved in organised crime.

The Crime and Disorder Act contains a number of measures intended to speed up justice and encourage greater co-operation between the police and the Crown Prosecution Service. There will be greater community involvement based upon locally conducted crime audits with crime reduction as the clearly defined outcome.

The last review of the criminal justice system under the Conservative government by a Royal Commission in 1993 was remarkably complacent, but within its 352 recommendations there were some which should reduce the risks inherent in the system. The implementation of these recommendations has been patchy to date but a new Criminal Justice Bill will provide the opportunity for this government to act on them. Some of the risks contributing to miscarriages of justice will be managed through the Criminal Cases Review Commission in an attempt to make the current adversarial system safer.

The sterility of the last Conservative government's right-wing policy that 'Prison works', was paralleled by the prevailing views of radical left-wing criminologists who were more concerned about police accountability than police effectiveness. This created a paradigm of justice where solid research evidence showing the potential for crime reduction by focusing on the role of the individual, family and community was ignored by successive Home Secretaries who for over 25 years emphasised only situational crime prevention and custody. The Crime and Disorder Act reflects in parts evidence-based policy formulation. It is a statutory framework built on solid research which emphasises the effectiveness of individual, family and community prevention. The use of restorative justice approaches to offending and disorder is likely to be more effective because it involves the offender, victim and community accepting their respective responsibilities in ways which are not possible in a criminal trial.

We now have the potential for a shift of paradigm which will see the adversarial system retained but with a new emphasis on diversion and multi-agency risk management of offenders. It is too early to say whether there has indeed been a paradigm shift but the potential will only be realised if the wider range of agencies empowered under the Act are able to work more effectively together with offenders.

The early indications are that the police service will respond enthusiastically to this new way of working. It will be a police service which will be less well funded, smaller, grouped into fewer, larger forces with an emphasis on local delivery but reliant on national information technology systems.

Some police officers appear to have an aspiration for the service to be considered a profession. This aspiration will continue to be marred by cultural impediments surfacing as corruption and discrimination of minorities. In turn, this will have an adverse effect on the way the service is perceived, not least by potential recruits. There is an ambivalence within the service as to whether it is truly professional or not. 'White collar' and 'blue collar' will continue to coexist as no formal qualifications have been developed for the workforce. Inquiries into police investigations reveal a workforce that frequently is neither skilled nor educated. The 1998 Home Affairs Select Committee on Police Training is likely to stimulate further debate together with a thematic inspection on training by one of Her Majesty's Inspectors of Constabulary. Savage and Wright (1998) in their evidence to the Home Affairs Committee make a number of relevant proposals for developing police professionalism through higher education in a way which builds on some existing schemes in this country and developments outside of the United Kingdom.

If the service is to remain unqualified and 'blue collar', it would be reasonable to anticipate that the future will produce examples of unprincipled behaviour of the kind which have been identified in most of the recent inquiries into miscarriages of justice. Unprincipled behaviour often reflects the failure of the service to develop an ethical and scientific approach to policing in general and investigation in particular. Alderson (1998) discusses a principled approach to policing while Crawshaw, Devlin and Williamson (1998) develop a human-rights-based approach to policing as a basis for setting standards for good law enforcement behaviour. If the service does not desire a view of its future as characterised by unprincipled behaviour it will need to progress its professional skills development and higher educational qualifications with much greater vision, effort and rigour. The last 25 years have provided too many missed opportunities.

The challenge of moving the police up-market and into a professional service culture delivering quality services is achievable. It is the biggest challenge which the service faces. The role of policing in the criminal justice system early in this new millennium will depend on how effectively policing meets the challenge of changing its culture. The assumed growth of professionalism (Williamson, 1996) must now be seriously questioned and remedial action taken urgently by others if the service is incapable or unwilling to do so itself.

'Tough on crime, tough on the causes of crime' does have the elements of a shift in paradigm which is clearly New Labour led in respect to the Crime and Disorder Act 1998, but other elements are event driven as seen in reactions to concerns about institutionalised racism in the police service. Both, however, call for greater police professionalism, which will also be necessary to manage the downward pressure on police budgets. A new Criminal Justice Act, the next flagship piece of legislation, will again reflect this mix of New Labour led evidence-based policy making, event-driven political expediency and measures which are Treasury-driven.

References

Alderson, J. (1998) *Principled Policing. Protecting the Public with Integrity.* Winchester: Waterside Press.

Bean, P. (1998) Discussion at East Midland Group of the British Criminological Society, Institute of Criminology, University of Loughborough.

Braithwaite. J. (1989) *Crime, Shame and Reintegrative Shaming.* Cambridge: Cambridge University Press.

Blair, T. (1998) *Bringing Britain Together: A National Strategy for Neighbourhood Renewal.* Report by the Social Exclusion Unit. Cm 4045. London: The Stationery Office.

Byford, L. (1982) *Report of Her Majesty's Chief Inspector of Constabulary on the Investigation into Crimes Committed by Peter Sutcliffe.* London: HMSO.

Charman, S. and Savage, S. (1999) 'New Politics of Law and Order: Labour, Crime and Justice' in Powell, M. (ed.) *New Labour, New Welfare State?* Bristol: Policy Press.

Clarke, R.V. (1995) 'Situational crime prevention' in Tonry and Farrington (1995b).

Crawshaw. R., Devlin, B. and Williamson, T. (1998) *Human Rights and Policing. Standards for Good Behaviour and as Strategy for Change.* The Hague: Kluwer Law International.

Farrington, D.P. (1998) 'Developmental crime prevention initiatives in 1997', *Forensic Update,* 54. Division of Criminological and Legal Psychology, British Psychological Society. Leicester.

Faulkner, D. (1994) Quoted in *Guardian,* 16 April.

Galaway, B. and Hudson, J. (1996) (eds) *Restorative Justice: International Perspectives.* Monsey, NY: Criminal Justice Press.

Glidewell, Sir Ian (1998) *Review of the Crown Prosecution Service.* Cm 3960. London: The Stationery Office.

Government's Annual Report (1997 and 1998). Cm 3969. London: The Stationery Office.

Her Majesty's Inspectorate of Constabulary (1999) *Police Integrity. Securing and Maintaining Public Confidence.* London: HMIC.

Home Office (1997a) *Preventing Children Offending: A Consultation Document.* London: Home Office.

Home Office (1997b) *No More Excuses: A New Approach to Tackling Youth Crime in England and Wales.* London: Home Office.

Hope, T. (1995) 'Community Crime Prevention' in Tonry and Farrington (1995b) *op. cit.*

Hutton, M. (1998) 'Virtual Incarceration – Tagging Offenders', *Criminal Justice,* II (I). Manchester: Partnership Media Group Ltd.

Leishman, F., Loveday, B. and Savage, S. (eds) (1996) *Core Issues in Policing.* 1st edn. Harlow: Longman.

Loeber, R. and Farrington, D.P. (eds) (1998) *Serious and Violent Juvenile Offenders: Risk Factors and Successful Interventions.* Thousand Oaks, CA: Sage.

Loeber, R. and Farrington, D.P (2000) *Studies on Crime and Crime Prevention, 7.* London: HarperCollins.

Macpherson, Sir William, of Cluny (1999) *The Stephen Lawrence Inquiry.* Cm 4262-I. London: HMSO.

Maguire, M. *et al.* (eds) (1997) *Oxford Handbook of Criminology.* 2nd edn. Oxford: Oxford University Press.

Michael, Alun (1998a) Home Office Press Release on Underlying Causes of Crime. London: HMSO.

Michael, Alun (1998b) Home Office Press Release on Overarching Aims and Objectives for the Police Service. London: HMSO.

Moxon, D. (ed.) (1995) *Managing Criminal Justice.* London: HMSO.

Narey, M. (1998) *Review of Delay in the Criminal Justice System.* London: Home Office.

Nathanson, D.L. (1992) *Shame and Pride. Affect, Sex, and the Birth of the Self.* New York: Norton and Co.

Powell, M. (1999) *New Labour, New Welfare State?* Bristol: Policy Press.

Rose, D. (1996) *In the Name of the Law. The Collapse Of Criminal Justice.* London: Jonathan Cape.

Savage, S., and Wright, A. (1998) *Evidence Submitted to the Home Affairs Committee Inquiry into Police Training and Recruitment.* Institute of Criminal Justice Studies, University of Portsmouth.

Scarman, Lord (1981) *The Brixton Disorders. 10-12 April 1981: Report of an Inquiry by Lord Scarman.* London: HMSO.

Stephenson, G.M. (1992) *The Psychology of Criminal Justice.* Oxford: Blackwell.

Stephenson, G.M. (1999) Discussion in *Forensic Update,* 55. Division of Criminological and Legal Psychology, British Psychological Society, Leicester.

The Royal Commission on Criminal Justice. Report. Cm 2263. London: HMSO.

Thompson, J. (1998) 'Chief Executive Viewpoint', *Criminal Justice,* II (I). Manchester: Partnership Media Group Ltd.

Tonry, R.E. and Farrington, D.P. (1995a) 'Strategic approaches to crime prevention' in Tonry and Farrington (1995b).

Tonry, R.E. and Farrington, D.P. (eds) (1995b) *Building a Safer Society: Strategic Approaches to Crime Prevention.* Chicago: Chicago University Press.

Travis, A. (1998) 'Criminal Justice Management into the 21st Century', *Criminal Justice,* II (I). Manchester: Partnership Media Group Ltd.

Tremblay, R.E. and Craig, W.M. (1995) 'Developmental Crime Prevention' in Tonry and Farrington (1995b).

Williams of Mostyn, Lord (1998) Home Office Press Release regarding the creation of a National Confiscation Agency, 10 November.

Williamson, T.M. (1994) 'Reflections on current practice', in Morgan, D. and Stephenson, G. (eds) *Suspicion and Silence: the right to silence in criminal investigations.* London: Blackstone.

Williamson, T.M. (1996) 'Police Investigation: The Changing Criminal Justice Context' in Leishman *et al., op. cit.*

Williamson, T.M. (1998) 'Restorative Justice – A Police Approach'. Paper presented to Diversion from Gaol Conference, 8 July, Winchester.

Woodcock, Sir John, Her Majesty's Chief Inspector of Constabulary (1992) 'Trust in the Police – the Search for Truth', IPEC '92. Metropolitan Police Library, 200, 12 December, 3–12.

Young, J. (1997) 'Left Realist Criminology: Radical in its Analysis, Realist in its Policy' in Maguire *et al.*, *op. cit.*

Chapter 3

The policy-making context: who shapes policing policy?

STEPHEN P. SAVAGE, SARAH CHARMAN AND STEPHEN COPE

Introduction

A central issue of police governance is the question of who or what shapes policing policy. This in turn is linked to the question of who *should* make or shape policing policy. These questions have been at the core of debates about British policing for many years, often overlapping, though not necessarily coterminus with, the issue of police accountability. Yet, with few exceptions (Jones *et al.* 1994), there is little research evidence or even close analysis of the external and internal processes engaged in police policy making. There is no shortage of what we might call 'tendential' analysis, which draws inferences from broader structural or legal changes in the world of policing as to the general 'drift' of policing policy. The best example of this is the 'centralisation thesis', much traded in the debate over the Police and Magistrates' Courts Act 1994 (PMCA), according to which the constitutional reforms embodied in the Act were seen to herald a new and more acute phase in the longer-term 'centralisation' of British policing (Reiner, 1991, 1992; Loveday, 1995). Important as such discourse has been (and we shall return to it in due course), it has not always been accompanied by an empirical assessment of the extent to which *formal* changes in the constitutional status of the police have impacted on the *substance* of policing policy.

In this chapter we draw upon research recently conducted by the authors on the changing role of the Association of Chief Police Officers (ACPO)[1] as a means of providing further insight into police policy making in the British police service. The term 'policy' is a contested concept; generally there are three competing and distinctive meanings of what constitutes policy. Policy can be seen as a set of goals to be pursued (Fischer, 1980: 183); as a set of actions embracing both its decisions (and 'non-decisions'), goals and effects (Dye, 1992: 2); and as a set of constructed symbols (Edelman, 1985). Policy is thus all about what policy makers want, what they do and/or what they appear to do. These multiple meanings are littered within the academic and, moreover, the so-called 'real-world' discourse of policy making, including police policy making.

No discussion of policing policy in the British context can ignore a central 'given' in the discourse of British policing, the principle of *constabulary independence*. Lurking around every corner of police governance, whether that be at local or national level, lies the 'untouchable' doctrine of the 'constitutional independence' of the police officer, whether that officer be an operational constable or a chief officer of police. The legal foundation for this still rests with what has become known as the 'Denning doctrine' (Lustgarten, 1986). This thesis stems from case law and has been embodied into a constitutional principle that chief police officers cannot be subject to any political authority in the determination of policing policies and operations and must remain fully independent of any such authority in the exercise of their duties. Lord Denning's original and infamous judgment stated that, with reference to the powers of a chief constable:

> Like every constable in the land, he [*sic*] should be, and is, independent of the executive ... he is not the servant of anyone, save of the law itself, no Minister of the Crown can tell him that he must, or must not, keep observation on this place or that he must, or must not, prosecute this man or that one. Nor can any police authority tell him so. The responsibility for law enforcement lies on him. He is answerable to law and to the law alone.   (*R* v *MPC, ex parte Blackburn* [1968])

Much has been written on constabulary independence (CI), most notably in relation to its legal foundations (Lustgarten, 1986; Marshall, 1965, 1984) and its central role in the structures of police governance and accountability (Jefferson and Grimshaw, 1984; Reiner, 1992). The 'Denning doctrine' has been taken as an axiomatic foundation of the constitutional principle of CI. Its status has been the subject of much debate and indeed has been heavily challenged. Regarding the quote above Lustgarten (1986) has commented that: 'Seldom have so many errors of law and logic been compressed into one paragraph' (*ibid.* 64).

Notwithstanding the legal propriety of the doctrine of CI, there is no doubting the discursive and political power of the principle, inside and outside of the police service. Most certainly the discourse of senior police officers is riddled with Denning-type interpretations of the role of the chief officer and his/her relationship with other authorities (Reiner, 1991; Savage *et al.*, 1999). Put simply, the doctrine of CI presumes that chief police officers are fully independent from other bodies when it comes to a matter of police decisions or policing policies. Our own research on ACPO has exposed a deep seam within the discourse of chief officers which constellates around the construction of CI. For example, one chief officer stated:

> [T]he Chief Constable is autonomous in his [*sic*] command and that is a very important aspect of the constitution of this country ... the chief constable's operational command ... cannot be usurped by anybody apart from a court of law ... this independence of the police service is unique to this country ... and I think that is the strength of the British police service, that it is not politically directed or manipulated ... it is a very sacred thing.   (P12)

The doctrine of CI has held sway despite the major structural changes in British policing over the past decade or so. Most notable in this respect are the reformed constitutions and responsibilities of the local police authorities and the Home Secretary contained in the PMCA on the one hand, and the formation of the new national police agencies on the other. The former are discussed in other chapters in this collection (see Chapter 13 by Loveday) and briefly later in this chapter. The development of national police agencies has inevitably shaken the old foundations of the essentially locally based nature of British policing. The creation of National Police Training (NPT), responsible for co-ordinating the core training of officers of all ranks, the National Criminal Intelligence Service (NCIS), a body which co-ordinates criminal intelligence on serious crimes, and the National Crime Squad, a centralised criminal investigation unit, has compromised to an extent the local autonomy of the 43 separate police services of England and Wales. At the very least, local police services have had to accede to a degree of policy-making power to those national agencies, even if not in a dramatic way. An issue we shall discuss towards the end of this chapter is how far that accession can go without a fundamental review of the whole doctrine of constabulary independence.

Against this backcloth we can now move on to consider the status and changing positions of the major 'players' in police policy making, what we have termed the *policy shapers*.

Policy shapers

We would identify five bodies as key players in the policing policy process and core shapers of policing policy: the Home Office/Home Secretary, Her Majesty's Inspectorate of Constabulary (HMIC), the Audit Commission, local police authorities (LPAs) and ACPO. Each has differing degrees of influence over police policy and decision making, and that influence has changed over time both absolutely and relatively.

1. The Home Office/Home Secretary

The Home Secretary has through much of the twentieth century held a position of substantial authority over the British police service, not least in terms of the formal powers the Home Secretary possesses in the 'tripartite' relationship between central government, local police authorities and chief police officers. The department for which the Home Secretary is responsible more generally has, as a number of authors have argued (Lustgarten, 1986; Reiner, 1991; Wall, 1998), accumulated power and influence over police decision making by stealth and through a variety of channels, including its influence over the appointment of chief police officers and training (Wall, 1998).

During the 1980s this process was accelerated under the Treasury-driven 'Financial Management Initiative' (Savage and Charman, 1996) whereby forces were 'encouraged' more and more aggressively to pursue this or that economy or efficiency, such as 'civilianisation' (*ibid.*). The vehicle for this increased assertiveness of the Home Office was to be the Home Office Circular, which, during the 1980s, was transformed from a gentle 'chief officers may consider this' type of *advice* to a role increasingly of a *directive* (Clark, 1991; Jones *et al.*, 1994). Furthermore, the impact of Home Office

Circulars was enhanced by HMIC increasingly adopting the role of 'enforcers' of such Circulars through their annual inspections (Weatheritt, 1986).

It is difficult to deny that, as time has gone on, the extent of influence of central government over the police policy-making process has grown, most probably more at the expense of local police authorities than at the expense of chief police officers (Lustgarten, 1986; Wall, 1998). Furthermore, recent legislation in the form of the PMCA has arguably raised the stakes of centralised power even higher. Under the Act the Home Secretary accumulated new formal powers to determine spending levels of police forces and local police authorities and, even more controversially, to set out 'national objectives' for the service as a whole (Jones and Newburn, 1997). At the very least, the national objectives set out an abstract framework within which chief police officers and police authorities must work on setting out policies for their areas and in that sense they act as formative parameters for the police policy-making process. However, as Jones and Newburn (*ibid.*) have made clear, it is important not to overstate the significance of the national objectives (and through them the power of the Home Secretary); they argue that, to date at least, they act as extremely broad and fairly non-contentious (even non-challengeable) expressions of good practice. Their actual impact on force policies, other than the referential, has yet to be demonstrated.

However, the formation of the national policing agencies NPT, NCIS and NCS almost by definition extends the influence of the Home Office over the national, and possibly the local, patterning of policing policy. Initially at least these agencies operated directly under the umbrella of the Police Department within the Home Office. The establishment of 'service authorities', currently for NCIS and the NCS and almost certainly in future for NPT, has clearly qualified that direct relationship. The service authorities incorporate representation from a range of bodies and thus to an extent dilute Home Office influence; nevertheless, the Home Office itself has both formal and informal involvement in the service authorities and the power and influence this generates should not be overestimated.

2. Her Majesty's Inspectorate of Constabulary (HMIC)

The influence wielded by the Home Office is also furthered through HMIC, despite the formal 'independence' of the Inspectorate from central government. In turn, HMIC has extended its role in the formation of British policing policy and decision making. Firstly, as has been indicated already, as it has taken more and more the position as the 'enforcer' of Home Office Circulars at force level, the power of HMIC has been enhanced and the scope for chief officers to ignore HMIC recommendations has diminished. The watershed in this respect was the notorious Circular 114/83, which set out the police service's version of the Financial Management Initiative (Leishman and Savage, 1993). Not only did the Circular state in no uncertain terms that chief officers had little choice *but* to pursue the '3 Es of Economy, Efficiency and Effectiveness', it charged HMIC with the responsibility of finding out whether forces were making sufficient steps in this direction through their annual inspections (*ibid.*). Since that point, HMIC has typically sought to discover how each force had responded to respective Home Office Circulars and to adapt its recommendations accordingly. No longer were HMIC inspections to be 'toothless tigers'; annual inspections had begun to shift from relaxed and casual reviews with predictable outcomes to inquisitive and challenging audits of police performance force by force (Weatheritt, 1986).

This is one of a series of developments which have enabled HMIC to become a more interventionist and less permissive body over the past decade or so (Jones *et al.*, 1994). In the early 1990s measures were taken for the first time to publish and widely disseminate HMIC annual reports, which up to that point had been restricted documents. This had the effect of energising the whole inspection process because any apparent 'underperformance' of a force could be made public knowledge. Publication also had the effect of imposing more constraints on the Inspectorate itself; in the words of one senior HMI we interviewed: 'It's been a huge discipline on the Inspectorate because every word is looked at.' Publication has been one factor in the increasing 'professionalisation' of inspection. Another has been changes in personnel within the Inspectorate. Prior to the late 1980s, Inspectors were appointed from the ranks of retired chief constables; from that point onwards that policy was changed to one of appointing younger chief officers who were at their peak and better briefed on new policing and managerial philosophies if not at the cutting edge in those fields. Additionally, 'Assistant HMI's', 'starred' middle-ranking officers from around the forces, were appointed who were to add robustness to the whole inspection process. Furthermore, in the wake of then Prime Minister John Major's 'Citizens' Charter', *lay* inspectors were added to the inspection team, ending the 'closed shop' of inspection by police officers only. The lay members, with specialist expertise in personnel, finance and information technology, have added a degree of external scrutiny and broadened the knowledge and skill base of HMIC. Another key development has been the creation in the early 1990s of a three-tier inspection framework: 'Performance Reviews [annual], Primary Inspections [triennial] and 'Thematic Inspections' [*ad hoc*]. The latter have been particularly significant in terms of influencing strategy and policy. They have embraced service-wide themes such as equal opportunities, police complaints and training and are undertaken through inspection of selected groups of forces. The thematic reports have been well publicised and powerful statements of HMIC 'philosophy' in a range of areas and their messages have been difficult to ignore at force level.

Taken together, these developments have served to transform HMIC into a more assertive and concerted agency of inspection and audit. The most tangible expression of this has been the role played by the Inspectorate in the whole business of performance measurement. As the performance culture spread across the public sector in the1980s and 1990s (Farnham and Horton, 1993; Horton and Farnham, 1999; Pollitt, 1993), the search for service-specific performance indicators (PIs) moved apace. In the case of the police service a number of agencies have made contributions to this process, including the Audit Commission (see below), ACPO itself and HMIC (Leishman and Savage, 1993). The Inspectorate not only made the early running in the formation of the first PIs for the police, it was HMIC which had the difficult task of 'softening up' a resistant police service to the whole culture of performance measurement. At the very least, HMIC acted as the 'messenger' of the philosophy of performance measurement and was 'shot at' accordingly. Eventually, perhaps in part because HMIs were still drawn largely from police ranks, that message was to be taken on board more positively by senior police management; in that sense the Inspectorate was to have a major impact on policing policy, given the pivotal position of the performance culture within contemporary police decision making.

A very interesting feature of the recent history of the police has been the 'competition' between the regulatory agencies involved in police governance. In particular, whilst HMIC has been the pre-eminent body responsible for oversight and effective 'audit' of British policing, given that it was formed in the nineteenth century, the late arrival on the scene of that other regulatory agency, the Audit Commission, was to spark a fascinating if discrete territorial battle. At this point we can consider the role of the Commission itself.

3. The Audit Commission

Under the Local Government Finance Act 1982, the Conservative government established the Audit Commission as part of its drive to curb public expenditure and its further attack upon local government, though its audit function can be traced back to the mid-nineteenth century. The Audit Commission's stated mission is 'to promote proper stewardship of public finances and help those responsible for public services to achieve economy, efficiency and effectiveness'. Within this mission it carries out two principal functions. First, the Audit Commission performs an audit function, ensuring the regularity and probity of spending of public monies. This watchdog role is principally concerned with legality, in that auditors check that public spending is sanctioned by statutory powers. Second, the Audit Commission undertakes a value-for-money function, promoting economy, efficiency and effectiveness within much of subnational government. This relatively new consultancy function gives the Audit Commission a roving brief to investigate and make recommendations on value-for-money issues. More recently, under the Local Government Act 1999, this function of the Audit Commission has been significantly extended with the introduction of 'Best Value' (replacing compulsory competitive tendering) within many public services, including the police service. The Audit Commission is charged with the task of overseeing the implementation of Best Value, which involves a continuing process of monitoring the performance of many public services (Boyne, 1999).

Our research suggests that the Audit Commission, though not as influential as any other policy shapers discussed in this chapter, 'punches above its weight', especially given that the investigative team working on the police comprises only a handful of dedicated researchers. Two Audit Commission officials stated:

> The take-up of our recommendations is much higher in the police world than it is in the rest of the local authority sector or in the health service ... (E04)

> ... the work we've done on the police has been some of our smartest work. We think it's been some of our most influential work ... (E13)

However, this record is perhaps better explained in terms of the police service policing the work of the Audit Commission than in terms of the Audit Commission auditing the police service. The Audit Commission and the police service have developed particularly close relations. This closeness reflects to a significant extent the political and professional power of the police service. The Audit Commission is highly dependent upon the police service (and particularly ACPO) for information, expertise, support, and implementation; and consequently it tends to work with (as opposed to against) the police service in its investigations. ACPO often welcomed an Audit Commission investigation to provide an external push for reform and a basis for claiming extra resources. Not only was ACPO increasingly consulted over the selection of topics for Audit Commission investigation, it was also given the opportunity to comment on draft reports to the extent that ACPO could claim a significant degree of 'ownership' of the final reports (including recommendations) published by the Audit Commission, thus demonstrating a significant degree of regulatory capture. However, there is sometimes tension between the Audit Commission and other bodies, such as the Treasury, Cabinet Office, Home Office and HMIC. The Audit Commission is nominally independent, though the Secretary of State for the Environment, Transport and the Regions can formally direct the Commission as he/she sees fit. However, no formal directive has yet been issued though it has been threatened at least on one occasion. Nevertheless, informal guidance has been evident – for example, the Home Office prevented the Audit Commission from investigating the Special Branch within the police service without recourse to formal mechanisms.

The Audit Commission has now conducted a wide-ranging series of investigations into the police. Its early papers tended to address rather 'peripheral' issues, such as vehicle fleet maintenance and the fingerprint service. However, over time it has increasingly conducted high-profile investigations into often very sensitive 'core' areas of police work, such as criminal investigation and police street patrol. This shift from 'peripheral' to 'core' issues was not accidental; it was partly a learning strategy before hitting major targets, and partly a legitimation strategy to gain a foothold in the police service. Our research sought, amongst other things, to gauge ACPO members' assessment of the Audit Commission in influencing policing policy. From a representative sample of ACPO ranks, we found that 73 per cent of those interviewed thought that the Audit Commission had been 'extremely influential' in policing policy. No less than 93 per cent of ACPO members interviewed expressed generally positive views of the work and influence of the Audit Commission. This satisfaction needs to be understood in light of the relatively short period of time that the Audit Commission has been interested in the police service. The first police-related reports written by the Audit Commission only appeared in 1988, though well over 20 reports have been published on the police service since then. Over a relatively short period of time, the Audit Commission's work has had a substantial impact upon the police. For example, two ACPO members typically observed:

> The Audit Commission in my view are the people of the future. They are extremely professional people, they are well qualified and they know what they are doing. We may not like what they do, we may not like their conclusions; you ignore what they do at your peril quite frankly. (M09)

> ... we accept them [the Audit Commission] now as I think an extremely useful, competent, objective body who do the job they do in a focused way, looking at particular issues and where we can actually get something of real benefit, we've picked up on the past and done things which have been positive and therefore if the Audit Commission produces something we take it on board quickly and fairly strongly. I think the Audit Commission has been a major success in the police service. (M10)

Though senior police officers often perceive the work of the Audit Commission as objective, such perceptions should not be taken as meaning that the forms of 'best practice' identified by the Audit Commission are somehow brought in from outside the police service. The Audit Commission makes no secret of the fact that its recommendations are often based on perceived 'best practice' found within the police service; its skill lies in identifying and disseminating such 'best practice'. However, this skill is not always valued within the police service. For example, one ACPO member said:

> I have yet to read an Audit Commission report which tells me anything I didn't know already. The Audit Commission goes around and steals your best ideas and puts it in a flashy, excellently prepared and beautifully presented document ... and they always seem to be able to present it in a way that they've discovered the meaning of life and the holy grail ... (M01)

Such views notwithstanding, there is little doubt that the Audit Commission is a significant actor in shaping policing policy. Its influence stems from three key sources. First, the police service, like other criminal justice agencies, had 'remained largely immune to market-orientated reforms' when compared to other public services (Loveday, 1999: 351). Significant reform of the police service was launched in the early 1990s, after the Conservative government became frustrated with its expensive policies to reduce crime (Baker, 1993: 450), and consequently the police service became targeted for new public management-inspired reforms that had already taken hold in other public services (Cope et al., 1996). The Audit Commission was a key component of this reform programme, and was used by central government to introduce a performance culture into the police service. Second, chief constables have become more managerialist, and thus far more receptive to the work of the Audit Commission (Reiner, 1991). Third, the strategy pursued by the Audit Commission of incorporating ACPO into its investigations (from design to implementation), allied with its relative dependence upon senior police officers to implement reform, greatly facilitated the acceptance of its recommendations. In general, the Audit Commission has been, and remains, a significant conduit for policy reform within the police service, though ACPO itself has to an extent used the Audit Commission as such a conduit for reform.

4. Local police authorities

We shall deal with local police authorities (LPAs) more briefly as the LPAs are examined in depth in another chapter of this book (see Chapter 13 by Loveday). The LPAs have always been the 'Cinderella' of the tripartite framework for police governance. In comparison to its partners in this triangle, chief officer and the Home Office, the LPAs have had little influence over policing policy. Indeed, the outcry which surrounded the PMCA, with its apparent 'diminution' of the powers of LPAs in general and the locally elected element in particular, seemed to ignore the fact that the *former* LPAs were no beacons of local accountability in terms of calling chief officers to account. The issue for contemporary policy analysis is whether that 'Cinderella' status for LPAs will continue to apply in the future under the new constitutional arrangements introduced by the PMCA and consolidated in the Police Act 1996. There are two dimensions to this debate: the role of the LPAs themselves and the emerging role of their representative body, the Association of Police Authorities (APA).

From the point of view of 'policy shaping', the key question relating to the role of the LPAs relates to the extent to which the reformed police authorities are able to exert effective levels of influence over the formation of policing policy in their respective localities. In turn, this concerns the capacity of the newly constituted LPAs, with their reduced locally elected components and 'independent members' (see Chapter 13 by Loveday) to equal or better the success of their predecessor bodies. Much attention in this respect has focused on the role and formation of the 'policing plan' which states policing priorities for each police service for the year ahead.

Formally the LPA has a responsibility for the setting of the annual budget and the drawing up of the local policing plan each year. The policing plan must embrace the national policing objectives as set by the Home Secretary. The chief police officer should 'have regard to' the policing plan in the determination of his or her operational priorities and resource allocation, although, on the grounds of 'operational independence', that officer may choose to ignore all or part of the plan. The LPA is now made up of a combination of elected members, magistrates and 'independent members'.

There are two schools of thought relating to these arrangements. One view, perhaps in academic circles at least the dominant view, is that the whole agenda for the policing plan is one characterised by a powerless LPA and an all too powerful chief officer. This is coupled with the assertion that the independent members are far from 'independent' and are either ineffective in influencing the direction of policing or essentially oriented to 'business' and managerial philosophies (Loveday, 1998). The other interpretation of the role of the new LPAs is more equivocal. This holds that the new arrangements, whilst far from establishing a model of local accountability and democratic influence, at least contain the *potential* to create a more challenging environment for the chief officer as he or she draws up policing policy. For example, Jones and Newburn (1997) conclude, on the basis of their study of six police authorities, that although the overall picture is one in which chief officers continue to dominate the policy and planning process, there are flickering signs of a new assertiveness in the LPAs. As they state:

> The PMCA has clearly given police authorities a number of important tools with which to enhance their input into the development of local policing policy ... [these] new tools available to police authorities have yet to be employed to their full potential ... our research has suggested that this is likely to change. As the new police authorities become more established, more experienced in dealing with the planning process ... we may well see police authorities play a more prominent role in the system of police governance of England and Wales.
>
> (Jones and Newburn, 1997: 222–3)

Our own research, also undertaken as the PMCA was unfolding, offered some, if limited, support for this latter thesis. For example, a chief constable of a large police force commented:

> ... because of the way we approach [the police authority] and the powers they've now got, they've got a fairly significant influence on what takes place either by discussion or resolution in the authority or merely by informal discussion with senior officers in the force. (M43)

Furthermore, one prominent chair of a police authority observed:

> ... the policing plan is a crucial part of how we deliver the policing service now ... [That] part of the legislation is very welcome, for many years ... [ACPO members] tended ... to take more and more powers to themselves ... but inevitably this part of the legislation has made them look hard at that. (E25)

We shall return to the relative influence of the LPAs over police policy-making below. Clearly the debate around the impact of the new LPAs will require further empirical investigation. This is particularly the case given the development of the new Police Authority for London, an innovation which has attracted remarkably little attention in the recent literature on local police accountability and police governance. It is likely that this new body will open up a Pandora's box of challenges to chief police officers' control of the local policy agenda and send messages across the country to the individual LPAs about just how far they can dare to go.

In this respect, the role of the APA will also, almost certainly, become a key factor in the shaping of LPA strategy and approcah, which will in turn affect the relationship between chief officers and their local authorities in setting local policy for policing. Prior to the formation of the APA, police authorities were represented by not one but two national bodies, the Association of County Councils and the Association of Metropolitan Authorities. This in itself served to weaken (in the same way as was found pre-1948 when senior police officers had two representative bodies (see Wall, 1998)) the capacity of the representative bodies to represent any collective interest and form a coherent platform. It is, however, more than a question of drawing together disparate interests under one umbrella. The APA, with apparent encourage-ment from central government, has clearly set out its stall with a view to mobilising the LPAs into much more assertive and interventionist bodies than has been the case (and arguably was the case with old LPAs). It has embarked on a programme to make the LPAs full, active and even 'equal' partners in the tripartite framework. In this respect the APA is in many ways about to ride on the crest of a wave. Not only has central government offered a clear steer for the APA to flex its muscles, particularly in relation to ACPO, the emerging agenda for local governance seems to be heading in a way fully conducive to the APA's ambitions.

Firstly the *best value* agenda places local authorities in the driving seat in determining whether local services are delivering 'best value' in terms of effectiveness, cost and responsiveness to local needs; this includes the police service. Secondly, the Crime and Disorder Act 1998 makes *local authorities* responsible for crime reduction in their domain, in terms of crime audits, the formulation of crime-reduction strategies and the mobilisation of the agen-cies (which *include* the police) in furtherance of that strategy. Both best value and the Act shift decision making, in what were exclusively 'police' matters, 'down' or 'across' to the local authorities. In this environment the APA is in a sense not only 'backing a winner' but is positioning itself to mobilise and direct how the local authorities should go about handling its new-found pow-ers. This is evident in the proliferation of reports and guidelines issued by the APA recently with documents such as: *Can You Manage it? A Review of the Approaches Police Authorities Take to Managing Performance* (APA, 1998a), *Objectives, Indicators, Targets: A Study of Policing Plans and Reports* (APA, 1998b) and *Guide to Youth Initiatives* (APA, 1999). When it comes to the APA and its role as a shaper of policing policy, it is very much a case of 'watch this space'.

5. ACPO

The Association of Chief Police Officers occupies a unique position in the roll call of key players in the field of police policy making. It is the only body of those examined here with little or no statutory basis. It is in many ways lit-erally an *association* in the sense that it is a voluntary assembly of chief officers – officers of the rank of assistant, deputy and chief constable in the 'provin-cial' forces and all officers of the rank of commander, deputy assistant commissioner, assistant commissioner and commissioner within the Metropolitan Police Service. Despite the impressions which may have been given in the past, the establishment of a corporate culture within ACPO is a relatively recent development. Past presidents of ACPO who had held office in the 1980s made it clear to us that a feature of their presidencies had been a sense of frustration with the reluctance of members to operate collectively – individual chiefs doing their own thing irrespective of ACPO policy was common. While ACPO undoubtedly gained a high profile during this period, this had more to do with the high visibility and notoriety of the chief constables who had held the presidency (the Oxfords and the Andertons) than with the nature of the *organisation* as such. Political pressures, including in the late 1980s a clear steer from the Home Office, and a variety of external forces (not least the threat of force amalgamations) encouraged ACPO to 'get its act together' and move in the direction of greater consensus and internal cohesion.

Conveniently, the pressures for change within ACPO coincided with a continuing cultural shift within the membership of ACPO to a different type of police manager. There seems little doubt that in the past a major obstacle in the way of ACPO developing into a more corporate and collective unit had been the traditional individualism of chief constables. Whether 'Barons', 'Bobbies' or 'Bosses', to use Reiner's typology (Reiner, 1991: 306–9), these chiefs fiercely defended their right to determine policing priorities and policing practices in their own forces against whoever sought to compromise that degree of autonomy. This applied to an extent even to their own professional association. Furthermore, it did not help that some of *the* most individualistic chiefs, perhaps ironically, held the office of president of ACPO. However, a common view of those we have interviewed both from within and without of ACPO is that such individualism is becoming a thing of the past. In its place, as Reiner has also identified *(ibid.)*, is the 'new breed' of officer, one more collectively oriented, more inclined to consider and accept competing perspectives. As a recent past president put it:

> We've grown up together, know each other pretty well … We've moved around a lot more so that we've served in different cultures, different forces. I think our approach is more broadly based. We're more receptive to new ideas as well. Some of our predecessors convinced themselves that there was only one way to do something. (MO4)

The 'new breed' of ACPO member is also more highly educated. In his research specifically on chief constables, Reiner found that only 20 per cent possessed a degree (although by the time the research was published that had reached nearly 50 per cent). All of the 20 per cent of chiefs possessing a degree had gained the qualification while serving as a police officer – half of them through the Bramshill Scholarship scheme. Our research, based on a sample of 41 ACPO members of all ACPO ranks, found that 71 per cent possessed a degree, a quarter of whom had joined the police service as graduates. Clearly, the non-graduate ACPO officer is becoming something of a rarity. Although possession of a degree is no guarantee of an open mind, it is more likely to be associated with receptiveness to alternative perspectives, including those of fellow officers. This is an attitudinal shift well suited to the development of a corporate culture within ACPO.

In addition to cultural changes, ACPO has experienced some key organisational developments which have furthered the pursuit of a corporate status; in total they constitute the 'professionalisation' of ACPO. Firstly, a decision made in the late 1980s established the principle of what we have termed the '*presumption in favour of compliance*'. This was introduced by Peter Wright who, as president of ACPO, argued that there were some areas of policing policy where it was important to have consistency across the service and not 43 different variations. Therefore, having discussed and agreed a particular policy at committee level and then ratified it at Chief Constables' Council, a chief was then bound by that policy in his or her force unless that chief wrote to the president of the day explaining the reasons why this was not possible. The adoption of this principle represented a major turning point in the development of ACPO. It began a general move towards policy consistency and the acceptance of such consistency which would otherwise not have been possible. However, the principle of independence is always stated and chief constables at no stage have to comply with ACPO policy. Despite the rhetoric of collectivism and the complicated committee and executive structures, a chief constable when back in force can ignore the advice of ACPO. This has been exhibited publicly, and since the completion of our interviews, with the chief constable of Greater Manchester Police deciding not to adopt a register of freemasons within his force, a policy adopted by ACPO and ratified in the Chief Constables' Council. In the words of the *Guardian,* he has 'defied his professional body'.

Secondly, and more recently, the 'new corporacy' of ACPO has been reflected in a more professional organisational structure. Starting with the establishement of a permanent secretariat in the early 1990s, the organisational machinery has been strengthened by an enhanced policy-making process and an improved research function. The committee structure, often criticised in the past for its over-bureaucratic nature and duplication of ideas, has streamlined into a more efficient matrix model with functional cross-representation. The large number of specialist committees, not to mention the many *ad hoc* committees set up for specific purposes and the sub-committees, demonstrate the significant changes that have taken place in recent years within ACPO. This has been supplemented by the greater use of focused seminars and conferences on particular subjects at which members are invited to attend and debate.

An important internal change within the Association has been the 'split' of ACPO into two distinct bodies: a staff association and a 'professional body'. Pressure for change within the organisation had been apparent for a considerable amount of time but, after a membership ballot in 1993, ACPO opted to approve the split and now two bodies represent senior police management: ACPO acts as the professional and policy arm and the Chief Police Officers' Staff Association, CPOSA, handles the represention of chief police officers' pay and conditions. This split was more than a symbolic gesture – ACPO could now more easily claim to be *the* 'voice of the service', in contrast to the other associations (the Police Federation and the Superintendents'

Association) which could be accused of speaking on behalf of 'vested interests' rather than for service-wide concerns.

All of these cultural and organisational developments have helped to place ACPO in an increasingly strong position as a representational agency. This has been reflected in ACPO becoming a much more effective campaigning body *vis-à-vis* government, as the Police and Magistrates' Courts Act and the Criminal Justice and Public Order Act make clear. In both cases ACPO's preferences on policing and criminal justice matters have ended up in statute. However, in the context of this chapter it is ACPO's *internal* influence as a policy-shaping body which is of greater relevance. What seems to have emerged is a much greater *consistency* in force policy making over the past decade. Generally this greater consistency has been recognised and welcomed by the membership. Typical sentiments from our research were:

> ... you're talking about a group of very independent people and each of the forty-three Chief Constables in his or her own area has quite a powerful voice as an influential person there, and they don't necessarily like to lose that voice if they go to the national level ... and it would be very difficult to get unity all the time but we have made progress in that respect, we do work more as an Association now than we did when I first came into it. (M07)

> ... when they were operating individually and not operating as part of ACPO, people on the outside as it were were able to pick ACPO off. Or, perhaps more relevantly, got frustrated because they couldn't get the service point of view. I think things have improved enormously in the past few years and ACPO can now fulfil that function. (M38)

> ... I think there's a recognition now of the strength of all really singing from the same hymn sheet. (M06)

In order to place these comments and the issue of ACPO's role in 'policy shaping' into context, we need to turn to an assessment of the comparative influence of each of the major players in police policy making on the policy process. One measure of this, albeit not the only one, is how chief officers themselves view the relative significance of the five bodies considered here: the Home Office, HMIC, the Audit Commission, LPAs and ACPO.

Who most shapes policing policy?

As a part of our research into the organisation of ACPO mentioned earlier, there was an opportunity for some quantitative analysis of the views of a sample of ACPO members (n=41). The sample of chief officers (sampled by rank and force size) were asked to assess where they felt the influence lay between the five bodies discussed above in relation to local policing policy. Respondents were asked to comment on the five bodies as to whether their influence was 'considerable', 'some' or 'negligible', and then to rate the organisations in terms of their influence over local policing policy on a one to five (most influential to least influential) basis. Fuller details of the results of these questions are discussed elsewhere (Savage *et al.*, 1998) but presented below are some of the most significant findings.

As mentioned previously, there are those who advocate that we have witnessed in recent years centralising tendencies within the police service. A result in line with their argument would show an increase in influence of the national bodies associated with policing. However, for those who believe that legislation has favoured a rise in the influence of force-level bodies, the results should show the opposite. As will be seen, the results in favour of either proposition are inconclusive. There are caveats to this. Clearly the answers may be very dependent on which area of policy is in question and the extent to which each of the five bodies has produced a definitive position on a particular issue. Furthermore, given that policy is influenced by a variety of factors, it is not always easy for policy makers to be able to identify precisely which factors have played key roles in policy making. The best that can be hoped for is an approximation of the extent of influence of each of the five players at force level. The results are notable nonetheless (see Table 3.1).

Table 3.1 Influence over local policy making

%	HMIC	Home Office	Local police authorities	ACPO	Audit Commission
Considerable	27	66	41	39	37
Some	63	34	37	46	58
Negligible	10	0	22	15	5
Total	100	100	100	100	100

In some ways this analysis replicates that of Reiner in his earlier study of chief constables (1991). Reiner used a rather different grading system from that employed within this research and the interviews were conducted with chief constables only rather than a sample within the ACPO rank; however, comparisons are useful in the sense of providing some form of analysis over time. Reiner found the Home Office to be the clear frontrunner in terms of influence on chief constables, with HMIC and ACPO having much less influence, but with ACPO notably a way behind HMIC (Reiner, 1991: 268).

Since that research took place in the late 1980s, we have perhaps seen a shift in the influence wielded by some of the players within this network of policy actors. The influence of the Home Office, whilst certainly significant, does not appear to have changed considerably since the time of the previous research. Where we have noticed changes is with the fluctuating influence of the older bodies, the newer bodies and those with radically altered roles and compositions. Local police authorities have, for example, undergone major restructuring and change since the time of Reiner's research. Although the full effects of the Police and Magistrates' Courts Act 1994 were not being felt during the time of our research, respondents seemed aware of the implications of these changes and answered accordingly. This is evidenced by the local police authorities coming second only to the Home Office in terms of bodies with 'considerable' influence. However, there is also a significant group of people who believe the influence of the local police authorities to be 'negligible', as given by over one-fifth of respondents and with local police authorities being most often cited fifth in the rank-order question.

Perhaps the winners and losers of this particular battle have to be ACPO and HMIC. The influence of HMIC has seen a decline since the late 1980s and this is confirmed within the interviewees' comments in addition to the quantitative analysis. Despite changes within HMIC – the introduction of lay inspectors and the decision to make HMIC reports public documents – ACPO members did not sense HMIC as being a particularly significant body within local policing policy making. This is not to deny earlier comments on the professionalisation of the Inspectorate or to dismiss its emerging role of 'enforcer' rather than merely an 'observer' of Home Office policy; however, it does perhaps confirm the Inspectorate's position as less than the 'master' of policing policy.

In terms of ACPO, there has been a notable increase in the perception of their influence. Methodologically, there are difficulties with asking a group of people to grade their own influence alongside that of other bodies, yet chief officers are known to be generally very critical of their own association. However, there was a general belief that ACPO's influence had grown and this is seen in it being placed third in terms of those having considerable influence over local policy making, and second in the rank-order question. Again, it must be remembered that comparisons are difficult but the changes from Reiner's research to our research point to a substantial level of influence which ACPO has over local police policy making, and one which compares well with the formal statutory bodies. Furthermore, it became apparent from other areas of our research that ACPO also had a significant degree of influence over some of the other bodies concerned, such as the Audit Commission, in such a way as its influence can be seen as both direct and indirect in shaping the agendas of the other bodies.

The Audit Commission, with the unenviable position of being the 'new kid on the block', fared surprisingly well within a policing organisation known for its suspiciousness of 'outsiders'. Comments were made about the 'professionalism' of the Audit Commission and its readiness to work 'with' the police rather than 'against' them. Clearly the amount of influence that the Audit Commission can wield over local police policy making is limited, yet, despite this, 95 per cent of respondents found its influence to be either 'considerable' or 'some'. The battle between the regulatory agencies mentioned earlier showed itself in our research and critical comments were made about the unnecessary situation of two regulatory agencies; however, opinion within the more detailed comments was more or less divided over which agency was 'unnecessary', with 37 per cent and 27 per cent viewing the influence of the Audit Commission and HMIC, respectively, as 'considerable' and 5 per cent and 10 per cent viewing the influence of the Audit Commission and HMIC, respectively, as 'negligible'.

Discussion

The police policy-making context has been and will undoubtedly in the future be a rapidly changing one. We would argue that the context which sets the parameters of policing policy and which provides the major sources of influence over policy is also an essentially complex one. There is no one simple direction in which policing policy is going or one unequivocal trajectory of the policy-making environment. As we have seen, there are numerous 'players' in the field of policing policy and in each case they have been reshaped and reoriented in recent years. Each has in some respect attempted to pull and push policing policy in different directions and with differing degrees of effectiveness. Some are dominant, others subordinate, but each has contributed to an extent to the total mosaic of policing policy. Chief officers have had to respond to the demands of an increasing number of 'masters' than ever before and there is no evidence of that changing in the future.

As we have noted, an overarching interpretation of the direction of policing policy in Britain is the 'centralisation thesis' (Reiner, 1992; Loveday, 1995). This postulates that police policy and decision making have, over a long period of time, become more and more dominated by central government at the expense of local influence and local diversity. The PMCA has, it is argued, done much to accelerate this trend, particularly with regard to the new powers it gave to Home Secretaries to set National Police Objectives. So too has the establishment of national police agencies, such as NPT, NCIS and the National Crime Squad. There is every chance that new nationally based policing agencies will emerge to take this process even further. At the time of writing, for example, a 'Police National Training Organisation' is about to be formed, which will take the role of nationally set training objectives much further than currently exists within NPT. As a result, there will be far less room for discretion and variation at force levels in training provision than at present. We are in broad agreement with the view that a process of centralisation has been under way but would argue that this process is far more complicated than at first appeared (see also Newburn and Jones, 1997). More recent developments have increased this complexity.

Firstly, as was mentioned in Chapter 1 of this book, the implementation of *devolution* and *regionalisation* will have a major impact on both policing policy and the delivery of policing as it unfolds. As we edge towards overarching bodies with responsibilities for regional strategy, or in the case of Scotland, Wales and Northern Ireland, national strategy, policing will be increasingly re-engineered along *supra*-force lines. The point here is that not only will this mean a diminution of *local* discretion over policing policy (to which we shall return), it may very well mean the *reduction* of *central* influences over policing. If devolution is to have any impact at all then some loss of power, or at least responsibility, from the centre to the nations/regions must flow. In which case the apparently inexorable 'drift' to the centre may, in part, be compromised. Secondly, *above* the level of nation state, policing decisions and policies are being increasingly shaped by *international* movements and processes. As Walker, in Chapter 6 of this book demonstrates, policing at both local and national levels is coming more and more under the rubric of *international governance* both in terms of the internationalisation of 'policing problems' – i.e. cross-border crime – and the expansion of supra-national policing organisations and international law. Inevitably, this will serve to undermine the degree of control and influence which the British central government can exert over policing nationally and locally.

The third complication to the 'centralisation thesis' relates more to the issues raised in this chapter. The growth in the cohesiveness and consequent influence of bodies such as ACPO and, increasingly, APA, should cause us to recast the centralisation argument. Instead of equating 'centralisation' with the process of accretion of power to *central government* we should begin to talk of *multiple centres of influence* which can *coincide, converge, overlap* but also *compete, contradict* and *counteract* each other. For example, with reference to ACPO, as we have argued elsewhere (Savage, Cope and Charman, 1996), to an extent the enhanced corporate status of ACPO both *centralises* policing policy through *standardisation* of policy across forces and protects the *decentralised* nature of British policing by offering itself as an alternative to a national police force. We know that one spur behind ACPO 'getting its act together' was the fear that 'if we don't, they will', meaning that unless ACPO could offer central government something closer to a standard system of policing across the country then government would be forced to impose it – with a consequent loss of police influence over policing policy. In this sense ACPO can be seen, at least periodically but always potentially, as a *counterweight* to central government.

Something similar may be emerging out of APA. As we have seen earlier, the bodies representing the local police authorities have, in the past, suffered in terms of power and influence because of the aggregated weaknesses of the police authorities they represent, the fact that not one but two bodies (AMA and ACC) were involved – with ensuing rivalries and divisions – and because of the 'Cinderella' status of the local police authorities in the tripartite framework. There is now evidence that this is changing: the unification of LPAs under one umbrella, APA, the gentle steer from the Labour government for APA to become more assertive in relation to chief officers and the police planning process, together with a growing inner determination to become more challenging and strategic (*perhaps* influenced in part by the participation of the 'infamous' independent members!) are all factors at work in this respect. We would argue that the field of policing policy will in the future witness a steady enhancement of the power and influence of both individual LPAs and their representative body. This will be at the expense both of the freedoms enjoyed by chief officers at the local level and, to some extent, central government. APA is emerging as another 'central' body which is pushing more and more to influence policing policy along national lines *without* necessarily following some central *government* line. Like ACPO, APA has emerged as a 'centralising' body which inhibits not only local discretion over policy but also the powers of the core central agency, government.

The point made here is that the 'centre versus local' dualism is increasingly an inadequate framework for the analysis of general trends in policing policy. There are *different forms of 'central' organisations* competing to influence policy making; at times operating within a 'corporatist' framework (Cawson, 1986) of inclusion and participatory governance, at others within a *neo-pluralist* framework of (limited) competition and counteractivity (Richardson and Jordan, 1979). The 'centralisation thesis' needs to be reworked in this respect and to take on board the growing complexity of the policing 'policy network' (Rhodes, 1997; Savage and Charman, 2000) as it has emerged and will continue to develop around the key 'players' in the shaping and making of policing policy.

We opened this chapter by stating the crucial role of the constitutional principle of *constabulary independence* for any discussion about police policy making. In some sense it is the 'bottom line' of the whole policy process for policing in the British context. We might talk about dominant or subordinate influences on policing policy but in the final analysis, tradition has it, only the chief police officer can decide on 'operational' matters. Few have dared, at least explicitly, to challenge this sacred principle, practically, analytically or empirically. We would argue that the hallowed status of constabulary independence is likely to come under increasing pressure as a result of emerging and future reformations of the context of police policy making, most of which we have already outlined. Each in different ways will make recourse to constabulary independence more and more problematic in the years ahead (Savage, 1998).

Firstly, there is the *regionalisation agenda*. As individual police services are subsumed either strategically or functionally under regional structures there will inevitably be a partial transference of policy making and discretionary management from local chief officers to the regional level. Indeed, regionalisation will also be accompanied by the continuing devolution of management *within forces* down to 'basic command' level. Chief officers may lose power 'upwards' and 'downwards', to the regions above and the command units below. In this context, it is difficult to see how the (accepted) tradition of chief officers' constabulary independence can survive in anything like its present form. One can imagine the problems created within regional governance if individual chief officers attempted to resist change and development by waving the card of constabulary independence.

Secondly, there is the *best value agenda*, discussed at various points in this book (but see DETR, 1998). Best value has many implications for police policy making and the delivery of policing services but we are yet to see how its adoption will impact on chief officers' 'right' to invoke the doctrine of constabulary independence. Best value in this respect poses two sets of challenges. On the one hand, the 'what matters is what works' philosophy behind best value means that *who* provides services is less important than *how* the service is provided and at what cost. This could be taken to mean that service providers other than the police are enabled (even more) to compete for police 'business' by offering 'best value'. In what may emerge as a highly competitive environment, a chief officer who insists on holding the line of constabulary independence and maintaining absolute authority over a field of operational decisions may place his or her organisation at a distinct disadvantage as the new environment unfolds. Competitor organisations would come in uncluttered by such 'bottom line' conditions of participation. On the other hand, best value places great emphasis on *consultation* with service users in the setting of priorities and action plans, a form of 'power sharing' with consumers of services. Of course, chief officers are no strangers to demands for consultation and in some cases have taken the initiative in developing consultation schemes. However, many of their colleagues would still wish to draw a line in policy formation and maintain that behind that line all is a matter of 'constabulary independence'. In the new world of best value, that will be an increasingly difficult position to cling to. Matters of policing policy will become more and more the 'property' of those outside of the service.

The same applies to the *crime and disorder* agenda. As mentioned in Chapter 1 of this book, the Crime and Disorder Act 1998 has become a sort of watershed in the British approach to crime and criminal justice. From the point of view of this discussion the Act's creation of new powers and responsibilities for *local authorities* in crime reduction and the statutory requirements for *partnerships* and *inter-agency* planning and delivery, both present serious challenges to the unconditional exercise of constabulary independence. A significant degree of *power sharing*, including the sharing of *policy, planning and performance review*, will flow, or is already flowing, as a consequence of the Act. Again, it is difficult to see how the established traditions of working to the principle of constabulary independence can survive intact in such an environment.

What this leaves is the question of whether the 'handed down' constitutional doctrines and the practices which have followed can be sustained in anything like their present form. We would argue that it is time to 'deconstruct' the principle of constabulary independence and subject the doctrine (and its invocation by chief police officers) to scrutiny. Already, as Loveday in Chapter 13 makes clear, the Patten Commission on policing in Northern Ireland has begun to 'unpick' the concept and question its veracity (HMSO, 1999). This analysis may have opened the floodgates and exposed deep flaws in the received wisdom which has surrounded the principle of constabulary independence. At the very least, we need to identify the points in the police decision-making chain where the principle of 'independence' is sustainable and conversely the points where it is not. This would most likely turn on a more clearly formed distinction between *constabulary* independence and *operational* independence. After all, the medical doctrine of 'clinical freedom' for medical practitioners can sit quite easily with the idea of a whole host of stakeholders having a say on medical and health *policy*. In the policing context, it is the conflation of 'operational' decisions with 'policy' and the ring-fencing of both within the doctrine of constabulary independence that is the source of difficulty. The principle can then be used to resist all sorts of 'interference' with police decision making in a way that reflects more a form of 'professional closure' (Johnson, 1972), to enhance chief officers' *autonomy* and authority, than a means of protecting police operational decisions as such from political or otherwise inappropriate influence. Police policy making is a sphere which will always be surrounded by ambiguity and idiosyncracy unless the 'sacred cow' of constabulary independence is put to the test, if not put to rest.

Note

1 The research involved interviews with a representative sample of ACPO members (n=41), interviews with a range of past and present role holders in ACPO and with representatives from all of the bodies associated with British policing. The research also involved observations of ACPO gatherings and documentary analysis.

References

Association of Police Authorities (1998a) *Can You Manage It? A Review of the Approaches Police Authorities Take to Managing Performance.* London: APA.

APA (1998b) *Objectives, Indicators, Targets: a Study of Policing Plans and Reports.* London: APA.

APA (1999) *Guide to Youth Initiatives.* London: APA.

Baker, K. (1993) *The Turbulent Years: My Life in Politics.* London: Faber and Faber.

Boyne, G. A. (ed.) (1999) 'Special Issue on Managing Local Services: from CCT to Best Value', *Local Government Studies,* 25 (2).

Cawson, A. (1986) *Corporatism and Political Theory.* Oxford: Basil Blackwell.

Charman, S., Savage, S. and Cope, S. (1998) 'Singing From the Same Hymn Sheet: The Professionalisation of the Association of Chief Police Officers', *International Journal of Police Science and Management,* 1(1) (March).

Clark, C. (1991) 'The Need for a National Policy', *Policing,* 2, Summer.

Cope, S., Starie, P. and Leishman, F. (1996) 'The Politics of Police Reform', *Politics Review,* 5 (4).

DETR (1998) *Modernising Local Government: Improving Local Services Through Best Value.* London: Department of the Environment, Transport and the Regions.

Dye, T. R. (1992) *Understanding Public Policy.* Englewood Cliffs: Prentice Hall.

Edelman, M. (1985) *The Symbolic Uses of Politics.* Urbana: University of Illinois Press.

Farnham, D. and Horton, S. (eds) (1993) *Managing the New Public Services.* Basingstoke: Macmillan.

Fischer, F. (1980) *Politics, Values and Public Policy.* Boulder: Westview Press.

HMSO (1999) *The Report of the Independent Commission on Policing for Northern Ireland: A New Beginning.* London: HMSO.

Horton, S. and Farnham, D. (eds) (1999) *Public Management in Britain.* Basingstoke: Macmillan.

Jefferson, T. and Grimshaw, R. (1984) *Controlling the Constable.* London: Frederic Muller.

Johnson, T. (1972) *Professions in Power.* London: Longman.

Jones, T., Newburn, T. and Smith, D. (1994) *Democracy and Policing*. London: Policy Studies Institute.

Jones, T. and Newburn, T. (1997) *Policing After the Act*. London: Policy Studies Institute.

Leishman, F. and Savage, S. (1993) 'The Police Service' in Farnham and Horton (1993).

Leishman, F., Cope, S. and Starie, P. (1996) 'Reinventing and Restructuring: Towards a New Policing Order' in Leishman, F., Loveday, B. and Savage, S. (eds) *Core Issues in Policing*. 1st edn. Harlow: Longman.

Loveday, B. (1995) 'Reforming the Police: From Local Service to State Police?', *Political Quarterly* 66 (2).

Loveday, B. (1998) '"Waving not Drowning": Chief Constables and the New Configuration of Accountability in the Provinces', *International Journal of Police Science and Management*, 1 (2).

Loveday, B. (1999) 'The Impact of Performance Culture on Criminal Justice Agencies in England and Wales', *International Journal of the Sociology of Law*, 27.

Lustgarten, L. (1986) *The Governance of the Police*. London: Sweet and Maxwell.

Marshall, G. (1965) *Police and Government*. London: Methuen.

Marshall, G. (1984) *Constitutional Conventions*. Oxford: Oxford University Press.

Newburn, T. and Jones, T. (1997) 'Police Accountability' in Saulsbury *et al.* (1997).

Pollitt, C. (1993) *Managerialism and the Public Services*. Oxford: Blackwell.

Reiner, R. (1991) *Chief Constables*. Oxford: Oxford University Press.

Reiner, R. (1992) *The Politics of the Police*. Hemel Hempstead: Harvester Wheatsheaf.

Rhodes, R.A.W. (1997) *Understanding Governance: Policy Networks, Governance, Reflexivity and Accountability*. Buckingham: Open University Press.

Richardson, J. and Jordan, A. (1979) *Government Under Pressure*. Oxford: Basil Blackwell.

Saulsbury, W., Mott, J. and Newburn, T. (eds) (1997) *Themes in Contemporary Policing*. London: Policy Studies Institute.

Savage, S. (1998) 'The Geography of Police Governance', *Criminal Justice Matters*, June.

Savage, S. and Charman, S. (1996) 'In Favour of Compliance', *Policing Today*, 2 (1).

Savage, S. and Charman, S. (1997) 'ACPO: The Views of the Membership'. Report Submitted to the Association of Chief Police Officers. Unpublished.

Savage, S. and Charman, S. (2000) 'The Bobby Lobby: Police Associations and the Policy Process' in Ryan, M., Savage, S. and Wall, D. (eds) *Policy Networks in Criminal Justice*. Basingstoke: Macmillan.

Savage, S., Charman, S. and Cope, S. (1996) 'Police Governance: the Association of Chief Police Officers and Constitutional Change', *Public Policy and Administration*, 11 (2).

Savage, S., Charman, S. and Cope, S. (1998) 'ACPO: Choosing the Way Ahead', *Policing Today*, 4 (2).

Savage, S., Charman, S. and Cope, S. (1999) 'The State of Independence: The Discourse of Constabulary Independence', unpublished paper presented to the British Criminology Conference, Liverpool, July.

Savage, S., Cope, S. and Charman, S. (1997) 'Reform Through Regulation: Transformation of the Public Police in Britain', *Review of Policy Issues*, 3 (2).

Wall, D. (1998) *The Chief Constables of England and Wales*. Aldershot: Dartmouth Press.

Weatheritt, D. (1986) *Innovations in Policing*. Beckenham: Croom Helm.

Chapter 4

Romantic realism: policing and the media

ROBERT REINER

> The romance of the police force is the whole romance of man.
>
> (Chesterton, 1901: 161)

Policing, especially in Britain, has always been a matter of symbolism as much as substance (Walker, 1996; Loader, 1997). Most sophisticated police leaders have always realised this. From the architects of modern British policing in the early nineteenth century, such as Colquhoun, Peel, Rowan and Mayne, up to today's ACPO, there has been a continuing concern with constructing and maintaining a favourable image of the police as benign and honourable providers of law enforcement and other services (Mawby, 1997a). This chapter will examine how the mass media have operated as a key vehicle for competing representations of policing, order and criminality.

The media–crime debate

During the twentieth century, the mass media have constituted the main arena in which public images of policing have been constructed and contested. Recognition of the potential impact of mass media of communication on order and policing is as old as the media themselves. In the late eighteenth century, Patrick Colquhoun, a leading advocate of the police idea, worried about a new wave of 'bawdy ballad singers' and their deleterious effects on 'the morals and habits of the lower ranks in society'. He advocated government support for rival groups of ballad singers who would tour the pubs with wholesome, uplifting lyrics to put right the damage done by their salacious counterparts (Reiner, 1997: 189).

During this century the successive waves of new technological forms of mass medium – cinema, radio, television, video, satellite, the Internet – have all been the stimulus for moral panics about their detrimental effect on morals and crime. Police spokespersons have often been in the vanguard of this alarm. In 1916 John Percival, Chief Constable of Wigan, declared in evidence to an enquiry by the 'National Council for Morals' that 'the cinema is responsible for the increase in juvenile crime' (Mathews, 1994: 27). That same year a report representing all chief constables concluded that 'The establishment of a central government censor of cinematograph films is essential and will conduce to the reduction of juvenile crime in the country' (*ibid.*: 25). These comments typify a long history of 'respectable fears' (Pearson, 1983).

Anxiety about the criminogenic consequences of the mass media are only one source of concern about their effects on order. Radical and liberal analyses of the media have often had the opposite concern. They see the media as fomenting exaggerated concerns about crime with the consequence of undermining popular support for the rule of law, thus legitimating undemocratic and authoritarian forms of policing and criminal justice.

One result of both these anxieties has been a veritable industry of research attempting to assess the content, effects and sources of media representations (recent reviews include Wartella, 1995; Livingstone, 1996; Reiner, 1997). Much of the research on media effects has been conducted within a positivist psychological frame of reference, seeking to establish whether exposure to particular images has clearly identifiable consequences either for 'anti-social' attitudes or actions or for fear of crime. Perhaps unsurprisingly the prodigious efforts to isolate a 'pure' media effect tend to result in such masterpieces of inconsequentiality as the conclusion of one major study that:

> for some children, under some conditions, some television is harmful. For some children under the same conditions, or for the same children under other conditions, it may be beneficial. For most children, under most conditions, most television is probably neither particularly harmful nor particularly beneficial.
>
> (Schramm *et al.*, 1961: 11)

The majority of studies, whether conducted in laboratory or 'natural' conditions *do* find some effects in the expected direction but usually very small ones. For example, one study of 34 matched sets of US cities between 1951–5 found that larceny increased by about 5 per cent in the cities that gained access to television for the first time, compared to cities without TV or which had been receiving it for some time (Hennigan *et al.*, 1982). The weight of evidence does also suggest some effects on fear of crime, although these are not unequivocal (Reiner, 1997: 217–19).

It is not surprising that the vast research enterprise on media effects has been rather inconclusive. Most of it has been focused on testing the allegations which have flourished for centuries in political debate, and indeed have been circulated by the media themselves, about direct causal relationships between exposure to images of deviance and subsequent behaviour. The implicit model behind such anxieties is extremely implausible: that the media act as an autonomous and powerful ideological hypodermic syringe, injecting ideas and values into a passive public of cultural dopes.

It is far more plausible to suggest that media images do indeed have profound consequences, but not in a pure and directly deterministic causal manner. They are interpreted by audiences in various ways according to their particular social experiences and interests. Media images do not develop autonomously but reflect changing social perceptions and practices which have other origins. The media–society relationship is dialectical: each interacts with the other in a complex loop of interdependence. This does not mean that media representations do not have significant consequences, but it does make the hunt for pure effects which can be experimentally isolated a chimerical quest. The question is not 'how the media make us act or think, but rather how the media contribute to making us who we are' (Livingstone, 1996: 31–2).

Police and the media before the Second World War

The media representation of the police has always been a key aspect of the general debate about media and crime. The nineteenth-century conflicts about the establishment and acceptability of the police were played out in the media of the day, the press, the novel, and the music hall (W. Miller, 1977; D. A. Miller, 1988). Popular literature and journalism began to feature the exploits of police 'detective officers' from the mid-1840s, and Dickens 'virtually appointed himself patron and publicist to the Detective Department' (Ousby, 1976: 65–6). The genre of police memoirs (pioneered by the celebrated 1828 *Mémoires* of Vidocq, head of the Sûreté in Paris from 1812–27), was imported to Britain in 1849 when a long-running series *Recollections of a Detective Police-Officer* first appeared in *Chambers's Edinburgh Journal* (Ousby, 1976: 66).

The advent of the cinema as the primary medium of mass entertainment early in the twentieth century stimulated the kind of respectable anxiety which has accompanied each successive form of technological innovation, from television to the Internet. As indicated earlier, the police were prominent in campaigns to censor cinema because of fears about its criminogenic consequences.

There was also continuing concern about the cinema's representation of the police, which was alleged to undermine their authority. As early as 1910, the International Association of Chiefs of Police adopted a resolution condemning the cinema's treatment of the police (Reiner, 1981: 197). Its president complained that 'in moving pictures the police are sometimes made to appear ridiculous, and in view of the large number of young people, children, who attend these moving picture shows, it gives them an improper idea of the policeman'. The police were alarmed by being lampooned as the Keystone Cops, and by appearing dull and ineffectual in comparison with heroic private investigators or glamourised gangsters.

These fears reached a height in the early 1930s with the cycle of classic gangster movies such as *Little Caesar, Public Enemy* and *Scarface*. Concern about these was a major factor in the enforcement from 1934 of the Hays Code, which laid down strict rules about how Hollywood could depict crime and law enforcement, as well as more general moral issues (Black, 1994: ch. 5). In the early 1930s the Director of the FBI, J. Edgar Hoover, the first of many media-conscious police chiefs, initiated a policy of co-operating with Hollywood in return for control over how his agency was represented (Powers, 1983: ch. 4). The result of the Hays Code and Hoover's moral entrepreneurship was the birth of the first cycle of films featuring law-enforcement heroes, beginning in 1935 with *G-Men*, a paean to the Bureau replete with documentary-style footage on FBI training and forensic methods (Reiner, 1981: 200–3). Despite this, police heroes remained rare in the cinema (and in popular literature) until the early 1970s. The only medium which has always represented the police as central characters in fiction has been television.

Police and the media since the Second World War

The media representation of policing has become an increasingly central aspect of the long-running debate on crime and the media in the period since 1945. This is related to the police becoming more prominent in all media during the second half of the twentieth century, in both fiction and news stories.

The same two broad perspectives which dominate the general debate about crime and the media are echoed in controversies about the representation of the police. On one hand, there has been a continuation of the long-running conservative anxiety about media images undermining authority, including the police as the front-line embodiments of the state's authority. On the other hand, there has been concern amongst liberal and radical commentators that the media presentation of crime and policing is detrimental to popular support for principles of legality and fosters authoritarianism.

There has been considerable research in Britain and North America in the last 30 years which has studied the content of media representations of policing (usually as an aspect of a more general concern with images of crime and criminal justice). There has also been some research on the processes of production, and the perception of media images by the public, and by police officers themselves.

The police themselves are generally very sensitive about their image in the media. Sir Robert Mark, the leading pioneer of a more open approach to the media, declared to the London Press Club in 1974 that the police were 'without doubt the most abused, the most unfairly criticised and the most silent minority in this country' (Chibnall, 1979). Police reactions to their media representation suggest a kind of 'catch-22' paranoia. Stories about police deviance are understandably regarded with concern, even though they are usually framed within a perspective that legitimates the police institution itself (Chibnall, 1977; Schlesinger and Tumber, 1994). Somewhat less predictably, officers are also worried about positive representations of policing, fearing that they lead the public to expect too much of the police, in terms of crime-fighting wizardry or superhuman patience, tact and integrity. They fear that TV 'cop shows' breed an assumption that crimes can be cleared up routinely in half an hour minus commercial breaks.

Anxiety about the media representation of policing has stimulated police leaders and professional associations to cultivate positive relations. The most common strategy in the post-war period has been to pre-empt problems by co-operation with media producers, and by training police spokespersons for media appearances (Chibnall, 1977; Schlesinger and Tumber, 1994; Mawby, 1997a and 1997b). Unfortunately, there is also a pattern of negative reactions to particular programmes stimulating periodic souring of police–media relations (Reiner, 1992: 177–82). A recent example is the 1998 BBC2 series entitled *The Cops*, which drew much criticism from police forces for its graphic portrayal of various forms of police deviance, from cocaine sniffing to violence against suspects. This echoed the similar hostile police reaction to the much less deviant images of policing in such earlier series as *Z-Cars*.

The numerous content analyses of news and fiction stories about crime suggest that the predominant representation of policing is an extremely favourable one, contrary to the perennial police anxiety about this. Interestingly, similar patterns of representation have been found in studies of both fiction and news/documentary stories about crime and law enforcement. Although there are some variations in the representation of crime and policing between different media, operating with varying technologies and in different markets, and between different genres, the following broad patterns have been found by studies at different times and places:[1]

1 Stories about crime and law enforcement are prominent in all media, although their precise proportion varies between different media and the markets they operate in (and because different studies use definitions of crime stories which vary in scope). As one study of newsmaking put it, 'deviance is *the* defining characteristic of what journalists regard as newsworthy' (Ericson, Baranek and Chan, 1987: 4). This is clearly almost tautologous: news implies some element of novelty and extra-ordinariness, and the same applies to fictional storytelling. In this sense deviance and control are intrinsic to narrative, and the empirical finding of media fascination with crime and police stories is hardly news.
2 The media concentrate on stories of serious crimes against the person, particularly homicide and sexual offences. These offences, which constitute only a small proportion of crime recorded in official statistics or victim surveys, are the focus of the overwhelming majority of media accounts.
3 The media concentrate on crimes which are solved. Offences which are reported in the news when they occur are typically the most serious cases of inter-personal violence, which have the highest clear-up rates. Most other offences are reported only at the stage of an arrest or trial, and the reports are usually filtered through the perspective of the police, prosecutor or judge. Fictional crimes are almost invariably cleared up, as a result of the exercise of remarkable skill and daring by law enforcement heroes. This contrasts with the picture given in official statistics, which shows that only 2 per cent of offences reported in victim surveys result in a conviction. Studies of detection show that few of these clear-ups are the product of skilful detection, but are either virtually self-clearing cases or due to interrogation tactics and bureaucratic processes (Maguire and Norris, 1992).

4 Offenders and victims reported in news stories are disproportionately older, white, middle or upper class. The same demographic pattern of offenders and victims features in most fiction. The media picture contrasts sharply with the characteristics of convicted offenders or victims portrayed in official statistics. These are mostly young, from the most marginal socio-economic groups, and disproportionately black.

The overall picture of crime and control presented in the media, whether fiction or news, is highly favourable to the police image. Crime is represented as a serious threat to vulnerable individual victims, but one which the police routinely tackle successfully because of their prowess and heroism. The police thus appear as the seldom-failing guardians of the public in general.

The police are sensitive about the regular appearance of stories which focus on police deviance. Corrupt police officers have high news value as do all stories of authority figures caught in wrongdoing. The press will ferret these out with enthusiasm. However, the overall framework within which news stories about police corruption is presented tends to legitimate the institution as a whole. Traditionally such stories have been depicted as 'one bad apple' in an otherwise sound barrel (Chibnall, 1977). As such stories have multiplied in the last three decades this narrative has become less credible. None the less, the overall framework of police deviance stories continues to legitimate the organisation. This is accomplished now by a narrative of progressive reform. The cases of deviance are presented with an accompanying theme of how organisational procedures are being changed to prevent the recurrence of malpractice in the future (Schlesinger and Tumber, 1994).

Police corruption features less often in fiction, but where it does the protagonists are often the cops who fight corruption (as in *Serpico* or *Between the Lines*). When the deviance takes the form of rule-breaking to catch criminals, this vigilante style of policing is often celebrated (as in *Dirty Harry* or *The Sweeney*). Thus, the presentation of police deviance by both news or fiction helps to reproduce the overwhelmingly favourable police image in the media of successful and heroic guardians of the public.

The sources of this overwhelmingly favourable police image lie more in the practical exigencies of production processes than any direct consequences of the ideology of those responsible for creating the content of media output. It is true that the British press has been predominantly Conservative and overtly champions 'law and order', and even more liberal newspapers support the police role although they also have a concern for civil liberties. Traditional crime reporters on the tabloids explicitly have seen it as their function to present the police in a favourable light whenever possible, representing them as the 'goodies' (Chibnall, 1977: 145). However as 'law and order' has become increasingly controversial as a political issue (Downes and Morgan, 1997), the broadsheet press at the 'quality' end of the market have also appointed specialist editors in this area. They are more commonly referred to as 'home affairs' or 'legal' correspondents than 'crime' reporters (Schlesinger and Tumber, 1994), and do not share the police-centred perspective of their tabloid counterparts. The producers of broadcast news, as well as the creators of crime fiction in any medium, do not intentionally act as police cheerleaders either. Their primary self-conception is as purveyors of objective information or non-ideological entertainment. Both values would lead to assiduous pursuit of police failure or malpractice, in exactly the way that the police themselves fear. If the outcome of their practices none the less is the overall legitimation of the police role found by content analyses, then the source of this cannot be the direct ideological intention of creative personnel.

The origins of the fundamentally favourable representation of the police in the media lie in a combination of professional conceptions of what counts as a 'good story' for news or fiction, and practical exigencies in the production process. The concentration of news on the most serious inter-personal crimes of violence, especially murder or sexual offences, is due to what reporters perceive as the essence of newsworthiness: individualisation, immediacy, drama, titillation and novelty (Chibnall, 1977: 22–45; Hall *et al.*, 1978; Ericson *et al.*, 1987, 1989 and 1991). These crimes are portrayed primarily as specific cases rather than in terms of broader social causes because the basic format of news schedules involves an event orientation – what's happened since the last news (Rock, 1973: 76–9). Perceptions of 'good stories' by writers and producers of popular fiction share a similar sense of what interests audiences (and audience interviews confirm this: Reiner and Livingstone, 1997).

Another ingredient of the conception of a 'good story' held by creators and audiences is a structure which resolves tension with a clear, satisfying outcome, as encapsulated in Miss Prism's celebrated definition of fiction in Wilde's *The Importance of Being Earnest*: 'The good ended happily, and the bad unhappily'. This inclines towards stories with crimes which are cleared up, since the majority of audience members are positioned with the victim or the law-enforcers by most crime stories (Sparks, 1992; Reiner and Livingstone, 1997).

In addition to the professional sense of what kinds of narratives interest and satisfy audiences, practical exigencies exert pressures on producers inclining towards a police-filtered perspective. The most overt of these have been formal and informal censorship pressures, deriving from a variety of moral entrepreneurs concerned about the criminogenic or destabilising consequences of media representations of crime and law enforcement. A clear example discussed earlier was the Hays Code, which in 1934 forced Hollywood to switch from producing films with gangster protagonists to ones featuring the FBI as heroes. More generally, it meant that until the Hays Code became ineffective in the mid-1950s, all Hollywood films had to conform to a message of 'crime doesn't pay'.

More consistently important than negative censorship pressures has been the need of producers of news and fiction to achieve and maintain practical co-operation with the police. The exigencies of news production in particular have several unintended pro-police ideological consequences. The focus on cleared-up cases, which creates a misleading image of police effectiveness, is primarily a result of the economics of allocating reporting resources, which requires the allocation of personnel to institutional settings, such as courts, where newsworthy events can be expected to recur regularly. Considerations of convenience and personal safety lead cameramen and reporters typically to cover incidents such as riots from behind police positions, creating an image of the police as 'us', and the people they are dealing with as 'them' (Murdock, 1982: 108–9).

Above all, the police control much of the information on which crime news reporters depend, which gives them an inevitable degree of power as essential and accredited sources (Chibnall, 1977; Ericson *et al.*, 1987, 1989 and 1991). This allows the police often to be the 'primary definers' of crime news, which is framed by their perspective (Hall *et al.*, 1978: 58). There is considerable variation between news production processes and procedures according to the medium and market in which they work, and contingency and cock-up play a central role in determining day-to-day content (Ericson *et al.*, 1991: 93–4). None the less, the most comprehensive study of the creation of crime news concluded that 'the news media are as much an agency of *policing* as the law-enforcement agencies whose activities and classifications are reported on' (Ericson *et al.*, 1991: 74). They reproduce order whilst representing it. Although there are no systematic studies of the production of crime fiction in any medium, the hallmark of police stories above all has been a realist style and the appearance of verisimilitude. It is likely that this too sets up pressures to obtain police co-operation which are analogous to those for news production, albeit not as pervasive or tight.

Whilst crime stories in both news and fiction have generally legitimated the police, as shown by studies of content and production, there have been considerable changes over time in the extent and the way that this has been accomplished (Reiner and Livingstone, 1997). There are also important differences between different media, and within any medium at different market levels, for example between popular and 'quality' newspapers (Ericson *et al.*, 1991).

Several commentators have noted the clear shifts in television representations of the police in particular (Hurd, 1979; Clarke, 1982, 1983, 1986 and 1992; Laing, 1991; Sparks, 1992, 1993; Reiner, 1992, 1994 and 1996; Leishman, 1995; Eaton, 1996). There has been a clear parade of contrasting images, from the cosily consensual world of *Dixon of Dock Green* in the 1950s, via the gradual hardening image in *Z-Cars* in the 1960s, to the tough vigilantism of *The Sweeney* in the 1970s. In contemporary representations there is a complex coexistence of a range of diverse images: the synthesis of several previous models in *The Bill*, as well as the nostalgic worlds of *Heartbeat* and classic sleuth stories like *Morse*, and the politicised policing portrayed in *Between the Lines* or *The Chief.*

Shifting media representations of policing since the Second World War: empirical data

A more systematic analysis of the changing images of police in the media is provided by a historical content analysis of changing representations of crime and criminal justice which I have recently conducted with Sonia Livingstone and Jessica Allen (Reiner and Livingstone, 1997; Allen et al., 1998[2]) We examined a random sample of all films released in Britain from 1945–91 to examine the extent to which they were concerned with crime, and carried out a detailed quantitative and qualitative content analysis of 84 out of the 196 crime films which have been top box-office successes in that period. We also analysed in detail a random sample of nearly 500 crime-related stories from *The Times* and the *Mirror* between 1945–91. Finally, we conducted an analysis of those crime series which featured in the ten top-rated shows on television from 1955–91.

The different media vary in the extent to which the police figure prominently in the stories analysed. The police typically played a minor role in cinema films until the mid-1960s. Hardly any films in our sample for the period 1945–65 featured police heroes, but after the late 1960s police protagonists became the most common type in the cinema. The police have, however, always been the most common protagonists of television crime series, though this is to a slightly decreasing extent. In the period up to 1979, 64 per cent of the top-rated TV crime series had police heroes, but in the 1980s this falls to 43 per cent. In newspapers the proportion of stories which were about the criminal justice system (as distinct from specific crimes) rose in the period since the war, but has always been greater in *The Times* than in the *Mirror*. Criminal justice stories rose from 2 per cent of all stories on average from 1945–51 to 6 per cent 1985–91 in the *Mirror*, and from 3 per cent to 9 per cent in *The Times*.[3] Overall the police are more frequently the central protagonists in stories in all the media now than in the immediate post-war period, but the change is most marked in the cinema, and least on television, where the dominance of police heroes has slightly receded.

In all, the media the representation of the police became *less* positive over the period as a whole, though still remaining predominantly positive. However, this declining trend in positive images of policing overall masks some important complexities. For most aspects of the representation of the integrity or the effectiveness of the police which we examined, there is a clear curvilinear pattern. The police are presented most positively in the first part of our period, from 1945–63. Their image is most negatively presented overall in the middle part of our period, from 1964–79. In the last years of our period, 1980–91, there is some recovery in the overall representation of police ethics and efficiency. However, this turnback is itself complex because the total figures mask a bifurcation of images in recent years from very negative ones to attempts to resuscitate the earlier pattern of representation.

The extent to which crime is cleared up in media stories illustrates this. In cinema films the offender was brought to justice in 39 per cent of cases in

1945–64, and killed in another 9 per cent. After 1965 offenders were brought to justice in less than 15 per cent of films, but killed in 35 per cent. In press stories the proportion of crimes not cleared up was 23 per cent during 1945–63; 37 per cent 1964–79; and 31 per cent in 1980–91. Thus, although the broad conclusions of previous content analyses are confirmed by our study – the police are typically represented as effective – there are complex patterns of change in the extent to which this is true between different periods.

Another example is the extent to which the police are portrayed as caring and socially responsible, as opposed to just doing a job. From 1945–63 the police were represented as caring and responsible in 56 per cent of films, and instrumental in only 8 per cent. During 1964–79 only 6 per cent of films presented the police as caring/responsible, and 44 per cent as instrumental. From 1979–91 the respective proportions reverted to 39 per cent and 23 per cent. The representation of internal conflicts in the police organisation shows the same curvilinear pattern. This was shown in only 15 per cent of films in the first period, 79 per cent in the second, and 56 per cent in the third.

Excessive use of force by police was shown in only 3 per cent of films in the early period, 44 per cent in the middle, and 25 per cent in the third. Illicit investigation methods were shown in 11 per cent of films between 1945–63; 80 per cent in 1964–79; and 67 per cent in 1980–91. Corruption featured in no films in our sample before 1963, 13 per cent from 1964–79, and 15 per cent for 1980–91.

The personal characteristics of the police in films show the same pattern. Until 1963 no films had police protagonists whose lifestyle was deviant in any way. From 1964–79 this appeared in 33 per cent of films, but only in 17 per cent from 1980–91. During 1945–63, 50 per cent of police protagonists were caring and pleasant in manner; only 19 per cent from 1964–79; and 39 per cent after 1980. In the earliest period only 26 per cent of police protagonists were reacted to as sexually attractive within the narrative, but this was 63 per cent in the middle period, and 59 per cent after 1980.

The overall pattern of representation of police since 1945 thus seems curvilinear. Positive images are increasingly challenged after the mid-1960s, but with some bifurcation after the early 1980s between attempts to restore the past and even more negative representations of policing as ineffective or unjust.

Romantic realism in the risk society

Overall media representations of crime and law enforcement exhibit profound processes of change since the Second World War. We have attempted to summarise these by suggesting a rough periodisation in terms of three ideal-type patterns of representation of crime (Reiner and Livingstone, 1997). The first post-war decade is a period of consensus and social harmony in representations of criminal justice. Crime stories – news as well as fiction –

present an image of society as based largely on shared values and a clear yet accepted hierarchy of status and authority. Criminals were normally brought to justice, crime did not pay. The police were almost invariably represented as righteous, dedicated and efficient.

During the mid-1960s the dominant mode of representation of crime and justice shifts as the values and integrity of authority increasingly come to be questioned, and doubts about the fairness and effectiveness of the police proliferate. Increasing prominence is given to conflict: between ethnic groups, men and women, social classes, even within the criminal justice system itself. Whilst street cops feature increasingly as protagonists, they are more frequently morally tarnished if not outright corrupt. However, the increasing criticism of the social order and criminal justice is from a standpoint of reform, the advocacy of preferable alternatives.

Since the late 1970s another shift is discernible, the advent of what could be called a post-critical era. Stories are increasingly bifurcated between counter-critical ones, which seek to return as far as possible to the values of consensus (like *Heartbeat*), and those which represent a hopelessly disordered beyond-good-and-evil world, characterised by a Hobbesian war of all against all (epitomised by the work of Tarantino). It is this division of narratives which accounts for the curvilinear pattern of many variables: there is some attempt to restore the values of the past, challenged by representations which extend the critiques of the middle period.

Underneath the shifts in the mode of representation of concrete aspects of crime and policing, however, can be discerned a more fundamental shift in discourse. This is a demystification of authority and law, a change in the conceptualisation of policing and criminal justice from sacred to secular. The marked changes in the representation of victims which we have found are the clearest emblem of this. Crime moves from being something which must be opposed and controlled *ipso facto* because the law defines it thus, to a contested category. Criminality comes to be seen less as an offence against the sacred and absolute norms of law and morality, and more a matter of one individual harming another. The image of policing shifts from being symbolic of one overarching conception of order to managing diverse risks facing individuals and institutions – a characterisation which has been attributed to the practices of police organisations themselves.

The media still generally represent crime as wrong, but this is a pragmatic issue, turning on the risk of harm which may be suffered by individual victims, not derived from the authority of the law itself. The moral status of the police and other characters in a story (news or fiction) is no longer conferred by their role in the social order. Rather, it is subject to negotiation and must be established from scratch in each narrative, turning upon the demonstration of serious suffering caused to the victims who increasingly occupy the subject position of the narrative. (In an increasing minority of stories, these may even be the legally defined offenders, who may be represented as victimised by a criminal injustice system.)

The majority of narratives continue to work to justify ultimately the police and criminal justice viewpoint. However, this must now be achieved by demonstrating particular harm to identifiable and sympathetic individual victims. This usually serves to provide a tentative and utilitarian legitimation of the police as their would-be protectors, though in an increasing number of stories the police are either irrelevant, ineffective or are themselves lawbreakers or rule-benders. In this sense the media both continue to reproduce order and to function as sources of social control, whilst also reflecting the increasing individualism of a less deferential and more desubordinate culture. The police image is no longer paragon or pig, but the practical provider of a product: the management of risk. The performance of the police is assessed pragmatically on a case-by-case basis in terms of its value to individual clients: policing for the age of the Audit Commission.

Notes

1 These conclusions are drawn mainly from Roshier (1973); Chibnall (1977); Dominick (1978); Pandiani (1978); Ditton and Duffy (1983); Garofalo (1981); Ericson *et al.* (1989, 1991); Marsh (1991); Surette (1992); Reiner (1992: ch. 5, 1997); Williams and Dickinson (1993); Lichter *et al.* (1994); Sacco (1995); Bailey and Hale (1998).
2 This research was supported by a grant from the Economic and Social Research Council (Great Britain), No. L/210/25/2029, to whom we are grateful.
3 The pattern for crime stories is the reverse of that for criminal justice stories. The proportion in the *Mirror* rose from 9 per cent in 1945–51 to 21 per cent in 1985–91, whilst in *The Times* it rose from 7 per cent to 21 per cent. There is a marked increase in both papers, but whereas crime stories used to be more common in the *Mirror* than *The Times,* the latter has now caught up.

References

Allen, J., Livingstone, S. and Reiner, R. (1998) 'True Lies: Changing Images of Crime in British Postwar Cinema', *European Journal of Communication,* 13 (1).

Bailey, F. and Hale, D. (eds) (1998) *Popular Culture, Crime and Justice.* Belmont: Wadsworth.

Becker, S. and Stephens, M. (eds) (1994) *Police Force, Police Service.* Basingstoke: Macmillan.

Bennett, T., Mercer, C. and Woollacott, J. (eds) (1986) *Popular Culture and Social Relations.* Milton Keynes: Open University Press.

Berry, G. Izat, J., Mawby, R. and Walley, L. (1998) *Practical Police Management.* London: Police Review Publishing Co.

Black, G.D. (1994) *Hollywood Censored: Morality Codes, Catholics and the Movies.* Cambridge: Cambridge University Press.

Brandt, G. (ed.) (1993) *British Television Drama in the 1980s.* Cambridge: Cambridge University Press.

Chesterton, G.K. (1901) *The Defendant.* London: Dent.

Chibnall, S. (1977) *Law and Order News.* London: Tavistock.

Chibnall, S. (1979) 'The Metropolitan Police and the News Media' in Holdaway (1979).

Clarke, A. (1982) *Television Police Series and Law and Order* (Popular Culture Course Unit 22) Milton Keynes: Open University.

Clarke, A. (1983) 'Holding the Blue Lamp: Television and the Police in Britain', *Crime and Social Justice*, 19.

Clarke, A. (1986) 'This is Not the Boy Scouts: Television Police Series and Definitions of Law and Order' in Bennett *et al.* (1986).

Clarke, A. (1992) '"You're Nicked!" Television Police Series and the Fictional Representation of Law and Order' in Strinati and Wagg (1992).

Cohen, S. and Young, J. (eds) (1973) *The Manufacture of News*. London: Constable.

Corner, J. (ed.) (1991) *Popular Television in Britain: Studies in Cultural History*. London: British Film Institute.

Curran, J. and Gurevitch, M. (eds) (1996) *Mass Media and Society*. London: Arnold.

Davies, P. and Neve, B. (eds) (1981) *Politics, Society and Cinema in America*. Manchester: Manchester University Press.

Ditton, J. and Duffy, J. (1983) 'Bias in the Newspaper Reporting of Crime News', *British Journal of Criminology*, 23 (2).

Dominick, J. (1978) 'Crime and Law Enforcement in the Mass Media' in Winick (1978).

Downes, D. and Morgan, R. (1997) 'Dumping the "Hostages to Fortune"? The Politics of Law and Order in Post-War Britain' in Maguire *et al.* (1997).

Eaton, M. (1996) 'A Fair Cop? Viewing the Effects of the Canteen Culture in *Prime Suspect* and *Between the Lines*' in Kidd-Hewitt and Osborne (1996).

Ericson, R., Baranek, P. and Chan, J. (1987) *Visualising Deviance*. Milton Keynes: Open University Press.

Ericson, R., Baranek, P. and Chan, J. (1989) *Negotiating Control*. Milton Keynes: Open University Press.

Ericson, R., Baranek, P. and Chan, J. (1991) *Representing Order*. Milton Keynes: Open University Press.

Garofalo, J. (1981) 'Crime and the Mass Media: A Selective Review of Research', *Journal of Research in Crime and Delinquency*, 18 (2).

Hall, S., Critchley, C., Jefferson, T., Clarke, J. and Roberts, B. (1978) *Policing the Crisis*. Basingstoke: Macmillan.

Hennigan, K., Delrosario, M., Heath, L., Cook, J. and Calder, B. (1982) 'Impact of the Introduction of Television Crime in the United States: Empirical Findings and Theoretical Implications', *Journal of Personality and Social Psychology*, 42 (3).

Holdaway, S. (ed.) (1979) *The British Police*. London: Edward Arnold.

Hurd, G. (1979) 'The Television Presentation of the Police' in Holdaway (1979).

Kidd-Hewitt, D. and Osborne, R. (eds) (1996) *Crime and the Media: The Post-Modern Spectacle*. London: Pluto.

Laing, S. (1991) 'Banging in some Reality: The Original "Z-Cars"' in Corner (1991).

Leishman, F. (1995) 'On Screen – Police on TV', *Policing*, 11 (2).

Lichter, S.R., Lichter, L.S. and Rothman, S. (1994) *Prime Time: How TV Portrays American Culture*. Washington, DC: Regnery Publishing.

Livingstone, S. (1996) 'On the Continuing Problem of Media Effects' in Curran and Gurevitch (1996).

Loader, I. (1997) 'Policing and the Social: Questions of Symbolic Power', *British Journal of Sociology* 48 (1).

Maguire, M., Morgan, R. and Reiner, R. (eds) (1997) *The Oxford Handbook of Criminology.* Oxford: Oxford University Press.

Maguire, M. and Norris, C. (1992) *The Conduct and Supervision of Criminal Investigations.* London: HMSO.

Marsh, H.L. (1991) 'A Comparative Analysis of Crime Coverage in Newspapers in the United States and Other Countries from 1960–1989: A Review of the Literature', *Journal of Criminal Justice,* 19 (1).

Mathews, T.D. (1994) *Censored.* London: Chatto and Windus.

Mawby, R. (1997a) 'Managing Police Media and Public Relations', *Focus on Police Research and Development No. 9.* London: Home Office, Police Research Group.

Mawby, R. (1997b) 'Managing Media and Public Relations in the Police Service', *Police Research and Management,* Autumn.

Mawby, R. (1998) 'Managing the Image' in Berry *et al.* (1998).

Miller, D.A. (1988) *The Novel and the Police.* Berkeley: University of California Press.

Miller, W. (1977) *Cops and Bobbies.* Chicago: Chicago University Press.

Murdock, G. (1982) 'Disorderly Images' in Sumner (1982).

Ousby, I. (1976) *Bloodhounds of Heaven: The Detective in English Fiction From Godwin to Doyle.* Cambridge, MA: Harvard University Press.

Pandiani, J. (1978) 'Crime Time TV: If All We Knew Is What We Saw', *Contemporary Crises,* 2 (2).

Pearson, G. (1983) *Hooligan.* London: Macmillan.

Powers, R.G. (1983) *G-Men: Hoover's FBI in American Popular Culture.* Carbondale, IL: Southern Illinois University Press.

Reiner, R. (1981) 'Keystone to Kojak: the Hollywood Cop' in Davies and Neve (1981).

Reiner, R. (1992) *The Politics of the Police.* Hemel Hempstead: Wheatsheaf.

Reiner, R. 1994) 'The Dialectics of Dixon: The Changing Image of the TV Cop' in Becker and Stephens (1994).

Reiner, R. (1996) 'Crime and Media' in Sasson and Diamond (1996).

Reiner, R. (1997) 'Media Made Criminality' in Maguire *et al.* (1997).

Reiner, R. and Livingstone, S. (1997) *Discipline or Desubordination? Changing Media Images of Crime.* End of Award Report: Grant L210252029. Swindon: Economic and Social Research Council.

Rock, P. (1973) 'News As Eternal Recurrence' in Cohen and Young (1973).

Roshier, R. (1973) 'The Selection of Crime News by the Press' in Cohen and Young (1973).

Rutter, M. and Smith, D. (eds) (1995) *Psychological Disorders in Young People.* London: Wiley.

Sacco, V.F. (1995) 'Media Constructions of Crime', *The Annals of the American Academy of Political and Social Science,* 539 (1).

Sasson, H. and Diamond, D. (eds) (1996) *LSE on Social Science.* London: LSE Publishing.

Schlesinger, P. and Tumber, H. (1994) *Reporting Crime.* Oxford: Oxford University Press.

Schramm, W., Lyle, J. and Parker, E.B. (1961) *Television in the Lives of Our Children.* Stanford, CA: Stanford University Press.

Sparks, R. (1992) *Television and the Drama of Crime.* Milton Keynes: Open University Press.

Sparks, R. (1993) 'Inspector Morse: *The Last Enemy*' in Brandt (1993).

Strinati, D. and Wagg, S. (eds) (1992) *Come on Down? Popular Media Culture in Post-War Britain.* London: Routledge.

Sumner, C. (ed.) (1982) *Crime, Justice and the Mass Media.* Cropwood Papers, 14. Cambridge University: Institute of Criminology.

Surette, R. (1992) *Media, Crime, and Criminal Justice.* Belmont, CA: Wadsworth.

Walker, N. (1996) 'Defining Core Police Tasks: The Neglect of the Symbolic Dimension', *Policing and Society,* 6 (1).

Wartella, E. (1995) 'Media and Problem Behaviours in Young People' in Rutter and Smith (1995).

Williams, P. and Dickinson, J. (1993) 'Fear of Crime: Read All About It? The Relationship Between Newspaper Crime Reporting and Fear of Crime', *British Journal of Criminology,* 33 (1).

Winick, C. (ed.) (1978) *Deviance and Mass Media.* Beverley Hills, CA: Sage.

Chapter 5

Private policing: problems and prospects

LES JOHNSTON

Introduction

By and large, popular and academic debate about private policing has displayed two tendencies. First, it has focused on the activities of uniformed security guards and, to a lesser extent, of private investigators. Secondly, it has explored controversial issues arising from the growth of private policing, including its lack of public accountability, its poor standards of recruitment and training, and its encroachment upon the traditional mandate of the public police. Though these questions are, undoubtedly, crucial – and remain underresearched – they also have to be situated in a wider context. For, without that wider reference, there is the danger that critics will be 'unable to see the wood for the trees'.

The basic proposition of this chapter is that the growth of private policing has to be considered within the context of late modern 'mentalities' or 'ways of thinking'. So considered, 'late modern policing' – the context within which private policing has to be situated – signifies a wider reconfiguration of governance. One effect of that reconfiguration is to undermine the very terms ('state' and 'society') through which the process of modern governance has been conceived. The chapter is in five sections. The first links the emergence of public (state) policing to the consolidation of modern societies. The second section considers some key features of late modern thinking, drawing particular attention to the significance of 'neo-liberal' and 'risk-based' thinking. The third section describes some significant developments in private policing, including those at the international and transnational levels. The fourth section explores the impact of risk-based thinking on both commercial and public police. The final section outlines some problems and prospects associated with the growth of late modern policing.

Modernity and state policing

Modern policing, as defined here, spans the period from the early nineteenth century to the last quarter of the twentieth, a pivotal stage in the development of what sociologists have termed 'modern society'. Throughout that period Western societies displayed the features identified by Durkheim, Weber and Marx as characteristically 'modern'. Thus, Britain could be depicted as a nation-state whose social relations were shaped by economic class divisions and whose social institutions were both functionally specialised and bureaucratically organised. As to the last of these, two institutions typified the image of the modern bureaucracy: military organisations, whose function was to secure the nation-state and its citizens from the external threats posed by invading armies; and police organisations, whose function was to protect the state and its citizens from the internal threats posed by acts of crime and disorder committed by the 'dangerous classes'.

Prior to the formation of specialised, professional police organisations, policing was organised on a relatively *ad hoc* basis. First, it was not perceived to be the direct responsibility of the state. Rather, responsibility for policing lay in local civil society, the police role being delegated to parish constables and other members of the local community. In effect, governmental functions such as policing were dispersed or 'distanciated' (Giddens, 1990): what one would nowadays call 'government (or rule) at a distance' (Rose and Miller, 1992; Shearing, 1996). Secondly, policing was very diverse in character. In the early nineteenth century, for example, Portsmouth was policed by the navy, the military, customs officers, and the yeomanry, as well as by borough police, municipal police, beadles, night watchmen and commercial security (Field, 1981).

The formation of the 'new police' in 1829 symbolised the shift to modern policing. This shift was inextricably linked to the establishment of the modern state and, through it, to the consolidation of modern society. The modernising project was driven by a complex of post-Enlightenment values (concerning rational action, scientific knowledge, behavioural predictability and governmental stability) which, having first located 'the social' as a field of action (whose study would, eventually, be undertaken by sociologists and other human scientists), then declared 'the state' to be the essential apparatus through which the bulk of social life was to be governed. Accordingly, one of the purposes of the legislation was to replace the past *ad hoc* system (the distanciated mixture of public and private, formal and informal provision) by one in which the state (through the police) bore responsibility for internal security. Thus began the period of the state's relative monopoly – never an absolute one – of policing. Of course, this did not produce 'state policing' in the Continental sense, where national police forces were controlled by a monarch or other dominant power. There was widespread resistance to the idea of a single, national police force in Britain on the ground that it would undermine liberty. Nevertheless, the new police reforms confirmed that policing was to be the prerogative of the state, albeit at the local level. In addition, two other things were striking. First, the new police's mandate was defined in moral as well as criminological terms – confirmation of the state's role in the wider governance of social life (Storch, 1975, 1976). Secondly, the uniformed police officer served as the routine embodiment of state sovereignty, personifying public authority at 'street level' by virtue of the legal powers residing in the office of constable.

Late modern thinking

It has been suggested by some writers that we are now living through a period of 'late', 'high' or 'post' modernity (Bottoms and Wiles, 1996; Giddens, 1990; Crook *et al.*, 1993). Some of the main factors which have led to the emergence of 'late modern policing' were identified in the previous edition of this book (Johnston, 1996a). Amongst these factors, three were of particular importance. First, changes at the economic level – notably the transfer of private business practices to the public sector by means of the 'New Public Management' (NPM) reforms – have required police organisations to behave, more and more, like commercial enterprises. Secondly, changes at the socio-cultural level have led to the suggestion that personal consumption has replaced economic class as the main form of social identity (Waters, 1995). Moreover, differentiation by age, gender, ethnicity, region, religion, lifestyle and nationality has grown in significance raising the question of whether a state-centred system of policing, designed to pacify the 'dangerous classes', is suited to cope with plural divisions and conflicts. Thirdly, there is the question of the state itself. Here, a number of developments appear to call 'state rule' into question: economic privatisation 'rolls back the state' in key functional areas; globalisation has an impact on the sovereignty of nation-states; and NPM reforms produce 'arms length' modes of administration. As a result, the imagery of state rule has been superseded by an altogether more complex picture of governance in which, it is said, the state is being 'hollowed out' (Rhodes, 1994), 'stretched' (Bottoms and Wiles, 1996), or 'unravelled' (Crook *et al.*, 1993).

One issue which also demands consideration is the impact of late modern 'mentalities' on governance, in general, and on policing, in particular. This issue can be illustrated, first by reference to the concept of risk and secondly by reference to neo-liberal forms of thinking. As to the first of these, it has now become commonplace for sociologists to argue that we live in a 'risk society' (Beck, 1992).[1] Beck, who coined the term, sees risk as one of the defining features of modernity since it (modernity) 'transforms everything into decisions and, therefore, into risks' (Beck, 1996: 35). What Beck seems to have in mind here is a distinction between pre-modern 'class societies' (dominated by the fatalistic acceptance of incalculable hazards, such as the Black Death) and modern societies (dominated by rational calculation as to how best to identify and avoid risks). This preoccupation with risk seems to be borne out by our everyday experiences. Eating is risky (pesticides, additives, 'E' numbers, BSE), and so is dieting (anorexia, bulimia). Work is risky (job-induced stress, fear of unemployment, sexual and racial harassment in the workplace, repetitive strain injury), but unemployment is more so (poverty and depression). Walking the streets is risky (robbers, muggers, stalkers, rapists), but so too is staying at home (burglars, domestic accidents, domestic violence, marital rape).

Our awareness of risk, whether real or imagined, and its associated insecurity is accompanied by the emergence of specialists whose professed aim is to manage and minimise risks: these include dieticians, ecologists, counsellors, therapists, investment and pensions advisers, commercial risk managers, credit-rating agencies, drug-testing services, crime-prevention experts, and the like. Both risk and the expertise for dealing with it are ubiquitous. Consider a mundane example. One might not consider walking to be a par-ticularly risky enterprise. Yet, the publicity material attached to a well-known brand of boots, popular amongst young people, warns potential buyers of the hazards associated with this dangerous activity. Walking, we are told, sends constant shock waves up the foot and leg causing pain and fatigue. Fortunately, these problems can be minimised by the technical qualities of the boots in question whose shock-absorbing track – designed, of course, by experts – is able to absorb impact and inject a spring into the step of poten-tial victims.

Beck (1992) maintains that, whereas class society was dominated by ideo-logical disputes about the equitable distribution of social products, members of a risk society have no interest in the attainment of 'good' normative ends, such as social equality or social justice. Instead, they are obsessed with mat-ters of personal security (what Beck terms 'preventing the worst') and, by implication, live in an order which is, effectively, asocial. This asocial view of human relations is also reflected in neo-liberal thinking, the impact of which has been dramatic throughout Western societies during the last two decades. The leading proponent of the neo-liberal position was Hayek (1960, 1976) who denied the justification for welfare-liberalism (state intervention for pur-poses of social welfare, social redistribution, social planning or social justice) on three grounds: first that such intervention usually undermined individual liberties and, as such, constituted coercion; secondly, that since government could not 'know' the individual preferences of its many citizens, social inter-vention had no valid epistemological foundation; and thirdly, that 'society' – in whose name governments invoked state intervention – was merely a form of words used to describe an aggregation of atomised individuals (or, as Mrs Thatcher was later to put it, 'There is no such thing as society').[2]

Early analysis of the neo-liberal project focused, understandably, on the issue of economic privatisation. Yet, it was increasingly clear that neo-liberalism aspired to the wholesale 'reinvention of government' (Osborne and Gaebler, 1993), rather than merely to the sale of state assets. Thus the 'privatisation of policing' was made up of a complex mixture of commercial, municipal and community-based developments occurring at a bewildering variety of sectoral and spatial levels, all of them featuring the dispersal or 'distanciation' of rule (Johnston, 1992). Such distanciation was apparent, not just in the commer-cialisation of public services, but also in attempts to disperse governmental responsibilities to communities through 'community policing', 'community education', 'community justice', 'punishment in the community', 'care in the community' and similar. This project of reinvention had major implica-tions for the state and society. On the one hand, demands to reimpose welfare-liberalism – by 'bringing the state back in' – were no longer tenable since the morphology of the state had been profoundly affected by the neo-liberal project.[3] On the other hand, the fragmentation of the social realm into disparate 'communities' and interest groups was indicative of what one writer termed 'the death of the social' (Rose, 1996).[4] Together, the implication of these two developments was clear. The basic assumption of modern governance – that the state was the essential mechanism for governing social life – was doubly unsustainable.

Late modern policing: developments in commercial security

This section and the following one consider some key features of late modern policing. One such feature is its diversity, something which was explored in detail previously (Johnston, 1996a). Though there is insufficient space to explore that issue further (see Johnston, 2000, for further discussion), it is clear that policing now consists of a complex network of security provision. At the local level, for instance, one finds public police, commercial security, 'special' police forces (such as parks constabularies), municipal security forces, and a plethora of community initiatives ranging from neighbourhood watch to organised vigilantism (Johnston, 1996b).

Obviously, the growth of commercial security has been a major factor in diversity. The industry grew quickly in North America during the 1960s and spawned a significant body of research (e.g. Kakalik and Wildhorn, 1972; Shearing and Stenning, 1981, 1983; Cunningham and Taylor, 1985; Cunningham et al., 1990). Commercial security personnel now outnumber public police in both the USA and Canada by a ratio of 2:1, and recent research suggests that average revenues for the US commercial security sector exceed $52 billion per annum, an amount nearly double that generated for public law enforcement through taxation (Kempa et al., 1999). In Britain, the industry's turnover stood at £5 million in 1950; had risen to £55 million by 1970 (Randall and Hamilton, 1972); and to more than £120 million by the middle of that decade (Home Office, 1979). Healthy growth continued during the next 20 years and turnover now exceeds £2 billion per annum (House of Commons, 1995). The wider European market has also grown rapidly. In 1992 the total market for security products and services in Germany, France, Italy, Spain and the UK stood at £11.2 billion, with Germany representing the largest market (£3.7 billion), followed by the UK (£2.4 billion) and France (£2.2 billion) (Narayan, 1994). Security services – mainly guarding and cash-in-transit – still retain the largest market share, though developments in the electronics field, such as CCTV (closed circuit television), access control and integrated security systems now display the highest annual rates of growth.

While the nations of north-western and north-central Europe have exhibited significant levels of overall growth, in eastern and southern Europe and in Asia – where the industry has only recently started from scratch – there has been a greater degree of relative growth (Kempa et al., 1999). In Japan, the first security company was only established in 1962, partly as a consequence of the security demands of the 1964 Tokyo Olympic Games (Miyazawa,

1991). Since then, the industry has experienced dramatic growth. Between 1989 and 1993 the number of commercial security companies grew from 5,248 to 7,062 and the number of guards from 232,617 to 321,721, this later figure exceeding the combined authorised police strength for the National and Prefectural Police by more than 60,000 (National Police Agency, 1994). Similar rapid development has occurred in Turkey, where enabling legislation was only passed in 1981 and where, by 1993, 2,227 institutions employed 34,928 people (Kempa *et al.*, 1999). The most dramatic growth has occurred, however, in post-apartheid South Africa where the industry now has an estimated value of just under 6 billion Rand. Official figures suggest that with 4,345 companies employing 363, 928 registered guards, numbers employed in commercial security exceed members of the South African Police Service by a ratio of about 3:1 (de Waard, 1999).

Important comparative research carried out in ten European countries (de Waard and van der Hoek, 1991; de Waard, 1993) has claimed that, despite rapid expansion in the last two decades, the commercial security industry in Europe – unlike that in North America, Japan and South Africa – remains the secondary, rather than the primary, protective source. In the course of that research the authors identified numbers of police personnel, numbers of commercial security personnel, total security personnel (police plus commercial security) and the ratio of public to commercial security for each individual country. Analysis of the data suggested that Germany had the highest numbers of commercial security personnel (307 per 100,000 population) followed by Sweden (182), Spain (165) and Portugal (150). As the authors admitted, however, one has to be cautious about comparison. Official data obtained from countries with rigorous regulatory systems (such as The Netherlands) are far more reliable than data obtained from jurisdictions without a licensing system (where the researchers were forced to rely on experts' estimates of numbers employed).

The latest findings from this continuing programme of research (de Waard, 1999) need to be assessed in this light. Now, it is suggested, northern European countries – Britain (275 commercial security personnel per 100,000 population), Germany (217), Luxembourg (201), Denmark (193) and Sweden (184) – occupy the top five positions in the commercial security 'league table'.[5] It is interesting to compare this estimate of employment in Britain with Jones and Newburn's (1998) recent study. This research, which adopts a broader definition of private security than de Waard's (1999), suggests that total employment in the British commercial security sector amounts to 333,631. Though the authors accept that this figure might be a 'significant overestimate', if accurate it would mean that Britain has 588 security personnel per 100,000 inhabitants (more than twice the figure cited in the Dutch research) and a public police to commercial security ratio of 1: 1.85 (Johnston, 2000). Such a conclusion would be significant for two reasons. First, it would bear comparison with North American ratios of the recent past. Secondly, it would suggest that commercial security in Britain is now a primary, rather than a secondary, protective source.

It is also important to note that while 51 per cent of companies sampled in Jones and Newburn's (1998) study employed five or fewer people and 88 per cent employed fewer than 50 people, a small number of large companies dominate domestic and international markets. At present, four companies in Britain (Williams Holdings: £372 million, Securicor: £310 million, Group 4: £158 million, and Rentokil Initial: £110 million) account for almost £1 billion of market turnover (Garrett, 1997). The domination of large multinational corporations over domestic markets is reflected in their increased penetration of overseas ones. The Securicor Group employs 41,000 staff in an organisation whose subsidiaries engage in a bewildering variety of security and non-security activities including guarding, alarms and electronic surveillance, cash-in-transit, the construction and design of prisons, hotel and leisure services and personnel recruitment. In recent years Securicor has undertaken an increasing number of joint ventures in South Africa, South-East Asia and the Americas. Developments in North America follow a similar pattern. The Pinkerton Organization employs 47,000 personnel in 250 offices throughout North and Central America, Asia and Europe (Business Wire, 1998). Its chief rival, the Wackenhut Corporation, employs 56,000 people in a variety of functions, including prison management and the provision of security services to nuclear installations. In 1997 Wackenhut enjoyed 24.4 per cent growth in international sales from its activities in 50 countries (Hoover, 1998).

One striking development has been the increased involvement of multinational security corporations in private correctional facilities. The effects of such involvement on company revenues is well-illustrated by the case of Wackenhut. Wackenhut set up a Corrections Division in 1984 and by 1995 the Division accounted for 12 per cent of the company's $797 million revenue. Two years later the annual revenue from corrections increased by 50 per cent (following a 38 per cent increase the previous year) to account for 19 per cent of a total revenue of $1,127 million. In effect, revenue from corrections is now almost double the revenue from all company sources recorded in 1976 (Wackenhut, 1998).

Another significant development has been the commercial penetration of national security, defence and foreign policy by 'professional service companies', such as Sandline, Military Professional Resources Inc. (MPRI), Defence Services Ltd and Executive Outcomes (EO). Such companies, unlike the mercenaries of the 1960s, select their personnel carefully and, in consequence, enjoy a degree of official endorsement. Thus, the US administration played a successful role in lobbying the Angolan government on behalf of MPRI (an American company), the Angolans having previously hired EO (a South African company) to reverse the military gains of the UNITA army. Subsequently, EO – having recruited large numbers of personnel from the South African Police and Defence Forces following their 'downsizing' – undertook work on behalf of the country's defence forces, mining companies and drugs enforcement agencies. Speculating on future market opportunities, EO's publicity material predicts that, in the future, there will be considerable scope for expansion in the field of 'peacekeeping and refugee operations' (Executive Outcomes, 1998).

Late modern policing: risk-based thinking

As was stated previously, we live in a society where organisations are predisposed to think in terms of the identification, management and minimisation of risks. This way of thinking has always been a defining characteristic of commercial security and latterly state agencies, like the police, have begun to follow suit. Such melding of commercial and public police mentalities has been evident for some time. A decade ago Cohen (1985) observed that situational crime prevention, far from being concerned with causal explanation of crime, was interested solely in its temporal and spatial manipulation through techniques such as defensible space and target hardening. This lack of concern about causality is reflected in Broder's classic definition of commercial risk management: 'Risk management is the anticipation, recognition and appraisal of a risk and the initiation of some action to remove the risk or reduce the potential loss from it to an acceptable level (Broder, cited in Nalla and Newman, 1990: 92).

Risk management has a number of objectives: to anticipate risk by proactive means, rather than merely to react to risks which have been realised; to calculate the potential losses arising from their occurrence; to establish a balance between losses and the costs of intervention; to minimise and control risks or, if needs be, to transfer them elsewhere. In the case of the last of these, it is not unusual for commercial risks to be transferred to insurance companies. But there are parallels in policing and crime prevention with citizens being given greater responsibility for purchasing their own security; and for providing for it by responsible means (e.g. joining a Neighbourhood Watch group) or through acts of autonomous citizenship (vigilante street patrols) (Johnston, 1996b).

Since this way of thinking is rational and pragmatic, its focus being on anticipation, proactive engagement, and careful actuarial calculation of the costs and benefits associated with particular decisions, it depends upon the systematic generation of information for analysis. In order to produce such information it is necessary to undertake systematic surveillance of those individuals, groups and locations which might be a source of risk; or, indeed, of those individuals who might consciously or unconsciously facilitate the occurrence of risks. This suggests that the target for surveillance is not merely wrongdoers, but those who might be victims of wrongdoing, or who might allow wrongs to occur. In this regard, Shearing and Stenning (1981) were right to define surveillance as the core function of (commercial) security. Increasingly, however, that core function cannot be separated from its wider role in providing information for risk analysis.

The public police's growing commitment to intelligence-gathering, anticipatory thinking, proactive intervention, systematic surveillance and rational calculation of the costs and benefits of particular operations, demonstrates an ethos comparable to commercial risk management. Consider the case of crime management. Here, the Audit Commission (1993) has encouraged forces to set up crime management desks in order to allocate resources more efficiently, to target prolific offenders, to make better use of informants and to develop integrated systems for compiling and interrogating databases. The head of the National Crime Faculty at the Police Staff College, Bramshill has stated that criminal investigation is undergoing a fundamental shift 'from an emphasis on resource allocation to [one on] detectability' (Pyke, cited in Gibbons, 1996: 4). According to this model the old system of categorising crimes according to resource availability and type of offence is replaced by one balancing available skills (personnel) with data quality (intelligence). By these means an assessment can be made of the costs and benefits of deploying a given investigative technique and, indeed, of whether the particular level of detectability justifies an investigation being undertaken at all.

Of course, such practices depend upon the production of high-quality intelligence. One key element of intelligence-led policing is the cultivation of informants, something which the Audit Commission, the Home Office, the Association of Chief Police Officers and Her Majesty's Inspectorate of Constabulary have supported in recent years. However, the use of informants is controversial for several reasons. First, there are problems at the organisational level: the danger that informants may control those who supervise them, rather than vice versa; the likelihood that officers who gain information from informants will use it for personal career advancement, rather than for the collective good of the organisation. Secondly, there are ethical considerations: the prospect that the deployment of informants may 'amplify deviance', facilitate criminal activity or encourage officers to become involved in 'noble cause corruption' (Dunnighan and Norris, 1997; Gill, 1994; Marx, 1988). Thirdly, the effectiveness and efficiency of informants may be called into question due to their high deployment costs, high attrition rates and natural tendency to overestimate the value of the information they give (Norris, 1996; Gill, 1994). Yet, on this third point, Gill (1994) reminds us that the productivity of informants is not to be measured solely in terms of the quality of the information they generate. A key function of informants – particularly those employed by state security services – has always been to create disruption amongst targeted groups (Gill, 1994: 155). Indeed, for Brodeur (1983), one of the defining elements of 'high policing' is that it deploys informants not only to collect information but also to create disruption.

It is useful to bear this in mind when assessing the impact of the Security Services Act 1996, under the provisions of which MI5 agents will work alongside police officers in the fight against terrorist and drug-related crimes. This development is important for two reasons. First, it is clear that 'techniques of disorganisation' (Johnston, 2000) may be deployed to undermine the activities of targeted criminal groups. Such techniques are commonplace in state security (where counter-intelligence, disinformation and misinformation are widespread). They are also well known in the commercial security sector where critics have long drawn a distinction between public-formal justice and informal-commercial justice (South, 1988). A comment from a 'Home Office source' regarding the enhanced role of MI5 suggested that 'disrupting the activities of organised criminals may be a desirable role if MI5 is unable to bring them to justice'. This idea of making life difficult for criminals whom the law cannot touch was illustrated in a recently reported incident in which the security services 'managed to identify a drug runner's bank account and remove all the funds from it' (Palmer, 1997). Secondly, this development – considered alongside the emergence of 'professional service companies' in the field of foreign and defence policy – is indicative of the growing inter-penetration of civil, military and commercial security at domestic and international levels, the significance of which has yet to be assessed (Johnston, forthcoming).

Two other areas of development – both linked to the growing importance of risk-based thinking – are worthy of brief comment. First, there is the increased deployment of electronic surveillance devices by commercial and public police alike. Closed-circuit television is the exemplar of a risk-based (actuarial) technology since, under it, aggregate populations, rather than particular offending groups, constitute the 'risky' community. Secondly, there is the question of how risk-based mentalities impact on the police themselves. Ericson and his colleagues (Ericson, 1994; Ericson and Carriere, 1994; Ericson and Haggerty, 1996) suggest that police organisations have become part of a network of information-based expert systems, seeking to produce knowledge for – and to collect reciprocal knowledge from – other security agencies. Since the police are, more and more, enmeshed in multi-agency information networks, they are, effectively, 'information-brokers' and, for that reason, Ericson (1994) suggests that 'community policing' could, more accurately, be described as 'communications policing'.

Problems and possibilities

Late modern policing combines diversity and risk. The former leads to the increased fragmentation of policing. The latter leads to similarity of thought and action between different security organisations.[6] It may also lead to the proliferation of security, since risk-orientation fuels the demand for 'more policing'.

These developments raise various problems which will need to be addressed in the future. Take first the issue of diversity. Fragmentation of policing, if left unchecked, may give rise to a patchwork system of security which combines ineffectiveness (due to a lack of co-ordination between the diverse elements) and injustice (due to inequities in the distribution of secu-rity and risk). The model of diverse policing described previously (Johnston, 1996a: 63) is one in which towns and cities are policed by a complex of agen-cies: public police; commercial security (contracted by groups of residents, by businesses or by local authorities); municipal constabularies; municipal security forces; activated neighbourhood watch groups; and groups of active citizens engaged in various forms of civil policing. The danger is, of course, that without effective governance that mixture might degenerate into an anarchic patchwork.

This governmental problem consists of two elements. First, there is the issue of equity. In a 'two-thirds-one-third' society where goods (including security) are already distributed unevenly, inequity will increase if the market is allowed to determine the distribution of security and risk. In these circumstances, it will be necessary to look for new solutions. Addressing that issue in a North American context, Bayley and Shearing (1996) have suggested that poor people should be given the means to participate in markets for security through the provision of block grants to communities. Such grants would empower the poor and, by so doing, enable them to purchase security according to their needs.

Secondly, there is a problem of functional co-ordination: the question of what tasks the different agencies might, legitimately, undertake? Obviously, such a question raises issues of principle, something which was little discussed in the Posen Enquiry (Home Office, 1995), set up to examine police core and ancillary tasks. By contrast, The Independent Committee of Inquiry into the Role and Responsibilities of the Police (Police Foundation/Policy Studies Institute, 1996) did discuss some basic principles, proposing that, while police should retain their monopoly of legal powers of arrest and coercion, municipal security and regulated commercial security companies should have a legitimate role to play in patrol. An alternative position put forward by Brogden and Shearing (1993) is that sworn police should concentrate on law enforcement ('bandit catching') leaving crime prevention and community safety ('community policing') functions to municipal, civil and commercial bodies. In future there may be some movement towards such a 'dual model'. However, there are limits to how far the police can be restricted to a reactive law-enforcement role. After all, their involvement in risk-based thinking involves them, more and more, in proactive engagement.

As to the issue of risk, two problems, again, arise. First, it needs to be emphasised that risk-based policing, when undertaken by public police, does not replace, but is combined with, other policing styles. This is well-illustrated in the example of zero tolerance policing (ZTP). Ostensibly, ZTP is an enforcement-led strategy which aims to re-establish order on the streets by tackling so-called 'quality of life' offences. However, it is also assumed that enhanced street-level capacity will generate significantly higher levels of information for use in proactive, intelligence-led, policing. This duality of purpose is reflected in the disparity between public and police discourses. For the public – as, indeed, for many rank and file police officers – ZTP is about the vigorous policing of 'quality of life offences' on the streets. For police managers, ZTP is part of an intelligence-led strategy linked to the targeting of offenders; crime-pattern analysis; the collection, collation and dissemination of intelligence; the reform of organisational structures; the initiation of resource sensitive thinking (prioritisation); and the reform of communication systems (notably through the deployment of the Compstat system, which was first initiated in the New York Police Department).[7]

This raises a question. If there are to be new combinations of enforcement-led and risk-based policing, what implications might follow for justice? The example given earlier ('techniques of disorganisation') involves discipline being imposed on criminals – or those believed to be criminal – without recourse to law enforcement: what in the commercial sector might be called 'informal justice'. No doubt this is an excellent practice when administered to drugs barons and terrorists. But what defines a legitimate target for the receipt of such discipline? Certainly not criminal activity *per se* since the whole objective of proactive policing is to anticipate deviance rather than merely to respond to it. This raises obvious problems. For example, Hudson (1996) has suggested that injustice might arise if social factors (class, age, ethnicity, homelessness) are used as a basis for risk definition and, then, as a justification for penal intervention.

Secondly, there is the question of security. On the one hand, security is unevenly distributed and, under conditions of diversity, might become more so unless properly governed. On the other hand, the demand for security – if left unchecked – might engender something akin to what Marx (1988) has called 'the maximum security society'. Such a society would combine a quantitative excess of policing (due to providers acceding to, or even encouraging, the public's insatiable demand for 'more security') with its qualitative distortion (due to the proactive employment of increasingly invasive security technologies). The worst possible future would be one in which 'too much policing' was done 'too invasively' and distributed 'too unevenly'.

The implication of this is that diversity and risk demand the 'good' – that is, the effective, just and democratic – governance of security. Under modern conditions the mechanism for securing good governance was the liberal democratic state – a 'public sphere' whose function was to govern 'society' and embody 'the public interest'. For reasons described earlier, however, the dominance of the state–society pair is challenged by late modern developments. While rumours of the 'death of the state' and the 'death of the social' may, certainly, be exaggerated (Hirst and Thompson, 1995), late modernity has altered the morphology of governance to a significant degree. In particular, the good governance of security cannot be reduced to the imposition or re-imposition of the state's authority over policing, for the simple reason that the state – as a unified, authoritative, exclusively public body, with an in-built capacity to exercise sovereign control – is becoming a fiction.

This indicates a paradox. Diversity is linked to certain policing problems (over-policing of some; under-policing of others; invasive policing of all; inequitable, ineffective and unaccountable policing). Yet, with weakening sovereign authority, governmental diversity is also the context in which those problems have to be resolved. In effect, the pursuit of 'good governance' under late modern conditions demands that we 'embrace diversity'. Such a conclusion has implications for policing and for democracy. As to the first, a critical question concerns how to secure public interests under conditions of diverse policing. Here, the need is to construct a model of 'optimum polic-ing' (Johnston, 2000) where security is neither quantitatively excessive (to the detriment of social values and objectives other than security) nor qualita-tively invasive (to the detriment of public freedoms) and which satisfies conditions of public accountability, effectiveness and justice. As to the sec-ond, it is important to provide a corrective to the negative and pessimistic view of diversity adhered to by the majority of police and academics. Diversity is to be embraced not only because it is inevitable, but also because it offers genuine prospects of re-inventing government. Undoubtedly, the dangers of diversity should not be ignored. Yet, we should not lose sight of the fact that the demise of state-centred governance provides the opportunity for public life to be organised in a more self-directed manner than before.

Notes

1 In some respects, too commonplace, since the concept of risk society has severe limita-tions in the criminological context (see Johnston, 2000).
2 While neo-liberalism and neo-Conservatism both deny the concepts of 'society' and 'the social', they have very different conceptions of governance, the former seeking to govern through the market, the latter through some conception of a reconstituted community. See Kempa *et al.* (1999) for further discussion of this point.
3 For one thing, this changing morphology – caused by the growing interpenetration of the state, the market and civil society – makes it increasingly difficult to equate the state with 'public interests' and the market with 'private interests'. For a discussion of the public–private dichotomy in a policing context, see Johnston (1992).
4 See Johnston (1997) for an analysis of how this view affects community policing.
5 Britain's rapid ascent to the top of the European 'league table' is almost certainly due to the earlier research's underestimation of numbers employed (de Waard and van der Hoek, 1991). In this case, the expert estimate was obtained from a representative of the British Security Industry Association which appeared to include only employees of BSIA member-companies.
6 Neither of these tendencies should be overestimated, however. Many police practices remain reactive rather than proactive and are, to that extent, incompatible with risk-based thinking. Likewise, there are structural and attitudinal obstacles to collaboration between commercial, military and civil security.
7 This disparity between popular and managerial discourses was emphasised during a major conference on ZTP held two years ago (IEA, 1997). On the one hand, senior police officers, repeatedly, emphasised the significance of these developments. On the other hand, all dissociated themselves from the concept of 'zero tolerance policing' (even those who had done much to popularise the term's use) and very few made any reference to 'quality of life' offences.

References

Audit Commission (1993) *Helping With Enquiries: Tackling Crime Effectively.* London: Audit Commission.

Bailey, V. (ed.) (1981) *Policing and Punishment in Nineteenth Century Britain.* London: Croom Helm.

Bayley, D.H. and Shearing, C.D. (1996) 'The future of policing', *Law and Society Review*, 30 (3), 585–606.

Beck, U. (1992) *Risk Society: Towards a New Modernity*. London: Sage.

Beck, U. (1996) 'Risk Society and the Provident State' in Lash *et al.* (1996), 27–43.

Bennett, T. (ed.) (1996) *Preventing Crime and Disorder: Targeting Strategies and Responsibilities*. Cambridge: Institute of Criminology.

Bottoms, A. and Wiles, P. (1996) 'Understanding Crime Prevention in Late Modern Societies' in Bennett (1996), 1-42.

Brodeur, J.P. (1983) 'High Policing and Low Policing: Remarks about the Policing of Political Activities', *Social Problems*, 30, 507–20.

Brogden, M and Shearing, C.D. (1993) *Policing For a New South Africa*. London: Routledge.

Business Wire (1998) 'Pinkerton Names McCormick Senior Management Director, Business Risks International'. URL: http://www.businesswire.com

Cohen, S. (1985) *Visions of Social Control*. Cambridge: Polity Press.

Crook, S., Pakulski, J. and Waters, M. (eds) (1993) *Postmodernization: Change in Advanced Society*. London: Sage.

Cunningham, W.C., Strauchs, J.J. and van Meter, C.W. (1990) *Private Security Trends, 1970 to 2000: The Hallcrest Report II*. Boston: Butterworth-Heinemann.

Cunningham, W.C. and Taylor, T. (1985) *Private Security and Police in North America: The Hallcrest Report I*. Boston: Butterworth-Heinemann.

de Waard, J. (1993) 'The Private Security Sector in Fifteen European Countries: Size, Rules and Legislation', *Security Journal*, 4 (2), 58–63.

de Waard, J. (1999) 'The Private Security Industry: International Perspectives', *European Journal on Criminal Policy and Research*, 7 (1).

de Waard, J.J. and van der Hoek, J. (1991) *Private Security: Size of Sector and Legislation in The Netherlands and Europe*. The Hague: Dept. of Crime Prevention, Ministry of Justice.

Dunnighan, C. and Norris, C. (1997) 'Subterranean Blues: Conflict as an Unintended Consequence of the Police Use of Informers', paper presented to British Criminology Conference, The Queens University Belfast, July.

Ericson, R. (1994) 'The Division of Expert Knowledge in Policing and Security', *British Journal of Sociology*, 45 (2), 149–75.

Ericson, R. and Carriere, K. (1994) 'The Fragmentation of Criminology' in Nelken (1994), 89–109.

Ericson, R. and Haggerty, K. (1996) 'The Population of Police', paper presented to the Joint Meeting of the American Law and Society Association and the Research Committee on the Sociology of Law of the International Sociological Association, Glasgow, 10–13 July.

Executive Outcomes (1998) URL: http://www.eo.com/about.html

Field, J. (1981) 'Police, Power and Community in a Provincial English Town: Portsmouth 1815–75' in Bailey (1981), 42–64.

Francis, P., Davies, P. and Jupp, V. (eds) (1997) *Policing Futures. The Police, Law Enforcement and the Twenty-First Century*. Basingstoke: Macmillan.

Garrett, A. (1997) 'When Rising Crime Equals Rising Profits', *Observer*, 8 June.

Gibbons, S. (1996) 'Change to Criminal Investigation Planned to Save Time and Money', *Police Review*, 23 August, 4.

Giddens, A. (1990) *The Consequences of Modernity*. Cambridge: Polity.

Gill, P. (1994) *Policing Politics: Security Intelligence and the Liberal Democratic State*. London: Frank Cass.

Gormley, W.T. (ed.) (1991) *Privatization and Its Alternative*. Madison: University of Wisconsin Press.

Hayek, F.A. (1960) *The Constitution of Liberty*. London: Routledge and Kegan Paul.

Hayek, F.A. (1976) *The Road to Serfdom*. London: Routledge and Kegan Paul.

Hirst, P. and Thompson, G. (1995) 'Globalization and the Future of the Nation State', *Economy and Society*, 243, 408–42.

Home Office (1979) *The Private Security Industry: A Discussion Paper*. London: HMSO.

Home Office (1995) *Review of Core and Ancillary Tasks*. London: HMSO.

Hoover (1998) Company Profiles: Wackenhut. URL: http://www.pathfinder.com/money/hoovers/corpdirectoryplus/w/wak.html

House of Commons (1995) 'First report of the Home Affairs Committee Session 1994–5', *The Private Security Industry*, Vol. 1. HC 17–1. London: HMSO.

Hudson, B. (1996) *Understanding Justice*. Buckingham: Open University Press.

IEA (1997) Zero Tolerance Policing Conference. London: Institute of Economic Affairs, 12 June.

Johnston, L. (1992) *The Rebirth of Private Policing*. London: Routledge.

Johnston, L. (1996a) 'Policing Diversity: The Impact of the Public–Private Complex in Policing' in Leishman *et al.* (1996) 54–70.

Johnston, L. (1996b) 'What is vigilantism?', *British Journal of Criminology*, 36 (2), 220–36.

Johnston, L. (1997) 'Policing Communities of Risk' in Francis *et al.* (1997), 186–207.

Johnston, L. (2000) *Policing Britain: Risk, Security and Governance*. Harlow: Longman.

Johnston, L. (Forthcoming) 'Transnational Private Policing' in Sheptycki (Forthcoming).

Jones, T. and Newburn, T. (1998) *Private Security and Public Policing*. Oxford: Clarendon Press.

Kakalik, J.S. and Wildhorn, S. (1972) *Private Police in the United States*. 4 volumes. Washington, DC: National Institute of Law Enforcement and Criminal Justice: US Dept. of Justice.

Kempa, M., Carrier, J., Wood, J. and Shearing, C. (1999) 'Reflections on the Evolving Concept of "Private Policing",' *European Journal on Criminal Policy and Research*, 7 (1).

Lash, S., Szerszynski, B. and Wynne, B. (eds) (1996) *Risk Environment and Modernity*. London: Sage.

Leishman, F., Loveday, B. and Savage, S. (eds) (1996) *Core Issues in Policing*. 1st edn. Harlow: Longman.

Marx, G. (1988) *Undercover: Police Surveillance in America*. Berkeley: University of California Press.

Miyazawa, S. (1991) 'The Private Sector and Law Enforcement in Japan' in Gormley (1991), 241–57.

Nalla, M. and Newman, G. (1990) *A Primer in Private Security*. New York: Harrow and Heston.

Narayan, S. (1994) 'The West European Market for Security Products and Services', *International Security Review*, Winter, 28–9.

National Police Agency (1994) *White Paper on Police 1994 (Excerpt)*. Tokyo: National Police Agency, Government of Japan.

Nelken, D. (ed.) (1994) *The Futures of Criminology*. London: Sage.

Norris, C.A. (1996) *The Role of the Informant in the Criminal Justice System*. London: Economic and Social Research Council.

Osborne, D. and Gaebler, T. (1993) *Reinventing Government*. New York: Plume.

Palmer, A. (1997) 'Global crusade that can never be won', *Sunday Telegraph*, 31 August, 17.

Police Foundation/Policy Studies Institute (1996) *The Independent Committee of Inquiry into the Role and Responsibilities of the Police*. London: Police Foundation/Policy Studies Institute.

Randall, W.E. and Hamilton, P. (1972) 'The Security Industry in the United Kingdom' in Wiles and McClintock (1972), 67–72.

Rhodes, R. (1994) 'The Hollowing out of the State: The Changing Nature of the Public Services in Britain', *Political Quarterly*, 65 (2), 138–51.

Rose, N. (1996) 'The Death of the Social? Re-figuring the Territory of Government', *Economy and Society*, 25 (3), 327–56.

Rose, N. and Miller, P. (1992) 'Political Power beyond the State: Problematics of Government', *British Journal of Sociology*, 42 (2), 172–205.

Saulsbury, W., Mott, J. and Newburn, T. (eds) (1996) *Themes in Contemporary Policing*. London: Independent Committee of Inquiry into the Roles and Responsibilities of the Police.

Shearing, C.D. (1996) 'Public and private policing' in Saulsbury, *et al.* (1996), 83–95.

Shearing, C.D. and Stenning, P.C. (1981) 'Modern Private Security: Its Growth and Implications' in Tonry and Norris (1981), 193–245.

Shearing, C.D. and Stenning, P.C. (1983) 'Private Security – Implications for Social Control', *Social Problems*, 30 (5), 493–506.

Sheptycki, J. (ed.) (Forthcoming) *Issues in Transnational Policing*. London: Routledge.

South, N. (1988) *Policing for Profit*. London: Sage.

Storch, R. (1975) 'The Plague of Blue Locusts: Police Reform and Popular Resistance in Northern England 1840–57', *International Review of Social History*, 20, 61–90.

Storch, R. (1976) 'The Policeman as Domestic Missionary: Urban Discipline and Popular Culture in Northern England 1850–1880', *Journal of Social History*, 9 (4), 481–509.

Tonry, M. and Norris, N. (eds) (1981) *Crime and Justice: An Annual Review of Research*. Vol. 3. Chicago: University of Chicago Press.

Wackenhut Corporation (1998) *Annual Report*, March.

Waters, M. (1995) *Globalization*. London: Routledge.

Wiles, P. and McClintock, F.H. (eds) (1972) *The Security Industry in the United Kingdom: Papers Presented to the Cropwood Round-Table Conference, July 1971*. Cambridge: Institute of Criminology.

Chapter 6

Transnational contexts

NEIL WALKER

Introduction: the boundaries of state policing

The very idea of transnational policing might appear incongruous from the state-centred perspective from which, explicitly or otherwise, the history of policing has typically been viewed. Traditionally, the integrity of the state and the viability of modern policing as a specialist institution have been seen as closely intertwined, even symbiotically linked. Most fundamentally, this connection is attributable to the pattern of coercive authority as it unfolded in the modern state system after the Peace of Westphalia in 1648. Theories of the state, ranging widely from the sixteenth-century analyses of the absolutist state by Thomas Hobbes and Jean Bodin to the current century of political sociology originating with Max Weber, have agreed that a key defining feature is its ultimate control over the legitimate use of force, which it exercises in order to ensure its security against internal and external threats (see e.g. Giddens, 1985). Correspondingly, theories of modern policing have stressed the importance of the specialist organisational form of the police as the vehicle through which the state asserts its title to the internal dimension of security (see e.g. Reiner, 1997: 997–1049; Walker, 1999).

A second and related reason for the close fit between policing and the modern state has to do with broader matters of governance. As the etymology of the term 'police' as a descriptor of a broader range of government administration suggests (see e.g. Pasquino, 1991), policing has been closely linked to the unprecedented claim of the modern state from the eighteenth century onwards to provide a *general* programme of detailed regulation of the population with a view to promoting tranquillity and security, or 'general order' (Marenin, 1992: 241–66, 258), expediting trade and communication, and enhancing health and prosperity (see e.g. Foucault, 1991: 173–214). The role of the police in this wider governance project is both at the foundational level, drawing on the authority of its latent coercive power to secure and guarantee the daily routines of general order which are prerequisite to the pursuit of the more specific goods (trade, communication, etc.) and also, to varying degrees at different times and places,[1] at the policy-generation and implementation levels, involving active co-ordination with, direction of and support or substitution for other agencies in the supply of the more specific state-guaranteed goods.

A third link between police and state is symbolic rather than instrumental. Because policing has been pivotal to the security of the state and integral to its project of governance, control over policing institutions has become central to the political and constitutional integrity of the state – a jealously guarded incident of its sovereign authority.[2] Further, as another feature of the development of the political form of the modern state since the eighteenth century has been its provision, in many instances, of a framework to nurture and sustain the cultural identity of the nation, the development of policing has also become interwoven with this wider project – the police officer or police institution often providing an important aspect of the iconography of the *nation*-state (see e.g. Walker, 1996: 251–84, 271–3; Loader and Walker, forthcoming).

If, in the ways set out above, 'police organizations around the world have had nation states as their nesting sites' (Sheptycki, 1998: 485–503, 498), this suggests very limited scope for transnational policing to flourish. Yet, from the outset, modern policing within the capsule of the nation state has been accompanied by a range of policing practices which cut across national boundaries, and this secondary domain is becoming wider and deeper. The developing transnational field has both professional and political roots.

Professionally, police officers and police institutions have always cultivated international contacts, however informally (see e.g. Nadelman, 1993: ch. 1). Partly, this has to do with the practicalities of law enforcement. The mobility of populations and the reach of criminal acts, strategies and networks across national boundaries has encouraged the exchange of criminal intelligence and the reciprocal supply of operational assistance. The propensity of police officers to co-operate is further enhanced by cultural factors. While the focus of policing on the neighbourhood community and the sense of loyalty to the 'local patch' might discourage, and in some instances has discouraged, the generation of mutual trust, interest and understanding required to forge transnational links (see e.g. Walker, 1993: 106–19), policing also has a social meaning which transcends state boundaries and which encourages a degree of transnational solidarity. Negatively, policework within every culture is 'dirty work' (Harris, 1973: 3) – an activity which many people find socially necessary but unpalatable and so consign to the margins of their consciousness. Further, the impersonal authority of the state borne by police officers creates an asymmetry of power in most of their professional dealings, so exacerbating the social distance between them and the public (see e.g. Reiner, 1992: 115–17). For both these reasons police officers tend to turn inwards to their own professional corps and are well equipped to empathise with the experiences of other officers regardless of national context. For more positive reasons, too, police officers may be receptive to the overtures of foreign colleagues. A strong sense of vocation and a keen perception of the centrality of their function to the maintenance of the fragile bonds of social order (*ibid.* 111–14) are two cultural traits which encourage mutual respect amongst police officers and which facilitate mutual appreciation across frontiers of the burdens of professional responsibility. Moreover, it is not insignificant that since, by and large, transnational police officers and institutions lack operational capacity, their work, accentuating a trend also evident in the intra-state context, is predominantly 'knowledge work'

(Ericson, 1994: 149–76) – mostly IT-based. That is to say, it is primarily concerned with the 'collection, collation and dissemination' (Sheptycki, 1998: 54–74, 71, fn2) within 'informated space' (*ibid.*: 60) of knowledge about specific cases or general patterns of insecurity or of security risk, and this shared technocratic imperative provides an additional basis for mutuality amongst transnational policeworkers.[3]

Politically, transnational links are encouraged for a number of reasons. Just as police officers find pragmatic grounds for informal co-operation, sovereign states find pragmatic grounds for formal co-operation in bilateral and multilateral arrangements to allow informational exchange, operational support or liaison between their separate police organisations and mutual assistance between their discrete criminal justice systems. This is facilitated by the fact that the framework of criminal law which defines the boundaries of general order shows a remarkable similarity from one state to the next, providing a common register in terms of which co-operation may proceed.[4] Even in those areas, such as terrorism and other forms of political crime, where a direct threat to the 'specific order' (Marenin, 1996: 258) of the state is posed and where the state is most jealous of its policing prerogative, the pronouncedly international context in which such crimes may be planned and perpetrated encourages co-operation.

Co-operation may also be encouraged for symbolic and strategic reasons. The development of an international agenda on law enforcement may reconfigure the politics of 'law and order' in a way which is helpful to national governments. In matters of internal security the flipside of the robust assertion of state sovereignty tends to be the attribution to national government of exclusive or predominant responsibility for the success of security policy. The opening up of a transnational policy arena may displace some responsibility upwards to the wider security community and, furthermore, may provide leverage to home affairs departments in the domestic politics of competitive resource allocation to seek the deployment of extra resources towards the new international security agenda.

Increasingly, however, the politics of transnational police co-operation are not only about the retrenchment of state sovereignty. They also reflect the gradual development of a new world order in which the nation state is no longer the unrivalled unit of political authority, but is challenged by new transnational or supranational regulatory regimes such as the United Nations, the North American Free Trade Association (NAFTA),[5] and the European Union (EU). These new entities assert authority of a type traditionally associated with state sovereignty and may even claim the label of sovereignty itself. As explored in detail below, this shift has been most profound, and with the most significant consequences for policing, in the context of the EU. It is important, however, to see the EU as but one instance of a global trend towards the relocation of political authority in multiple levels of governance and in non-state sites, in which altered configuration policing and its regulation is no longer securely domiciled within the nation state (see, e.g. Loader, forthcoming; Walker, forthcoming).

In the remainder of this Chapter, I trace the development of transnational policing, and in so doing reflect upon the nature and consequences of the tension between the statist tradition in policing and the social forces which encourage policing activities between and beyond nation states. In the first place, a brief historical overview of transnational policing is provided. In the second place, the conflicting pressures attending contemporary developments in police organisation and co-operation in the key site of the EU are analysed. Finally, the ways in which these tensions are likely to be played out in the future constitution and regulation of EU policing are assessed.

A brief history

The earliest concerted attempt to institutionalise trannsnational policing involved a series of initiatives amongst European states in the late nineteenth century to secure co-operation in the fight against terrorism, revealing a common concern to address the danger posed to national security by nationalist and socialist revolutionary movements (Fijnaut, 1991: 103–20, 104). In contrast, with the exception of mutual extradition treaties and cross-border controls, for which the regulatory resources of governments were indispensable, early forms of co-operation with regard to 'ordinary crime' tended to involve professionals – lawyers, academics and police officers – rather than politicians. The predominance of professionals was evident in the first major International Police Conference hosted by Prince Albert of Monaco in 1914, and, more significantly, was reflected in the organisation of the first permanent international agency – the International Criminal Police Commission (ICPC) – established in Vienna in 1923. Both the ICPC and its post-Second World War successor, the French-based International Criminal Police Office (ICPO) – or Interpol, as it soon became known – supplied a communication network for the participating national police organisations, as well as providing a 'policeman's club' (Anderson, 1989: 43) in which senior officers could cultivate social and professional contacts with international colleagues. Formal international legal agreements prepared between state authorities were conspicuous by their absence from the foundations of these organisations, and, with the notable exception of the Nazi take-over of the ICPC in 1938, the involvement of governments in these organisations remained 'minor or low-key' (*ibid.*: 37).

In the contemporary age, Interpol has expanded its activities significantly. Its membership, originally 19, has grown tenfold, it has exploited new forms of information technology to expedite and broaden its flow of communications between national forces, and it has attempted to rationalise and augment its activities in the crucial European field within a separate organisational unit (Anderson *et al.*, 1995: 49–53). However, such is the overall development of the network of transnational policing that it is no longer the pre-eminent player. Its influence has been lessened by two developments in particular. First, there is the marked internationalisation of United States law enforcement. The United States were slow to become involved in matters of transnational law enforcement, partly for reasons of geography and partly because of the fragmented nature of the national law enforcement effort and the attendant difficulties of identifying the most appropriate and legitimate representative of federal law enforcement interests. In recent years, however, particularly since the explosion of international drug-trafficking in the 1960s and 70s and President Nixon's declaration of a 'war on drugs', there has been a sharp increase in activity, only a modest proportion of which is realised in greater American involvement in Interpol.[6] Instead, internationalisation of American criminal justice policy is most marked in the increased concentration of resources upon international work in existing federal law enforcement agencies dealing with drugs, internal revenue, organised crime, immigration etc., including the widespread placement of liaison officers, training units and other support agencies in embassies and law enforcement institutions abroad (see e.g. Nadelman, 1993: chs 2–3; Anderson, 1989: ch. 2).

The second major development, which, unlike the American intervention, is not predominantly marked by bilateral arrangements but which involves multilateral and, increasingly, supranational initiatives, has taken place within the European field, particularly within the EU, undoubtedly the most ambitious experiment the modern world has seen in polity building beyond the state. Yet the beginnings were inauspicious. While the Pompidou Group pioneered policy-level collaboration in the area of drug trafficking, the Trevi organisation provide the first major initiative in the policing field in 1975, a full 18 years after the signing of the Treaty of Rome, the foundational document of European supranationalism. Trevi provided a forum for member states to develop common measures with regard to counter-terrorism, and later, with regard also to drugs, organised crime, police training and technology and a range of other matters. The intensification of Trevi's activities coincided with the development of the European Commission's Single Market Programme after 1985. Whereas previously, Trevi had been isolated from the mainstream of Community policy making, now its security concerns were integral to the doctrine of compensatory measures through which the Co-ordinator's Group on the Free Movement of Persons responded to the 'security deficit' of open internal frontiers (see e.g. Anderson *et al.*, 1995: ch. 4).

A second important step towards a European law enforcement capacity, the Schengen system, is even more closely associated with the Single Market initiative. The initial Schengen Agreement of 1985 embraced a core of five member states which sought to take the initiative in abolishing border controls and so accelerate the completion of the internal market. A more detailed Implementation Agreement of 1990 established a number of associated law enforcement measures including the Schengen Information System and police co-operation in matters such as 'hot pursuit', cross-border observation and controlled delivery of illegal goods. After various false promises, Schengen eventually became operational in March 1995, though even then a zone entirely free of permanent border controls was not immediately achieved amongst the seven fully participating members. Despite these problems, Schengen's sphere of influence grows ever wider. All except the United Kingdom and Ireland of the 15 members of the EU have now joined and are at various stages of the implementation process,[7] while the two non-EU members of the Nordic Passport Union – Norway and Iceland – have been granted associate status. Further, as explained below, recent developments in the EU Treaty architecture have reversed the longstanding assumption that the gradual extension of the frontier-free regime of the internal market would lead to the eclipse of Schengen by the EU acting as a whole.

While Trevi and Schengen are noteworthy advances in the development of a European law enforcement capacity, the European Police Office (Europol) constitutes the most ambitious plan yet conceived in this field. Its foundations were laid at Maastricht in the Treaty on European Union of 1992 (hereinafter 'Maastricht'), which included policing within a new Third Pillar[8] of EU competence over Justice and Home Affairs (JHA) (Peers, 2000). Whereas Trevi, to which the Third Pillar is the institutional successor, was an intergovernmental arrangement in the shadow of the 'official' Community, the Third Pillar was built into the stonework of the new EU. Under Maastricht, the major EU institutions – Commission, Council, Parliament and Court of Justice – were less central than in the traditional First Pillar, where the Union has full legislative, executive and judicial authority. Nevertheless, the Council and Commission, in particular, continue to exert a significant influence over the decision-making process alongside the individual member states (Anderson et al., 1995: chs 6, 8).

Under the Third Pillar, there is an elaborate administrative structure – originally spanning five organisational levels. Beneath two familiar Community executive organs – the Council of EU Justice and Interior Ministers, and the Committee of Permanent Representatives (Coreper) – lies the Article 36 (previously K4) Committee, which comprises permanent representatives of the justice and interior ministries of the member states. In turn, the Article 36 Committee has generated a number of sub-groups which constitute the lower levels of the hierarchy. Initially, there were three steering groups, one dealing with police and customs co-operation and the others with immigration and asylum and with judicial co-operation in criminal and civil matters respectively. This fourth tier of decision making was abolished under the Luxembourg presidency of the EU in the second half of 1997, but the various specialist Working Groups which had been formed under each of these functional heads remain, and indeed have expanded in number. In the area of police co-operation these include permanent groups on Europol, police co-operation (more generally), police technology, terrorism and drugs.[9]

This structure has spawned various initiatives, ranging from the adoption of high-profile legal Conventions[10] to new networks of exchange of information and ideas on practical issues. The focal initiative in policing, however, has remained Europol, the development of which was in fact one of the few clearly stated *specific* objectives of the Third Pillar (see e.g. Cullen, forthcoming; Monar, 1998: 320–35). Yet, the history of the birth of Europol offers an instructive example of the halting progress of co-operation under the Third Pillar generally. Maastricht envisaged Europol as a system of information exchange for the purposes of preventing and combating terrorism, drug trafficking and other serious crimes within the EU, and as a means of providing co-operation in aid of criminal investigations and analyses more generally. Nevertheless, and notwithstanding Chancellor Kohl's strong support for the prompt establishment of Europol, it was soon evident that progress would be achieved only in modest increments.

The early institutional ambition was a limited one, to establish the Europol Drugs Unit (EDU) as a precursor to a fully fledged Europol, but even here the timetable slipped. Originally intended to be established by the end of 1992, the EDU did not become operational at The Hague until November 1993, and it was not until 1995 that it was granted formal recognition under the Third Pillar as a joint action. By that time, the remit of the fledgling organisation had been extended beyond drug trafficking and associated criminal organisations and money laundering activities to cover nuclear crime, illegal immigration networks and international vehicle crime, and it was further extended in December 1996 to cover traffic in human beings for sexual and other purposes. Despite the extension of the breadth of the EDU's competence, the depth of its powers over these matters remained strictly limited. While the Hague organisation provided a focus for liaison officers from each state to exchange information and provide mutual support for police investigations with a transnational element in the various jurisdictions, there was no power to hold personal data centrally and to allow the EDU as an *independent* entity to communicate criminal data with third states and organisations.

The full Europol Convention, which conferred these additional powers, and which also supplied a mechanism for the wide-ranging extension of the criminal jurisdiction of Europol beyond the EDU core provided these crimes involved an 'organised criminal structure',[11] was not ultimately signed until July 1995, following protracted debate over the mandate and powers of a mature Europol and over the adequacy of its data protection systems and its framework of legal and political accountability. Even then, there were obstacles to overcome before the process of ratification and implementation could be completed. Given its Eurosceptic stance, the United Kingdom had opposed any role for the European Court of Justice – the EU's 'Supreme Court' – throughout the negotiation of the Convention, and when a solution was eventually found in a protocol of July 1996, it effectively took the form of an agreement to differ. The United Kingdom would not itself recognise the jurisdiction of the Court, but acknowledged the right of the other 14 member states to accept its jurisdiction over a limited range of questions. However, important questions about the legal capacity and immunities of Europol officials and about the powers of the central data protection agency – the Joint Supervisory Board – remained unresolved, delaying the formal implementation of the Convention until October 1998, and even then preventing its operationalisation until July 1999.

These unresolved matters do not exhaust the contest over the new European policing framework. Just as the various policing initiatives began to take shape within the context of the Maastricht Third Pillar, that overarching context was altered by the latest round of EU constitutional politics – the Treaty of Amsterdam. Signed in October 1997, and entering into force in May 1999, this latest adornment to the architecture of the EU heralds a new Treaty chapter on the so-called 'area of freedom, security and justice'. The new chapter contains both a new First Pillar Title on visas, asylum, immigration and other matters related to free movements of persons, most of which competences have been transferred from the Maastricht Third Pillar, and a revised and truncated Third Pillar restricted to police and customs co-operation and judicial co-operation in criminal matters.

This new dual structure within justice and home affairs might seem to distance policing yet further from the mainstream of EU governance. As one of the few non-transferred matters, it does not share the majority-voting procedures, the exclusive policy-making role of the Commission and the system of parliamentary and judicial supervision associated with the First Pillar. Yet, within the limits set by the retention of the multi-pillar structure, there is some recognition of an enlarged and more integrated European policing capacity. Largely in acknowledgement of the aspirations set in the EU's Action Plan on Organised Crime of April 1997,[12] police co-operation between national authorities is extended to cover operational co-operation. Europol is allocated a range of new functions, including the authority to establish joint operational teams to support national investigations, the power to ask the competent authorities of the member states to conduct and co-ordinate investigations in specific cases, and the capacity to develop specific expertise which may be put at the disposal of member states to assist them in investigating organised crime.[13] Further, this extended police jurisdiction applies within an institutional context less distinct than previously from that of the First Pillar. The power to legislate is reinforced, with 'framework decisions' (i.e. decisions to approximate national laws) joining Third Pillar Conventions as available mechanisms. The consultative role of the European Parliament in policy making is clarified and strengthened. The Commission acquires the same authority as the member states to initiate decision taking. And, for the first time, general provision is made for the Court of Justice to decide Third Pillar cases, though member states retain extensive discretion to 'opt out' of this jurisdiction, and the Court is explicitly prohibited from adjudicating on the operations of national police forces or other aspects of internal national security.

Finally, the complexity of the new institutional framework under the Amsterdam Treaty is thickened by the incorporation of the Schengen system into the new dual justice and home affairs structure. This reaffirmation and communitisation of Schengen flows from the decision at Amsterdam to allow Britain and Ireland to retain their border controls within the EU while allowing the other member states to proceed at their own pace, and with the full authority of the EU, to manage the consequences of the abolition of such controls. As the competences of Schengen cut across the new division within the justice and home affairs structure, one consequence of the new flexibility is to provide Britain and Ireland with an 'opt out' in respect of Schengen-associated policing measures. As we shall see, this and other elements of 'variable geometry' within the field of European police regulation demonstrate that the present structure – with Europol at its apex – offers no more than a provisional design for the new order, and reinforces doubts about the potential of the emergent system to address the various legitimate concerns which have become associated with the practice of transnational policing.

Tensions within the emergent order

In accounting for the unprecedented yet uneven progress towards a 'state-like' policing capacity within the EU we are faced with a paradox. Some of the relevant explanatory factors are those traditionally associated with the growth of transnational policing *between* states while others are those traditionally associated with the idea of policing as a domestic function *of* the state. This paradox is explicable by reference to the ambiguous political status of the EU. In so far as it retains the attributes of a classical international organisation, the well-worn pragmatic explanations for transnational co-operation – or intergovernmentalism – are appropriate. Yet, in so far as it has acquired some of the characteristics of a state, the arguments which link policing to the state become relevant. In turn, this explanatory duality is reflected in the peculiarly hybrid quality of Third Pillar institutions in general and the policing provisions in particular. More pronouncedly than any of the other aspects of the political architecture of the EU, the Third Pillar sends conflicting messages about its political pedigree. The Third Pillar, unlike its predecessor Trevi, is part of the institutional machinery of the EU, but stands at some remove from the First Pillar. The constitutional organs of the new European order – Parliament, Commission and Court of Justice – have a role to play in the Third Pillar, but less significant than in other areas. The Third Pillar confers institutional autonomy and some operational powers upon EU policing, but in contrast to other areas of European policy reserves supreme law-making authority to the member states.

What, then, are the conflicting causal factors which have left European policing under the Third Pillar delicately poised between classic intergovernmentalism and supranational polity building? On the side of intergovernmentalism, there have been numerous factors to encourage pragmatic co-operation between sovereign states, including the common threat of international terrorism in the 1970s, the subsequent growth of 'clandestine markets' (Sheptycki, 1998: 93) in drugs and other forms of organised crime, the development of international computerised financial transactions and associated crimes, and increasing concern in all western European countries about patterns of immigration (see e.g. Guyomarch, 1997: 123–50, 137–41). Further, as rising official crime rates and the findings of successive victimisation studies render increasingly implausible the myth of the capacity of the bounded state to provide 'sovereign crime control' (Garland, 1996: 445–71), the fostering of a new international agenda against matters which appear to challenge the social, economic and political order of the state as profoundly as terrorism, drug trafficking, money laundering and organised crime is of strategic value to beleaguered national authorities in reallocating part of the political burden of crime control beyond the state. As noted earlier, the construction of a new site for crime control projects, unsullied by association with past failures and disappointments at national level, also provides a basis from which fresh support and new resources for the security project can be mobilised.

At the professional level too, the Third Pillar structure has proved conducive to the maintenance and extension of international collegiate ties. In one sense, the Third Pillar might seem an unlikely host to nurture the professional police community as an autonomous influence in developing international ties. The Third Pillar announces a formalisation of law enforcement co-operation, which implies subordination of the work of the operational professional to a framework of legal and political control. In practice, however, the ideological context, organisational structure and policy innovation of the Third Pillar encourage the thickening of transnational professional networks. Ideologically, as we shall see, a number of the main political discourses associated with European police co-operation provide a facilitative context for the linkage of a wide range of issues in and around policing – drugs, organised crime, terrorism, smuggling, immigration, asylum – which previously had been treated separately. Organisationally, this is acknowledged in the wide-ranging structure of the Third Pillar which broadens and strengthens professional connections, especially at working group level[14] where police and other and other relevant operational experts are directly represented. At the policy level, the establishment of Europol as a dedicated organisational unit with an expanding remit provides for the first time a permanent international facility within which a solidary professional culture can develop.

What of the supranational influences underpinning the Third Pillar? In earlier writings I have discussed at length three main public political discourses in terms of which arguments for and against police co-operation in the context of an increasingly integrationist EU have tended to be framed (see e.g. Walker, 1998a: 165–86; Walker, 1998b: 141–60). These discourses are important not only as evidence of the ideas that genuinely structure and motivate this debate, but also because they tend to dominate the agenda, and so provide the ideological context in which, regardless of their underlying motives, interested parties must conduct their argument if they wish to influence the debate. What is more, each of the three discourses draws upon one of the main rationales linking police to state – security, governance and symbolic association, in so doing adapting the rationale in question to the quasi-state context of the EU polity.

To begin with, there is the discourse of *internal security*, which, naturally, connects to the security rationale linking police and polity. The fashioning of a new Treaty objective 'to develop the Union as an area of freedom, justice and security',[15] and the provision of a separate Treaty chapter to that effect, together with a similar commitment to external security through a common foreign and security policy, is indicative of a wider project which focuses on the EU as a self-contained 'security community' (see e.g. Adler and Barnett, 1998). This project is premised upon the identification of a range of common interests amongst the states and populations of western Europe, the perception of a series of threats to these common interests, and the selection as appropriate of a 'security-oriented' response to these threats.

There are powerful political and economic strands within this ideological matrix. The stable prosperity of the EU in the more fluid post-Cold War world order stands in stark contrast with the insecurity and poverty of the polities and economies to the South and East. In particular, the 'arc of instability'[16] along the eastern flank of Europe during the 1990s, from Russia through Ukraine, the Balkans and Turkey into the south and eastern Mediterranean, has begun to provide the 'dangerous other' of EU politics. While one response is incrementally inclusionary – there are at present 11 candidate states of central and eastern Europe which are on track to join the 15 of the EU in the early years of the twenty-first century and others in more distant anterooms – a parallel response views exclusion and resistance to migratory pressures as prerequisite to the maintenance of western Europe's political pedigree and economic advantage (see e.g. Anderson *et al.*, 1995: ch. 5).

The use of a discourse centred on the idea of insecurity, with its connotations of crisis and the need for 'extraordinary means' (Waever, 1996: 103–32) to counter threats, has provided the political class with a usefully reductionist method of viewing complex multi-faceted problems. The power of the security metaphor has also encouraged the treatment of a range of relatively discrete issues, each with a security dimension, as one, indivisible problem. Thus, the core economic and political anxieties associated with the prospect of sharing the European space with outsiders has become connected to more specific concerns about the development of intra- and extra-EU cross-border criminal organisational links. In this vein, Bigo has argued on the basis of emerging practice and rhetoric of the EU security community that the elaboration of an 'internal security ideology' around the institutional complex of the Third Pillar has allowed a number of concerns, ranging from immigration and asylum to terrorism, organised crime and public order[17] to be located along a single 'security continuum' (Bigo, 1994: 161–73, 164) and treated to a one-dimensional response. On this view, it is nothing less crucial than the security of the western European *way of life* that is the foremost priority across a range of JHA policies, from reinforcing the hard outer shell of the EU's external frontiers to conducting systematic internal checks and developing an autonomous policing capacity.

A second public discourse closely associated with the development of EU policing, and which resonates with the governance rationale for linking police and polity, is the discourse of *functional spillover*. Since its inception, a key argument associated with the extension of the European project into new domains has been that the optimisation of a programme of intervention in one sector requires adjustments in related policy sectors (see e.g. Lindberg, 1963). The development of an efficient and effective common market – the founding mandate of the EU – was deemed to require spillover policies as diverse as anti-discrimination measures to ensure a level playing-field within the labour market and common welfare and environmental measures to ensure some equivalence of 'externalities' across enterprises located in different states. The argument about the need for security measures, including common policing measures, to compensate for the opening of internal frontiers is but one more instance of the functionalist theme.

Further, if we move beyond the particular policy framework of the EU, we may demonstrate how the logic of functionalism, and, more broadly, the logic of a multi-purpose programme of governance within a polity, is generally favourable to enhanced police co-operation. Given their flexible capacity to provide an authoritative solution and their round-the-clock accessibility, the police tend to exercise a '"stand-in" authority' (Cohen, 1985: 27–42, 37) within all polities, plugging the gap wherever the normal authoritative solution or practice has failed. Or in functionalist language, there is inevitable spillover into the policing domain from a wide range of other policy sectors or social activities. Whether the argument is that the growth of business enterprise across western and, increasingly, eastern Europe leads to a corresponding increase in crime connections, or that the development of international leisure has produced the international football hooligan and the international paedophile ring, or that the information revolution has led to increased use of computers in the commission of international crimes, there is a persuasive case to be made for policing measures to compensate for dysfunctions in other sectors.

For present purposes, the political efficacy of these arguments is more significant than their intrinsic validity. Indeed, as indicated by the expansion of the scope for police co-operation amongst all 15 EU members in the new Treaty of Amsterdam alongside its explicit acknowledgement of the right of the United Kingdom and Ireland to retain border checks, the removal of which was the classical functionalist justification for a Third Pillar, such reasoning may not bear close scrutiny. Yet a functionalist rhetoric of governance remains influential because it appeals to a technocratic vision of policing (see e.g. Sheptycki, 1995: 613–35), and a similar 'Eurocrat' vision of European public policy in general (see e.g. Weiler, 1991: 2403–2483), as the performance of a range of necessary but neutral tasks, and as such beyond the ken and critique of partisan politics.

The third and most general public political discourse affecting the development of European police co-operation, which corresponds to the general symbolic rationale linking police and polity, is the discourse of *European integration* itself. Unlike the other two discourses, it does not operate in a manner generally favourable to the expansion of an EU policing capacity. The discourse of European integration is directly and unequivocally concerned with the growth of the European polity as a rival to the state, and inasmuch as policing is seen as one of the crucial building blocks of statehood, the continuing emphasis upon state sovereignty as the bottom line of political commitment within the international order has acted as a brake upon the development of a European police capacity. Indeed, the resurgence of nationalist sentiment against a strong EU which coincided with the ratification difficulties of the Maastricht Treaty in the early 1990s have provided an important subtext to the erratic progress of the Europol Convention. And, tellingly, in the pre-Amsterdam negotiations, despite broader disagreement about the future of justice and home affairs, there was a considerable degree of consensus that, while pragmatic considerations favoured an extension of police co-operation, it should remain firmly grounded in the intergovernmental soil of the Third Pillar (Monar, 1998: 322).

Yet, the discourse of European integration can also work in favour of European policing. The balance between pro-EU and pro-state sentiment is complex and unstable. The general Euroscepticism of the second half of the 1990s may be seen as a prelude to a renewed federalist drive associated with the deepening of economic integration and the launch of the European single currency in 1999. Euroscepticism is also in part a reaction to an earlier period in which the European project was buoyant, and where European policing prospered in a favourable macro-political climate. Thus, it is no mere coincidence that the crucial Third Pillar initiatives took place at the high tide of European institutional self-confidence in the integration process, following the Commission's audacious success in marketing the 1992 project. In particular, German Chancellor Kohl's proposal for a European Police Office (Europol) in 1991 was in tune with the political mood, typifying the ambitions of the increasingly dominant EU member state at a point when a significant deepening of the integration project appeared politically viable (see e.g. Cullen, 1992). It was intended, and partly succeeded, as a symbol of integrationist virility, precisely because it was so audacious, promising to transfer authority in an area which was one of the most traditional and closely guarded preserves of the state.

There is a second and more subtle sense in which policing connects favourably with a macro-political integrationist discourse. Just as from the nineteenth century policing has been symbolically connected not only to the political project of state-building but also to the linked cultural project of nation-building (Emsley, 1999), so as we enter the twenty-first century, policing at the EU level may be connected not only to the political project of suprastate-building but also to the linked cultural project of building a European identity and a cohesive European civil society. This project has assumed a greater urgency in recent years not only because of the questionable legitimacy of the move towards a more integrated Europe but also because the ambitious programme of EU expansion has had to confront head-on the challenge of the significant resurgence of the politics of national identity in the fragmented post-Communist eastern Europe (see e.g. Brubaker, 1996). Yet, in the absence of the vivid, readily accessible and well grounded mythology and symbolism from which a common identity is typically constructed at national level, the development of a European identity is a pioneering and precarious exercise. In the absence of more positive material and given the economic and political background, it tends to accentuate certain tones found in all identity politics, namely exclusion and otherness (see e.g. Cable, 1994). In turn, this resonates with the anxieties and distinctions of European security politics, in which, as we have seen, European policing is deeply implicated. In other words, the idea of a security community also has a cultural dimension; it provides one way of defining European identity beyond the level of the nation state, and in so far as this cultural project is important to the development and legitimation of the European polity – however ambitiously defined – this provides a further, if indirect, current encouraging the growth of European policing.

Prospects

The emergence and regulation of a significant European policing capacity, therefore, has been determined by a wide range of factors. Pragmatic, strategic and professional arguments in favour of classical state-centred international co-operation have combined, and in some cases vied, with the internal security, functional and integrationist discourses of a very new form of polity to leave European policing uneasily poised between intergovernmentalism and supranationalism. From such a complex and internally contradictory position the future cannot be anything but deeply uncertain, but this very complexity and internal tension ensures that certain interrelated themes will be to the fore. Ironically, given the context of profound change, these themes identify areas which have given perennial cause for concern in international policing, and which may indeed throw up even greater difficulties in the foreseeable future.

A first such theme is *informalism*. As we have seen, international police co-operation was initially driven by a professional 'old boys network' (Anderson *et al.*, 1995: 74–6), and, due to the pragmatism inherent in functionalist and internal security discourses and the opportunity for close and continuous operational liaison provided by the Third Pillar structure, the new, and apparently formalised, European framework helps to sustain such an approach. On one view, this might seem to be a transitional matter. Once the Treaty framework is in place and the institutional structure is properly bedded down, it might be argued, the formal framework will establish a much clearer influence over professional practice.

The difficulty with this approach is that it fully appreciates neither the dynamics of European law-making nor the nature of police practice. As regards the formal rules, there is a general tendency in the international policing domain, not restricted to the particular circumstances of recent Europolitics, towards the symbolic affirmation of consensus, leading to the premature conclusion of agreements on 'incompletely theorised' terms (Sunstein, 1996: ch. 2), 'watered down to carry as little legal obligation as possible' (Turnbull-Henson, 1997). The Schengen Implementation Agreement, the Ministerial Agreement founding the EDU, the Europol Convention, and the new operational powers of the Amsterdam Treaty, were all endorsed before important matters of principle had been resolved and at a point when a considerable delay could be anticipated prior to implementation. The main attraction of premature and diluted agreements is that they strike a compromise between pro-integrationist and anti-integrationist tendencies, a formal record of progress to add to the integrationist vision balanced against the guarantee of no practical advance pending agreement on the matter of principle.[18] Yet, as the busy preparatory schedules undertaken by the various new European police organisations prior to their official commencement date indicate, the public affirmation of an international commitment to action, however premature, provides a sense of permission for those committed to enhanced co-operation to proceed in anticipation of a final resolution of outstanding disputes. In this vein, the extension of police co-operation under the Treaty of Amsterdam was repeatedly invoked as a legitimising device for the preparation of new co-operative initiatives in the early post-Treaty period, even while the ratification process remained incomplete and the process of formal development of new measures and arrangements under the new institutional context had yet to commence.[19]

The problem of regulatory 'lag' is compounded by the tendency of operational practice not merely to anticipate the implementation of new rules, but also to move beyond these regulatory thresholds in a series of incremental shifts of practice and strategy, the cumulative effect of which may be for a professionally driven agenda to cross important policy thresholds without rounded public debate or candid acknowledgement of the consequences. For example, while under the original Convention it was determined that Europol should be without executive powers (arrest, search, questioning, etc.) or operational competence, but should instead provide a service function in matters of information exchange and intelligence analysis to national operational units, the co-ordinator of the EDU, Jurgen Storbeck (Storbeck, 1996: 28–31), was soon advocating the practical inevitability and desirability of an extension. In suggesting the establishment of *ad hoc* Europol task forces to direct operations in particular states, Storbeck contended that since in its intelligence co-ordination role Europol would acquire a unique overview of certain transnational crime patterns and incidents, so it would be better placed than any national policing units to respond operationally. As we have seen, Storbeck's argument appears to have borne fruit in the Amsterdam Treaty, where the idea of task forces is endorsed and additional authority is given to Europol to direct national authorities towards specific investigations post-Amsterdam trends provide further confirmation of a gradualist agenda. The landmark Tampere summit of October 1999 built upon the implementation of Amsterdam to call for the speedy establishment of joint investigative teams, the establishment of a European Police Chiefs Operational Task Force, the receipt by Europol of operational data from member states, co-ordination between Europol and a new co-operative unit called EUROJUST (composed of prosecutors and magistrates from each member state), and the establishment of a European police college. (*Statewatch European Monitor,* 2000.) In an additional move, the Third Pillar Convention on Legal Assistance was signed in May 2000, having been extended beyond its initial draft brief to cover matters such as the interception of communications and interviews with suspects across borders by national police forces.

In some part, this apparently relentless incrementalism is due to the so-called 'law of inevitable increment', whereby 'whatever powers the police have they will exceed by a given margin' (Reiner, 1992: 217). To the extent that this is fair comment, it is so in recognition that, where the police possess a broad general mandate but their specific legal powers are significantly restricted, as has been the case until now in the European context, they are likely to acquire both the wherewithal, in this case a developing resource base of intelligence and expertise, and the ambition to initiate practices which will take them beyond the limits of these powers. And while there has already been significant slippage from a service to a directive role, it may well be that the same incrementalist logic will be used in the future to argue that, alongside intelligence and operational co-ordination, Europol should be granted the third and final dimension of control over national units, namely executive powers.

The gap between the official form and actual practice connects with a second theme which is likely to dominate future discussion of international policing arrangements, namely *weak accountability*. However, this is not simply a matter of the professional desire for autonomy and the consequent frustration of political aspirations. It is also indicative of the ambiguous quality of these political aspirations. Neither the discourse of functional spillover, with its privileging of technocratic expertise and its denial of grand politics, nor the discourse of internal security, with its emphasis upon the uncompromising pursuit of a narrow objective, is particularly receptive to the idea of an elaborate framework of external accountability, with detailed overview of tasks and consultation of a wide range of opinions.[20]

If this helps to explain why even after the Treaty of Amsterdam, Europol, like its predecessors and competitors, allows only a relatively modest role to those institutions best placed to exercise an external overview of its functions – in its case the European Parliament and the Court of Justice – it does not account for the lack of resistance to this prospect by the strong anti-integration forces within the wider ambit of European politics. After all, surely the Eurosceptics have particular reason to be wary of the empire building of powerful and relatively unaccountable Third Pillar institutions. The answer to this conundrum lies in the fact that from the perspective of national sovereignty, the proper lines of accountability are through national channels, which means domestic parliaments and domestic courts. On this view, the strengthening of *any* European institution, even those which are designed to reduce the deficit in accountability and democracy, may be perceived in narrow zero-sum terms as contributing to the erosion of national self-determination, and for that reason resisted. There is, therefore, a refusal, or at best a reluctance, to contemplate that the locus of power has already shifted so much to the European centre, that the accountability system must adapt accordingly, even if that entails empowering particular European institutions, or developing a dual framework of governance linking national and supranational institutions.

A final problematic theme of the new international policing agenda is *flexibility and pluralism*. If a key promise of European police co-operation was the eclipse of the tradition of fragmented organisation and rival facilities and the imposition of a stable hierarchy of transnational policing mechanisms, with the Third Pillar and Europol clearly foremost, then this ordered solution became blurred and was in danger of being supplanted even before its full implementation. The Treaty of Amsterdam has built on a number of recent developments, such as the European Monetary Union opt-outs, the individual Europe Agreements with candidate states and the opt-out of the previous British government from the Social Protocol, to endorse a general principle of flexible integration, whereby different states can integrate at different rates in different combinations in different policy spheres. The reasons for this are many and varied (see e.g. Walker, 1998c: 355–88), but the most important is that in the current finely-balanced political debate over the future of Europe flexible integration as a broad strategy appeals to both pro-integration and anti-integration forces. For those in favour of greater integration, flexibility avoids institutional stagnation, with the overall European project proceeding at the pace of the most reluctant member state. For those opposed to greater integration, particularly in the context of an ever expanding EU, flexibility promises a more loosely structured set of arrangements. On the latter view, if states are allowed to co-operate on an *à la carte* basis, not only will this arrangement be more respectful of divergent national interests, but it will also begin to dilute the significance of the Union as a distinctive and cohesive entity with particular interests and a common set of institutions.

Whichever view is more plausible, a situation is clearly emerging where the debate over European sovereignty can no longer be perceived in traditional vein as the relationship between two fixed entities – the EU and the member states. The EU increasingly means different things in different sectors, while the member states, together with a number of non-member states, now find themselves in variable relationships with the institutions of the EU. In order to understand this changing mosaic, we need to forge more subtle and flexible concepts of political authority (Walker, 2000).

The move towards flexible integration in a post-national Europe applies as much, and perhaps more – given its long history of influence by the shifting sands of state expediency – to policing and JHA matters as it does to any other area of EU activity. This is demonstrated by the opt-out on the jurisdiction of the Court of Justice negotiated by the UK under the Europol Convention. It is also indicated by the general willingness of the IGC negotiators, recorded in the Florence summit of June 1996, to accept the idea of flexible integration more readily in the context of the Second and Third Pillars than in the traditional sphere of the First Pillar, where the perceived need to preserve the essentials of the single internal market reduces the scope for differentiation. In turn, this willingness was reflected in the final form of the Amsterdam Treaty, which as well as providing a general permission for particular states to forge ahead with advanced forms of co-operation, allows the full incorporation of a non-EU structure, Schengen, together with a range of more detailed opt-outs and opt-ins (see e.g. Monar, 1998). For example, in May 2000 the United Kingdom concluded an agreement with the other member states to apply some aspects of the Schengen Agreement, including those relating to the strategically-important Schengen information systems, but not others. The upshot is a structure of Byzantine complexity, with the JHA Council, which is supposed to provide some overall level of policy coherence at the political level, wearing as many as ten different hats and boasting ten variable memberships depending upon the subject matter (*Statewatch*, 1998, 8(5): 28–9; see also Peers, 2000).

The prevalence of a flexible and diversified approach in policing and Third Pillar matters is also apparent at a more detailed level from the spate of security agreements and liaisons recently negotiated between the EU and other states. Recent prominent examples include an agreement between Europol and third-party states concerning exchange of data, a developing dialogue on police co-operation between the UK and the main non-European player in transnational co-operation – the USA – and the launch of a strategy to exploit a new provision of the Amsterdam Treaty[21] to allow the eleven candidate states of central and eastern Europe to join in Third Pillar co-operation with the existing 15 member states. These, however, are only the tip of a large and expanding iceberg (see e.g. Walker, 1998b: 159–60).

While it seems highly likely that these trends towards the diversification and fragmentation of political authority will continue, and indeed accelerate, it is very difficult to predict what their implications will be for the long-term future of police co-operation in and beyond Europe. It is likely that, increasingly, we will have to try to understand trends in police co-operation not simply in relation to the shifting balance of sovereign authority, but against a background of increasing challenges to the very idea of sovereign authority. What is clear, however, is that unless new regulatory tools are crafted which are adequate to this complexity, the growing intransparency and renewed diversity of transnational policing arrangements will exacerbate the problems of informalism and attenuated accountability which have shadowed the entire history of transnational policing.

Notes

1 For example, community policing, problem-oriented policing and multi-agency policing are but three modern labels which seek to describe and develop a more expansive version of the police project, actively engaged in public policy making.
2 The idea of sovereignty is invariably invoked in official governmental discourse concerned with justifying a conservative approach to the governance of police institutions in contexts in which the ultimate authority of the state is under challenge or reassessment, whether between the UK and the EU (see text below) or, for example, between the UK and Ireland in the context of the current peace process (see Walker and Telford, 2000).

3 Although Sheptycki (1998: 66–70) notes that even within this specialist context there is scope for the development of a number of different policing styles and attitudes.

4 It is this common register which has made possible the proliferation of extradition and mutual legal assistance treaties in and beyond the EU in recent years, a development which complements the growth in police co-operation. For a recent overview, see Cullen and Gilmore (1998).

5 On policing and security developments associated with the development of NAFTA, which in its present form embraces USA, Canada and Mexico, see, for example, Taylor (1992: 181–93); Andreas (1996: 51–69).

6 Although between 1967 and 1991, the US national central bureau of Interpol increased its staff from 6 to 110; Nadelman (1993: 3).

7 The target date for the final wave of implementation of the Nordic members is October 2000.

8 The informal term for JHA co-operation coined during the negotiation of the Maastricht Treaty, with the Second Pillar representing common foreign and security policy and the First Pillar representing the traditional economic core of the common market.

9 For a full list, see *Statewatch European Monitor* (1999) vol. 1, No. 2, p. 21.

10 The most significant of which for policing purposes are the 1995 Europol Convention and the Mutual Legal Assistance Convention, eventually signed in May 2000.

11 Europol Convention (1995, OJ C 316) Article 2(1). Since the Convention was signed, Europol's remit has been extended to cover terrorism, counterfeit currency and, following the Tampere summit in October 1999, money-laundering as a general offence.

12 OJ C 251, 15.8.97.

13 New Article 30, Treaty on European Union.

14 The independent authority of the working group level has arguably been augmented by the addition of the three Third Pillar steering groups.

15 New Article 2, Treaty on European Union.

16 Michael Emerson, former EU ambassador to Moscow, quoted in *The Economist*, 7 November 1998, p. 50.

17 Public order is a growing area of Third Pillar co-operation, as reflected in the Joint Action on Public Order and Internal Security of 26.5.97 (8012/97 ENFOPOL 111).

18 As with the unresolved status of the European Court of Justice under the original Europol Convention.

19 See e.g the Austrian Presidency Work Programme for the K4 Committee (July–December 1998), discussed in *Statewatch European Monitor* (1998, 1(1): 6–8).

20 The continuing reluctance of Third Pillar politicians and administrators to permit a high level of external scrutiny of their activities, despite consistent criticism of their weak accountability, can be seen in the failure to consult the European Parliament and other interested bodies as to the content of the strategically important Action Plan to Combat Organised Crime: European Parliament, Committee on Civil Liberties and Internal Affairs, *Report on the Action Plan to Combat Organised Crime*, Session Doc. A4-0333/97.

21 New Article 38, Treaty on European Union, the application of which in this context is discussed in the Austrian Presidency Work Programme for the K4 Committee (*Statewatch European Monitor*, 1998, 1(1): 6–8).

References

Adler, E. and Barnett, M. (eds) (1998) *Security Communities*. Cambridge: CUP.

Anderson, M. (1989) *Policing the World: Interpol and the Politics of International Police Co-operation*. Oxford: Clarendon.

Anderson, M. and Bort, E. (eds) (1998) *The Frontiers of Europe*. London: Pinter.

Anderson, M. and den Boer, M. (eds) (1994) *Policing across National Boundaries*. London: Pinter.

Anderson, M., den Boer, M., Cullen, P., Gilmore, W.C., Raab, C.D. and Walker, N. (1995) *Policing the European Union: Theory, Law and Practice*. Oxford: Clarendon.

Andreas, P. (1996) 'US–Mexico: Open Markets, Closed Borders', *Foreign Policy*, 103, 51–69.

Bigo, D. (1994) 'The European Internal Security Field: Stakes and Rivalries in the Newly Developing Area of Police Intervention' in Anderson and den Boer (1994).

Brubaker, R. (1996) *Nationalism Reframed: Nationhood and the National Question in the New Europe*. Cambridge: CUP.

Burchell, G., Gordon, C. and Millar, P. (eds) (1991) *The Foucault Effect*. Brighton: Harvester.

Cable, V. (1994) *The World's New Fissures*. London: Demos.

Cohen, H. (1985) 'Authority: The Limits of Discretion' in Elliston and Feldberg (1985).

Cullen, P.J. (1992) *The German Police and European Cooperation*. Edinburgh Police Working Paper, No. 2.

Cullen, P.J. (forthcoming) 'The Third Pillar: Criminal Law Aspects of "Convention law", in Usher (forthcoming).

Cullen, P.J. and Gilmore, W.C. (eds) (1998) *Crimes sans Frontières: International and European Legal Approaches*. Edinburgh: Edinburgh University Press.

Elliston, F.A. and Feldberg, M. (eds) (1985) *Moral Issues in Police Work*. New York: Rowman and Allanheld.

Emsley, C. (1999) *Gendarmes and the State in Nineteenth-Century Europe*. Oxford: OUP.

Ericson, R.V. (1994) 'The Division of Expert Knowledge in Policing and Security', *British Journal of Sociology*, 45, 149–76.

Fijnaut, C.J. (1991) 'Police Co-operation within Western Europe' in Heidensohn and Farrell (1991).

Foucault, M. (1991) 'Governmentality' in Burchell *et al.* (1991), 173–214.

Garland, D. (1996) 'The Limits of the Sovereign State: Strategies of Crime Control in Contemporary Society', *British Journal of Criminology*, 36, 445–71.

Garland, D. (1997) '"Governmentality" and the Problem of Crime: Foucault, Criminology and Sociology', *Theoretical Criminology*, 1, 173–214.

Giddens, A. (1985) *The Nation State and Violence*. London: Polity.

Gilmore, W. (ed.) (1993) *Action against Transnational Criminality*. Vol. 11. London: Commonwealth Secretariat.

Guyomarch, A. (1997) 'Cooperation in the Fields of Policing and Judicial Affairs' in Stavridis *et al.* (1997), 123.

Harris, R.N. (1973) *The Police Academy: An Inside View*. London: Wiley.

Heidensohn, F. and Farrell, M. (eds) (1991) *Crime in Europe*. London: Routledge.

Lindbergh, L.N. (1963) *The Political Dynamics of European Integration*. Stanford: Stanford University Press.

Loader, I. (forthcoming) 'Plural Policing and Democratic Governance', *Social and Legal Studies*.

Loader, I. and Walker, N. (forthcoming) 'Policing as a Public Good: Reconstituting the Connections between Policing and the State', *Theoretical Criminology*.

Maguire, M., Morgan, R. and Reiner, R. (eds) (1997) *Oxford Handbook of Criminology*. 2nd edn. Oxford: OUP.

Marenin, O. (1992) 'Parking Tickets and Class Repression: The Concept of Policing in Critical Theories of Criminal Justice', *Contemporary Crises*, 6, 241–66, 258.

Marenin, O. (ed.) (1996) *Policing Change, Changing Police: International Perspectives*. London: Garland.

Monar, J. (1998) 'Justice and Home Affairs in the Treaty of Amsterdam: Reform at the Price of Fragmentation', *European Law Review* 23, 320–35.

Nadelman, E. (1993) *Cops across Borders: The Internationalization of US Criminal Law Enforcement*. Pennsylvania State University.

Pasquino, P. (1991) 'Theatricum Politicum: The Genealogy of Capital – Police and the State of Prosperity' in Burchell *et al.* (1991).

Peers, S. (2000) *EU Justice and Home Affairs Law*. Harlow: Longman.

Reiner, R. (1992) *The Politics of the Police*. 2nd edn. Brighton: Wheatsheaf.

Reiner, R. (1997) 'Policing the Police' in Maguire *et al.* (1997), 997–1049.

Sheptycki, J.W.E. (1995) 'Transnational Policing and the Making of a Postmodern State', *British Journal of Criminology*, 35, 613–35.

Sheptycki, J.W.E. (1998) 'Policing, Postmodernism and Transnationalization', *British Journal of Criminology*, 38, 485–503, 498.

Statewatch European Monitor (1998) 1 (1).

Statewatch European Monitor (1998) 8 (5).

Statewatch European Monitor (1998) 2 (1).

Stavridis, S., Mossialos, E., Morgan, R. and Machin, H. (1997) *New Challenges to the European Union: Policies and Policy-Making*. Aldershot: Dartmouth.

Storbeck, J. (1996) 'Part of the Union', *Policing Today*, 2(1), 28–31.

Sunstein, C.R. (1996) *Legal Reasoning and Political Conflict*. Oxford: Oxford University Press.

Taylor, I. (1992) 'The International Drugs Trade and Money Laundering: Border Controls and Other Issues', *European Sociological Review*, 8, 181–93.

Turnbull-Henson, P. (1997) 'Negotiating the Third Pillar: The Maastricht Treaty and the Failure of Justice and Home Affairs Cooperation among EU Member States', paper to the ECSA Conference, Tampa: Florida, USA.

Usher, J.A. (ed.) (forthcoming) *The State of the European Union: Structure, Enlargement and Economic Union*. Harlow: Longman.

Waever, O. (1996) 'European Security Identities', *Journal of Common Market Studies*, 34, 103–32.

Walker, N. (1993) 'The Dynamics of European Police Co-operation: The United Kingdom Perspective' in Gilmore (1993), 106–19.

Walker, N. (1996) 'Policing the European Union: The Politics of Transition' in Marenin (1996), 251–84, 271–3.

Walker, N. (1998a) 'The New Frontiers of European Policing' in Anderson and Bort (1998).

Walker, N. (1998b) 'European Policing and the Politics of Regulation' in Cullen and Gilmore (1998).

Walker, N. (1998c) 'Sovereignty and Differentiated Integration in the European Union', *European Law Journal*, 4, 355–88.

Walker, N. (1999) 'Decoupling Police and State', in E. Bort and R. Keat (eds) *The Boundaries of Understanding: Essays in Honour of Malcolm Anderson.* Edinburgh: International Social Sciences Institute.

Walker, N. (2000) 'Flexibility within a Metaconstitutional Frame: Reflections on the Future of Legal Authority in Europe', in G de Burca and J. Scott (eds) *Constitutional Change in the EU: From Uniformity to Flexibility?* Oxford: Hart.

Walker, N. (forthcoming) *Policing in a Changing Constitutional Order.* London: Sweet and Maxwell.

Walker, N. and Telford, M. (2000) 'Designing Criminal Justice: The Northern Ireland System in Comparative Perspective', *Review of the Criminal Justice System in Northern Ireland, Research Report 18.* Belfast: HMSO.

Weiler, J. H. H. (1991) 'The Transformation of Europe', *Yale Law Journal,* 100, 2403–2483.

Part II
CORE FUNCTIONS

Chapter 7

Core policing: the seductive myth

R.I. MAWBY

Introduction: a comparative perspective

When Sir Richard Mayne issued his instructions to the newly formed Metropolitan Police in 1829, he identified the prevention of crime, the protection of life and property, and the preservation of public tranquillity as the core responsibilities of the police (quoted in Cassels, 1994: 9). From this initial broad remit, the functions of the police expanded. The introduction of paid police forces across the country, often with the grudging consent of local politicians, led to a situation where county and urban authorities, eager to get value for the money they were required to expend, burdened their new 'employees' with a wide range of additional work (Steedman, 1984). Alongside this, efforts to accredit the new police with legitimacy in the eyes of a sceptical public resulted in the fostering of the myth of the police as 'citizens in uniform', performing a plethora of public services and epitomised in the untarnished image of 'community policing' as the English heritage. The music-hall song that advised those wanting to know the time to ask a policeman, originally a sceptical reference to police dishonesty, became adopted as illustration of the extent of help one could expect from the police. While controversies such as that surrounding the role of the police in the 1926 General Strike acted as reminders that control and the maintenance of public order lay at the heart of police functions, early sociological studies, such as Banton's (1964), confirmed the broad responsibilities that had accrued to the police. Similarly, studies of police workloads (Comrie and King, 1974; Martin and Wilson, 1969) demonstrated the myriad of tasks they undertook, while Punch and Naylor (1973) argued that the primary role of the police was a social service one. More recently, in an analysis of British Crime Survey data on police/public contacts, Skogan (1990) demonstrates how the public contact the police for a variety of reasons, many of which are not crime-related.

This view is not without its critics. To a large extent, whether the police are carrying out crime-related work or not depends on how this is defined. Punch and Naylor (1973), for example, contentiously considered 'domestics' as non-crime, while Shapland and Vagg (1990), among others, note that many calls to the police that are not, at first sight, crime-related, in fact concern 'potential crime'.

Be this as it may, there exists a widespread feeling that British policing does – and should – have a broad mandate. Allied to this is the implicit notion that this is in some sense distinctive and that the roles of other countries' police are more confined. Nothing could be further from the truth.

For example, the functions performed by the embryonic US police were equally broad. Monkkonen (1981) describes the early police as fulfilling crucial welfare responsibilities, and Meyer's (1974) account of policework in the 1970s parallels British studies in noting the extent of non-crime work. Perhaps the most graphic illustration of this acknowledgement is Cummings *et al.*'s (1965) account of the police officer as 'philosopher, guide and friend', a first port of call to those in difficulty and a key gatekeeper in referring the public on to more appropriate agencies. Moreover, recent trends towards the adoption of community policing (Bayley, 1994; Sadd and Grinc, 1996) – referred to by Kelling and Moore (1988) as the 'community problem-solving era' – have accentuated this position, with acknowledgement that effective policing requires officers to address community problems that underpin crime and that sole emphasis on crime results in the treatment of the symptom rather than the cause (Eck and Spelman, 1987; Goldstein, 1979).

Excursions further afield into less familiar police systems reveal different, but no less diverse, patterns (Mawby, 1990; *ibid.*, 1992). Thus, police systems of continental Europe, where there has traditionally been little evidence of a welfare orientation, have tended to emphasise the maintenance of public order and control alongside 'crime fighting', but at the same time have incorporated a number of administrative responsibilities. While the original responsibilities of the German police for fire and health services, building controls and lodging houses (Fosdick, 1969) were curtailed under Allied occupation (Fairchild, 1988), they remain extensive. And while the Soviet policing model has retained most of its political and order-maintenance priorities in Russia and the independent states (Shelley, 1999), alternative communist systems incorporate an additional welfare orientation (Mawby, 1990). Yun (1983: 22), for example, describes how in China the police often help older people 'wash their clothes, buy food grain, clean their houses, manage their household affairs and get to hospital when they fall ill'. Elsewhere, colonial policing systems have tended to prioritise political control, as well as maintaining responsibility for a range of welfare tasks (Cole, 1999), and the Japanese police has a renowned reputation for its service orientation (Bayley, 1991).

The evidence from a myriad of studies is unequivocal. At different points of time and in police systems across the world, the police have been expected to carry out functions far wider than those pertaining to crime alone. The fact that, by the mid-1990s, the British government considered the roles that its police performed as too extensive, and raised the spectre of a police with responsibilities curtailed around a set of 'core tasks', requires explanation.

Policing in the 1990s

The suggestion that policing should be organised around a designated and limited series of 'core tasks' flowed from what was perceived to be a crisis in policing in Britain in the early 1990s (Cassels, 1994; Home Office, 1995).

Expenditure on the police increased dramatically in the 1980s, partly as a result of the recommendations of the Edmund Davies Committee regarding pay levels. However, far from helping to curtail the crime problem, both British Crime Survey (BCS) data and – especially – official statistics revealed a persistent rise in crime rates (Mirrlees-Black *et al.*, 1998). Indeed, research studies questioned the impact that a police patrol presence had on crime levels (Clarke and Hough, 1984) (echoing earlier US research) and the extent to which the police themselves were responsible for detecting crime (Burrows, 1986; Mawby, 1979).[1] At the same time, successive BCSs revealed a decline in public satisfaction with police services (Bucke, 1995; Southgate and Crisp, 1993), and urban riots, the deployment of the police during the Miners' Strike, and a number of high-profile cases in which police investigations came under critical scrutiny, raised concerns that questioned the long-standing complacency that the 'British' police were 'the best in the world'.

The 1980s also saw a change in the balance between the public police, sworn officers employed by the 43 police forces in England and Wales, and other people involved in a policing role. This had a number of dimensions to it. First, the number of civilians employed within police forces rose dramatically, trebling in the 15 years up to 1995 (Home Office, 1995: 8). Second, private security increased both in terms of the numbers of private police and the range of work undertaken, evidencing a shift in the public/private balance (Johnston, 1999; Jones and Newburn, 1995). Finally, encouraged by successive Conservative governments, the police looked to the public to become more involved in crime prevention through Neighbourhood Watch schemes (Dowds and Mayhew, 1994), the Special Constabulary (Gill and Mawby, 1990; Mirrlees-Black and Byron, 1995) and other permutations (Southgate *et al.*, 1995).

In this context, it was perhaps not surprising to find the government starting to question the effectiveness and efficiency of the police. This was illustrated in 1993 with reviews, including the Royal Commission on Criminal Justice, the Sheehy Inquiry into Police Responsibilities and Rewards and the White Paper on Police Reform.

One issue fundamental to these reviews was the appropriate roles and responsibilities that should be expected of the modern police. The Sheehy Inquiry saw policing as encompassing four main aims: to prevent crime; to pursue and bring to justice those who break the law; to keep the peace; and to protect, help and reassure the public. In contrast, the White Paper prioritised 'fighting crime', albeit noting that this should be done in partnership with the public. Flowing from this, the Home Secretary announced a further Home Office Review of Police Core and Ancillary Tasks, to be chaired by Ingrid Posen from F1 Department of the Home Office (Posen, 1994). Its terms of reference were:

> To examine the services provided by the police, to make recommendations about the most cost-effective way of delivering core policing services and to assess the scope for relinquishing ancillary tasks.　　　　　　　　(Home Office, 1995: 7)

The Posen Inquiry

In introducing its terms of reference, Posen noted the traditional social service orientation of the police but considered that this created difficulties in terms of setting proper boundaries, with 'the police called on to fill any vacuum left by other services, acting as out-of-hours social workers, mental health nurses, housing officers' (Posen, 1994: 15). In attempting to distinguish between core and ancillary tasks she asked whether any specific task contributes in some significant way to the achievement of police aims and objectives and, if so, whether it needs to be performed by the police. That is, the inquiry concerned whether or not the task should remain under the control of the police, not whether it had to be performed by a police officer. However, even where an alternative provider may make sense on practical grounds, Posen noted that it is also important that the public should have confidence in that alternative.

This raises the issue of consultation. However, while Posen described the review as falling into three stages of consultation between the committee and the police and Police Authorities, she avoided committing herself to any public review. Consequently, while ACPO had argued in favour of public consultation, consultation was largely internal (Travis, 1994). Chief constables were sent a questionnaire spelling out 85 alternative tasks and asked to identify these as core or ancillary. If core, a further distinction was made between inner-core and outer-core tasks. In each case tasks were also subdivided according to their primary function: bringing offenders to justice, fighting or preventing crime, upholding the law, and protecting, helping and reassuring the community.

There would therefore seem to have been three issues central to the review. First, as Home Office minister David Maclean put it, 'we need to prioritise ... and find out which tasks are key to policing and which could either be dropped altogether or allocated to others to do' (Mason, 1994: 22). Second, according to Home Secretary Michael Howard, the emphasis was on 'tasks – not officers – which can be shed'.[2] But, third, as Ingrid Posen admitted, tasks that the police relinquish would not be paid for through *additional* public expenditure (Travis, 1994).

Controversies over cost, arguments that savings can only be made by substituting inferior services or that the issue is more one of redirecting expenditure rather than cutting it, are central to this debate. One further major issue concerns the nature of the police/public relationship itself. For example, the fact that the regular police deal with routine traffic incidents provides an opportunity for them to gather crime intelligence (Howe, 1994). Moreover, as the president of ACPO at the time noted:

As the review team are rapidly discovering, policing does not divide easily. 'Ancillary' tasks have a vital role to play in forging links between officers and the communities they serve and it is increasingly apparent that neat divisions of labour do not provide solutions to setting priorities.   (Hoddinott, 1994: 21)

This has crucial implications for policing by consent:

If work is hived off which brings us into contact with decent, law-abiding people, we lose that information, we lose that support and, ultimately, we lose that consent.[3]

Concern over the widespread implications stemming from the Posen Inquiry led the Police Foundation and Policy Studies Institute to set up a separate Independent Committee of Inquiry into the Roles and Responsibilities of the Police, chaired by Sir John Cassels (1994).

However, while public perceptions of the police role are implicit to any review of 'policing by consent' and police/public relationships, neither Posen nor Cassels sought the views of the public.[4] Yet, research evidence clearly shows that people do see the value of the police performing a broad range of tasks, rather than limiting themselves to 'fighting' crime. The Operational Policing Review, for example, found that, given a choice between the officer who 'detects and arrests offenders' and one who 'works with local people to solve crime', three times as many chose the latter (Joint Consultative Committee, 1990). The Devon and Cornwall Constabulary, therefore, decided to task its Quality of Service Unit with conducting a survey of different publics' views on the current style and functions of the police, the importance of different police tasks, and the potential for hiving off some of these to other agencies.

The research in Devon and Cornwall

A survey that focuses on the minutiae of detail regarding police tasks is a challenge. On the one hand lies the danger of assuming too much public knowledge; on the other hand, the possibility of putting words into people's mouths is ever-present. A survey carried out for the Cheshire Constabulary (Smith and Allison, 1993) amply illustrates the difficulties (Redshaw *et al.*, 1997: 286–7).

The Quality of Service Unit constructed a questionnaire based on earlier discussions of the tasks carried out by the police. Five questions related to the functions and styles of the police. The first simply asked respondents to choose between two alternative police styles: one crime focused, the other community oriented. The second was an open-ended question where respondents were invited to state what they felt should be the main functions of the police. The third, and most complex, question listed 36 'jobs the police are asked to do' and asked respondents, 'How important is it that the police carry out each of these jobs?', using a four-point scale from 'very important' to 'not at all important'. Next they were given a similar list of jobs and told, 'There are obviously many activities which people think *could* be carried out by other agencies. However I would like you to consider whether or not any of the following activities *should in your view* be carried out by organisations other than the police'. For each job they were offered five alternatives:

(i) should *only* be done by the police;
(ii) police should be responsible but in *partnership* with other authorities;
(iii) should only be done by some *other* authority;

(iv) parts should be subcontracted out to some other authority *but under the control of the police;*

(v) all parts of this activity should be discontinued.

In the case of six of the activities, answers (ii), (iii) and (iv) were asterisked, and those ticking a box marked with an asterisk were then asked to elaborate on what they had in mind.

Finally, respondents were asked their opinions on 12 statements, ten of which referred to police tasks and styles, two to private security firms.

Clearly, the questionnaire was extremely complex and contained information that required time to digest and possibly also some background knowledge on which to base answers. For these reasons the Unit decided that self-completion was preferable to an interview. It was also felt that the questionnaire was most suitable for use with groups with an appropriate knowledge base and should be used with the general public only with caution.

We, therefore, decided to target three populations: police officers, Neighbourhood Watch co-ordinators and Police Consultative Committee members. Questionnaires were therefore sent to a random sample of 300 police officers in Devon and Cornwall, 584 Neighbourhood Watch (NW) co-ordinators in four divisions in the force area, and 19 Police Consultative Committee members from one division. Completed questionnaires were returned by 154 police officers, 342 Neighbourhood Watch co-ordinators and 13 Police Consultative Committee members, giving response rates of 57 per cent, 59 per cent and 68 per cent respectively. The questionnaire was also piloted with members of the public attending a crime prevention display at the Cornwall County Show at Wadebridge, being given out to 114 people who completed it on the spot, and given the lack of problems experienced through this purposive sample, a random sample of 400 residents in the North Devon area were mailed the questionnaire, resulting in 188 replies, a response rate of 47 per cent. The remainder of this article concentrates on the three largest samples, of police, Neighbourhood Watch co-ordinators and North Devon public.[5]

General perceptions of police tasks and responsibilities

One starting point for discussion of core policing tasks is a consideration of the extent to which the police should concentrate more on crime fighting rather than community-based initiatives. We therefore began by asking respondents which of two alternative statements came '*closest* to the way you think the police *should* be dealing with crime'. As is evident from Table 7.1, while almost half NW co-ordinators opted for an arrest-and-prosecute strategy, only about one-third of police did so. In fact, in all three samples, the majority felt that the police should maintain close links with the public and not exclusively concentrate on arrest and prosecution.

Nevertheless, there is some degree of disagreement or ambiguity here, and this is confirmed if we consider responses to the general statements positioned at the end of the questionnaire (Table 7.2). Asked if 'the police

Table 7.1 Preference on how the police should deal with crime

	Police	NW co-ordinators	Public
The police should concentrate on arresting and prosecuting offenders	30.8	48.8	43.1
The police should maintain close links with the public rather than exclusively concentrate on arrests and prosecution strategies	69.2	51.2	56.9

should become more streamlined and concentrate on core tasks only ... relinquishing ancillary tasks for privatisation or in liaison with other agencies', the majority of all three samples agreed: 67 per cent of police, 76 per cent of NW co-ordinators and 73 per cent of the public. Similarly, there was agreement that 'the occupational role of the police covers too wide an area', with 73 per cent of the police, 77 per cent of NW co-ordinators and 76 per cent of the public agreeing. However, a majority of police and NW co-ordinators also agreed that 'the idea of policing by consent would be eroded if the police just concentrated on core policing tasks'. Indeed, respondents also had very clear views on the duties and working styles expected of their police. They strongly felt that 'the state has a responsibility to provide a standardised and comprehensive police service unrelated to where you live' and 'it is important that the police make the public feel safe' and also felt that:

(i) 'It is important that the police take an interest in community issues in general and not just crime.'
(ii) The police should provide a 'caring service'.
(iii) 'The police should concentrate on providing a personal local service.'
(iv) 'The social service function of the police is important.'

Finally, they were firmly of the view that 'policing should not be motivated by profit' (see Table 7.2).

Ranking police tasks

Responses to these general statements suggest that the various samples are concerned that the police emphasise their crime fighting role but not to the detriment of community and service orientations. But what about when they are asked to prioritise tasks?

We aimed to distinguish more clearly between different police tasks through our listing of 37 jobs the police are asked to do. In each case respondents were asked to rate the job on a five-point scale from 'very important' to 'not at all important'. While this allowed us to compare the percentage of responses in each category for the different samples, it did not provide an easy way of ranking jobs and comparing samples. We, therefore, scored answers from 1 ('very important') to 4 ('not at all important'). Low scores thus denote jobs that respondents felt it was particularly important that the police carried out, with 2.5 the mid-point. The mean scores for the police, NW and public are illustrated in Table 7.3.

Table 7.2 Percentage agreeing or disagreeing with the following statements

	Police		NW co-ord.		Public	
	A	D	A	D	A	D
The police should become more streamlined and concentrate on core tasks only	67.4	26.8	75.5	17.7	72.6	16.1
The occupational role of the police covers too wide an area	73.2	19.6	77.3	13.1	76.4	12.0
The state has a responsibility to provide a standardised and comprehensive police service	74.5	17.0	89.6	6.8	88.0	7.1
Policing should not be motivated by profit	94.8	4.6	96.2	2.1	93.5	3.8
It is important that the police make the public feel safe	98.7	0.6	98.8	0	100	0
It is important that the police take an interest in community issues in general	85.7	3.2	82.3	4.7	78.6	5.8
I place great emphasis on the provision of a caring service	84.4	3.9	85.2	4.2	83.3	5.4
The police should concentrate on providing a personal local service	74.7	7.8	75.6	4.2	76.5	6.0
The social service function of the police is important to me	55.2	16.2	58.4	14.8	50.3	17.3
The ideas of 'policing by consent' would be eroded if the police just concentrate on core policing tasks	54.5	31.8	55.3	19.3	43.4	25.0

As is evident, mean scores for each sample were relatively low, demonstrating that most jobs were considered of some importance. For police respondents, scores ranged from 1.02 to 3.56, with only eight activities at over 2.5. For NW co-ordinators, the scores ranged from 1.03 to 2.90 with only six scored at over 2.5. Finally, among the public the scores ranged from 1.2 to 2.95 with nine scored at over 2.5.

That said, however, there was a marked level of agreement between the three samples. Overall, the tasks rated as core policework were:

(i)   respond immediately to emergencies;
(ii)   detect and arrest offenders;
(iii)   investigate crime;
(iv)   set up squads for serious crimes;
(v)   collect criminal intelligence information and keep records;
(vi)   patrol the area on foot;
(vii)   get to know local people;
(viii) deal with rowdy behaviour;
(ix)   deal with public disturbances;

Table 7.3 Mean scores and ranks of importance placed on police carrying out each job (Score of 1 equates with extremely important, 4 not at all important)

	Police		NW co-ord.		Public	
	Mean	Rank	Mean	Rank	Mean	Rank
Respond immediately to emergencies	1.02	1	1.03	1	1.02	1
Investigate crime	1.10	3	1.20	3	1.10	3
Control and supervise road traffic	2.09	18.5	2.35	28	2.54	31
Give advice to the public on how to prevent crime	1.90	13	1.83	12	1.99	17
Patrol the area on foot	1.58	8	1.51	6	1.66	9
Patrol the area in cars	1.76	9.5	2.01	19	1.86	13
Provide help and support to victims of crime	2.02	15	2.05	21	2.14	21
Detect and arrest offenders	1.08	2	1.15	2	1.03	2
Work closely with local schools	2.15	20	1.86	13	1.95	16
Get to know local people	1.44	7	1.54	7	1.73	11
Set up squads for serious crime	1.88	12	1.33	4	1.33	4
Work with local council departments such as housing to plan crime prevention	2.21	21	2.03	20	2.15	22
Preparing cases for prosecuting criminals through the courts	2.09	18.5	1.88	15	1.90	14
Dealing with lost/found property	3.36	36	2.90	37	2.95	37
Advising householders on crime prevention	2.39	24	2.09	23	2.24	23
Advising businesses on crime prevention	2.47	26	2.11	24	2.27	35
Dealing with traffic accidents	1.76	9.5	1.74	11	1.70	10
Maintaining traffic flows	2.48	27	2.39	29	2.52	29
Escorting heavy loads	3.56	37	2.76	36	2.83	36
Policing motorways	2.00	14	1.96	17.5	2.13	20
Advising highway and other planning authorities on road safety	2.43	25	2.22	25	2.43	27
Collecting criminal intelligence information and keeping records	1.28	5	1.42	5	1.53	8
Dealing with rowdy behaviour	1.31	6	1.57	8	1.49	5
Dealing with prostitution, indecency, etc.	1.67	9	1.96	17.5	1.92	15
Dealing with public disturbances	1.23	4	1.58	9	1.49	7
Attendance at public events (e.g. football matches)	2.61	29	2.60	33	2.54	30
Monitoring licensing arrangements (e.g. monitoring those people holding licences)	2.83	31	2.55	32	2.70	34

Continued

Table 7.3 continued

	Police		NW co-ord.		Public	
	Mean	Rank	Mean	Rank	Mean	Rank
Monitoring firearms and explosives	1.88	11	1.60	10	1.49	6
Monitoring licensed premises	2.48	28	2.46	31	2.48	28
Monitoring betting shops, dangerous dogs	3.06	32	2.61	34	2.66	33
Missing persons	2.07	16	2.07	22	2.07	19
Crime recording service	2.32	23	1.86	14	2.04	18
Sudden deaths	2.29	22	1.95	16	1.78	12
Looking after prisoners in custody	2.72	30	2.41	30	2.26	25
Executing court processes (e.g. serving summonses)	3.32	35	2.70	35	2.63	32
Escorting prisoners from police stations to court	3.12	33	2.35	27	2.24	24
Providing enquiry/advice points	2.08	17	2.33	26	2.32	26

(x) monitor firearms and explosives;
(xi) deal with traffic accidents.

What then of those tasks seen as least important for the police to carry out? In fact, all six activities scored at over 2.5 by NW co-ordinators were similarly rated by police and public:

(i) deal with lost/found property;
(ii) escort heavy loads;
(iii) execute court process (e.g. serve summonses);
(iv) monitor betting shops, dangerous dogs;
(v) attendance at public events (e.g. football matches);
(vi) monitor licensing arrangements (e.g. monitor those holding licences).

Responses suggest that while police tasks concerning 'fighting crime' are prioritised, and none rated low in the list, in other respects high and low priorities span a range of police activities. With one or two exceptions, these findings are perhaps not surprising. That is, given a long list of tasks that the police carry out, police, NW co-ordinators and public saw some of those jobs as fundamentally the responsibility of the police, others less important. That does not, however, mean that they necessarily felt that such activities should be discontinued or carried out by agencies external to the police.

Hiving off police tasks

The feeling that it was inappropriate for the private sector to take over police tasks was illustrated in responses to two statements about private security firms. When it was suggested that these firms were 'quite capable of maintaining law and order by patrolling the streets', only a minority agreed, confirming the findings of an earlier study in Plymouth (Dale and Mawby,

1994). In fact 73 per cent of NW co-ordinators, 92 per cent of police and 70 per cent of the public disagreed. Similarly, while rather less disagreed with the statement, 'Private security firms are quite capable of being impartial', the proportions of respondents endorsing this viewpoint were far lower than those disagreeing with it. These views complement the concern noted earlier that 'policing should not be motivated by profit'.

Who then, if anyone, should be charged with carrying out so-called ancillary police tasks? We can consider this on two levels. First, for those tasks given low priority, we can assess who respondents felt should carry them out, according to the alternatives provided. Second, for the tasks initially specified, we can review respondents' more detailed comments.

We have identified who respondents felt should be responsible for each of the ten low-priority tasks. It was evident that overall the most popular of the alternatives provided were that the activity should be carried out by the police in partnership with other authorities, or by some other authority. The partnership model was the most popular choice among all three samples for attendance at public events and the top choice of the three non-police alternatives for monitoring licensed premises and control and supervision of traffic, where the public and police respectively gave the police as their first choice. Two tasks – escorting heavy loads and dealing with lost/found property – were considered by all three samples as best done by some other authority. Monitoring licensing arrangements was felt by police and NW co-ordinators to be an appropriate job for another authority, although the public felt this could best be done by the police in partnership with other authorities. Monitoring betting shops and dangerous dogs was felt by the police to be an appropriate job for some other agency while the public tended to favour a partnership approach; NW co-ordinators were split on this. Maintaining traffic flows was considered by all three samples to be a police task. NW co-ordinators and the public also were inclined to agree that executing court processes and looking after prisoners in custody were police tasks, although the police were more likely to favour the work being carried out by some other agency, in the latter case under the control of the police.

Looked at in another way, the police opted for police responsibility with regard to two of the ten activities, police partnership for 2, other authority for 5 and police control for one. NW co-ordinators opted for police responsibility for 3, police partnership 3/4 and other authority 3/4. The public opted for police responsibility four times, police partnership four times and other authority twice. Ironically this suggests a greater willingness among the police to abdicate responsibilities than among the other groups.

The notion of partnership is, of course, of wider contemporary relevance, and it is no contradiction to accept that the partnership approach would be favoured for some core policing tasks. This was certainly the case. Thus, all three of our main samples felt that partnership was important *vis-à-vis*:

(i)   giving advice to the public on how to prevent crime;
(ii) providing help and support to victims of crime;

(iii)   working closely with local schools;
(iv)   working with local councils to plan crime prevention;
(v)   advising householders on crime prevention;
(vi)   advising businesses on crime prevention;
(vii) advising highways and other planning authorities on road safety.

There was also a broad degree of endorsement of the partnership approach towards the preparation of cases for prosecution and dealing with missing persons. With these exceptions, though, clearly those activities associated with crime prevention were considered most appropriately addressed through the partnership approach, an endorsement of current police and government initiatives.

Having asked respondents to state who should carry out the various activities specified, we then focused on six specific tasks that had featured in earlier discussions and asked those who had felt that these tasks should continue to be carried out, but not solely by the police, to provide, in their own words, additional details of what they had in mind. The six activities we chose were: (i) Monitoring of firearms and explosives, seen as a core police task; (ii) Providing help and support for victims of crime; providing enquiry/advice points; advising businesses on crime prevention; control and supervision of road traffic: generally ranked intermediate–low; (iii) Executing the court process: generally ranked low.

Any assessment of these verbatim statements runs the danger of becoming a subjective exercise. However, two themes run clearly through the replies. First, while many felt that the police did carry out tasks which could appropriately be done by someone else, in most cases respondents felt that the task should remain the *responsibility* of the police and saw the exercise of choosing alternatives as difficult:

> 'Core tasks': this means many things to different people. In dealing with 'core tasks' police invariably touch on social areas and provide a service in these areas.
>
> (NW 763)

and dangerous:

> Police should be responsible for nearly every activity ... The responsibility difference between various functions is often marginal ... I see no objection to letting out work functions ... but police surely cannot lose control of any or part of these jobs. This must be a questionnaire brought about by strong financial pressures, which is deplorable.   (PUB 1029)

Second, and reiterating the points made earlier, except in the case of crime prevention advice for businesses there was widespread reluctance to extend the role of the private sector in areas traditionally associated with the public police. For example:

> Strongly supportive of our police forces and do not agree with present policy towards hiving off parts of their duties to private firms who are profit driven first and foremost.   (NW 121)

There are services the police currently attempt to provide that could be passed to others but my definition of 'core services' includes such things as routine patrolling etc. and I do not approve of the private security approach at all.   (PUB 1016)

I am strongly opposed to the creation of yet more quangos and to the making of private profit from socially necessary activities. The past few years have seen far too much of both trends. They are harmful and divisive.   (PUB 1012)

The research: summary and conclusions

Clearly, it is dangerous to generalise from our surveys, first because they are confined to the Devon and Cornwall Police area, but also because the subject matter is difficult to tackle through surveys of any sort. Nevertheless, the extent of agreement between our different samples and the internal consistency of replies suggest to us that a few conclusions are justifiable.

First there is recognition that in order to carry out 'crime control' policing tasks the police need to engage in a wide range of other activities and that separating 'core' from 'ancillary' tasks is a dangerous, if not impossible exercise. Second, even where activities appear to have no immediate 'crime control' payoffs, there is widespread acceptance that the British tradition of local community-based, service-oriented policing needs to be preserved. In these respects the concerns expressed by Reiner (1994) are reflected in the views of our samples. Third, while many members of the public – and even NW co-ordinators – do not appear aware of the extent to which civilianisation has taken place already, there is far greater support for transferring tasks from the police to civilians working *within* the police service than there is for hiving off tasks *from* the police service. Fourth, a partnership approach receives considerable support both in the context of many 'core' activities and for 'ancillary' tasks which might be taken away from the police. Finally though, in such cases or others where respondents felt activities could be hived off, other public agencies were usually preferred and – with one or two exceptions – expansion of private sector involvement was viewed with unease.

It is not difficult to agree that some police activities are more important than others. However, to assume that those ranked lower should be carried out by other agencies is a logical jump that the government of the time appeared willing to make. Interestingly, our apparently less sophisticated respondents seemed more reluctant to make this jump; there is no widespread endorsement of any policies that might hive off significant aspects of policework and even less enthusiasm for the privatisation of ancillary tasks.

Core policing: a continuing debate?

The Independent Committee of Inquiry into the Roles and Responsibilities of the Police published its findings in 1994 (Cassels, 1994). The Posen Inquiry produced its final report in 1995 (Home Office, 1995). Ironically, the former was the more radical document. In attempting to head off recommendations for extensive privatisation, it offered instead two alternative models of two-tier policing, that would involve the establishment of locally based, less well trained forces to carry out routine and less demanding police tasks, as is the case in many continental countries (Mawby, 1990). The first alternative it spelt out would involve the 'establishment of local patrolling forces ... to some extent under the direction of the public police' (Cassels, 1994: 19); the latter 'involves the creation of "designated" patrol officers' who 'would be part of the local constabulary' (*ibid.*: 21).

In contrast, the Posen Inquiry was much more cautious:

> The Review started from the proposition that the existing style and character of British policing is based on a broad interpretation of the police role. The community is helped, protected and reassured by the police carrying out a wide range of everyday duties including responding to calls for service, visibly patrolling, restoring order and tackling crime. Such work develops numerous links between the police and public which contribute to building trust. Trust is an essential condition for policing by consent; and policing by consent is fundamental to preserving order and the liberty and property of every citizen.   (Home Office, 1995: 9)

> What emerged from the subsequent discussion of tasks is that there are relatively few areas where complete police disengagement could be achieved easily with no corresponding disadvantage.   (*ibid.*: 11)

As a result:

> The review team concluded that there was little scope for the police service, broadly defined, to withdraw completely from large areas of current police work.
> (*ibid.*: 5)

Twenty-six areas were, however, identified where police involvement could be reduced, including responsibility for dealing with stray dogs, noise nuisance, defendant and witness summonses, and court security, and regarding the policing of public events and escorting abnormal loads.

At first sight, the assumption that the British police carry out a wide range of miscellaneous tasks that could be hived off – to the private sector, other public-sector agencies, or the public – is appealing, offering as it does the promise that the police could then concentrate on their 'real' job, fighting crime, but police the world over are routinely expected to fulfil a comprehensive set of responsibilities, and – as our survey in Devon and Cornwall indicated – police and public appreciated, to a greater extent than the government of the day, the difficulties and dangers associated with attempting to disentangle these tasks.

Nevertheless, there is little sign that the new Labour (or New Labour) government is any less inclined to re-open the debate. The 1998 Crime and Disorder Act takes the issue forward as far as partnerships are concerned, and as our research indicates this seems to have widespread public support, but there is every indication that the private sector's role in policing will be extended, a move that our respondents viewed with concern. Moreover, with the likelihood of a move to a smaller number of regionalised forces, the prospect of a second tier of local, city or town police, as suggested by Cassels (1994), comes nearer to becoming reality. That such a model has been adopted in continental European countries with more militaristic and centralised police is perhaps indicative of the dangers of widening the gap between police (or top-tier police) and public. Ironically, while the Home Office (1995) inquiry came to recognise the dangers associated with such moves, the Cassels (1994) inquiry that was set up to counter it may well have played hostage to fortune. In either case, it is clear that debates over core policing tasks will continue into the twenty-first century. Historical and international review combines with research on public perceptions to suggest that the idea that policing can be pared down to a 'core' is more myth than a practical option; it is, nevertheless, a seductive myth.

Notes

1 Similarly, in the USA, see Greenwood and Chaiken (1977).
2 Speaking to the Police Federation Annual Conference, 1994, as reported in *Police*, June 1994, pp. 16–17.
3 Ray Oakley speaking to Inspectors Annual Conference, 1994, as reported in *Police*, June 1994, p. 24.
4 The Salford research is detailed in Smith and Allison (1993) and critiqued in Redshaw *et al.* (1997).
5 A more detailed review of the Devon and Cornwall surveys is contained in Redshaw *et al.* (1997).

References

Banton, M. (1964) *The Policeman in the Community*. London: Tavistock.

Bayley, D.H. (1991) *Forces of Order: Police Behaviour in Japan and the United States* (2nd edn). Berkeley: UCLA Press.

Bayley, D.H. (1994) *Police for the Future*. New York: Oxford University Press.

Bottomly, K., Fowles, T. and Reiner, R. (eds) (1992) *Criminal Justice: Theory and Practice*. London: BSC/ISTD.

Bucke, T. (1995) *Policing and the Public: Findings from the 1994 British Crime Survey*. Research Findings No. 28. London: Home Office, Research and Statistics Department.

Burrows, J. (1986) *Investigating Burglary: Tthe Measurement of Police Performance*. Home Office Research and Planning Unit Papers, No. 88. London: Home Office.

Cassels, Sir J. (1994*) Independent Committee of Inquiry into the Role and Responsibilities of the Police*. London: Police Foundation.

Clarke, R. and Hough, J.M. (1984) *Crime and Police Effectiveness*. Home Office Research Studies, No. 79. London: Home Office.

Cole, B.A. (1999) 'Post-Colonial Systems' in Mawby (1999) 88–108.

Comrie, M.D. and King, E.J. (1974) 'Urban Workloads', *Police Research Bulletin*, 23, 32–8.

Cummings, E. *et al.* (1965) 'Policeman as Philosopher, Guide and Friend', *Social Problems*, 12, 276.

Dale, P. and Mawby, R.I. (1994) 'Backing the Bobby', *Police Review*, 2 September, 26–8.

Davidoff, L. (1993) 'Performance Indicators for the Police Service', *Focus on Police Research and Development*, 3, 12–17.

Davidson, N. (1993) 'Feeling Quality: Measuring Public Satisfaction with Police Service Delivery', paper to British Criminology Conference, Cardiff.

Dowds, L. and Mayhew, P. (1994) 'Participation in Neighbourhood Watch: Findings from the 1992 British Crime Survey', Research Findings, No. 11. London: Home Office, Research and Statistics Department.

Eck, J.E. and Spelman, W. (1987) 'Who Ya Gonna Call? The Police as Problem-Busters', *Crime and Delinquency*, 33 (1), 31–52.

Fairchild, E. J. (1988) *German Police*. Springfield, MA: Charles C. Thomas.

Fosdick, R.B. (1969, original 1915) *European Police Systems*. Montclair, NJ: Patterson Smith.

Gill, M. and Mawby, R.I. (1990) *A Special Constable: A Study of the Police Reserve*. Aldershot: Avebury.

Goldstein, H. (1979) 'Improving Policing: A Problem-Oriented Approach', *Crime and Delinquency*, 25(2), 236–58.

Greenwood, P. and Chaiken, J. (1977) *The Criminal Investigation Process*. Lexington, MA: D.C. Heath.

Hoddinott, J. (1994) 'Core Questions', *Police Review*, 5 August, 20–2.

Home Office (1990) *Victim's Charter*. London: HMSO.

Home Office (1993a) *Inquiry into Police Responsibilities and Rewards*. (Sheehy Report.) London: HMSO.

Home Office (1993b) *Police Reform: A police Service for the Twenty-First Century*. Cmnd 2281. London: HMSO.

Home Office (1995) *Review of Police Core and Ancillary Tasks*. London: HMSO.

Howe, S. (1994) 'Hidden Agenda', *Police Review*, 4 March, 20–1.

Johnston, L. (1999) 'Private Policing: Uniformity and Diversity' in Mawby (1999), 226–38.

Joint Consultative Committee (1990) *Operational Policing Review*. Surbiton: Police Staff Associations.

Jones, T. and Newburn, T. (1995) 'How Big is the Private Security Sector?', *Policing and Society*, 5, 221–32.

Judge, T. (1994a) 'New Force for Motorways and London?', *Police*, June, 9, 39.

Judge, T. (1994b) 'Gnawing at the Core', *Police*, July, 12.

Kelling, G.L. and Moore, M.H. (1988) 'The evolving strategy of policing', *Perspectives on Policing*. Washington, DC: US Department of Justice.

Martin, J.P. and Wilson, G. (1969) *The Police: A study in Manpower*. London: Heinemann.

Mason, G. (1994) 'Home Truths', *Police Review*, 12 August, 22–3.

Mawby, R.I. (1979) *Policing the City*. Farnborough: Saxon House.

Mawby, R.I. (1990) *Comparative Policing Issues: The British and American Experience in International Perspective*. London: Unwin/Hyman (Routledge).

Mawby, R.I. (1992) 'Comparative Police Systems: Searching for a Continental Model' in Bottomley *et al.* (1992), 108–32.

Mawby, R.I. (ed.) (1999) *Policing across the World: Issues for the Twenty-First Century*. London: UCL Press.

Merseyside Police Authority (1993) *Residents' Attitudes to the Police Service*. Liverpool: Merseyside Police Authority.

Meyer, J. (1974) 'Patterns of Reporting Non-Criminal Incidents to the Police', *Criminology*, 12.

Mirrlees-Black, C., Budd, T., Partridge, S. and Mayhew, P. (1998) *The 1998 British Crime Survey*. Home Office Statistical Bulletin, 21/98. London: Home Office.

Mirrlees-Black, C. and Byron, C. (1995) *Special Considerations: Issues for the Management and Organisation of the Volunteer Police.* Home Office Research and Planning Unit Papers, No. 88. London: Home Office.

Monkkonen, E. (1981) *Police in Urban America, 1860–1920.* Cambridge, MA: Cambridge University Press.

Posen, I. (1994); 'What is Policing?', *Police Review,* 11 February, 14–15.

Punch, M. and Naylor, T. (1973) 'The Police: A Social Service', *New Society,* 24 (554), 358–61.

Redshaw, J., Mawby, R.I. and Bunt, P. (1997) 'Evaluating Core Policing in Britain: The Views of Police and Consumers', *International Journal of the Sociology of Law,* 25, 282–301.

Reiner, R. (1994) 'What Should the Police Be Doing?', *Policing,* 10 (3), 151–7.

Runciman, Lord (1993) *Royal Commission on Criminal Justice: Report.* Cmnd 2263. London: HMSO.

Sadd, S. and Grinc, R.M. (1996) 'Implementation Challenges in Community Policing', NIJ Research in Brief, URL: http: //www.ncjrs.org/txtfiles/implcp.txt

Shapland, J. and Vagg, J. (1990) *Policing by the Public.* London: Routledge.

Shelley, L.I. (1999) 'Post-Socialist Policing: Limitations on Institutional Change' in Mawby (1999), 75–87.

Skogan, W. (1990) *The Police and Public in England and Wales: A British Crime Survey Report.* Home Office Research Study, 117. London: HMSO.

Smith, L. and Allison, B. (1993) *Core Activity Survey.* Salford: University of Salford.

Southgate, P., Bucke, T. and Byron, C. (1995) *The Parish Special Constable Scheme.* Home Office Research Studies, No. 143. London: Home Office.

Southgate, P. and Crisp, D. (1993) *Public Satisfaction with Police Services.* Home Office Research and Planning Unit Papers, No. 73. London: Home Office.

Steedman, C. (1984) *Policing the Victorian Community: The Formation of English Provincial Police Forces, 1856–80.* London: Routledge.

Travis, A. (1994) 'Public May Have to Pay for the Former Police Services', *Guardian,* 11 July.

Yun, T. (1983) 'The Police and the People', *Beijing Review,* 23 May, 22–7.

Chapter 8

Policing, crime prevention and partnerships

DANIEL GILLING

Introduction

The police service has held a statutory duty for the prevention of crime since it first gained a permanent presence in London in 1829. The aim of this chapter is to examine how this duty has been interpreted, and with what consequences. Although the chapter begins with an historical review of crime prevention within the police service, its main focus will be upon the present, and especially upon the direction in which crime prevention is moving as a consequence of the ongoing implementation of the 1998 Crime and Disorder Act. The present is undoubtedly the most important focus of the chapter, but the contextualisation of the present within the past usefully serves to demonstrate the range of influences – occupational, organisational, environmental and socio-political – that have contributed and continue to contribute to the shaping and moulding of the police service and its crime preventive role. These influences constitute the major issues for crime prevention, and for policing more generally, at the beginning of the 21st century.

History lessons

It is from the 1829 Metropolitan Police Act, and the force instructions (quoted in Reith, 1956: 135–6) which first accompanied it, that the importance of the prevention of crime was first emphasised to police recruits:

> It should be understood, at the outset, that the principal object to be obtained is the prevention of crime. To this great end every effort of the police is to be directed. The security of person and property, the preservation of the public tranquillity, and all the other objects of a police establishment, will thus be better effected, than by the detection and punishment of the offender, after he has succeeded in committing the crime. This should constantly be kept in mind by every member of the police force, as a guide for his own conduct.

However, as is so often the case with statute and administrative regulations – and the 1998 Crime and Disorder Act may be no exception in this regard – the guidance was vague and in need of interpretation, yet it was by no means clear what specifically was meant by the prevention of crime, other than that it was to be regarded as preferable to detection and punishment. The force instructions made a clear distinction between crime prevention and detection, although such a perception would not necessarily hold across all quarters of the modern police service.

Historical analysis, and particularly the contribution of so-called 'revisionist' historians (see Reiner, 1992), has made it apparent that this early emphasis on the prevention of crime in the 1829 force instructions and subsequent policy developments probably had much less to do with an elaboration of operational practice than with the legitimation of an institution which was welcomed with less than open arms by a civil society quite rightly suspicious of an over-powerful central state. Seen in this light, the prevention of crime was about playing down the power of this potentially strong arm of the state – hence the emphasis, for example, on a 'gentlemanly' uniform as opposed to a militaristic one, and hence the limited arming of the new police. This was about the presentation of an acceptable face of policing to a potentially hostile public, and to this extent Reith's assertion that the notion of the prevention of crime was essentially a conduct principle may be correct. Reith believed (1956: 200) that the principle meant 'defined behaviour on the part of administrators and servants of the law ... who reduced to slight proportions ... the need for using the weight of the law'. There is a clear parallel between this principle of 'defined behaviour' and the principle of order maintenance which Reiner (1992) contrasts with law enforcement in demonstrating one core element of the politics of policing. This 'defined behaviour' effectively meant achieving a deterrent influence through the symbolisation of the rule of law, gaining the respect and compliance of ordinary people.

Essentially, then, the initial emphasis on the prevention of crime was a political rather than an operational matter, yet it required a translation into practice. It is unlikely that the earliest recruits to the police service would have been that well versed in the art of 'defined behaviour', or in the finer points of the distinction between order maintenance and law enforcement, or for that matter in the 'new science' of policing which the likes of Patrick Colquhoun (1969) had been writing about since the end of the eighteenth century. For these new recruits, the notion of the prevention of crime translated into the practice of foot patrol, or what Reiner (1992) unglamorously refers to as the 'scarecrow function'. Occupationally, this was less than attractive – in *The Wizard of Oz* the scarecrow gave up his job to follow Dorothy, and he did not even possess a brain! Those with brains and senses were no more likely to greet the task with greater enthusiasm: patrolling variously could be boring, lonely and dangerous, and uncomfortable when the streets were cold and wet. Potential offenders soon learnt to avoid the thin blue line, and it is of little surprise that it took only a short time for some officers to disregard the force instructions, to adopt the 'Ways and Means Act', and instead to turn to plainclothes detection. This was an important moment in police history: the political emphasis on the prevention of crime was subverted at the occupational level by those officers who saw detection as a more rewarding form of policing.

The nascent occupational preference for detection brought to light the important issue of effectiveness. As is now well recognised, it is extremely difficult to measure success in crime prevention, because the success criterion is a non-event, a crime that does not happen. In contemporary practice, the solution to this problem has been to focus effort upon crime reduction rather than crime prevention, with the reductive intent usually being focused upon high-crime areas, identified through police statistics and, sometimes, crime surveys. In the mid-nineteenth century, for various reasons, not least of which was the rudimentary nature of crime data (see Emsley, 1983), there was no similar emphasis upon crime reduction, and in its absence detection served as an indicator of success. Detection, therefore, became increasingly important to the police service when the 1856 'Obligatory Act' brought permanent policing to the whole of England and Wales. The reason for this is that the 1856 Act was accompanied by a 'sweetener' of an Exchequer grant, but only in return for demonstrably efficient forces, and detection and the clear-up rate became the currency of efficiency.

In other words, the nationalisation of permanent policing in the mid-nineteenth century had the unintended organisational consequence of institutionalising detection as the basis of the police service's professional credibility. This might have been deeply problematic had the same socio-political climate prevailed as it had in 1829, when the principle of crime prevention had been emphasised for political reasons. Perhaps fortunately for the police service, however, what had started life as a 'plague of blue locusts' in the public's eyes was, in the second half of the nineteenth century, becoming more publicly accepted as 'our boys in blue' (the women's police service had yet to be established), as the police entered their consensual golden age. This is not to say that there were not pockets of resistance (Cohen, 1981; Clarke, 1987), but rather, that the police had won the support of 'respectable society'.

So, by the second half of the nineteenth century, a combination of occupational and organisational pressures had conspired to thwart the political emphasis on the prevention of crime, something which with the benefit of hindsight could be seen as inevitable given the narrow interpretation of this principle as foot patrol. The cast was thus set for a police service which, as the twentieth century progressed, came to develop a stronger and stronger action orientation, particularly within the occupational culture. Before we move to look at these more recent developments, however, it is worth drawing attention to an alternative vision of the police role which emerged in the mid-nineteenth century, and which, had it been taken seriously, might have plotted a very different course for crime prevention and policing.

This alternative vision was proffered by the utilitarian reformer Edwin Chadwick, who had been a member of the Constabulary Force Commission whose report preceded the 1856 Act, and who maintained an interest in police reform throughout this period. Chadwick recognised what we now take for granted, namely that the police require the co-operation and participation of the public to prevent crime. In the 1839 Constabulary Force Commission report he co-wrote (Lefebre *et al.*, 1839: 55) the following:

> It is the honest portion of the community only who are in ignorance, who require to be put on their guard and convinced of the necessity of taking effective measures for the abatement of the evil. More effectual measures than have yet been

taken can only be founded in more close inquiries than have yet been made, and a better knowledge of the habits and practices of the classes to be guarded against than has yet been obtained.

Chadwick envisaged a role for the police service in helping this 'honest portion of the community', and it is apparent that his ideas attracted the interest of the then Home Secretary Palmerston, who according to a Home Office document quoted by Reith (1956: 260) was keen to commission further research:

> Viscount Palmerston is especially desirous that you should investigate and distinguish in your report as closely as the evidence will permit –
>
> 1 What offences admit of prevention by the action of a police alone.
> 2 What by a police in concert with the public.
> 3 What offences must be prevented, if at all, by the care taken by the public themselves.

The research was never completed, but had it been it might not have looked too different from the kind of research conducted in the 1970s into designing out crime (Clarke and Mayhew, 1980) or in the 1980s into specific categories of offending (e.g. Bennett and Wright, 1984).

The emergence of the crime prevention specialism

Although police officers have always had to balance the sometimes conflicting demands of order maintenance and law enforcement, and have, therefore, been minded of the preventive principle, and although the scarecrow function of foot patrol has continued to be an integral element of policing, and of particular public-relations value, any notion that the police had a more specific role to play in practical crime prevention remained buried until the 1950s. In that decade, the Home Office and the insurance industry launched the first high-profile national publicity campaigns, aiming to get across the message that the public had an important role in stemming the post-war tide of crime by protecting their own property. Some police forces recognised that the police service was a natural conduit for this publicity, and consequently one or two established their own Crime Prevention Departments (CPDs) and Crime Prevention Officers (CPOs) for this purpose (Greater London Council, 1986).

The establishment of CPDs was strongly encouraged by the Home Office's internal Cornish Committee on the Prevention and Detection of Crime, which had been set up in 1961 and finally reported in 1965 (Home Office, 1965). Faced with the twin pincers of rising crime and bulging prisons, the Home Office was desperate to make an impact upon the crime problem, and practical crime prevention was regarded as one possible way forward. It was not, however, the most important. The 1960s saw a flurry of activity against crime, including developments in probation and post-release supervision of offenders, reforms to the youth justice system, and, significantly, the introduction of unit beat policing. Set against these modernisations and developments, crime prevention in the form of practical guidance and advice had a rather archaic ring to it, and certainly did not capture the moment of Harold Wilson's white heat of technology. Nevertheless, police forces did establish their own CPDs in the 1960s, some placing them within the CID, others within Community Affairs sections.

While the establishment of CPDs provided a foothold for crime prevention in the police service, it also brought problems. As is not infrequently the case, the establishment of a specialism within an organisation can lead to an abrogation of responsibility elsewhere: crime prevention could easily be regarded as the sole responsibility of the CPDs, even though there was a good case for others, notably permanent beat officers, to take an interest. According to Harvey *et al.* (1989), moreover, the work done in CPDs hardly merited the label crime prevention: it was heavily demand-led, and as likely to be motivated by public relations as anything else.

The difficulty was that crime prevention was forced upon the police service at a time – or at least not much before it – when its character was just about to undergo a major transformation, as a result of more significant changes taking place across criminal justice and public policy in the 1970s and 1980s.

The rise of crime prevention within criminal justice policy

Where, in the 1960s, great stock had been set in the capacity of reformed and modernised criminal justice (and in the case of youth justice also social work) agencies to tackle the crime problem, by the mid-1970s the prognosis looked altogether more pessimistic. The 1976 Review of Criminal Justice Policy (Home Office, 1977: 9–10) made this point abundantly clear:

> In view of the limitations in the capacity of the agencies of the criminal justice system to reduce the incidence of crime, the scope for reducing crime through policies which go beyond the boundaries of the criminal justice system merit particular attention. In recognition of this, work is already in hand exploring how the Home Office could more readily involve other Government Departments, local authorities, and agencies outside government in the crime prevention field ... Work on the broader aspects of crime prevention should be pressed forward as speedily as possible.

The work alluded to in the above quote entailed, in particular, the work of Home Office researchers led by Ron Clarke, the former Head of the Home Office Research Unit. Inspired by a notion of crime as opportunity, stripped of its broader social context, and informed in turn by diverse interests including Oscar Newman's (1973) theory of defensible space, these researchers established a problem-oriented methodology (Gladstone, 1980) which was labelled the situational approach to crime prevention. Because the situational approach was generally used in such a way that required or suggested the deployment of 'target hardening' or 'opportunity reducing' measures, there appeared at first sight a natural affinity between it and the perceived role of CPDs. This affinity was, however, more apparent than real, because where the situational approach was problem-oriented, proactive and targeted at high crime areas, the work of the CPDs was, as already noted, generally demand-led and unfocused.

The important thing about the situational approach was that it required a sea change in the way crime problems were generally addressed. It acknowledged that routine, reactive, practice-led approaches to policing were not particularly effective at reducing crime, at least not at a level that could reasonably be afforded given the harsher economic climate of the 1980s. Instead, it required an innovative and flexible, tailored approach to different crime problems in different areas. Equally important, it recognised that the police service could not effectively control crime by itself, but required the active co-operation of the public, but also other agencies that had access to information about crime, and resources which could be deployed to tackle it. This included agencies with access to target-hardening and opportunity-reducing technologies, but given the social crime prevention rejoinder of the mid-1980s (situational crime prevention was a label originally given to the problem-oriented methodology, not specific crime prevention measures – see Weatheritt, 1986) it also included agencies whose focus was more traditionally social policy-oriented, and whose interest, either directly or indirectly, lay with offender motivations. Again, these were details that set situational crime prevention apart from anything that police CPDs had been doing to this point in time.

The 1980s witnessed a concerted effort by successive governments to bring crime prevention into the criminal justice mainstream. The landmark Home Office Circular 8/84 urged the police service, alongside local authorities and the probation service, to work collaboratively towards the goal of crime prevention, although there were to be no additional resources. The Home Office worked hard to encourage local activity, funding, for example, a range of demonstration projects, the Five Towns Initiative, and, from 1988, the Safer Cities Programme (Gilling, 1997). It also instituted a series of regional seminars in 1988, targeted at the police service and local authorities. In 1990 it issued practical guidance through the semi-independent body Crime Concern, together with a new Circular 44/90, which repeated the message of 8/84 but this time required a response from the police and local authorities to indicate what action they had taken.

However, despite all of the promotional activities of central government, the concern was that there was insufficient action 'on the ground'. The crime prevention message was being listened to, but not translated into action, other than in the case of neighbourhood watch, where the Thatcher–Hurd emphasis upon active citizenship eventually resulted in numbers of neighbourhood watch schemes being incorporated into Her Majesty's Inspectorate's (HMI) performance indicators. It was apparent that there were a number of blocks on progress, to which we now turn.

Confusion in the 1980s

Ironically, given its statutory responsibility, the police service was ill-equipped to take crime prevention forward in the 1980s. Weatheritt (1986) identifies two histories of police crime prevention: one where there has been strong rhetorical support, and the other where achievements have been poor. This situation pertains because CPOs have been trained in a way philosophically at odds with the crime prevention promoted in the 1980s. Their training was until comparatively recently unfocused and generalised (Harvey *et al.*, 1989), and lacking a research grounding or any sort of preparation for partnership working. In short, it was all the things that situational crime prevention strove not to be, reducing CPOs to little more than information brokers (Ericson, 1992).

Since the late 1980s training has improved as the curriculum at the national training centre has been brought up to date (Heal and Laycock, 1986), but such change has failed to overcome the basic problem that CPDs are marginalised within the police organisation. The crime prevention specialism does not lie at the heart of professional claims-making, or the preferences of the occupational culture; and CPOs do not attain senior ranks within the organisation. Consequently, given the high profile accorded by government to crime prevention, there was inevitably a degree of cognitive dissonance: such a status made no sense to the police service, barring a handful of converts who had 'seen the light'. Hence, Jones *et al.* (1994: 88) observed 'little evidence of concrete policy initiatives' in this area. The police service was used to ritualised statements of support for crime prevention, both from themselves and the Home Office. It took a while for them to recognise that the Home Office utterances in the 1980s were for real – the principle really was expected to be translated into practice.

Jones *et al.* (1994: 95) alternatively suggest that police inertia was attributable to 'the wider confusion of government policy'. There is undoubtedly some truth in this. The Home Office was less than explicit about how the police, local authorities and others were to take crime prevention forward. It fudged the issue of the possible conflict between social and situational approaches; it provided little in the way of resources beyond the high-profile initiatives which had the look of one-offs; and it refused to be drawn on the issue of local leadership, because of its antipathy to local government and because of a concern that it would result in unrealistic expectations of the police's preventive potential. The quasi-militaristic structure of the police service can make it slow at the best of times. Adding a dose of confusion risked making it positively slothful.

Another source of confusion may be found in the more general pressures the police service came under in the 1980s, inspired in part by government dissatisfaction that so much had been invested in the police with so little return (Loveday, 1996). The police variously faced financial constraint; privatisation in the form of civilianisation, voluntarisation and, in the early 1990s, threatened load-shedding; the unleashing of the Audit Commission; the application of the Financial Management Initiative and the pressure to reorganise along the lines of policing by objectives (Weatheritt, 1986); and internal pressures (Newman, 1983; Alderson, 1983) to adopt a community policing style as a response to a legitimacy crisis. There was also the small matter of the implementation of the 1984 Police and Criminal Evidence Act to contend with. Without seeking to be an apologist for the police service, it faced many other issues, a lot higher on its agenda. Besides, it was not only the police service that was slow to respond.

The Morgan Report and beyond

The Home Office's frustration at the lack of local progress led to the appointment of a committee of the standing conference on crime prevention to consider and monitor progress in the light of police and local authority responses to Circular 44/90. The findings were published in 1991 as the Morgan Report, and its tone was critical, identifying the fundamental problem that 'crime prevention is a peripheral concern for all of the agencies and a truly core activity for none of them' (Home Office, 1991: 15). It was also critical of the short-termist and unco-ordinated nature of government policy; and amidst a number of practical recommendations proposed that the government should fund local crime prevention, giving local authorities a lead statutory responsibility. It also suggested that crime prevention was a misnomer for activities which were beginning to attract the more generic term 'community safety'.

The report may have been expected to galvanise local action, had it not been ignored by a government in no mood to hand over additional resources to local authorities. Indeed, having been vigorously promoted in the 1980s, in some ways it entered the doldrums at the beginning of the 1990s, with little significantly new in the way of policy development, excepting the announcement of a second phase of Safer Cities, although one could argue this had more to do with urban policy than crime prevention. The logic of the Morgan Report was difficult to resist, especially as the model of community safety it proposed was similar to that pursued elsewhere in western Europe and further afield, but central governmental ideological antipathy to local government was a major block in the UK.

In addition, government criminal justice policy took a decisive shift to a harsher law and order stance, especially following the arrival of Michael Howard. Penal policy progressed in accordance with the dubious assertion that 'prison works' while, significantly for our purposes, a police White Paper baldly stated that 'the main job of the police is to catch criminals' (Home Office, 1993: para 2.3). This was followed by an influential Audit Commission report (1993) which promoted a model of crime management and intelligence-led policing based upon an assumption that a disproportionate amount of crime was committed by a hard core of offenders who could be closely tracked and monitored. If the police had been dazed and confused about crime prevention in the 1980s, this must have completely befuddled them, at least at first sight. The message of the 1980s, that the police could not be expected to control crime by themselves and should therefore engage in collaborative action, was now contradicted by this message, that they could control crime by themselves if they managed it more effectively, and that this meant prioritising detection (Morgan and Newburn, 1997; Crawford, 1998).

Although this posed a major dilemma for the police, it is now in the process of being resolved on two main fronts. At the policy level, the doldrums have now been cleared, thanks to the new Labour government's commitment to implement the Morgan recommendations in the 1998 Crime and Disorder Act, which gives the police and local authorities a joint statutory responsibility to prevent and reduce crime and disorder. We shall return to this Act below.

The second front on which the dilemma is being resolved is the local level, comprising the actions of the police and their partners. Taking the partners first, it is evident that in spite of, or quite possibly because of, the cool governmental response to Morgan, local authorities have enthusiastically embraced community safety. Hence, in 1996, a survey showed that nine out of ten authorities recognised it as a legitimate policy area (Local Government Management Board, 1996), while local authority associations developed a very clear supportive manifesto in the run-up to the 1997 General Election.

Within the police service, there has also been a groundswell towards crime prevention, helped initially by ACPO's decision to establish a Crime Prevention Sub-Committee in 1989, and the police service's general commitment to become more responsive and consumerist, made apparent in the Operational Policing Review (Joint Consultative Committee, 1990) and motivated by the general drift towards new public management and more specific concerns about the declining level of public support for the police (Waters, 1996). On this more solid base, crime prevention could establish firmer foundations. An example of this can be seen in Johnston *et al.*'s (1993) action research project in which the crime prevention specialism was moved organisationally centre stage, into the crime management mainstream. Although this project may have succeeded mainly because of the heavy resource investment and the high profile it attracted, it offers a model for bringing crime prevention in from the cold, and integrating it with detection in the kind of way envisaged by the Audit Commission.

The key to this integration lies in the concept of crime reduction, and the use of intelligence information and crime-pattern analysis to support this. In an enforcement-oriented model of policing, effectiveness inevitably tends to be conceived of in terms of detection and clear-up rates (Fielding, 1996). However, in addition to the changes described above, which have focused public minds more upon what the public wants, a very significant influence in the 1990s has followed in the wake of the 1994 Police and Magistrates' Courts Act, and in particular in central governmental objective-setting, accompanied by annual local policing plans. While the shift to a performance culture is not all good, and carries with it certain dangers, especially when objectives may be set centrally rather than locally, one benefit may have been to force the police service to take crime reduction more seriously. Thus, the first national police objectives included a reduction of violent crime, although it also included an increase in the number of detected burglaries (Loveday, 1996). Loveday warns of the danger of reifying the crime rate as an indicator of effectiveness, and is concerned that clear-up rates may be prioritised, but it may well be that the danger has been over-stated, in view of subsequent and contemporaneous developments.

The first of these developments may be found in the publication of *Towards 2000: A Crime Prevention Strategy for the New Millennium* (Association of Chief Police Officers, 1996). In this strategy document, ACPO's Crime Prevention Sub-Committee clarifies its intention of enhancing the status of crime pre-vention within the police service. This includes working towards seven key objectives, which incorporate a desire to work in partnership with other agencies, and, importantly, 'to seek to change the culture of the police serv-ice, so that crime prevention and community safety enjoys a higher status and is accepted as a responsibility of all officers'. Although it does not explic-itly state how this is to be achieved, one might surmise that one element could entail a shift from clear-up rates to crime reduction.

A second development may be found in the publication of Her Majesty's Inspectorate of Constabulary's (HMIC) thematic inspection report *Beating Crime*, published in 1998 as a companion document to the 1998 Crime and Disorder Act. *Beating Crime* reviews police performance in what it terms 'sus-tainable crime reduction' and shows that while many forces have yet to come up to par, there are several examples of good practice based upon problem-solving partnerships. The report argues that crime reduction should become a core policing function, and that 'the Home Secretary's Key Objectives for Policing need to keep shifting their emphasis towards reduction of crime and disorder' (HMIC, 1998: 11). This position may not yet have been reached, but it is a dynamic that is very much in evidence in the present, and is strongly supported by the Crime and Disorder Act.

Thirdly, as Bennett (1996) has argued on the basis of an extensive national survey, the fact remains that the police service, even when generally not working in partnership with other agencies, has been engaged in a consider-able amount of crime prevention work, even if it has not automatically been conceived of in such terms. In particular, he identifies five forms of such pre-ventive work, including general situational initiatives (something I am sure Ron Clarke would find a contradiction in terms), organisationally driven problem-oriented policing, generally directed routine patrols, targeted prob-lem-oriented policing, and targeted patrols. Of these, the last two are perhaps the most contemporary and demonstrate the greatest promise, and significantly they generally do so because of their focus on crime reduction. Bennett is correct to draw attention to the ever present threat of displace-ment, but Pease (1996) soundly argues that the threat should be no excuse for inaction, since the diffusion of benefits may be just as likely.

The Crime and Disorder Act 1998

As previously noted, the Crime and Disorder Act marks the enactment of the Morgan Report's key recommendation, to give local authorities a statutory duty to form crime reduction partnerships, though it does not offer additional resources to this end. The Act expects local partnerships to audit crime and disorder problems in their areas, to consult with the community, and to present three-year plans, together with clear objectives and performance targets. For the first sets of plans, all of this was to have been completed between the autumn of 1998 and 1 April 1999, always an inauspicious date for important documents.

The logical implication of the 1998 Crime and Disorder Act is that it will succeed where other policy initiatives have failed in pushing crime prevention firmly up the policing agenda, particularly because, as argued above, policing has already started to move in this direction. In this sense, the Act provides legislative backing to established good practice, at least in some areas. However, although it is always difficult to predict the future, it is unlikely that it will all be plain sailing. A number of commentators, including for example Crawford (1998), have noted the contradictions and tensions inherent in seeking to advance crime prevention within the police service. It is most unlikely that these will disappear. Rather, they are likely to concretise around a number of key issues which will follow in the wake of the Act. Here we focus upon two particular issues, namely, partnership and disorder.

Partnership

A key if not dominant theme of the Act is partnership, both at operational and strategic levels. A considerable amount has been written in the past about partnerships (see Gilling, 1997; Crawford, 1998; Hughes, 1998) and it is not intended to rehearse those arguments here, although many are relevant. Rather, the discussion will be limited to a few key points related to the Act.

First, it has often been alleged that the police service only works in partnership on its own terms, because of its power which partly accrues from its custodianship of information about crime, and its established expertise in crime control. It has been suggested, moreover, that the police service has previously made clear that it would not be prepared to work with others as lead agencies, and this may well be why the government opted for an open and equal partnership structure rather than nominating local authorities in the lead role, as Morgan had proposed. Interestingly, *Towards 2000* declares, somewhat pointedly it may be argued, that '[t]he police service continues to occupy the most prominent place within the partnership framework' (Association of Chief Police Officers, 1996).

It remains uncertain whether this dominant position will manifest itself in the new partnerships, or if it does, with what consequences. In the past, for example, it has been suggested that the police service has a natural inclination towards detection and opportunity reduction rather than social crime prevention, but policy documents imply this is now less likely to be the case. There are grounds for arguing, however, that even if the police do not show a bias in one way or another, they may nevertheless remain the dominant interest. This is because the crime reduction plans are expected to fit with the annual policing plan which the police service currently works towards. Cramphorn (1998) argues that the notion of community safety is now so all-encompassing that the community safety strategy (with its crime reduction plans) should be superordinate to all other plans and strategies, but while this makes good sense it is not guaranteed. The question arises as to what might happen in a situation where the annual policing plan is badly out of step with what partners proposed for the crime reduction plan. The position of the Home Secretary as final arbiter (and incidentally as the framer of national police objectives to which annual policing plans must conform) might suggest that the police position is the stronger one.

On a similar note, it is recognised that other likely partners, such as probation services, health authorities and so forth, also have their own plans which will need to accommodate or be accommodated by the community safety strategy. Can community safety really accommodate and contain all of this in a coherent way? Certainly community safety is so broadly conceived that it might, but it has been recognised for a long while that criminal justice is more of a fragmented, contradictory process than a co-ordinated system. There is no reason to assume that the absorption of even more agencies under the community safety umbrella will result in greater co-ordination, but some logic in suggesting it might result in less.

Now, one important element of the community safety partnership is the community itself, and Cramphorn's (1998) proposed consumerist framework implies that the possible discordance suggested above may be avoided because in the final analysis it will be the community that decides upon the strategy and the plans, because of the importance attributed to consultation. The idea that this kind of consumer accountability will be paramount is, however, deeply questionable. First, the final arbiter is the Home Secretary, and it is (currently) he rather than the community that has the power of veto. Second, experience of community consultation through Police Community Liaison Panels, which may continue to have a significant role in the consultation preceding the crime reduction plans, does not inspire confidence in the ability of the community to challenge police definitions of problem and solution. Quite understandably, the Home Office, while providing volumes of guidance with the Act, has opted for a post-modern approach to governance, where localities have been left to decide what their crime and disorder problems are (subject to certain modernist central concerns), what disorder actually means and exactly what bureaucratic model should be adopted for each local partnership, based on district council areas. In the case of bureaucratic models, this allows a flexibility which may prevent bureaucratic goal displacement and ossification, and it is laudable that partnerships are not seen as an end in themselves, but rather as a means of adding value to the activities they address. However, localities will still have to contend with the basic facts of partnership working (Hough and Tilley, 1998: v):

> Whilst partnership has been advocated for many years and receives almost universal support, it has often proved difficult to establish robust, routine, trusting and

open-minded multi-agency groups. They require hard work and realism about the obstacles and difficulties that are likely to be encountered.

Disorder

True to the fairy story, having been for so long the Cinderella, crime prevention is now the belle of the ball, attracting the interest and commitment of those who see within it a lasting opportunity to bring about a safer society. One reason for this remains crime prevention's definitional elasticity. In the past I have discussed the elasticity of the idea of prevention, but the same point applies to crime, which is ultimately a social construct. It has to be recognised that the Act, in focusing upon disorder, opens up another avenue for debate over definitions. It would appear that in the drafting of the legislation ACPO suggested a definition of disorder, perhaps in recognition of the possible difficulties that may lie ahead. The suggestion was rejected.

Rather like the inclusion of fear of crime in the purview of community safety, the inclusion of disorder threatens to expand police responsibilities and its sphere of influence in unwelcome directions (not least of all to the police service itself). In addition to the various by-laws and powers already available to local authorities to tackle nuisance neighbours, alcohol consumption in public places and so forth, the Crime and Disorder Act introduces a wealth of other instruments – including child safety orders, child curfew schemes, and the already notorious anti-social behaviour order (originally conceived as a community safety order, but presumably changed because of a concern it would give community safety a bad name) – to tackle disorder.

On ethical grounds one might object to the potential further criminalisation of the discourse of social policy (see Gilling and Barton, 1997) which this Act may engender, and on practical grounds the police may find themselves under more pressure to 'do something' about disorder problems which they would rather not be tackling. Since one motivation for participation in the partnership approach is the need to spread responsibility in view of limited police resources, the thought of the police having to police disorder more rigorously than before would seem particularly self-defeating and disingenuous. On the other hand, a less kindly view might suggest that the police service has brought this upon itself through the over-enthusiastic adoption of zero tolerance policing, which after all only 'worked' in New York because of a massive investment in new policing resources. That situation does not currently pertain in the UK.

It is apparent that the police service has been drawn into crime prevention only through a careful examination of the benefits of working in partnership, and the benefits of combining prevention and detection to achieve the crime reduction which is now a requisite part of national objectives. While the statutory character of crime reduction partnerships means that they are forced to collaborate, if it is perceived to be too great a disadvantage the police may not be particularly willing or active participants, and the local flexibility allowed in the construction of local partnership infrastructures potentially gives 'partners' a way out. Alternatively, and this may be more likely, the police service may find it easier to manage its new-found responsibilities through a division of labour which may ultimately result in two-tier policing, where the police service seeks to manage serious crime, as now through a combination of prevention and detection, while a combination of other agencies, including local authority patrols and other bodies, private security organisations and the local community itself, take on the major responsibility for minor crimes and disorder.

Conclusion

In 1829 crime prevention was institutionalised within the police service as an important principle underpinning its legitimacy, and then, barring a degree of lip service, promptly ignored for the next century and a bit. Home Office attempts to resurrect the principle as a form of practical action failed to make it any more than a marginal concern until it could no longer be ignored as evidence that patrolling and detection were largely ineffective reached a wide audience, as did evidence that a problem-oriented approach, typified by the Home Office's original formulation of situational crime prevention, was potentially effective. The police struggled against a burden of policy ambiguity and rapid organisational and environmental change in coming to terms with crime prevention, and it was not until the early 1990s that events took a decisive turn for the better, as the police, pressured from below by a less accepting public, and from above by central government's managerialist agenda, at least embraced crime prevention, or community safety as it is now more frequently called – ACPO's subcommittee could not quite bring itself to change its name.

Now, as in 1829, the 1998 Crime and Disorder Act has once more emphasised crime prevention, but this time less as a principle than as a practical project. The problem is, however, that just as a particular socio-political context framed the 1829, and caused some difficulty for the police service in interpreting the message, so the 1998 Act has its own socio-political context, and raises its own issues. In particular, the Crime and Disorder Act cannot be disentangled from broader changes taking place within criminal justice which have been referred to by some as the 'new penology' (Feeley and Simon, 1994), and by others as 'responsibilisation' (Garland, 1996). Here is not the place to explore their full implications, but the essence they seek to capture is of a changing state role in crime control, shifting from an aspiration to eliminate crime to a more modest desire to manage it in the most efficient, and economical way, something which fits the idea of two-tier policing outlined above. The difficulty is that agencies such as the police service, while themselves being a contributor to these structural movements, must also reflexively respond to them, and it is here that the difficulties of interpreting the crime prevention role have to be negotiated. The Crime and Disorder Act appears to bring crime prevention to the fore, but there remains doubt about what it means now that it is entwined with disorder, and now that partnerships have been cast with local authorities and others. It is time for Edwin Chadwick to carry out that research.

References

Alderson, J. (1983) 'Community Policing' in Bennett (1983).

Association of Chief Police Officers (1996) *Towards 2000: A Crime Prevention Strategy for the New Millennium.* Lancaster: ACPO.

Audit Commission (1993) *Helping with Enquiries.* Police Paper No.12. London: HMSO.

Bennett, T. (ed.) (1983) *The Future of Policing.* Cambridge: Institute of Criminology.

Bennett, T. (1996) 'Problem Solving Policing and Crime Prevention' in Bennett, T. (ed.) *Preventing Crime and Disorder.* Cambridge: Institute of Criminology.

Bennett, T. and Wright, R. (1984) *Burglars on Burglary.* Aldershot: Gower.

Clarke, M. (1987) 'Citizenship, Community and the Management of Crime', *British Journal of Criminology,* 27, 136–47.

Clarke, R. and Mayhew, P. (eds) (1980) *Designing Out Crime.* London: HMSO.

Cohen, P. (1981) 'Policing the Working Class City' in Fitzgerald *et al.* (1981).

Colquhoun, P. (1969) *A Treatise on the Police of the Metropolis.* Montclair: Patterson Smith.

Cramphorn, C. (1998) 'Positioning Community Safety Strategies: a Planning and Process Model', *Police Research and Management,* 2 (3), 3–12.

Crawford, A. (1998) *Crime Prevention and Community Safety.* Harlow: Addison Wesley Longman.

Dolling, D. and Feltes, T. (eds) (1992) *Comparative Aspects of Community-Oriented Police Work.* Holzkirchen: Felix-Verlag.

Emsley, C. (1983) *Policing and its Context 1750–1870.* London: Macmillan.

Ericson (1992) 'Community Policing as Communications Policing' in Dolling and Feltes (1992).

Feeley, M. and Simon, J. (1994) 'Actuarial Justice: the Emerging New Criminal Law' in Nelken (1994).

Fielding, N. (1996) 'Enforcement, Service and Community Models of Policing' in Saulisbury *et al.* (1996).

Fitzgerald, M., McLennan, G. and Pawson, J. (eds) (1981) *Crime and Society.* London: RKP.

Garland, D. (1996) 'The Limits of the Sovereign State: Strategies of Crime Control in Contemporary Society', *British Journal of Criminology,* 36 (4), 445–71.

Gilling, D. (1997) *Crime Prevention: Theory, Policy and Politics.* London: UCL Press.

Gilling, D. and Barton, A. (1997) 'Crime Prevention: A New Home for Social Policy?', *Critical Social Policy,* 17 (1), 63–83.

Gladstone, F. (1980) *Co-ordinating Crime Prevention Efforts.* London: HMSO.

Greater London Council (1986) *Policing London: Collected Reports of the GLC Police Committee.* London: Greater London Council.

Harvey, L., Grimshaw, P. and Pease, K. (1989) 'Crime Prevention Delivery: the Work of CPOs' in Morgan and Smith (1989).

Heal, K. and Laycock G. (eds) (1986) *Situational Crime Prevention: From Theory into Practice,* London: HMSO.

Her Majesty's Inspectorate of Constabulary (1998) *Beating Crime.* London: Home Office.

Home Office (1965) *Report of the Cornish Committee on the Prevention and Detection of Crime.* (Cornish Report). London: Home Office.

Home Office (1977) *Review of Criminal Justice Policy 1976.* London: HMSO.

Home Office (1991) *Safer Communities: the Local Delivery of Crime Prevention Through the Partnership Approach.* (Morgan Report). London: HMSO.

Home Office (1993) *Police Reform: a Police Service for the Twenty-First Century.* Cmnd 2281. London: HMSO.

Hough, M. and Tilley, N. (1998) *Getting the Grease to the Squeak.* London: Home Office Police Research Group.

Hughes, G. (1998) *Understanding Crime Prevention.* Milton Keynes: Open University Press.

Johnston, V., Shappland, J. and Wiles, P. (1993) *Developing Police Crime Prevention Management and Organisational Change.* Paper No. 41. London: Home Office Crime Prevention Unit.

Joint Consultative Committee (1990) *Operational Policing Review.* Surbiton: Joint Consultative Committee.

Jones, T., Newburn, T. and Smith, D. (1994) *Democracy and Policing.* London: Policy Studies Institute.

Lefebre, C., Rowan, C. and Chadwick, E. (1839) *First Report of the Constabulary Force Commissioners.* London: Charles Knight.

Leishman, F., Loveday, B. and Savage, S. (eds) (1996) *Core Issues in Policing.* 1st edn. Harlow: Longman.

Local Government Management Board (1996) *Survey of Community Safety Activities in Local Government in England and Wales.* Luton: LGMB.

Loveday, B. (1996) 'Crime at the Core?' in Leishman *et al.* (1996).

Morgan, R. and Newburn, T. (1997) *The Future of Policing.* Oxford: Clarendon Press.

Morgan, R. and Smith, D. (eds) (1989) *Coming to Terms with Policing.* London: Routledge.

Nelken, D. (ed.) (1994) *The Futures of Criminology.* London: Sage.

Newman, K. (1983) *Report of the Commissioner for the Metropolitan Police 1982.* London: HMSO.

Newman, O. (1973) *Defensible Space.* London: Architectural Press.

Pease, K. (1996) 'Opportunities for Crime Prevention: the Need for Incentives' in Salisbury *et al.* (1996).

Reiner, R. (1992) *The Politics of the Police.* 2nd edn. Hemel Hempstead: Harvester Wheatsheaf.

Reith, C. (1956) *A New Study of Policy History.* Edinburgh: Oliver and Boyd.

Saulisbury, W., Mott, J. and Newburn, T. (1996) *Themes in Contemporary Policing.* London: Policy Studies Institute.

Waters, I. (1996) 'Quality of Service: Politics or Paradigm Shift?' in Leishman *et al.* (1996).

Weatheritt, M. (1986) *Innovations in Policing.* Beckenham: Croom Helm.

Chapter 9

Mood swings: debates and developments in drugs policing

FRANK LEISHMAN AND TOM WOOD

Since 1980, my position has veered between optimism and pessimism. Enforcement alone has not solved and will not solve the drugs problem. The best the police can do is to disrupt the drugs trade. (Grieve, 1998: 9)

Introduction

That drugs constitute a core issue in policing is a proposition with which few would disagree. Globally, trafficking in illicit drugs is said to rank alongside the oil and gas industries in terms of its share of world economic activity, while the British government estimates that serious drug misuse costs the country £4 billion annually (UKADCU, 1998). A fleet of official statistics testifies to widespread usage of drugs among young people, with evidence of a drop in the average age of first use (Home Office, 1997). Indeed, during the 1990s, the thesis of 'normalisation' of drug-taking, and in particular patterns of poly-drug use, gained wide acceptance (Parker *et al.*, 1995). Though 'normalisation' is not an uncontested concept (Shiner and Newburn, 1999), the notion that there is far from a consensus about the extent to which the law and police should intervene in drug use seems to gain credence with successive opinion polls. A recent MORI survey, for instance, suggested that as many as 80 per cent of the public want some relaxation of the laws against cannabis (*The Economist*, 2000). At the same time, however, research also indicates growing levels of public concern about drug-related crime, with higher levels of anxiety in the North than the South (Charles, 1998). All the while, a hurricane of headlines in broadsheet and tabloid newspapers buffets about a veritable raft of 'respectable fears' about the drugs issue. It is not surprising, then, as Waters (Chapter 16) points out, that drug-related crime has reached the top three in the over-arching Ministerial Priorities for the police.

Developments in drugs policy and law enforcement over the last 40 years have taken place in the context of a debate which has often seemed like a 'dialogue of the deaf' in which 'for prohibitionists and reformers alike, the way the drugs scene is currently policed is seen as being often counterproductive, inconsistent and largely unworkable' (Davies, 1997). This chapter begins by outlining three broad perspectives which continue to shape and influence debates about how drugs should be policed. It then maps out key developments, focusing particularly on the last two decades, and attempts to illuminate emergent divergences in drugs policing in post-devolution Scotland, where the mood may be swinging in a slightly different direction from the rest of the UK.

Key perspectives on drugs policy options

There are doubtless many inside and outside of the police service who, from their own observations and experience, will echo the sentiment expressed by DAC John Grieve in the opening quotation. Coomber makes the point that 'where "debate" has taken place, it has often been disappointingly shallow, tending to concentrate on dichotomous argumentation. Thus simple prohibition is counter-posed with simple legalisation, and vice-versa' (1998: xv). The common-sense ideology which underpins crime news reporting encourages precisely this sort of simplification and polarisation (Chibnall, 1977; Reiner, 1992). As the police have come to take an increasingly proactive approach in 'news management' (Dorn and Murji, 1993; Schlesinger and Tumber, 1994) in respect of drugs enforcement, this has brought them both benefits and costs, as Karim Murji has suggested:

> For example, following their role in the spectacular representation of drugs as a problem and continuing evidence that usage has not declined, the police are faced with two possibilities: either to 'give up' and join the drug legalisation lobby, or to campaign for even more powers and resources, etc. Both options position them in a posture of defeat: the 'problem' is either insoluble, or so overwhelming that only further special powers, the limits of which can never be specified, will do
> (1998: 131)

Nevertheless, many of the leading and more reflective contributors to the drugs debate have been serving and retired senior officers, many of whom have had extensive operational experience in the drugs policing sphere. In this section we map out three broad orientations – which need not be mutually exclusive – which will continue to have an influence on drugs policing in the twenty-first century.

Drug warriors

Our 'drug warriors' adopt an uncompromisingly prohibitionist stance: drugs are a dangerous menace which the state must control through tough enforcement. This approach to social problem solving tends to rely upon the passing of restrictive laws, the argument being that legislation backed by tough and escalating penal sanctions prevents and deters – a classic 'drugs war' scenario. Regimes of total prohibition, however, seem doomed to failure, not least because the law is being targeted in the main at willing participants in drug-taking activity: after all, there are few, if any, direct complaints about *individual* drug transactions. The 'drugs war' approach holds many implications for policing in terms of objective-setting, use of resources, officer discretion, and the scope for questionable and corrupt enforcement practices (Boyd and Lowman, 1991). In the context of the 'drugs war', Mike Collison sounded a cautionary note about the development of policing skills which:

may, on occasion, test the boundary between acceptable and unacceptable police practice (buy-bust operations, covert surveillance, the manipulation of informants and so on) and certainly test the officer's presentational ability in providing satisfactory accounts (from the point of view of law and senior officers) of activity: an ability honed to 'make sure the wheel does not come off". (1994: 34)

In addition to and, in some instances, because of the ethical dilemmas presented, police officers may themselves become drugs war casualties on account of the high levels of stress and danger associated with such methods.

A 'drug warrior' perspective on drugs control is typically associated with harsh penal measures which can often result in inequitable treatment of drugs offenders relative to those processed and convicted of other crimes and may – as has happened spectacularly in the United States – contribute significantly to increased overall rates of imprisonment with little or no reduction in drug-related violence and criminality on the outside (Bullington, 1998; Concar and Spinney, 1994).

It can be argued that during the 1980s and through into the 1990s, the drugs phenomenon in the UK has been unhelpfully stereotyped as a war, a war fought between the army of law enforcement against evil drugs barons and their cohorts. One cannot claim that the police have been inactive combatants: far from it. Home Office figures indicate a four-fold increase in dealing offences over the last decade, from 3,900 in 1987 to 14,100 in 1997 (Home Office, 1999: 23). Precisely because the drugs phenomenon has been conceived of as a 'war', many of those involved – in statutory and voluntary agencies alike – have found themselves sucked at some time into a blinkered mind-set similar to that of First World War generals. Everyone, it seems, had to be seen to be doing *something*, the problem being that that often meant doing different things. Such pulling and heaving in different directions defuses energy and has often resulted in inertia. Drug warriors' faith in eliminating markets through a combination of tougher laws and aggressive supply-side enforcement is both naive and misplaced. The dynamics of the world drugs trade act against the likely effectiveness of any enforcement-driven 'drug warrior' strategy. With opiates at their cheapest, purest and most plentiful, with a greater number of international cartels apparently protected by national governments, and with open EU borders facilitating greater transnational mobility of goods and passengers, trade in illicit drugs seems virtually unstoppable. As Grieve (1994) has argued, the best that the police can hope to do is to 'sit on the lid'. It may be possible to disrupt supply, but for a longer-term solution, tackling demand seems the more fruitful possibility.

Law softeners

In the context of drugs debates, there are those who argue, often from quite diverse political and moral points of view, that more rational and consistent policing of drugs can only result from some 'softening' of the current drugs laws. Broadly speaking, there are 'legalisers' and 'decriminalisers', the former envisioning something altogether more radical than the latter.

Supporters of legalisation span a spectrum of positions, from those who extol the virtues of free-market economics for all commodities, to others who regard criminalisation as an invasion of civil liberties, through to those who are simply frustrated with the costly and counter-productive consequences of prohibition. Legalisers have suggested a number of possible scenarios, including the possibility of 'drug off-licences', with police control being exerted through systems of licensing and regulation as with alcohol (see, for example, Blanchard, 1994). Proponents of legalisation argue that the creation of a legal market would reduce the health risks posed by adulterated street supplies and, by removing the profit motive, would also have the positive effect of removing 'criminal diversifiers' from the scene. Benefits would accrue to the Treasury from increased taxation, a proportion of which could be hypothecated for drugs research and rehabilitation programmes.

On the other hand, critics voice concern that legalisation might lead to increased consumption and addiction as a result of inevitably lower prices and freer availability of current Class A and, very probably, a new generation of synthetic drugs. State drug-related health and welfare expenditure would rise, as might drug-related crimes of violence and traffic accidents. Moreover, so long as the prospect of illegal profits remained from avoiding duty on drugs, criminal entrepreneurs would not be deflected from exploiting new market opportunities. However, as Mott and Bean (1998) and Pearson (1992) have observed, out-and-out legalisation of drugs is simply not going to happen without major revision or repeal of existing international treaty obligations: 'one can therefore waste a great deal of brainpower and breath in arguments about legalisation' (Pearson, 1992: 16).

Decriminalisation, however, is a form of 'law softening' (usually linked to cannabis, but more recently to some 'dance drugs') which need not bring nation states into conflict with international conventions on drugs. *De facto* partial decriminalisation of cannabis possession is often referred to as 'Hollandisation', after the situation in The Netherlands, where cannabis is still technically illegal, though the 'principle of expediency' in the Dutch Criminal Code empowers the public prosecutor to refrain from prosecuting possession of small amounts (up to 5 grammes) in the public interest (Trimbos Institute, 1997). The main aim of this approach is to bring about 'market separation' between cannabis supply and that of other more harmful drugs (Dorn, 1992).

In the case of cannabis, the argument goes that a criminal market suppressed only results in a vicious cycle. Prices are kept high by illegal untaxed profits. Distribution is facilitated by networks of low-level workers, whose arrests only provide work for the criminal justice system, while the resultant vacancies offer employment opportunities for a steady supply of poorly educated (often black) inner city youth (see Ruggiero and South, 1995).

According to Home Office statistics, cautioning for cannabis possession in Britain has increased from 31 per cent to 58 per cent between 1987 and 1997 (Home Office, 1999), a trend which could be taken as indicative of a shift in the direction of *de facto* decriminalisation. However, the statistics also reveal an over-concentration on cannabis which accounts for the bulk of the 90 per cent of offenders processed for possession of drugs. Against this backcloth, many would argue that there is a compelling case for decriminalising possession of cannabis. There is, for example, research evidence to suggest that, whereas alcohol is closely associated with violence, cannabis use does not 'significantly increase, instigate, precipitate or enhance aggressive behaviour' (Schlaadt and Shannon, 1994). Moreover, some within the medical profession have argued that although cannabis may offer positive benefits to patients suffering from a range of degenerative conditions, at the moment they or their family and friends currently risk prosecution if caught in possession or being concerned in its supply. At the same time, there do remain uncertainties over the effects of long-term cannabis use, including not least the carcinogenic risks attached to smoking it. Opponents of *de jure* decriminalisation would argue also that this would merely increase overall numbers of drug abusers, hardly a prescription for a healthier society.

Harm reducers

More recent thinking on drugs-policy options in Britain and elsewhere has been significantly influenced by an overarching concern to adopt harm reduction or harm minimisation goals, a perspective manifested in the growth of needle exchange and arrest referral schemes, for example (O'Hare *et al.*, 1992). Some harm reducers might agree with drug warriors that abstinence from drugs is best, but would urge that if a person is going to use them they should do so safely. In this respect they would argue for credible and consistent messages in drugs education and information programmes. Though controversial, Hartnoll (1998: 245) notes that, against a general background of some convergence in drugs policy, certainly in the EU:

> Various harm reduction measures have expanded markedly in almost all countries. the major driving force behind these changes has been concern about HIV and AIDS.

One of the longer established harm-reduction measures relates to methadone substitution, which remains a controversial area of policy. Some point to its role in drugs-related deaths and rightly draw attention to the fact that there exists a lucrative black market for methadone. However, a methadone programme, properly supervised, can be seen to have potential advantages in bringing order to chaotic lifestyles, some gradual reductions in both dependency and drug-related criminality (especially acquisitive crime) and a lessening of the health risks associated with injection. Though the current mood may be optimistic, it should be pointed out that the research evidence on methadone is still far from clear-cut (South, 1997).

Harm reducers want to see closer alignment of criminal justice and policing policies with those of other agencies involved in drugs treatment and education. Pearson, for example, argues for more focused low-level enforcement strategies directed at keeping the 'not-yet-user' out of the local market, while at the same time seeking to contain a contracted drugs market in the locality to avoid the harm associated with displacement into adjacent neighbourhoods (see also Murji, 1993). Instead of excessive and counter-productive use of imprisonment, harm reducers advocate new and more effective community-based diversion, education and intervention schemes as a means of reducing drug-related harm to communities as well as to individuals.

So far as the police and wider criminal justice system is concerned, Pearson (1992) offers a useful framework of four principles which, he argues, policy makers should aspire to follow:

- contain the numbers of new users;
- encourage existing users to 'retire';
- minimise law enforcement's counter-productive effects;
- reduce harm to the wider community.

As Nigel South suggests, from these flow the proposition that rather than ponder 'how can we eradicate drugs?' *à la* 'drugs warrior', police, wearing a harm-reducer's helmet, ought to be asking 'how can we shape drug markets in the least undesirable direction?' (1997: 951).

Drug-control developments 1960–2000

Whereas the American approach to drug control has typically tended more towards penal 'solutions', the 'British system' has always included a prominent therapeutic paradigm. As far back as the 1920s, drug-control policy in Britain has demarcated – *in theory at any rate* – between 'victims' (dependent users and addicts) in need of help, and 'villains' (those involved in illicit supply) deserving of punishment (Collison, 1993: 383). Up until the late 1950s, it appears that Britain had no great illegal drug problem, a perception confirmed by the Brain Committee in 1961, which concluded that illegal supplies of drugs were, at the time of its deliberations, very limited (South 1997: 927–8). However, as the 'swinging sixties' got under way and concern grew about changing patterns of drug availability and drug-taking, the Brain Committee reconvened and its second report led to the Dangerous Drugs Act of 1967 which, among other things, legislated for compulsory notification of addicts and the restriction of opiate and cocaine prescribing to designated clinics. To an extent catalysed by a high-profile student-overdose case at Oxford University (Rose, 1998), provincial police forces began to establish specialist drug squads which, suggests Malcolm Young, quickly 'followed established traditions of police work by homing in on easily identifiable members of their traditional enemy in the "dangerous classes"' (1994: 58). The passage of the Misuse of Drugs Act (MDA) in 1971 – still the primary legislation in Britain – marked a consolidation of previous drugs legislation. In addition to classifying drugs and distinguishing between offences of possession and supply, thus underlining the 'victim/villain' dichotomy, the MDA established the influential Advisory Council on the Misuse of Drugs (ACMD) to advise ministers on how to tackle problems associated with drug misuse. During the 1970s, however, Britain began to follow the United States in its approach to both drugs victims and villains. Firstly, it adopted the American treatment system of methadone substitution for opiate addicts. Secondly, it became markedly influenced by US ideology on crime control.

The late 1970s and early 1980s saw the emergence of drugs as a highly political issue on both sides of the Atlantic, a development tellingly attested to by the 'war against drugs' rhetoric of the administrations of President Ronald Reagan and Prime Minister Margaret Thatcher. Of particular concern in Britain around this period was a glut on the streets of cheap, high-purity heroin (following the fall of the Shah of Iran) and a shift from injecting the drug to smoking it, leading to the popularisation and enhanced accessibility of heroin in many urban areas. The 1980s also witnessed the entry into illicit drugs markets of 'criminal diversifiers', lured by the prospect of high profits at much less risk than traditional criminal pursuits such as armed robbery (Dorn *et al.* 1992). As South has suggested, this was very much a 'decade of developments' characterised by 'a dramatic assertion of penal power in drugs control in Britain' (South, 1998: 92), a tendency which had hardly diminished in the closing years of the twentieth century. The 1980s generated a number of important documents which have shaped significantly the direction and structures of contemporary British drug enforcement.

Firstly, the Hodgson Committee, named after its chair Sir Derek Hodgson, was set up in the aftermath of the notorious 'Operation Julie' drugs case (*R* v *Cuthbertson*, 1980) to examine and report upon the confiscation of criminally generated profits. Its report (Hodgson *et al.*, 1984) contained a number of ground-breaking proposals in relation to the seizure and recovery of assets deemed to be the proceeds of drug-related crime, including the exceptional provision of a reversal of the burden of proof on the accused. While the latter measure paralleled anti-racketeering and anti-corruption laws in other jurisdictions, it marked Britain out from practice in other EU member states which place responsibility on the prosecution to prove unlawful provenance (Europol Drugs Unit, 1996). The Hodgson Committee recommendations provided much of the substance of the wide-ranging Drug Trafficking Offences Act 1986 (DTOA). However, the committee's view that asset confiscation could be at least a partial *alternative* to incarceration was overshadowed by the Controlled Drugs (Penalties) Act 1985 which further escalated prison sentence maxima suggesting, as Dorn *et al.* argue, 'an excess of gung-ho sentiments over careful analysis' (1992: 199–200). The application of the Act and subsequent legislation have raised concerns about erosion of civil liberties and due process. However, although the number of confiscation orders issued has grown from 200 in 1987 to over 1500 in 1996, recent reports suggest that investigators are finding seizure increasingly more difficult and that even tougher laws may be in the pipeline (Campbell, 1999: see also Williamson, Chapter 2 in this volume).

Influential in tilting the balance of British drugs policing further in a crime control direction was the report of the 1984 ACPO Working Party on Drugs Related Crime, more usually referred to after its chair, the then Chief

Constable of Avon and Somerset, Ronald Broome (ACPO, 1985). In addition to its commentary on the Hodgson Committee proposals, the Broome Report recommended that police operational strategy should be based formally on a co-ordinated three-tiered approach: divisional, force, and regional/national – the so-called 'Broome triangle'. There was considerable debate at the time about the need for a National Drug Squad, but Broome and his colleagues recommended instead a revised regional structure with the addition of dedicated drugs wings on to existing regional crime squads to tackle 'cross-boundary' cases. (The establishment of a National Crime Squad was to come a little over a decade later (Murji, 1998: 1).) With regard to intelligence efforts, Broome urged that the former Central Drugs Intelligence Unit become the National Drugs Intelligence Unit (NDIU), which has been superseded in turn by the creation of the National Criminal Intelligence Service (NCIS) and, indeed, by more recent transnational developments at European level which raise interesting new questions about police discretion and accountability (den Boer, 1999; Walker, Chapter 6; Loveday, Chapter 13).

For a number of years, the Broome triangle was the benchmark against which HM Inspectors of Constabulary, during their routine inspections, would evaluate (and on occasions castigate) forces for the efficacy (or otherwise) of their drugs strategies. However, in 1996 a thematic report by Her Majesty's Inspectorate of Constabulary (HMIC) on drugs policing confirmed what many operational officers had for some time recognised as the increasing irrelevance of the Broome model, a view already shared by academics such as Ruggiero and South (1995) whose study *Eurodrugs* had found the hypothesis that drugs markets are dominated or controlled by cartels directed by shadowy 'Mr Bigs' to be largely invalidated. HMIC reported that:

> Examples were given of drugs offenders 'moving up and down' the scale of seriousness, from simple users to minor suppliers, then major dealing and back down to simple possession again. Similarly, examples were given of force drugs squads investigating drug dealers moving all round the country and abroad. Divisional personnel mentioned that it was not unusual for offenders traditionally regarded as low tier users/dealers, to travel across the channel to obtain supplies of cannabis or ecstasy for personal use or 'minor' supply to associates, further evidence of the blurring of the 'Broome' model. (1996: 14)

The 'blurring' is reflected to some extent in the recent enthusiasm for more focused, low-level drug enforcement (LLDE) strategies aimed at transforming rather than eliminating local markets, an objective which seems more realistic and in tune with the harm reduction principles discussed earlier (see also Edmunds *et al.*, 1996; Lee, 1996; Murji, 1998).

Finally, in the same year that the ACPO Working Party reported, *Tackling Drug Misuse* (Home Office, 1985) outlined the government's strategy which proposed simultaneous action on five fronts:

- supporting international efforts to reduce supplies from abroad;
- increasing the effectiveness of police and Customs enforcement;

- maintaining tight domestic controls and effective deterrents;
- developing prevention through publicity, education and community action;
- improving treatment and rehabilitation.

As this list of aims and the concomitant expenditure profile would suggest, by the mid-1980s and on into the early 1990s, Britain was placing primacy on enforcement (and, in particular, on the role of the police), with considerably less emphasis (and spending) on education, prevention and treatment responses: around 70 per cent on enforcement measures, compared with 30 per cent going into education, treatment and rehabilitation.

Corporacy and co-ordination

In the 1990s, the provisions of successive pieces of legislation are suggestive of oscillations in mood between penal and more therapeutic responses toward drugs offenders. One of the more innovative elements of the 1991 Criminal Justice Act with its 'punishment in the community' agenda, for example, was its provision for conditioned probation orders. Such a sentence, which requires alcohol or drugs offenders to attend treatment programmes, remains an option that seems surprisingly underused (South, 1998). The 1994 Criminal Justice and Public Order Act, on the other hand, gave the police new powers to deal with, among other things, open air 'raves' and the emergent 'dance culture', while the Crime (Sentences) Act 1997 introduced mandatory minimum seven-year prison sentences for repeat Class A drug traffickers. More recently, the Crime and Disorder Act 1998 introduced Drug Treatment and Testing Orders (DTTOs) aimed at reducing the amount of acquisitive crime committed by problem misusers. Pilot studies are still under evaluation, with a view to national implementation from late 2000, but provisional findings seem encouraging (Turnbull, 1999). However, ironically, the concept of further extension of drug testing into the workplace sparked off an interesting debate in the columns of *Police Review*, between those who regard its introduction to the police's own workplace as an essential tool in guaranteeing high quality of care and service (Oliver, 1999), and others who see it as a dangerous infringement on police officers' civil liberties (Pater, 1999).

On the broader policy front, the government White Paper, *Tackling Drugs Together*, appeared in May 1995 and mapped out a three-year strategy for England. (Action for Scotland, Wales and Northern Ireland, though tailored to the specific needs of those countries, was to be broadly consistent with this.) Better co-ordination and multi-agency partnership approaches were seen as holding the key to effective drugs policing, by bringing together disparate elements which had, until then, been undertaken in different policy areas, such as health and education. The Statement of Purpose was:

> To take effective action by vigorous law enforcement, accessible treatment and a new emphasis on education and prevention to:
>
> - increase the safety of communities from drug-related crime;

- reduce the acceptability and availability of drugs to young people;
- reduce the health risks and other damage related to drug misuse.

(Lord President *et al.*, 1995: vii)

Drug Action Teams (DATs), which include high level representation from local authorities, police, probation and health authorities, were created to deliver the strategy locally. One declared aim of the White Paper was to promote greater consistency between police forces, each of which was required to publish a drugs strategy aimed at ensuring that drugs enforcement activity articulated with their equal opportunities policies. Three years on, reported Newburn and Elliott (1998), the police had come to play a central role in the DATs and forces had generally reoriented their enforcement practices away from simple possession offences to higher-level traffickers. At the same time, they appeared to be balancing enforcement with education and harm reduction goals, though the development of more sophisticated arrest referral schemes and more effective performance measures were identified as two key issues for future anti-drugs strategies (Newburn and Elliott, 1998).

The managerial politics associated with New Labour and its 'joined-up government' project were in a sense epitomised by the appointment in January 1998 of Keith Hellawell (former Chief Constable of West Yorkshire) as the first UK Anti-Drugs Co-ordinator (or 'Drugs Czar'), tasked with developing a new ten-year strategy to build on the earlier White Paper. The resultant document, *Tackling Drugs to Build a Better Britain* (Cm 3945), which has more the feel of a glossy corporate prospectus than its predecessor, sets out four aims:

- to help young people resist drug misuse in order to achieve their full potential in society;
- to protect communities from drug-related anti-social and criminal behaviour;
- to enable people with drug problems to overcome them and live healthy and crime-free lives;
- to stifle the availability of illegal drugs on the street.

The strategy document, which like so much else in contemporary policing places firm emphasis on the 'best value' and 'what works' principles, highlighted in the introduction to this volume, acknowledges that better co-ordination and integration are needed to shift resources from 'reactive measures' (expenditure on policing, prisons, etc., which still accounts for about 62 per cent of the annual drugs budget) towards prevention and treatment. To achieve this, the police were encouraged to redirect resources towards drugs-specific partnership projects and to emphasise in Annual Policing Plans the Home Secretary's national objectives, and key performance targets and indicators. This recommendation resonates with the strategy's underlying principle of 'evidence-based' decision making, an aspect of policy implementation and monitoring which seemed set to become embedded with the establishment during 2000 of a dedicated Home Office Drugs Research and Statistics Unit.

149

As other contributors to this volume have argued, the development of 'performance culture', a trend associated with the rise of New Public Management (NPM) in the 1980s, has had a significant impact on policing (Leishman, *et al.*, 1996a). Indeed, there were signs, at the close of what Nicholas Dorn and Maggy Lee have memorably dubbed the 'nervous 1990s' (Dorn and Lee, 1999: 97), that NPM may also be serving to 'reinvent' drugs enforcement and the discourse that surrounds it:

> The development at national level of criteria and strategies other than seizures and arrests parallels the new 'community' strategies at local level. In both cases, new goals are being constructed, in a sense retrieving the enforcement agencies from their posture of apparent defeat in the drug war. The new approaches, aiming to reduce harm which may be associated with drug trafficking (unsafe streets, troubled communities, organised crime, violence, laundering of super-profits, etc.), provide a basket of indicators – some of which may be expected to be encouraging even if others turn out not, in any particular year.   (Dorn and Lee, 1999: 92–3)

The shift towards more corporate and co-ordinated goals for drugs policing informed by harm-reduction principles, has been reflected in many of Keith Hellawell's public statements. For example, in an interview some weeks before the publication of the report of the Police Foundation's Independent Committee of Inquiry to Review the Effectiveness of the Misuse of Drugs Act 1971, he spoke of the 'need to discriminate between different drugs and the relative harm caused and then talk openly about the difference we can make', a remark that was widely interpreted as lending tacit support for the idea of eventual 'depenalisation' of cannabis possession (*Observer*, 2000). Although the 'drugs czar's' remit extends to the whole of the UK, developments in post-devolution Scotland suggest that there may be limits to the prospects for complete corporate consistency in British drugs policing in the years ahead.

Caledonian considerations

As Hammersley (1997) has noted, Scotland has always tended to 'use the law a lot' in relation to drugs, a feature which was exemplified in the 1980s by energetic enforcement and some fairly tough sentencing outcomes in its High Court. For a while there seemed to be a mood more inclined towards a 'zero tolerance' approach to drugs which placed primacy on robust supply-side policing. However, the discovery of high rates of HIV/AIDS transmission among intravenous drug users in Edinburgh (Robertson, 1987) resulted in guidelines from Scotland's chief law officer, the Lord Advocate, urging forces to be more circumspect about the need to seize needles and syringes during drugs raids, and at the same time facilitating the inception of some of the earliest needle exchange schemes in the UK. As Hammersley suggests, 'the relatively left-wing or at least liberal traditions of Scotland mean that social justice is still seen as a valid orientation to social problems' (1997: 83) and this latter aspect is arguably reflected in *Tackling Drugs in Scotland: Action in Partnership* (Scottish Office, 1999).

While sharing the same key aims and evidence-based aspirations as the UK strategy, *Tackling Drugs in Scotland* seems to place an even greater emphasis on harm reduction goals and the importance of education (particularly at primary level) than does its Southern counterpart (ISDD, 2000). This may well be a foretaste of subtle divergences in mood about drugs policy between post-devolution Scotland and the rest of the UK, a feature that may become more apparent following the establishment of the Scottish Drug Enforcement Agency in 2000, headed by a Director accountable to the Crime Committee of the Association of Chief Police Officers in Scotland (ACPOS). Significantly, the new Scottish Executive has demonstrated its preparedness to take hard decisions, by switching funding from the prison service to strengthen community-based enforcement efforts.

What may also prove to be an absorbing issue in the early years of the twenty-first century is the direction that the decriminalisation debate may take in Scotland, where politicians have shown a greater willingness to at least ventilate the issue than others at Westminster, in particular government ministers. Significantly, senior political figures as well as church leaders and High Court judges have all contributed to the discussion. When Lord McCluskey, one of Scotland's most distinguished judges, called for a Royal Commission on the drugs laws, he received support from the Deputy First Minister and Justice Minister, Jim Wallace MSP (Hannan, 1999). Indeed, there has been open acknowledgement that minor possession of cannabis has effectively been decriminalised in parts of Scotland, where the matter is now more likely to be dealt with by police confiscating the drugs and issuing a warning, rather than reporting alleged offenders, thus allowing police to concentrate on targeting higher level suppliers of heroin (Laing, 1999). However, though the mood in Scotland may have been swinging in the direction of decriminalisation, with heroin related deaths running at an all time high at the end of the 1990s, many consider that the cannabis debate is not the priority issue. There remains a feeling that whatever debate is eventually held, it must be an exhaustive one since there will be only one opportunity to 'get it right'. Once decriminalised, there would be no going back: the genie could not be put back in the bottle. On a more optimistic note, Scots law has shown itself to be adaptable in the past in relation to substance abuse policy and the time could soon be right for a new and significant demonstration of this facet of its nature. Measures adopted during the height of the glue-sniffing 'panic' of the early 1980s may offer a useful template for new means of ensuring that drug misusers who enter the criminal justice system are channelled in the most appropriate direction at the earliest possible juncture to address what is seen by many as a social phenomenon rather than individual acts of criminality (Burns, 1996).

Finally, the inclusion in Scotland (as elsewhere in the UK) of alcohol in the remit of DATs has been broadly welcomed and encouraged. Alcohol prevention and education has long been a poor relation to programmes geared towards controlled drugs, but now the two are beginning to be delivered together. There have also been serious debates about over-provision of licensed premises and the mixed messages sent out by sponsorship of major sporting teams and events by manufacturers of alcoholic drinks. In Scotland, as elsewhere, the links between lager and athleticism remain difficult to reconcile!

Conclusion

Transported by time machine to the present, an assistant commissioner from the early years of the 'new' Metropolitan Police would most likely be astonished at the extent to which drugs have come to dominate the contemporary policing agenda. After all, in 1839 all manner of now controlled substances were freely available across the counter and Britain had just embarked on the first of two wars against China to protect its own role as one of the world's major sponsors of international trade in opium and morphia (South, 1997). Arriving several unsuccessful drugs wars later, our Victorian visitor might also perhaps be dismayed by the comparative neglect of attention paid to alcohol and drink-related criminality, especially that associated with those new-fangled horseless carriages!

In the latter half of the twentieth century, drugs undoubtedly became a core issue in policing, though, as we have discussed, the late 1990s witnessed a shift from their use and supply being viewed as essentially a 'police problem' to be tackled primarily by enforcement, to an issue defined by limiting harm to communities and to be dealt with in partnership. The 'drugs warriors' with their martial metaphors may, for the time being at least, have been muted by the now familiar mantra of 'best value' and 'what works'. As Dorn and Lee (1999: 97) have suggested, in relation to drugs as with other areas of policing and criminal justice, we may now be more prepared simply 'to settle for modest improvements at the margin'. Cynics will inevitably dismiss this view and the performance measures associated with it as a way of letting politicians and police officials 'off the hook' for policy failures. However, many others may harbour more optimism that such an approach to drugs policy monitoring is a welcome advance on reading seemingly endless and depressing despatches about casualties and skirmishes from the trenches of the drug-war front.

References

ACPO (1985) *Final Report of the Working Party on Drugs Related Crime* (unpublished).

Blanchard, S. (1994) 'A Thinkable Solution', *Police Review*, 3 June.

Boyd, N. and Loman, J. (1991) 'The politics of prostitution and drug control' in Stenson and Cowell (1991).

Braggins, J. (ed.) (1997) *Tackling Drugs Together: One Year On*. London: ISTD.

Bullington, B. (1998) 'America's drug war: fact or fiction?' in Coomber (1998).

Burns, P. (1996) 'Break the Brutal Circle of Addiction and Crime', *Scotland on Sunday*, 13 October.

Campbell, D. (1999) 'Criminals Getting More Ingenious at Holding on to Loot', *Independent*, 9 January.

Charles, N. (1998) *Public Perceptions of Drug-Related Crime in 1997*. HORS Research findings, No. 67. London: Home Office.

Chibnall, S. (1977) *Law and Order News*. London: Tavistock.

Collison, M. (1993) 'Punishing Drugs: Criminal Justice and Drug Use', *British Journal of Criminology*, 33 (3).

Collison, M. (1994) 'Drug Crime, Drug Problems and Criminal Justice: Sentencing Trends and Enforcement Targets', *The Howard Journal*, 33 (1).

Concar, D. and Spinney, L. (1994) 'The Highs and Lows of Prohibition', *New Scientist*, 1 October.

Coomber, R. (ed.) (1998) *The Control of Drugs and Drug Users: Reason or Reaction?*. Amsterdam: Harwood.

Davies, S. (1997) 'The War on Drugs is a Dialogue of the Deaf', *Independent*, 28 August.

den Boer, M. (1999) 'Internationalisation: A Challenge to Police Organisations in Europe' in Mawby (1999).

Dorn, N. (1992) 'Clarifying Policy Options on Drug Trafficking: Harm Minimisation is Distinct from Legalization', in O'Hare (1992).

Dorn, N. and Lee, M. (1999) 'Drugs and Policing in Europe: From Low Streets to High Places', in South (1999).

Dorn, N. and Murji, K. (1993) 'Low Level Drug Enforcement', *International Journal of the Sociology of Law*, 20 (2).

Dorn, N. Jepsen, J. and Savona, E. (eds) (1996) *European Drug Policies and Enforcement*. Basingstoke: Macmillan.

Dorn, N., Murji, K. and South, N. (1992) *Traffickers: Drug Markets and Law Enforcement*. London: Routledge.

The Economist (2000), 'Going Dutch?', 15 January.

Edmunds, E., Hough, M. and Urquia, N. (1996) *Tackling Local Drugs Markets*. Crime Detection and Prevention Series, Paper No. 80. London: Home Office.

Europol Drugs Unit (1996) *Operational Practices and Techniques Relating to Drugs Matters in the European Union*. The Hague: Europol.

Grieve, J. (1994) 'Sitting on the Lid', *Policing Today*, 1 (1).

Grieve, J. (1998) 'Intelligence as Education for All? Government Drugs Policies 1980–1997' in O'Connor (1998).

Hammersley, M. (1997) 'The Scottish drugs scene: an overview', in Braggins (1997).

Hannan, M. (1999) 'Decriminalise Cannabis Call from Judge', *Scotland on Sunday*, 11 July.

Hartnoll, R. (1998) 'International Trends in Drug Policy' in Coomber (1998).

Hodgson, D. *et al.* (1984) *The Profits of Crime and their Recovery*. London: Heinemann.

HMIC (1996) *An Examination of Police Force Drugs Strategies*. London: Home Office.

Home Office (1985) *Tackling Drug Misuse*. London: HMSO.

Home Office (1997) *Drug Misuse Declared in 1996: The Latest Results from the British Crime Survey*. Research Study 172. London: Home Office.

Home Office (1999) *Drug Seizure and Offender Statistics, United Kingdom, 1997*. Home Office Statistical Bulletin 8/99. London: Home Office.

ISDD (2000) *Drugs Situation in the UK – Trends and Update*. http://www.isdd.co.uk/trends

Laing, P (1999) 'Police Forces Turn Blind Eye to Cannabis Use', *Scotland on Sunday*, 25 July.

Lee, M. (1996) 'London: 'Community damage limitation' through policing?' in Dorn *et al.* (1996).

Leishman, F., Cope, S. and Starie, P. (1996a) 'Reinventing and Restructuring: Towards a 'New Policing Order', in Leishman *et al.* (1996b).

Leishman, F., Loveday, B. and Savage, S. (eds) (1996b) *Core Issues in Policing*. 1st edn. Harlow: Longman.

Lord President *et al.* (1995) *Tackling Drugs Together.* London: HMSO.

Maguire, M. *et al.* (eds) (1997) *The Oxford Handbook of Criminology*. 2nd edn. Oxford: Oxford University Press.

Mawby, R. (ed.) (1999) *Policing across the World: Issues for the Twenty-First Century*. London: UCL Press.

McDonald, M. (ed.) (1994) *Gender, Drink and Drugs*. Oxford: Berg.

Mott, J. and Bean, P. (1998) 'The Development of Drug Control in Britain' in Coomber (1998).

Murji, K. (1993) 'Drug Enforcement Strategies', *The Howard Journal*, 32 (3).

Murji, K. (1998) *Policing Drugs*. Aldershot: Ashgate.

Newburn, T. and Elliott, J. (1998) *Police Anti-Drugs Strategies: Tackling Drugs Together Three Years On*. Crime Detection and Prevention Series Paper 89. London: Home Office.

Observer (2000) 'Lay Off Cannabis Users – Drug Tsar', 6 February.

O'Connor, L. *et al.* (eds) (1998) *Drugs: Partnerships for Policy, Prevention and Education*. London: Cassell.

O'Hare, P. *et al.* (eds) (1992) *The Reduction of Drug-Related Harm*. London: Routledge.

Oliver, I. (1999) 'Tried and Tested', *Police Review*, 20 August.

Parker, H., Measham, F. and Aldridge, J. (1995) *Drugs Futures: Changing Patterns of Drug Use amongst English Youth*. London: ISDD.

Pater, M. (1999) 'Gone to Pot', *Police Review*, 30 July.

Pearson, G. (1992) 'Drugs and Criminal Justice: A Harm Reduction Perspective' in O'Hare (1992).

Reiner, R. (1992) *The Politics of the Police*. 2nd edn. Hemel Hempstead: Harvester Wheatsheaf.

Robertson, R. (1987) *Heroin, AIDS and Society*. London: Hodder and Stoughton.

Rose, D. (1998) 'The Real Inspector Morse', *The Force*, Episode 2, first broadcast on BBC2, 28 January.

Ruggiero, V. and South, N. (1995) *Eurodrugs*. London: UCL Press.

Schlaadt, R. and Shannon, P. (1994) *Drugs: Use, Misuse and Abuse*. Englewood Cliffs, NJ: Prentice Hall.

Schlesinger, P. and Tumber, H. (1994) *Reporting Crime: The Media Politics of Criminal Justice*. Oxford: Clarendon Press.

Scottish Office (1999) *Tackling Drugs in Scotland. Action in Partnership*. Edinburgh: HMSO.

Shiner, M. and Newburn, T. (1999) 'Taking Tea with Noel: The Place and Meaning Of Drug Use In Everyday Life' in South (1999).

South, N. (1997) 'Drugs: Use, Crime and Control' in Maguire (1997).

South, N. (1998) 'Tackling Drug Control in Britain: From Sir Malcolm Delevingne to the New Drugs Strategy', in Coomber (1998).

South, N. (ed.) (1999) *Drugs: Cultures, Controls and Everyday Life.* London: Sage.

Stenson, K. and Cowell, D. (eds) (1991) *The Politics of Crime Control.* London: Sage.

Trimbos Institute (1997) *Cannabis Policy Update.* Fact Sheet 7. Utrecht: Trimbos.

Turnbull, P. (1999) *Drug Treatment and Testing Orders – Interim Evaluation.* HORS Research Findings No. 106. London: Home Office.

UKADCU (UK Anti-drug Coordinator Unit) (1998) *Tackling Drugs to Build a Better Britain.* London: HMSO.

Young, M. (1994) 'The Police, Gender and the Culture of Drug Use and Addiction' in McDonald (1994).

Chapter 10

Public order policing: citizenship and moral ambiguity

P.A.J. WADDINGTON

Introduction

Policing is morally ambiguous and profoundly so. The police officer occupies a unique position in society: he or she is licensed by other citizens to exercise coercion over them. The police officer is duty bound to act in ways that would be exceptional, exceptionable or downright illegal if undertaken by anyone else (Waddington, P.A.J., 1999). For example, police officers may legitimately intrude into the privacy of others: it would be quite abnormal for anyone other than a police officer to approach strangers in a public place and to demand (however politely) that they give an account of themselves. It is unimaginable that any other citizen could find himself or herself *duty bound* premeditatedly to kill fellow citizens, as might a firearms officer acting as a sniper.

Routinely acting in ways that other citizens would not dream of doing means that policing is *precarious*. The authority that the officer exercises is underwritten by the fact that police officers are 'monopolists of force in civil society' (Bittner, 1990). A police officer may *ask* for the compliance of other citizens, but if they refuse he is able to *compel* compliance to a degree that virtually any other citizen is denied. However, if and when the police resort to the use of overt force the *legitimacy* of their actions is always questionable, and sometimes questioned. For example, an officer who instructs a group of boisterous youths to 'move on' may be regarded as the servant of the community *or* be accused of gratuitously throwing his weight around (Waddington and Braddock, 1991; Choongh, 1997).

In no other aspect of policing is this moral ambiguity more apparent than the policing of public order. When police battle with protesters and rioters, not only are they likely to be physically injured, the police organisation is also likely to suffer harm.

Whose order?

Public order policing enjoys a moral ambiguity that crime fighting has traditionally lacked. Why are these two aspects of policing so different? Put simply, the criminal occupies a position outside the moral community, whereas protesters, pickets and possibly even rioters may be considered the moral equals of other citizens. It is virtually true by definition that criminals are castigated as immoral predators on the moral community. Criminalising certain activities is an effective means of denuding them of any social or political legitimacy they might otherwise have. The typical strategy adopted by modern states to terrorism has been to deny it political significance and to treat it as *merely* criminal. Terrorists, on the other hand, strive to attain political status for their acts. They insist, for example, that terrorist prisoners are 'prisoners of war' who should be treated as such and *not* as common criminals.

Whatever it is that distinguishes the 'common criminal' from protesters and pickets, it certainly is not simply that criminals violate the criminal law and protesters do not, for those who protest also commit offences, sometimes very serious crimes. What distinguishes them is that protest is a *conspicuous act of citizenship*. Far from preying on the moral community, the protester is actively participating in that moral community, however misguidedly. Pickets, protesters and rioters do not serve purposes that are selfishly malign, but principled. Even when acting in pursuit of their self-interest – for example, by improving pay – pickets and protesters are usually acting on behalf of the *collectivity* and possibly suffering (or risk suffering) individually in doing so. Moreover, the collective aim that is being pursued is often morally defensible even if the means employed to achieve it violate moral precepts and the criminal law. 'Defending jobs and communities' is a perfectly legitimate aim, even if the violent means used to pursue it are morally dubious (*Sunday Times* Insight Team, 1985). However, not even the means are indisputably improper. The use of force (or, to give it a less euphemistic description, 'violence') is also employed by the state and its agents, the police, to pursue its, often contrary, goals.[1] Thus, a riot can be characterised as a battle between two groups (rioters and police), both of whom are willing to use violence for what they each regard as 'the common good'. Protesters and pickets can, therefore, claim to be the moral equal of the police with a degree of success rarely achieved by criminals.

The series of confrontations that took place during early 1995 between police and protesters aiming to halt the export of live animals to Continental Europe illustrates the general point. Opposing the export of calves destined to be reared in cramped 'veal crates' is clearly a moral purpose. Few spokespeople for any of the parties attempted to justify the practice of rearing calves in such a way; indeed the practice had been illegal in Britain since 1990. There was, in other words, agreement about the *aims* of the protesters. The dispute was solely about *means*: the government, farmers' representatives and exporters claimed that what they were doing was legal. If the law was to be changed, there were constitutional means of doing so. However, protesters appealed to a higher morality: while the wheels of the legislative machine slowly turned, calves were being reared in morally indefensible conditions. This posed the moral conundrum: if adherence to constitutional means allows a moral wrong to continue, should the moral person abandon those means to achieve a moral end?

In this case, it was not at all clear that adherence to moral means would resolve the issue, even in the long term. The government claimed that jurisdiction of this issue lay not with them, but with the European Union. It was clear that some member states had little sympathy with the aims of the protesters. Unable to exert influence by other means, protesters opted for 'direct action'. For the majority, this amounted to lying in front of trucks transporting calves at the port entrance. This is in the tradition of non-violent 'direct action' and was also unlikely to prompt moral indignation. Indeed, the willingness of protesters to experience discomfort and expose themselves to risk of arrest or injury for a cause with which many felt sympathy reflected a commitment that enhanced, rather than detracted from, their moral status.

On the other hand, the role of the police in removing protesters and ensuring that the trucks reached their destination was morally dubious: they were in the position of promoting immoral acts – albeit unintentionally – for without the assistance of the police the trucks would not have got through and the calves would not have been reared in 'veal crates'. When some protesters reacted with violence against the police and the trucks, their individual actions may have been denounced, but is it more morally reprehensible to use force in pursuit of a moral goal than to use force (the removal of sit-down protesters from the highway) in pursuit of an admittedly immoral goal? That is the moral ambiguity of policing public order.

The extent to which police and protesters, pickets and rioters may be considered moral equals is apparent when disorder is viewed from a broad historical and comparative perspective. Few would now suggest that those who rioted periodically throughout the nineteenth century in pursuit of the franchise or of trade union rights were morally wrong, although illegal violence was certainly used in doing so. Those who opposed Mosley's Fascists in the 1930s are rarely considered in hindsight to have been a riotous mob, but are credited as defending higher political ideals (Thurlow, 1987; Panayi, 1993a). On a broader canvas, black civil rights activists who systematically defied racist laws are sanctified and their leader, Martin Luther King, has acquired the status of a secular saint whose memory is honoured each year by a public holiday in the USA. The protesters in Leipzig who hastened the collapse of the East German state achieved democracy by defying their communist rulers. The verdict of history is that the 'bad guys' in these and many other confrontations between states and their respective citizens are the forces of repression – principally the police.

It is the police of authoritarian and totalitarian regimes that have justifiably earned the reputation of the 'bad guys', since they are the instruments used to suppress progressive democratic movements. However, their unenviable moral status arises from two analytically distinct sources: the means they use to suppress dissent and on whose behalf they do so. Wholesale slaughter, such as that which occurred in Tiananmen Square, Peking, obviously provokes outrage because it is difficult to imagine how such a use of force could possibly be justified. The police of authoritarian regimes are prone to heavy-handedness, but it is not this alone that leads to their repudiation by democrats. Even when the police of an authoritarian state use no more force than their counterparts in democracies, the fact that they defend authoritarianism by force is sufficient justification for moral repudiation. For example, police in many countries use teargas, water canon and baton charges to disperse illegal assemblies and rioting crowds, but when, say, the South African police did so in defence of apartheid, their actions were widely regarded as utterly reprehensible.

The order that protesters challenge need not, of course, be reprehensible. Right does not always lie with the protester. For example, when police and troops enforced the decision of the Supreme Court to desegregate schools in the southern states of the USA, they were instruments of enlightened liberalism defeating reactionary racism. Nevertheless, they were in the midst of a clash of moral orders in which they effectively took sides.

Where does all this leave us? It points to a fundamental distinction between crime fighting and order maintenance. The former is rarely morally questionable, but the latter is almost invariably morally ambiguous. Contrary to the usual police justification, public order policing is *not* the maintenance of order, but maintenance of *a particular order*. Police cannot shelter, as they often attempt to do in public utterances, behind the claim that they are merely enforcing the law. For if the law is itself unjust or sustains injustice, then enforcing it is tainted. Inevitably, that means defending the vested interests that are inherent within the established order and resisting the alternative order that protesters wish to establish. The clash of opposing moral orders leaves public order policing in a morally ambiguous position.

Riots: causation and blame

It is this moral ambiguity of public order policing that provides the context for understanding debates about the causes of riot and large-scale disorder, for this extensive literature, which masquerades as a search for causation, is mainly an exercise in attributing blame.

Academic researchers have long sought the causes of riot. In the late nineteenth century Gustave Le Bon suggested that the crowd liberates primordial passions in its members making them easy prey to manipulation by agitators (Le Bon, 1895). Later social scientists elaborated the theme that riots arose from irrational behaviour by emphasising how rioters were the playthings of forces beyond their comprehension and control. Perhaps the most prominent exponent of this view was Neil Smelser who explained riots as arising from strains in the social system. Rioters and protesters rarely understood the origins of their discontent, but were mobilised by beliefs that had the capacity to arouse emotional commitment (Smelser, 1962). The structural origins of such strains were regarded by some researchers as quite perverse: for example, actual deprivation turned out to be less influential than *relative* deprivation (Gurr, 1969) and the 'reverse J-curve' postulated that riot and revolution were most likely to occur when social conditions began to *improve* (Davies, 1962, 1969). Meanwhile, psychologists concentrated on how members of a crowd would be freed from social constraint by processes such as 'de-individuation' (that is, being anonymous and not directly or individually responsible for harm to others) (Zimbardo, 1970).

This traditional view of social disorder is now widely repudiated (see, for example, Currie and Skolnick, 1972, but note also Smelser, 1972). According to this repudiation, conceptualising the crowd as an irrational mob simply reflects a conservative élitist view that fails to recognise the grievances that lead to protest, disorder, riot and rebellion. In the aftermath of the race riots of America's long hot summers of the 1960s, it was regarded as both empirically untrue and morally offensive to suggest that black Americans were mindlessly responding to strains in the social structure of which they were unaware. It seemed to observers that these rioters were all too acutely aware of the deprivation, discrimination and police brutality that they routinely suffered (Allen and Adair, 1969; Skolnick, 1969; Fogelson, 1970, 1971). Similarly, in the aftermath of riots in British inner cities, a consensus emerged amongst academics, journalists and other commentators that emphasised how the riots represented a rational response to deprivation, discrimination and police harassment (Cowell et al., 1982; Kettle and Hodges, 1982; Benyon, 1987). It was argued that, viewed in its historical context, the inner-city riots of the early 1980s belonged to a long tradition of resistance to oppression. As Kettle and Hodges (1982) put it:

> Throughout British history, powerless people, feeling themselves oppressed and seeing no effective response to their grievances, have despaired of any improvement, formed themselves into crowds and physically challenged the world that seemed to deny them what they wanted.

However, this alternative to the traditional view (what I have elsewhere christened the 'critical consensus' (Waddington, P.A.J., 1991), is not free from criticisms. As Berk (1972) has pointed out, severe methodological problems are encountered by *any* theory that claims to explain crowd behaviour. First, the notion of 'a crowd' is open to question, for, as McPhail (1991) has observed, individuals frequently attend gatherings in the company of others with whom they remain throughout the event. It is also a common observation that protesters often participate in protest demonstrations as members of *distinct* factions, frequently maintaining their distinct identity by displaying their own banners and placards, and by maintaining physical segregation from others. In such circumstances, can it be said that there is a single crowd, or a collection of crowdlets?

Secondly, whether the crowd is a single entity or a multiplicity of distinct components, it is extremely difficult (not to say hazardous on occasion) to discover whether members share a common point of view. The claim that a crowd was motivated by a common grievance is almost invariably an attribution imposed on the crowd by the theorist. In some circumstances such an attribution seems quite reasonable: when tens of thousands gather and march to protest against some wrong, then few would dispute that they are voicing a common grievance. The reason is, as McPhail and Miller (1973) point out, that the means by which the protesters assembled indicates purposeful intent. This is, however, in stark contrast to 'community disorders'. These rioters did not assemble in an organised fashion, but were recruited haphazardly as the riot developed. As McPhail has also observed, the best predictors of riot participation are environmental – they take place on warm summer weekend evenings near major intersections where people gather and those participating in them tend to be those who because of their age, sex and social status are most likely to be found in the vicinity (McPhail, 1971). His reasoning is compelling, albeit incompatible with that of the 'critical consensus'; it is that, for an incident to spark a riot, there needs to be a critical mass of bystanders capable of assembling at the scene. The fact that they assemble is not *in* itself evidence of a common grievance.

Of course, it might be argued that the fact that an incident led to the spontaneous assemblage of a crowd suggests a common response to the incident that is, perhaps, symptomatic of a shared grievance. Benyon, for example, insists that injustice was the issue during the 1981 inner-city disorders (Benyon and Solomos, 1987a) and so it might have been. Certainly, black and Asian people in Britain suffer the injustices of discrimination and deprivation. The problem lies in linking injustice to the behaviour of rioters on the streets of inner cities. There are two oft-quoted links: the 'precipitating incident' that supposedly sparks a riot and the pattern of riotous behaviour.

The notion that an otherwise insignificant incident acts as the 'flashpoint' (Waddington, D. *et al.* 1987, 1989; Waddington, D., 1992) for a riot to occur is of pivotal significance, for it attempts to resolve difficulties in conceptualising riots as expressions of injustice. These problems are two-fold: first, injustice may not be perceived as such and, secondly, even when perceived, injustice tends to be a long-running state of affairs which leaves unanswered the question of why the riot occurred when and where it did. The concept of a 'precipitating incident' addresses both of these explanatory difficulties. First, the incident acquires significance from its symbolic import. Thus, a raid on a café suspected of selling illicit liquor (Joshua *et al.*, 1983) and the searching of a taxi driver suspected of possessing drugs (Scarman, 1981) both allegedly sparked riots because they represented the oppression and harassment suffered by black people at the hands of the police. Secondly, once crystallised by such an incident, diffuse frustration arising from persistent injustice becomes focused as anger at a *particular* wrong.

Although far from implausible, the notion of a 'flashpoint' is not strong enough to sustain the explanatory weight it is called upon to bear. How does the analyst identify which of the myriad incidents that occurred immediately prior to the outbreak of rioting constituted the flashpoint? The Scarman report accepts that it was the searching of the taxi driver that provided the flashpoint for the Brixton riot in 1981 (Scarman, 1981). What goes unexplained is why the hundreds of other searches conducted by police during the ill-fated operation 'Swamp 81' *did not* spark a riot. Why did they *not* symbolise police oppression and harassment, when the search of the taxi driver did? At least in the cases of the Bristol and Brixton riots, the proximity between the fateful police action and the commencement of the riot lends credibility to these incidents being the flashpoints. On other occasions this crucial link is far from secure. Apart from a brief altercation between traffic police and a black motorist some hours before the outbreak of the Handsworth riot in 1985, no credible flashpoint was identified in that case (Dear, 1986; Silverman, 1986). In other cases, the events that are credited with sparking the rioting are not proximate. For example, the Broadwater Farm riot erupted over 24 hours after the tragic death of Mrs Cynthia Jarrett (Gifford, 1986). The suspicion remains that, once disorder erupts, a credible flashpoint can retrospectively be discerned at will, since *any* event (however apparently insignificant) will serve the purpose. Most orderly political demonstrations are accompanied by many incidents which, if disorder were to break out, could be qualified as possible 'flashpoints'. Since, however, disorder is rare they go unacknowledged and unrecorded (Waddington, P.A.J., 1994, 2000; Waddington D., 1998b).

Let us now turn to the supposedly selective behaviour of rioters: it is maintained that rioting is far from indiscriminate and that in selecting targets for attack rioters reveal their grievances (Rainwater, 1967; Dynes and Quarantelli, 1968; Quarantelli and Dynes, 1968; Reicher, 1984). Impressionistically, it seems that buildings are selectively fire-bombed and/or looted because of their specific associations or general symbolic significance. However, Berk and Aldrich's (1972) systematic research on patterns of looting during the American ghetto riots suggests an explanation both more prosaic and plausible, for they discovered that the most significant predictor of looting is the value of the goods stolen. Keith (1993) suggests that the 1981 riots consisted of several stages that involved different participants with divergent motives and engaged in different actions.

As a purely explanatory theory of why riots occur when and where they do, the notion that they are expressions of common grievances – the ballot box of the poor (Bachrach and Baratz, 1970) – is deeply flawed. It is either untrue or untestable, but perhaps this is to apply inappropriate evaluative criteria. The aim of analysts might not be to explain, but to excuse and justify. Many social scientists explicitly eschew any pretensions to value-neutrality, arguing that analysis should be the servant of moral and political causes. Taylor identifies three 'theories' of riot voiced by academics, journalists, politicians and officials alike that correspond to radical, liberal and conservative ideologies (Taylor, 1984; see also Grimshaw and Bowen, 1968). Conservatives favour the view that rioting is no more than opportunistic criminality. On the other hand, the insistence that rioting is the expression of unresolved grievances is a reflection of radical and liberal ideology. The selectivity with which this explanation is invoked to excuse and justify only 'politically correct' rioting is a further indication that such theorising is ideologically driven (Waddington, P.A.J., 1991, 2000; see also Ingleton, 1996). From this perspective, the notion that riots are expressions of common grievances serves an obvious ideological purpose: it transforms rioters from perpetrators to victims.

This analysis of the ideological basis of riot explanations draws attention to a crucial feature of riots – that is, that they are highly contestable and often contest events. What is contested is the moral status of the various parties.

Were the riots justified eruptions of anger at injustice and oppression, or mindless hooliganism? Did police heroically defend law and order, or did they engage in an orgy of indiscriminate brutality? Inquiries such as those undertaken by the Kerner Commission (Kerner, 1968) and Lord Scarman (Scarman, 1981) are not exercises in dispassionate analysis. Their function is political, it is *authoritatively* to *adjudicate* on contending alternative accounts that are brought to their attention (Platt, 1971). When no such authoritative adjudication takes place, rival accounts are still contested, possibly with the assistance of 'independent' inquiries (Dummett, 1980; McCabe *et al.*, 1988), which are, in fact, not at all independent since they are established by one party to the dispute and rarely hear official evidence (Waddington, P.A.J., 1986). Almost inevitably, the immediate aftermath of a riot will be accompanied by news reportage, analysis and speculation. However the post-riot inquiry is conducted, *all* parties have an equally political purpose – to legitimate *their* violence and delegitimate the violence of others (Turner, 1969; Ball, 1976).

It is in the post-riot contesting of rival accounts that the political reality of the riot is constructed with equally political consequences (Keith, 1993). For example, the authoritative version of the 1981 riots laid blame unequivocally upon social deprivation and discrimination, together with police racism and heavy-handedness. As a direct result, changes were introduced into police training, the introduction of local consultation arrangements and 'lay visitors' to police stations. These reforms are, of course, modest compared to the political consequences of outbreaks of disorder elsewhere, for example the student riots in France in May 1968 (see Hanley and Kerr, 1989; Tarrow, 1993, 1989). However, without the catalyst of the inner-city riots, it is unlikely that even such modest reforms would have been introduced.

Might is *not* right when it comes to the suppression of rioting. The police may 'win the battle' but lose the war if their actions are widely perceived as excessive. Whether or not rioters were actually motivated by a sense of injustice, if they can be portrayed in this light after the event, then it is *they* who become the victims. This illuminates the crucially important fact, not only for public order policing but policing *per se*, that during a riot the police confront not an enemy, but fellow citizens.

Riot control: militarisation

The distinction between an 'enemy' and 'fellow citizens' seems to have been one of the considerations that motivated the establishment of a professional police force in the early nineteenth century. When the Yeomanry charged the unlawful gathering at St Peter's Field near Manchester in 1819, casualties were not enormous. At 'Peterloo', 11 people died and dozens more were injured, but it could hardly be described as a slaughter when compared, for example, to the Gordon riots of 1780 when civilian casualties exceeded 400 (Critchley, 1970; Palmer, 1988). What shocked public opinion seems to have been the fact that fellow citizens were treated like an enemy and were hacked down indiscriminately. Indeed, it is a paradox that, as the capacity for the state effectively to suppress dissent by overwhelming military might has increased, so the military has progressively disengaged from a domestic public-order role. In modern liberal democracies military involvement is typically restricted to states of emergency, or dealing with strictly delineated situations. For example, in Britain the intervention of the SAS is restricted to terrorist incidents.

The distinction between enemies and citizens (even if they happen to be heinous criminals) can be glimpsed in the difference between contemporary military and police tactics. Military tactics are broadly to create a 'field of fire' designed to eliminate the enemy. Military weapons and munitions reflect that purpose: from battlefield nuclear weapons to the assault rifle, the imperative is to maximise the 'body count'. Police, by contrast, do not create a field of fire, even when confronting armed adversaries. Fire is returned at a specific target who is presenting an immediate threat to life (Waddington, P.A.J., 1991). Although both police officers and soldiers may, in certain circumstances, kill their adversaries, what distinguishes police action from that of the military is the discrimination with which police use force. The circumstances that justify its use are specific: a citizen can only be killed when *necessary;* an enemy can be killed when *possible.* The necessity principle also applies to the *amount* of force that is used: it must be proportionate to the gravity of the offence (Harlow, 1974; Ashworth, 1975) and cease once the adversary has been subdued (Waddington, P.A.J., 1990). These principles extend to *any* use of force, not just lethal force (Waddington, P.A.J., 1991). When the military acts in aid of the civil power, as it has done in Northern Ireland for over a quarter of a century, soldiers find themselves constrained by rules that reflect their 'policing' role. Unlike wartime, soldiers are instructed only to fire single shots from automatic weapons (Everlegh, 1979; Rowe, 1985; Whelan, 1985; Babington, 1990).

Not all policing systems maintain this clear distinction between the police and the military, and the blurring of this line tends to be indicative of a fundamentally different relationship between the state and the population in these countries. A good example of this was to be found throughout the British Empire where colonial police forces shared many of the characteristics of an 'army of occupation' (Anderson and Killingray, 1991, 1992). This was to be seen in their deployment, weaponry and use of force. Colonial forces were typically housed in barracks from which they patrolled the territory for which they were responsible as a squad and for the purpose of 'showing the flag'. Weaponry was typically military, sometimes including artillery. When it came to the use of force, colonial police suffered few of the restraints that were imposed on their metropolitan counterparts. The exemplary destruction of villages so as to compel the compliance of local chiefs was just one example of the non-specific use to which force was put (Ahire, 1991). Of course (and this is crucial), colonial police were not policing citizens: their task was to suppress subject populations. Until the recent demise of apartheid, the South African Police (SAP) performed much the same role with regard to the non-white population – a process of 'internal colonialism' (Brewer, 1994). The militarism of the SAP was displayed by the assault rifles individual officers carried, the general purpose machine guns mounted on their armoured personnel carriers, and officers' familiarity with such weapons of war as mortars (Cawthra, 1993).

It follows from the distinction between the police and the military that any blurring of that distinction represents a threat to the general public. This is precisely what critics claim has occurred in recent years in public order policing in Britain. They argue that public order policing has become noticeably *paramilitary* (or, perhaps more accurately, militarised (Hills, 1995). Although the argument seems to concern deployments, weaponry and tactics, it is actually about citizenship. This is clearest in Northam's account (1988), for despite its other manifold deficiencies (Waddington, P.A.J., 1991) he clearly expresses the genuine fear that adoption of a colonial style of public order policing reflects a view of the public as a rebellious subject population, *not* citizens. Jefferson, too, concluding his protracted debate with me (Jefferson, 1993), correctly identifies the crucial issue as being whether recent changes in British public order policing are symptomatic of the declining health of democracy. Democracy rests upon the uncoerced consent of citizens. If a significant proportion of those citizens need to be coerced, then is democracy failing?

Genuine though these fears undoubtedly are, they rest on a set of false assumptions and confuse superficial appearance with underlying realities. The first false assumption is that democracy rests on the uncoerced compliance of virtually *all* its citizens. As Reiner (1992) has remarked, if there was this measure of consent, there would be little need for a police force at all. The second false assumption is that the acquisition of riot-control equipment and training in its use are inimical to democracy. If that were true, virtually every other liberal democracy would need to be expelled from the democratic club. The CRS (Companies Républicaines de Sécurité) may not be the most acceptable face of France, but this specialist riot police does not render France undemocratic. The third false assumption is that which equates the possession of riot-control equipment with suppression of the population. Such an assumption relies upon an unstated belief in technological determinism: if police possess certain weapons, they will feel compelled to use them; and they will use them in the most aggressive manner possible. Not only is this a crude equation, but the truth may point in the opposite direction: the acquisition of paramilitary paraphernalia may actually serve the purpose of restraint.

What confuses the debate are the different meanings that attach to the term 'paramilitary'. At one level the British police have undoubtedly become militarised; indeed militarisation is more profound than many critics seem to appreciate. It is the overt appearance of riot police – equipped with visored helmets, flame-retardant overalls, and carrying shields – to which critics point. However, beneath that appearance lies the growth of a military style of command, with commanding officers arranged in 'gold', 'silver' and 'bronze' tiers, and a division of responsibility between 'slow time' and 'fast time' decision making. (For details, see Waddington, P.A.J., 1991.) Major pre-planned public order operations are now accompanied by 'strategy meetings' (Waddington, P.A.J., 1994) and extensive contingency planning has been developed for dealing with spontaneous disorder. In London, the Metropolitan Police have installed a computerised Special Operations Control Room from which major public-order operations can be controlled. It is these largely invisible developments that have brought about the greatest changes in the policing of public order. No longer are officers deployed as a collection of individuals acting more or less at their own discretion; police now act as squads under superior command and control (Waddington, P.A.J., 1987). However, this militarisation does not mean that citizenship is denied; indeed these developments are more conducive to ensuring restraint (Waddington, P.A.J., 1987, 1993a). First, centrally co-ordinated strategy and tactics are able to minimise the likelihood of police taking *ad hoc* self-defeating actions such as that which occurred at Red Lion Square when different groups of officers pushed the crowd from opposite directions, causing panic and anger (Scarman, 1975). Secondly, officers acting as members of a disciplined body under the direct supervision of senior officers are less likely to succumb to acts of individual indiscipline. Thirdly, senior officers are more accountable for the actions of those whom they command when they have the means of commanding subordinates.

The argument that the recent militarisation of the British police is *more* consistent with the restraint normally reserved for citizens can paradoxically be made even more strongly with respect to weaponry and tactics. As responsibility for suppressing disorder gradually shifted from the military to the police throughout the nineteenth and early twentieth century, so the police inherited some military tactics. The most obvious of these is the baton charge, which is the civil equivalent of the military tactic of routing an enemy (Palmer, 1988). Despite its dubious legality (Waddington, P.A.J., 1991), such indiscriminate use of force to disperse an unruly crowd has compelling tactical appeal. The crowd is scattered, losing its coherence, and officers are not detained by the need to arrest large numbers of individuals. However, the arbitrariness with which force is distributed among members of the crowd and the encouragement the baton charge gives to indiscipline on the part of individual officers (Gregory, 1987; Jefferson, 1990) make it unsuitable in a liberal democracy. For example, the picture of a woman shielding her head against the imminent blow from the truncheon of a mounted police officer during the miners' strike did much to portray picketing miners as 'victims'. The alternative of using CS irritants and water cannon to apply a mildly noxious stimulus to everyone in a crowd is more consistent with the tenets of 'minimum force' (Waddington, P.A.J., 1991), despite its escalatory and military associations.

It is even more paradoxical that the most criticised public-order weapon – the plastic baton round (PBR), colloquially known as the 'plastic bullet' – is even more consistent with minimum force criteria. Unlike CS irritant and

water cannon, the PBR is not indiscriminate, but is used selectively to inca-
pacitate specific individuals against whom that measure of force can be
justified. For example, someone about to throw a petrol bomb could be inca-
pacitated by a blow from a PBR without exposing officers (or other members
of a crowd) to the danger of close-quarter combat. Criticism of the PBR has
focused upon the number of people (especially children) killed during the
'troubles' in Northern Ireland (Rosenhead, 1981, 1985; Northam, 1986).
However, even campaigners concede that between 1970 and 1984 fatalities
occurred in less than one in 4,000 firings (Curtis, 1987). More recently, the
RUC and police forces on the mainland have acquired more accurate
launchers that are less likely to inflict injury by mistake. Moreover, the
European Commission of Human Rights concluded, in a case concerning
the death of a 13-year-old boy, that 'the weapon is less dangerous than
alleged' (see Brittan, 1985).

Indeed, the history of the PBR illustrates quite nicely the pressures to act
with discriminate and proportionate force towards citizens. The origins of
the PBR lie in a weapon used by the colonial police in Hong Kong. This consisted of a piece of hard wood fired so as to ricochet off the ground and
strike the lower limbs of rioters. When the 'troubles' broke out in Northern
Ireland, the British Army decided to adopt this weapon, but felt it necessary
to adapt it to conditions in Northern Ireland. The Hong Kong hardwood
variant was found sometimes to fracture on impact with the ground, causing
'*unacceptable injuries*' to rioters from the shards of wood that struck them. So
was born the *rubber* baton round (PBR). This, too, was intended to be ricocheted off the ground and to strike the lower limbs of rioters. The problem
was that it struck people indiscriminately and resulted in three deaths that
were also regarded as 'unacceptable'. What appears to have made the rubber
variant unacceptable was *not* the fatality rate, since only one fatality was
caused for every 18,000 rounds fired (Curtis, 1987). It was that by the nature
of the weapon, each fatality was almost bound to occur indiscriminately.
Further modification led to the PBR that was designed to be fired directly
and selectively at individual targets. Ironically, the fatality rate of the PBR is
four-and-a-half times greater than that of its rubber predecessor. Yet, it
appears to be more acceptable, since injuries (even if fatal) can be justified
in terms of the specific behaviour of a particular person. It is also instructive
to consider developments of the weapon that were *not* proceeded with. In
the early 1980s the then nationalised company, the Royal Ordnance,
designed a replacement baton round. Shaped like a tadpole, with a bulbous
head and slender tail, it was far more accurate than the slab of plastic it was
designed to replace. However, government was concerned that if the round
ricocheted off a hard surface it might strike rioters tail first, causing potentially serious injury. This, quite remote, likelihood of causing injury to those
whose actions did not justify it, was sufficient to deter government from
authorising its use. Despite its reputation, what the history of the PBR
reveals is that the more rioters are regarded as citizens, the more careful the
state is in using force against them. What was 'acceptable' when inflicted

indiscriminately upon the colonial Hong Kong Chinese is 'unacceptable' when applied to dissident residents of Northern Ireland. Equally, the trepidation with which police on the mainland of Britain regard the use of this weapon (Waddington, P.A.J., 1991) reflects the continued distinction that is drawn between Ireland and the mainland.

Public order

So far, I have concentrated exclusively upon the suppression of disorder, but outbreaks of disorder are comparatively rare. In London alone, there are three major protest demonstrations each week, of which only a tiny minority result in any disorder at all. Yet the police still achieve remarkably extensive control over the conduct of virtually all these demonstrations. They do so not by the threat of law or force, but by guile. During negotiations with protest organisers that typically precede any demonstration, the police subtly employ advice and guidance to steer the conduct of the protest in a direction compatible with police aims. By the clever orchestration of traffic flows around demonstrators, they control their movement while appearing to safeguard protesters from inconsiderate motorists. Even when the law is invoked to restrict a demonstration, steps are taken to balance legal coercion with accommodation of the democratic rights of demonstrators (Waddington, P.A.J., 1994; see also della Porta and Reiter, 1998).

By acting in this way, contemporary police officers continue traditions of policing built up over a century. Compared to the late nineteenth century, civil disorder has declined enormously in Britain, despite an upturn during the past two decades (Dunning *et al.*, 1987). This reduction in disorder and violence has been most apparent in that cauldron of class conflict – strikes. According to Geary (1985), the twentieth century has witnessed the transformation of picketing from 'stoning and shooting' to 'pushing and shoving', complemented by a progressively less coercive police response. Wider institutional changes appeared to lie behind this mutual agreement to 'cool it' on the picket-line, for, as the Labour Movement grew in constitutional influence, neither the trade unions nor the authorities had any vested interest in being associated with violence. For the trade unions, picket-line violence threatened to damage the Labour Party's appeal to the electorate, whilst the authorities sought to avoid any suggestion that they were violently suppressing legitimate union grievances. Thus, violent class conflict was largely avoided by the *incorporation* of the organised working class into the political system.

When senior police officers seek to avoid confronting political demonstrators by using guile in preference to force or law, they are responding to much the same institutional pressures. They are sensitive to accusations of police provocation and conscious that disorder will lead to inquiries that might threaten careers (Waddington, P.A.J., 1993b). Equally, protest organisers appear tacitly to accept the institutional definition of peaceful protest, sometimes colluding with the police to exclude or constrain 'extremists' who might threaten to breach those institutional boundaries.

Thus, while police, protesters and pickets play their respective crucial roles in the maintenance of orderly dissent, they do so within an institutional structure and political culture that not only facilitate it, but also marginalise the role of law. For although the police in Britain have never lacked ample legal powers to suppress protest and disorder, they have remained largely unused (Waddington, P.A.J., 1994). While institutional restraints remain effective, law is largely unnecessary. If those institutional restraints crumble, then control is likely to be enforced through law and physical coercion.

Changes in economic institutions have resulted in the institutional structures of class relations crumbling. Since the 1960s strikes have been increasingly regarded as a major cause of Britain's relative industrial decline. The collapse of traditional 'smoke stack' industries has undermined trade union power and their virtual exclusion from a position of influence over government during the Thatcher administration marginalised them even further. More and more unable to succeed by appealing to labour solidarity and exerting parliamentary pressure, unions (finding themselves with little to lose) have reverted to picketing methods designed forcibly to close premises. This, of course, has brought them into overt confrontation with the police (Scraton, 1985).

Meanwhile, disadvantaged and deprived sections of the population increasingly find themselves excluded from institutions rooted in class relations that are ill-suited to their needs and unresponsive to their problems. For a decade prior to the eruption of the inner-city riots of the early 1980s, black groups had been complaining about police harassment and heavy-handedness – complaints which went unheeded (Lea and Young, 1982). New issues – feminism, environmentalism, animal rights – find little expression within these established institutional structures. Accordingly, excluded groups and those pursuing issues unrelated to employment relations have little incentive to 'play by the rules'.

Furthermore, as protests against live animal exports illustrate, institutional power is also shifting in ways that make incorporation into the institutions of the nation-state increasingly irrelevant. Even when animal rights protesters successfully convince government ministers of the rectitude of their cause, this is to no avail if power rests in the European Union: Environmentalists who persuade their own government to eliminate 'acid rain' win a pyrrhic victory if sulphurous clouds originate from beyond national boundaries. In an increasingly global economy, national political institutions are inevitably marginalised.

This suggests that protest is unlikely to remain within the 'rules' of a 'game' that is increasingly ill-suited to the needs of participants. Therefore, police strategies based upon the existence and maintenance of those rules will become redundant. As these institutions decay, so the police will become more vulnerable to external pressures and unable to deflect demands for vigorous enforcement by appeals to consensual values of 'democracy'. The principal danger in the Criminal Justice and Public Order Act 1994 is that, by blurring the distinction between the private and the public, private interests will be able to commandeer police resources by demanding that obviously illegal protests be suppressed.

Nor should it be assumed that confrontation will necessarily be between the public police and new generations of protesters. The police itself is not immune to institutional change and may be marginalised as the state pulls back from its involvement in society and the economy. The private security industry may increasingly recognise a 'market opportunity' in protecting vested interests from the activities of protesters. Increasingly cash-strapped police forces find it difficult to maintain large and costly public order operations. In 1972 the Chief Constable of Birmingham ordered the closure of Saltley coke works rather than risk continued confrontation and possible escalation. Thus, mass picketing succeeded and the miners won a crucial victory. Today his successors might decide that they, too, must allow protesters to succeed because the police lack sufficient resources to prevent it. However, it would be naively optimistic to assume that private interests will comply as meekly as did the National Coal Board at Saltley. Under the commercial pressure of global competition, companies may very well conclude that if the public police are unable to protect them, they must protect themselves. Private detective agencies played a long and ignoble role in labour conflicts in the United States (Weiss, 1986, 1987) and there is no reason in principle to suppose that they could not fulfil an equivalent role in Britain. Indeed, private security companies have already played a leading role in some of the protests by environmentalists against new roads and similar developments (Vidal, 1996b, 1996a).

Conclusion

Riot-control tactics have never been simply a matter of rational efficiency, but have always been suffused with *political* considerations. The Yeomanry at 'Peterloo' achieved their aim: the radical rabble-rouser, Henry Hunt, did not deliver his speech and the unlawful assembly was dispersed. It was the political ramifications of their actions that snatched defeat from the jaws of victory. Peel's 'New Police' were lightly and covertly armed, not because London was a tranquil city – on the contrary, London could be a violent and disorderly place, and policing was a dangerous occupation. The 'New Police' did not carry the sabres and pistols that some of their contemporaries, such as the famous Bow Street Runners, found indispensable. The 'New Police' carried only a truncheon and rattle, secreted in the tails of their frock coat, as an explicitly political gesture. Peel determined that his new force should not appear as militaristic. They were to be the antithesis of the continental gendarmeries, symbolising by their appearance and vulnerability a relationship between state and citizen that was non-oppressive. Contemporary public order policing continues that tradition, for the appearance of officers and the weapons they use continue to be fraught with political overtones. Police dogs are not used in riot control, not because they might be unsuitable (after all, other police forces throughout the world have found them very suited to the task), but because they evoke connotations that policymakers would rather avoid. Used against black rioters, the sight of dogs might evoke in the minds of spectators images of the suppression of civil-rights protests in the American South. Visored helmets, shields and flame-retardant overalls are essential protective equipment that police forces throughout the world have adopted for the purposes of riot control, but they also symbolise a relationship between police and public that is the antithesis of the 'Dixon of Dock Green' myth.

Public order policing is irreducibly political; it is a highly visible representation of the relationship between state and citizen. Its future is inextricably intertwined with how the British state develops.

Notes

1 Indeed, it is a moot point whether such a use of violence is necessarily illegal, since any citizen may use 'reasonable force' in self-defence or to prevent the commission of a crime; protesters who genuinely believe that the police are acting unlawfully could lawfully use force to resist unlawful police action.

References

Ahire, P.T. (1991) *Imperial Policing: The Emergence and Role of the Police in Colonial Nigeria 1860–1960. New Directions in Criminology*. Milton Keynes: Open University Press.

Allen, R.F., and Adair, C.H. (1969) *Violence and Riots in Urban America*. Worthington, OH: Charles A. Jones.

Anderson, D.M., and Killingray, D. (eds) (1991) *Policing the Empire: Government, Authority and Control, 1830–1940*. Manchester: Manchester University Press.

Anderson, D.M. and Killingray, D. (eds) (1992) *Policing and Decolonisation: Politics, Nationalism and the Police, 1917–65*. Manchester: Manchester University Press.

Arnold, W.J. and Levine, D. (eds) (1970) *Nebraska Symposium on Motivation*. Vol. 17. Lincoln, NB: University of Nebraska.

Ashworth, A.J. (1975) 'Self-Defence and the Right to Life', *Cambridge Law Journal* 34 (2), November, 282–307.

Babington, A. (1990) *Military Intervention in Britain. From the Gordon Riots to the Gibraltar Incident*. London: Routledge.

Bachrach, P. and Baratz, M.S. (1970) *Power and Poverty: Theory and Practice*. Oxford: Oxford University Press.

Ball, T. (1976) 'Power, Causation and Explanation', *Polity*, 8 (Winter), 189–214.

Ball-Rokeach, S.J. (1972) 'The Legitimation of Violence' in Short and Wolfgang (1972) 100–11.

Benyon, J. (ed.) (1984) *Scarman and After*. Oxford: Pergamon.

Benyon, J. (1987) 'Interpretations of Civil Disorder' in Benyon and Solomos (1987) 23–41.

Benyon, J. and Solomos, J. (eds) (1987) *The Roots of Urban Unrest*. Oxford: Pergamon, 181–95.

Berk, R.A. (1972) 'The Controversy Surrounding Analyses of Collective Violence: Some Methodological Notes' in Short and Wolfgang (1972), 112–18.

Berk, R., and Aldrich, H. (1972) 'Patterns of Vandalism During Civil Disorder as an Indicator of Selection of Targets', *American Sociological Review*, 37, 533–47.

Bittner, E. (1990) *Aspects of Police Work*. Boston: Northeastern University Press.

Brewer, J.D. (1994) *Black and Blue: Policing in South Africa*. Oxford: Clarendon.

Brittan, T.R.H.L., MP (1985) Letter to Rt. Hon. David Owen, MP. House of Commons, 25 June.

Cawthra, G. (1993) *Policing South Africa*. London: Zed Books.

Choongh, S. (1997) *Policing as Social Discipline. Clarendon Studies in Criminology*. Oxford: Clarendon.

Cowell, D., Jones, T. and Young, J. (eds) (1982) *Policing the Riots*. London: Junction Books.

Critchley, T. (1970) *The Conquest of Violence*. London: Constable.

Currie, E. and Skolnick, J.H. (1972) 'A Critical Note on Conceptions of Collective Behaviour' in Short and Wolfgang (1972) 61–71.

Curtis, L. (1987) *They Shoot Children*. London: Information on Ireland.

Davies, J.C. (1962) 'Toward a Theory of Revolution', *American Sociological Review*, 27, 5–18.

Davies, J.C. (1969) 'The J-Curve of Rising and Declining Satisfactions as a Cause of Some Great Revolutions and a Contained Rebellion' in National Commission on the Causes and Prevention of Violence (1969).

Dear, G.J. (1986) *Report of the Chief Constable West Midlands Police, Handsworth/Lozells – September 1985*. Birmingham, West Midlands: West Midlands Police.

della Porta, D. and Reiter, H. (eds) (1998) *Policing Protest: The Control of Mass Demonstrations in Western Democracies. Social Movements, Protest, and Contention: Volume 6*. Minneapolis: University of Minnesota Press.

Dummett, M. (1980) *Southall 23 April 1979*. London: National Council for Civil Liberties.

Dunning, E., Murphy, P., Newburn, T., and Waddington, I. (1987) 'Violent Disorders in Twentieth Century Britain' in Gaskell, and Benewick (1987), 19–75.

Dynes, R. and Quarantelli, E.L. (1968) 'What Looting in Civil Disturbances Really Means', *Transaction*, May, 9–14.

Everlegh, R. (1979) *Peacekeeping in a Democratic Society*. London: Hurst.

Fine, B. and Millar, R. (eds) (1985) *Policing the Miners' Strike*. London: Lawrence and Wishart.

Fogelson, R.M. (1970) 'Violence and Grievances: Reflections of the 1960s Riots', *Journal of Social Issues*, 26, 141–63.

Fogelson, R.M. (1971) *Violence as Protest*. Garden City, NY: Doubleday.

Gaskell, G. and Benewick, R. (eds) (1987) *The Crowd in Contemporary Britain*. London: Sage.

Geary, R. (1985) *Policing Industrial Disputes: 1893 to 1985*. Cambridge: Cambridge University Press.

Gifford, L. (1986) *Report of the Independent Inquiry into Disturbances of October 1985 at the Broadwater Farm Estate, Tottenham*. London: The Broadwater Farm Inquiry.

Gregory, F.E.C. (1987) *Policing the Democratic State: How Much Force? Conflict Studies: 194*. London: Institute for the Study of Conflict.

Grimshaw, A.D., and Bowen, D.R. (1968) 'Three Views of Urban Violence: Civil Disturbance, Racial Revolt, Class Assault' in Masotti and Bowen (1968).

Gurr, T.R. (1969) 'A Comparative Study of Civil Strife' in National Commission on the Causes and Prevention of Violence (1969), 544–99.

Hanley, D. and Kerr, P. (eds) (1989) *May '68: Coming of Age*. London: Macmillan.

Harlow, C. (1974) 'Self-Defence: Public Right or Private Privilege?', *Criminal Law Review*, 528–38.

Hills, A. (1995) 'Militant tendencies', *British Journal of Criminology*, 35 (3), Summer, 450–8.

Ingleton, R. (1996) *Arming the British Police: the Great Debate*. London: Frank Cass.

Jefferson, T. (1990) *The Case Against Paramilitary Policing*. Milton Keynes: Open University.

Jefferson, T. (1993) 'Pondering Paramilitarism', *British Journal of Criminology* 33 (3), 374–81.

Joshua, H., Wallace, T. with the assistance of Booth, H. (1983) *To Ride the Storm*. London: Heinemann.

Keith, M. (1993) *Race, Riots and Policing: Lore and Disorder in a Multi-Racist Society*. London: UCL Press.

Kerner, O. (1968) *The Report of the National Advisory Commission on Civil Disorders*. Washington, DC: US Government Printing Office.

Kettle, M. and Hodges, L. (1982) *Uprising*. London: Pan.

Lea, J. and Young, J. (1982) 'The Riots in Britain 1981: Urban Violence and Political Marginalisation' in Cowell *et al.* (1982), 5–20.

Le Bon, G. (1895) *The Crowd*. Revised English translation 1995. With a new introduction by Robert A. Nye. New Brunswick: Viking.

Masotti, L.H. and Bowen, D.R. (eds) (1968) *Civil Violence in the Urban Community*. Beverly Hills: Sage.

McCabe, S., Wallington, P., with Alderson, J., Gostin, L. and Mason, C. (1988) *The Police, Public Order and Civil Liberties: Legacies of the Miners' Strike*. London: Routledge.

McPhail, C. (1971) 'Civil Disorder Participation', *American Sociological Review*, 36, 1058–72.

McPhail, C. (1991) *The Myth of the Madding Crowd*. Hawthorne, NY: Aldine de Gruyter.

McPhail, C. and Miller, D.L. (1973) 'The Assembling Process: a Theoretical and Empirical Examination', *American Sociological Review*, 38, 721–35.

National Commission on the Causes and Prevention of Violence (ed.) (1969) *Violence in America*. New York: Signet.

Northam, G. (1986) 'Plastic Bullets – A Shot in the Dark which Could Prove Fatal', the *Listener*, 17 July.

Northam, G. (1988) *Shooting in the Dark*. London: Faber and Faber.

Palmer, S.H. (1988) *Police and Protest in England and Ireland, 1780–1850*. Cambridge: Cambridge University Press.

Panayi, P. (1993a) 'Anti-Immigrant Riots in Nineteenth- and Twentieth-Century Britain' in Panayi (1993b), 1–25.

Panayi, P. (ed.) (1993b) *Racial Violence in Britain, 1840–1950*. Leicester: Leicester University Press.

Platt, A. (ed.) (1971) *The Politics of Riot Commissions, 1917–1970*. New York: Macmillan.

Quarantelli, E.L. and Dynes, R. (1968) 'Looting in Civil Disorder: An Index of Social Change' in Masotti and Bowen (1968).

Rainwater, L. (1967) 'Open Letter on White Justice and the Riots', *Transaction*, September.

Reicher, S.D. (1984) 'The St. Paul's Riot: An Explanation of the Limits of Crowd Action in Terms of a Social Identity Model', *European Journal of Social Psychology*, 14, 1–21.

Reiner, R. (1992) *Politics of the Police*. 2nd ed. London: Wheatsheaf.

Rosenhead, J. (1981) 'The Technology of Riot Control', *New Scientist*, 91, 210.

Rosenhead, J. (1985) 'Plastic Bullets – A Reasonable Force?', *New Scientist*, 17 October, 26–7.

Rowe, P.J. (1985) 'Keeping the Peace: Lethal Weapons, the Soldier and the Law' in Rowe and Whelan (1985), 197–215.

Rowe, R. and Whelan, C.J. (eds) (1985) *Military Intervention in Democratic Societies*. London: Croom Helm.

Scarman, RH the L. (1975) *The Red Lion Square Disorders of 15 June 1974*. London: HMSO.

Scarman, RH the L. (1981) *The Brixton Disorders 10–12 April 1981: Report of an Inquiry by the Rt. Hon. The Lord Scarman, OBE* Cmnd 8427 ed. London: HMSO.

Scraton, P. (1985) 'From Saltley Gates to Orgreave: A History of the Policing of Recent Industrial Disputes' in Fine and Millar (1985), 145–60.

Shearing, C.D. and Stenning, P.C. (eds) (1987) *Private Policing. Sage Criminal Justice System Annuals. Volume 23*. Newbury Park, CA: Sage.

Short, J.F., Jnr. and Wolfgang, M.E. (eds) (1972) *Collective Violence*. Chicago: Aldine-Atherton.

Silverman, J. (1986) *Independent Inquiry into the Handsworth Disturbances, September 1985*. Birmingham: City of Birmingham District Council.

Skolnick, J.H. (1969) *The Politics of Protest: A Task Force Report to the National Commission on the Causes and Prevention of Violence*. New York: Simon and Schuster.

Smelser, N.J. (1962) *Theory of Collective Behaviour*. London: Routledge and Kegan Paul.

Smelser, N.J. (1972) 'Two critics in search of a bias: a response to Currie and Skolnick' in Short and Wolfgang (1972), 73–81.

Sunday Times Insight Team (1985) *Strike*. London: Coronet.

Tarrow, S. (1989) *Democracy and Disorder: Protest Politics in Italy, 1965–1975*. Oxford: Oxford University Press.

Tarrow, S. (1993) 'Social Protest and Policy Reform – May 1968 and the Loi d'Orientation in France', *Comparative Political Studies*, 25 (4), 579–607.

Taylor, S. (1984) 'The Scarman Report and Explanations of Riots' in Benyon (1984), 20–35.

Thurlow, R. (1987) *Fascism in Britain: A History, 1918–1985*. Oxford: Blackwell.

Turner, R.H. (1969) 'The Public Perception of Protest', *American Sociological Review*, 32, 815–31.

Vidal, J. (1996a) 'The Bypass of Justice', *Guardian*, 9 April, 13.

Vidal, J. (1996b) 'In the Forest, in the Dark', *Guardian*, 25 January, 2–3.

Waddington, D. (1992) *Contemporary Issues in Public Disorder*. London: Routledge.

Waddington, D. (1998) 'Waddington versus Waddington: Public Order Theory on Trial', *Theoretical Criminology*, 2 (3), 373–94.

Waddington, D., Jones, K. and Critcher, C. (1987) 'Flashpoints of Public Disorder' in Gaskell and Benewick (1987), 155–99.

Waddington, D., Jones, K. and Critcher, C. (1989) *Flashpoints: Studies in Public Disorder*. London: Routledge.

Waddington, P.A.J. (1986) 'It Depends What You Mean by "Independent"', *Police*, xix, 1 September, 32–4.

Waddington, P.A.J. (1987) 'Towards Paramilitarism? Dilemmas in Policing Civil Disorder', *British Journal of Criminology*, 27 (1), Winter, 37–46.

Waddington, P.A.J. (1990) '"Overkill" or "Minimum Force"?', *Criminal Law Review*, October, 695–707.

Waddington, P.A.J. (1991) *The Strong Arm of the Law.* Oxford: Clarendon.

Waddington, P.A.J. (1993a) 'The Case Against Paramilitary Policing Considered', *British Journal of Criminology*, 33 (3), October 14–16.

Waddington, P.A.J. (1993b) 'Dying in a Ditch: The Use of Police Powers in Public Order', *International Journal of Sociology*, 21 (4), 335–53.

Waddington, P.A.J. (1994) *Liberty and Order: Policing Public Order in a Capital City.* London: UCL Press.

Waddington, P.A.J. (1998) *Policing Citizens.* London: UCL.

Waddington, P.A.J. (1999) 'Orthodoxy and Advocacy in Criminology', *Theoretical Criminology*, 4 (1), 93–111.

Waddington, P.A.J. and Braddock, Q. (1991) '"Guardians" or "Bullies"?: Perceptions of the Police amongst Adolescent Black, White and Asian boys', *Policing and Society*, 2, 31–45.

Weiss, R.P. (1986) 'Private Detective Agencies and Labour Discipline in the United States, 1855–1946', *Historical Journal*, 29 (1), 87–107.

Weiss, R.P. (1987) 'From 'Slugging Detective' to 'Labor Relations': Policing Labour at Ford, 1930–1947' in Shearing and Stenning (1987), 110–30.

Whelan, C.J. (1985) 'Military Intervention in Democratic Societies: The Role of Law' in Rowe and Whelan (1985).

Zimbardo, P.G. (1970) 'The Human Choice: Individuation, Reason and Order versus Deindividuation, Impulse and Chaos' in Arnold and Levine (1970), 237–307.

Chapter 11

Policing force: rules, hierarchies and consequences

IAN McKENZIE

It is the purpose of this chapter to examine two principal issues. First, the extent to which British police officers' concerns about firearms use *against them* is in itself a sufficient justification for a movement towards a more highly armed force; and second, the application of 'rules of engagement', including the application of hierarchies of force by the police. The chapter takes as its starting point the doctrine of minimum force and the evidence of use of firearms against the police. It is argued that there has been some 'over-egging of the pudding' in connection with claims that the police are with any regularity exposed to firearms turned against them. Calls for a fully armed police force may have been ill-informed. Furthermore, there is concern that the police may not be the appropriate body to decide whether arming is an option and that both the public and Parliament, which currently may be excluded from the debate, must participate in the decision-making process. In addition, the chapter will consider the extent to which the police are prepared, through both selection and training, for such a change. Finally, the nature and effectiveness of current police procedures for controlling those seeking to use force against the police and the reporting of such incidents by the police will be examined.

The doctrine of minimum force

Some writers have contended that, in the early days of organised policing in England, the strategy of minimum force was part of an 'engineering of consent' (Reiner, 1992: 61), an act of social architecture, producing a 'benign and dignified English police image' which was predicated upon a need to pacify the strength of opposition felt at the inception of Peel's 'New Police'.

Reiner argues that this engineered consent (involving dimensions in addition to the concept of 'minimum force') has never represented universal approval of police activity. He recognises that *at its best*, policing by consent is

> ... the wholehearted approval of the majority of the population who do not experience the coercive exercise to any significant extent, and the *de facto* acceptance of the legitimacy of the institution by those who do. (Reiner, 1992: 60)

However, there is a problem with this, albeit pragmatic, assessment of the situation. Societal approval of the minimum use of force is one thing, but it does not follow that the application of higher levels of 'deadly' force will receive approval, produce consensus, or even garner legitimacy.

There is a conflict between, on the one hand, a sociological view of consensus and, on the other, a more legalistic view, seeking 'proof' of such consent. This is particularly so when in order to apply an 'appropriate' level of force, the arming of police officers will irrevocably alter more than just the number of guns deployed by the police.

It may be useful here to draw a contrast between consensus based upon whole-hearted approval in the absence of debate, discussion and information, and the quasi-consensus achieved in the absence of those elements. The words 'whole-hearted approval' used in the manner of Reiner are, for example, the reverse of the 'informed consent' requirement attached to application of the 'valid waiver' clause forming part of the Miranda Warnings in the USA (*Miranda* v *Arizona*, 383 US 436, 1966). Although a suspect's right to remain silent and to have counsel present throughout the interrogation process is 'unfettered' (Robin, 1980: 150), individuals may remain unsupported by legal advice if they provide a 'valid waiver' of their Miranda rights. The notion of a valid waiver, in its turn, rests upon the concept of 'informed consent', such that, in general terms, a decision made (to give consent) must be based upon adequate information about the pros and cons of that decision.

Seen in that way, it is possible to argue that there is little in policing, including questions about the validity or otherwise of arming police officers, that is truly the subject of *informed* consent. Furthermore, it is possible to construe most aspects of the British people's consent to police activity more in terms of apathetic disinterest than as a decision based upon information and open debate.

However, in a Parliamentary democracy, individuals hand to their elected representatives responsibility for the gathering of information, such that they, the Parliamentarians, may make their decisions on the basis of such information and with the benefit of broad debate. To put it another way, constitutionally, decisions are made, on the basis of informed debate, by those elected as representatives of the people. It does not follow, however, that in handing to their elected representatives such decision-making capacity, the population *always* provides a valid waiver of its right to make a decision. Neither does it follow that any Parliamentary concern about a policing issue is either informed or even the subject of debate.

The principle of constabulary independence, established in a series of cases,[1] is important here. This may be coupled with the debate generated by the division in the Police Act 1964 between police 'policy' matters and police 'operations' (Lustgarten, 1986) and seen as (despite the existence of the Police and Magistrates' Courts Act 1994) continuing and substantial autonomous control by each chief officer of his or her force.

Case law suggests that a request made by a chief constable to move to a fully armed police force – i.e. for the Home Office to supply the arms – might, quite legitimately, take place in the absence of any, let alone 'whole-hearted', approval of the majority of the population. Furthermore, such an operational/policy decision could avoid attracting even Parliamentary debate, let alone support. The sole caveat upon such an occurrence would be that the chief officer in question would require backing, couched in terms of an improvement in efficiency, from Her Majesty's Inspectorate of Constabulary.

Arming an unarmed police

The question of a fully armed police force may not, however, rest upon the decisions of three individuals – a chief constable, an inspector of constabulary and the Home Secretary. In the very recent past there has been an augmentation – at least in London – of the availability of firearms to the police.

In the early 1990s a number of senior police officers made pronouncements about arming their officers or about the prospect of a fully armed force before too long. (See, for example, *Independent*, 18 May 1994; *London Evening Standard*, 17 May 1994; McMahon, 1994; Bennetto, 1994). These developments were made against a background of the alleged desire of a large number of officers to carry guns (Leppard, 1994). Claims were made about 'an increasing number of armed incidents' (Condon, 1994) and about officers facing 'Kalashnikovs, Armalites and Uzis, on a fairly regular basis'. (Bennetto, 1994).

Much of the argument was later revealed to be hyperbole when a poll of Police Federation members showed far from unanimous approval of such a proposition.[2] The results of that wide-ranging survey suggested that 79 per cent of the federated ranks rejected the notion of a routinely armed police, but 83 per cent did support an increase in the number of officers trained and issued with firearms (Police Federation of England and Wales, 1995). However, 34.4 per cent of Metropolitan Police officers were in favour of routine arming, and a further 20 per cent approved of the training of '... all officers, to be issued with guns as and when necessary'. In effect, this means that in excess of 50 per cent of Metropolitan Police officers supported a substantial shift in the status quo. Overall, the 1995 Federation survey suggested that 83 per cent of respondents supported the proposition that 'Firearms should not be issued to all police officers, but [that] more officers should receive appropriate training and be issued with firearms as and when necessary' (Bennetto, 1995). The principal interpretation of this survey is that there was overwhelming support for a slow, but inexorable movement, 'click-by-click' of the ratchet, towards a more fully armed police, though with the qualifier from many respondents of 'but I don't want to do it'!

Furthermore, research showed that:

> Although there is widespread concern about the criminal use of firearms, and the public perception, or at least the media portrayal, is of a relentless rise in the incidence of armed crime, it is salutary to state at the outset that the use of firearms in crime is comparatively rare in England and Wales. According to *Criminal Statistics* for 1992, the most recent year for which data are available about 0.2 per cent of recorded notifiable offences involve a firearm, and one third of these were cases of criminal damage, often trivial in nature, over 90 per cent of which were caused by air weapons.   (Morrison and O'Donnell, 1994: 1)

In their study of armed robberies in London, Morrison and O'Donnell found that:

- firearms were only discharged in 45 of 1,134 incidents (4 per cent);
- in 90 per cent of cases they were fired without causing physical injury;
- the shots fired were not always live rounds (36 per cent);
- in only 2.5 per cent of the cases studied did the weapons fired have a 'lethal potential';
- 60 per cent of robbers either carried a replica firearm or merely intimated that they were armed. (1994: 82, 86)

The authors further stated that:

> In the light of interviews with convicted robbers, it appeared that the proportion of real guns used was just over half the estimate based upon our study of police records. (p. 86)

Although the forcefully raised voices appear for the time being to have fallen silent, it is important to point out that when the day of a fully armed police force comes there may be certain consequences, unanticipated by those seeking such an outcome. Bayley (1977) suggests that 'as long as police [officers] are afraid of being shot they will favour pre-emptive action ...' but that whilst the police may be afraid of being shot, 'the citizens will be afraid of being shot by mistake'. The presence of guns, he writes,

> ... adds a real but incalculable amount of emotion to any police–citizen encounter ... The gun on the hip is a visible reminder that the police have other things to do, that non-enforcement activities are a distraction from main purposes. (p. 222)

Furthermore, he adds:

> ... [a] disarmed police [officer] will be better prepared to provide mediation not involving enforcement. (p. 223)

It may be significant here that although 80 per cent of police activity is associated with the non-enforcement, 'mediation' provision of 'social-role' police activity, much of that work is assigned to the category of 'rubbish' by police officers *of the Metropolitan Police* (PSI, 1983: 62, 64–6), officers of which force gave stronger approval to the idea of a fully armed police force than did their provincial colleagues (McMahon, 1994; Connett, 1994).[3]

The calls by the Police Federation for the routine arming of 'all officers in dangerous inner cities' (Leppard, 1994) would in London alone, Scotland Yard estimated, cost £17m (at 1994 rates). This may be a gross underestimate. Furthermore, the cost may be more than financial.

The selection and training of firearms officers

It has long been recognised that not all officers are suitable to become 'authorised shots'. Thus, following the Waldorf incident in 1983, (in which an innocent man was wrongly identified as an armed criminal and was severely injured when police officers opened fire on him) and at the recommendation of the ACPO Joint Standing Committee on Police Use of Firearms (ACPO, 1983), a degree of psychological evaluation was introduced into the selection of firearms officers (Recommendation 5.8 and 5.9).

The application of psychometric techniques to the selection of firearms officers is beset with difficulty. This is so mostly because of a lack of data or improper application of the test materials which as a consequence are unable to demonstrate a correlation between test scores and involvement in the inappropriate use of force. However, despite Geller and Scott's (1992) criticism that 'virtually none of the empirical research to date establishes a strong correlation between individual officer characteristics and the outcome of police civilian encounters', the authors do concede that the advantage of the use of such tests is that '... the most obviously maladjusted personalities will be screened out by written tests or by interviews with psychologists' (p. 287).

However, importantly, Geller and Scott suggest that:

> The best guide to future conduct seems to be, as it has long been, *past* conduct.
> (Geller and Scott, 1992: 287, emphasis in original)

and that there are various pointers in an officer's past conduct which can be used to assess a propensity to misuse force. These include:

- civilian complaints against the officer;
- rates of charges filed by an officer for resisting or assaulting the officer and rates of disorderly conduct charges filed by the officer against arrestees;
- officers' involvement in ... incidents resulting in injury ... and in-custody injury.

The major point of correlation between these past events and the occurrence of excessive use of force and of deadly force is probably that summarised by Fyfe (1989: 467) when he writes:

> While [intentionally excessive] police violence is egregious, it probably occurs far less frequently ... than does police violence emanating from simple incompetence. Such violence occurs when police lack the eloquence to persuade temporarily disturbed persons to give up their weapons, but shoot them instead. It occurs when, instead of pausing to consider and apply less drastic alternatives, officers blindly confront armed criminals in the midst of groups of innocent people. It occurs when officers called to quell noisy but non-violent disputes act in a way that provokes disputants to violence to which the police must respond in kind. In short it occurs when well meaning police officers lack – or fail to apply – the expertise required to resolve as bloodlessly as possible the problems their work requires them to confront.[4]

It is thus the case that any attempt to move towards an arming of 'all officers' even 'in dangerous inner cities' must address the potential problems of suitability. What, as Waddington (1994) asks, happens to those found to be unsuitable?

Furthermore, the problem of the alleged lack of expertise of some officers in the USA, must be seen against a background of police training in that country. The inability properly to respond to threats of force from drunken or mentally disturbed persons, the tendency to take precipitate action in circumstances when innocent others are placed at risk, or the provocation of disputants by an officer's own lack of interpersonal (or policing) skills, must be viewed against a backcloth of 'officer safety training'; training, which teaches a hierarchy (or continuum) of the use of force and which must in turn be placed against the needs of the police department to protect itself from litigation in the form of multimillion dollar claims seeking to allege negligence against the Police Department as a consequence of the inadequacy of its training.

The continuum of force

Although there is considerable variation in the content of recruit training within and between the American states (see McKenzie and Gallagher, 1989), it is a foolish police department/academy that does not teach to its rookies some variation of the hierarchy or continuum of force. By contrast, a request made to British police officers to define such an hierarchy, would until quite recently commonly have produced a look of incomprehension[5] in some places it may continue so to do.

However, it is possible that something like the continuum, discussed below, is taught to *some* police officers in the UK. For, as Midgley (1995: 6) puts it:

> There is also *believed to be* a 10 stage set of operational guidelines which advises on oral commands and 'violent stances' [that] the officer should take up before opening fire as a last resort, *but it is not publicised.* (Emphasis added)

The 'secrecy' of these guidelines will further be discussed below, but it should be noted that this is a typical example of the operations/policy dichotomy discussed above. The confidential nature of the guidelines is made even more strange when it is recognised that the continuum, if taught, applies only to firearms officers – that is, only to those expected, and perhaps who themselves expect because of their unique, 'specialist' position, to be involved in firefights (i.e. expect and are expected to use their expertise).

In the USA, although, of course, firearms carriage is universal, there is no expectation that the continuum serves as a model only to those involved in firefights. It applies to all officers, in all circumstances. It is foolish in the extreme to confine instruction in the continuum only to those deployed with firearms. Many of the dynamics are considered to be 'unarmed control tactics', an area of British police training which, not to put too fine a point on it, is sadly wanting.[6] Geller and Scott, for example, preface their discussion of the continuum with the following words:

> Entire books have been written about the 'force continuum' and unarmed control tactics ... It is clear, however, that a wide variety of verbal (both oral and written) communications skills and unarmed physical control tactics *must be a core part of any professional basic training for police.* (p.309, emphasis added)

To fail so to do opens the door to litigation, and the principal losers are the police and those who hold their purse strings.

The 'force continuum' is best summarised as consisting of a range of control tactics commencing from body language and oral communication, through weaponless physical control, to non-lethal weapons, and finally to lethal measures. Although there is some internal variation in the various texts, particularly with regard to the extent and detail with which the levels of force are defined, the core of each remains the same. It is that, starting from some point at which the application of force is non-existent, there is a step-by-step, incremental process which defines the behaviours which are appropriate for an officer to use, which are themselves based upon the behaviour of the actor or actors with whom the officer is dealing. The key element is that, for many police departments, an officer will be expected to articulate and describe the reason why he or she escalated from one level of force to the next.[7]

Clede and Parsons (1987) outline the key categories of the non-lethal tools available to an officer as control techniques *prior* to the application of deadly force. These are, in summary, as follows:

- body language (including stance, posture and eye contact);
- oral control (including the use of a 'command voice' and clear instructions);
- unarmed restraints (i.e. 'forms of pain compliance' used to escort individuals for short distances);
- neck restraints;
- short sticks and batons;
- handcuffing techniques;
- mechanical devices (including, but not limited to, rubber rounds, stun grenades (flash-bangs));
- electronic devices (such as stun guns and TASERs);
- chemical devices (e.g. mace, tear gas, smoke, and capsicum (pepper spray)).

In a simplified paradigm (see Table 11.1), Parsons (1980) proposed a six-level model of escalating use of force options (called 'tactical objectives'), which are available to the on-street police officer. An important dimension of

Table 11.1 Escalating levels of tactical objective and their action correlates

Tactical objective	Activity/Instrument
1 Persuade	Dialogue
2 Compliance	Escort
3 Compliance	Inflict pain
4 Compliance	Use of mechanical devices (stun grenades, etc.)
5 Impede	Use of baton, CS gas, TASER (i.e. electronic stun-gun), etc.
6 Stop	Use of firearm

(Adapted from Parsons, 1980.)

the application of Parsons' six levels is that, throughout their use, officers should 'strive to maintain the ability to disengage *or* escalate'.

The teaching of these and other 'force' continua is undertaken by a police department as a form of protection against civil liability claims. It is done in order to ensure that there is an ability to defend against multimillion dollar claims for unjustified use of force. If the material is taught and the officer can be shown to be in breach of the instructions, then, although the officer may remain liable on a personal basis, the police department (and the municipality, city or county, etc.) is protected from liability. Similarly, many police departments include in their Department General Orders, Department Manual or whatever the official document is called, a graphic description of the application of the continuum.

Table 11.2 shows a typical verbal description of the application of the continuum of force.[8]

Disciplinary issues

The inclusion of hierarchies of force in an American police department's General Orders is both public and managerial. The instructions are openly published for all to see and read (they are an official public document) and, because they are part of a department manual, may be cited as a lawful order, breach of which may, at a minimum, result in internal disciplinary action against the officer(s) involved:

> A violation of these rules will be grounds for administrative discipline ...
> (para 306.01, General Orders, Fort Worth Police Department, TX)

This openness, and the declared consequences of non-compliance, contrast markedly with the guideline approach taken in the UK. Whilst many of the instructions contained in the UK guidelines echo those in the USA (e.g. a prohibition on shooting at, or from, moving vehicles) they remain a 'secret' document not available to those outside the police service. As a set of guidelines, the items have little coercive authority and despite the suggestion that the Police Complaints Authority would use the guidelines to judge an officer's performance in a case of alleged excessive use of force, there is little evidence to support that contention. In any case, not only do the guidelines not fall into the category of lawful written orders, they also seem, as we have seen, not to apply to unarmed officers!

Similarly, at this level (i.e. below deadly force), we have much to learn from American practice. In April 1994 at the conference 'Preparing Policing for the 21st Century', Reiter outlined the comprehensive use of force reports required to be completed by officers in most major, and many smaller, police departments in the USA:

> Many people in the audience were struck by the extent to which it is possible ... to examine in considerable detail the way in which all types of force are used by officers. The data examined in many studies included a blow-by-blow breakdown of the parts of the body to which an officer had applied force and the manner in which

Table 11.2 An example of a verbal description of the continuum of force

Label	Verbal description
Level 1	OFFICER PRESENCE – Best illustrated when the officer arrives at the scene. The actor sees the officer and does not alter his/her illegal behaviour. The assumption is that the actor knows that the person who has just arrived at the scene is a police officer. The actor acknowledges the officer's presence because of the marked patrol vehicle, the uniform or the visible badge/identification. If the actor continues the illegal actions, the officer may advance – or escalate – to Level 2.
Level 2	VERBAL COMMANDS – Best illustrated when the officer advises the actor to 'keep quiet', 'move along', etc. The assumption is that the actor can clearly hear the officer's directions. If the actor continues the illegal actions, the officer may advance – or escalate – to Level 3.
Level 3	CONTROL AND RESTRAIN (empty hand) – Best illustrated when the officer applies a wrist lock taken down or pressure point technique. Most police officer defensive techniques will fall in this area since they are designed for gaining control of the individual and do not have a high potential of injury.
Level 3a	A slight increase in the level of resistance by the suspect (punching or increased struggling) may cause the arresting officer to respond by striking the suspect. These blows should be directed towards areas which are not likely to cause great bodily harm, i.e. motor points, navel area. If these techniques are not effective or if the officer feels that he cannot control by using these techniques, he may advance to Level 4.
Level 4	CHEMICAL AGENTS (MACE) – Creates a low-level option with minimal chance of injury. Care should be taken that any time a technique is used (at any level in the continuum) that may cause an actor to fall, his head should not be allowed to strike the ground with a high level of force. If control cannot be achieved at this level, the officer may advance – or escalate – to Level 5.
Level 5	TEMPORARY INCAPACITATION – Best illustrated when the officer is forced to strike the actor with an impact weapon (i.e. a night stick) when it is the weapon of necessity. These strikes should be directed toward approved striking points. Any blows to the head, neck, throat, spine, kidneys or groin areas are to be avoided. Should the actor pull a knife, draw a firearm or attempt to otherwise kill or seriously injure the officer or the citizen, the officer may advance – or escalate – to Level 6.
Level 6	DEADLY FORCE – Best illustrated when the officer must shoot the actor or strike the suspect with an instrument in a manner that is likely to cause death or great bodily harm. The use of 'Choke Holds' are not condoned by the Fort Worth Police Department as an application of Deadly Force. It is important to note that often, because of the suspect's actions, it is necessary to skip levels, i.e. Level 1 to Level 3. All actions by an officer are predicated by a suspect's actions. Also, the continuum of force works both ways. At all times an officer should be issuing loud verbal commands in an attempt to gain voluntary compliance by the actor. Any time the level of resistance by the actor is increased or decreased, the officer must adjust his/her level of response accordingly.

Source: Fort Worth Police Department, TX. General Orders. Para 306.84.

that force had been applied. Data generated showed the effectiveness of and the specific injuries caused to people, by everything from fists, through flashlights to firearms. (reported in McKenzie, 1994)

Even though the majority of these reports are self-generated by the officer involved, scrutiny by internal and external experts allows lessons to be learned about particular applications of force and about individual officers. Reiter pointed out that the early identification of 'problem' officers made good managerial sense and that although the 'blue wall of silence' protected some officers, diligence and commitment on the part of first and second line supervisors is the key to developing strategies to limit and control the application of unjustified force. (See Geller and Scott, 1992: Appendix L, for an example of a typical non-lethal use of force report form.)

Although there is no criticism of *reports* of the lethal application of deadly force in the UK, much could be done to improve reporting of the application of non-lethal force. Commenting on the errors in Hollywood cop movies, Albrecht (1992) points to the classic non-report scenario:

> Our hero saves the city after a 75-car pileup, a 5,000 round shootout, and a 15 minute wrestling match with Godzilla's brother-in-law. Wiping the sweat from his sturdy brow, he heads home for a cold one.

It is too common, in England and Wales, for reports on the application of non-lethal force to be little more than a requirement to inform a supervising officer about the *use* of a truncheon and then to 'head home for a cold one' or at least to head for the canteen for a 'cuppa'. Even though some forces have introduced more comprehensive reporting requirements, *post hoc* analysis of the use of force in the UK remains, not to put too fine a point on it, problematic.

Secrecy and the application of hierarchies

As was noted in the opening section of this chapter, much is made, usually by the police themselves, of the consensual nature of policing in the UK. Unfortunately, the acceptance of police legitimacy, particularly in the application of force, is more a consequence of apathy than democracy and is far from the idea of 'informed consent' discussed above.

Winston (1997: 181) argues that it is mistaken to believe that:

> ... police officers – or public officials generally – should have privileged status in determining which set of rules of conduct will regulate their activities. In my view, it is no more their prerogative to set such rules than it is for them to be exclusive determinants of their social function. These matters, especially in a democracy, are to be settled by the ongoing (and mostly informal) deliberations of all citizens.

But it is the case that not only are the 'rules of engagement' circulated and (possibly) taught under the cover of secrecy, but also that, as a consequence, their development and interpretation is not the subject of informed, *public* debate; rather, it is the consequence of discussion and consensus in private between the police and their political and legal advisers. Whilst such a process, particularly in a parliamentary democracy, may be legitimate, it remains unacceptable. The question remains whether, in what is truly a matter of life and death, such should be the case with respect to the police use of force. The guidelines, it is argued, should have a similar legal status to the codes of practice made under the Police and Criminal Evidence Act 1984 and under the Criminal Prosecutions and Investigations Act 1996. The creation of *codes of practice for the deployment and use of firearms by the police* should (at a minimum) be the subject of discussion, if not debate, in Parliament. They should be subject (because they are a matter of life and death) to proper democratic processes.

The open publication of the rules of engagement, resisted by the police on the basis that it would give the 'bad guys' too much information and make resolution of incidents more problematic, is merely a part of a bigger 'culture of secrecy' (see Vincent, 1998 for a full exposition of this notion) and the continued absence, despite a Labour Party manifesto commitment to introduce one, of a Freedom of Information Act.[9]

One consequence of the restricted nature of the rules of engagement and of the application of hierarchies of force is that modification and interpretation of them take place for both administrative and practical reasons under cover of secrecy. Deviation from guidelines becomes a matter for the application of operational pragmatism, and through an uncontrolled process of 'slippage' the hierarchy is distorted and deformed. For example, it will be noted that in Tables 1 and 2, the use of 'incapacitant' CS spray is an option placed near the top of the hierarchy, either as an effort to impede (Parsons, 1980) or as the level before use of an impact weapon. Early use of the spray is not acknowledged as a substantive problem. John Giffard, Chief Constable of Staffordshire, wrote, in response to an article in the *Independent*, 'No empirical evidence, as opposed to individual and sometimes anonymous anecdote, has been produced in support of the proposition that there is a trend towards officers using CS unnecessarily and as a soft option.' (Giffard, 1998)

The rejection of 'individual anecdote' is here a tad obtuse. There are many press reports suggesting that early deployment of CS has become too commonplace (see for example, Johnston, 1998; O'Neil, 1998; Pook, 1998; Stokes, 1998) and, whilst some may be fiction, it seems anomalous to deny their value as evidence (the vast majority of evidence presented in a court is, after all, individual anecdote). One presumes that the distinction between empirical evidence and individual anecdote is achieved by making a comparison of personal evidence with quantified, university research-based examination of the topic. This stance is both mistaken and misleading. Over the last 18 months, I have spoken to more than 40 police officers about issues associated with the police application of force. Many acknowledged early CS deployment as a reality. One officer even told me, 'As a woman, faced with the threat of injury, I have to be concerned about my ability to use physical force: CS is a useful option.' Furthermore, the chair of the Police Complaints Authority – which received 254 complaints about the use of CS in 1997 (PCA, 1998) – suggested that in some cases the use of CS spray was 'neither justified nor appropriate' (Johnston, 1998). There does seem to be a problem, and one which needs urgently to be addressed.

Finally, there is some ground for consideration of a further 'problem' at the highest level of the hierarchy. The use of deadly force is legally authorised (and produces, if death occurs, an outcome of justifiable homicide) if an officer can argue that the threat posed to someone (including the officer) is sufficient to apprehend the occurrence of death or serious injury. In such a case, for the armed officer, opening fire becomes an option. What this means in practice is that an officer, seeing a weapon, particularly a firearm, raised towards him or her, is, on the basis that it *might* be discharged (leading to death or serious injury) entitled to open fire. In some cases, an officer may do so because, and only because, necessary and sufficient legal requirements have been satisfied. Thus, a legalistic definition of the legitimate application of deadly force may, *post hoc*, be used as a justification for it. But such a *legal entitlement* to take action fails to take into account the possibility that other dynamics might be important. For example, if the officer (and all his or her colleagues as well as members of the public) have taken cover, if the threat is to an animal not a human, if the threat is of dubious legitimacy, or in any circumstance where deadly force is not *necessary* (though it may be *legal*) the possibility of a *supra-legal* response exists. Thus, in the absence of real threat, even though the emitted behaviour of the 'actor' may meet one of the hierarchical levels, a 'don't shoot, do something else instead' option arises.

This supra-legal dimension (a question of ethical behaviour rather than legalistic behaviour) is absent from traditional hierarchical approaches to the use of force because, whilst personal safety and the safety of others is a key dimension, such hierarchies fail to allow consideration of the *legitimacy* of any threat. (For example, the hierarchy in Table 11.2, where it addresses the issue at all, speaks only of the behaviour of the 'actor' – see also McKenzie and Gallagher, 1989: 196–8 – and of responses to 'resistance' by him or her.)

The balancing of personal safety and protection of others with the extent to which the actor(s) may be seen at any moment to be a legitimate and real threat is key. Take, for example, the 'everyone under cover' scenario: a man with a gun call-out, a house, the sole occupant the 'actor', no family present. If all deployed police personnel have taken cover, if warnings ('Armed Police' and so on) have been given and if then the 'actor' appears at a window pointing a gun, is it really *necessary* (albeit that it may be legal) to open fire? The giving of an additional warning, or simply inaction, may be an appropriate response, if only because the level (or legitimacy) of the threat is insufficient to warrant any other action.

This balancing of danger with legitimacy is graphically shown in Fig. 11.1. Where the legitimacy/reality of a threat (of a particular level of force) is high and the danger (of death or serious personal injury) to self and others is equally high (top right quadrant of Fig. 11.1), the officer may, without reservation, legitimately and without criticism, use deadly force. Where one dimension (threat or danger) falls, even though the other remains high, alternative uses of either force or tactics may be deployed.

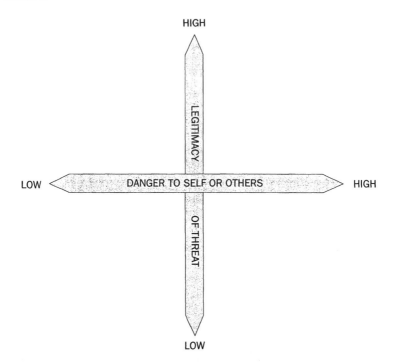

HIGH

LEGITIMACY

LOW ◁ DANGER TO SELF OR OTHERS ▷ HIGH

OF THREAT

LOW

Figure 11.1 Dimensions of the hierarchy of force

Where the legitimacy/reality of the threat (of a particular level of force) is high but where danger (of death or serious personal injury) is low (e.g. a siege without hostages), then negotiation is the key (top left quadrant of Fig. 11.1).

Where the legitimacy/reality of the threat (of a particular level of force) is low, but where danger (of serious personal injury) is high (e.g. a 'family' siege, no weapons, even though the threat may be to 'kill 'em all'), then the use of force, but at a non-deadly level is appropriate (bottom right quadrant).

Finally, where both the legitimacy/reality of the threat (of a particular level of force) is low, and where danger (of serious personal injury) is similarly low (a drunken person threatening to fight everyone) communication/interpersonal skills come into play (bottom left quadrant).

Conclusion

Many of the issues discussed above have been alluded to by contemporary writers. With regard to the permanent arming of the police, Waddington (1994), for example, has suggested that the problems of maintaining a rigorous training programme so that all officers are 'authorised shots', and the financial costs associated therewith, would be excessive. Similarly, he points to the personal problems associated with regular or routine arming of police officers. Personal problems are an acute issue. Green (1995) cites the following statistics:

> The suicide rate for NYPD police officers between 1960 and 1967 was 21.7 per 100,000 per year. The rate between 1950 to 1965 was 22.67 per 100,000 per year ... This is higher than the suicide rate of 16.7 [per 100,000 per year] for all males in the Unites States during these periods. (Green, 1995: 1)

More recent studies suggest that the suicide rate among police officers in the USA is 'three times as high as that of the general population'. According to Green (1995: 1), '... shooting is by far the most common method of suicide, and survival of the attempt is rare'.

Although it is relatively easy to show that the justification for more readily available firearms for police officers is limited, and that, in any case, the nature of training and selection of officers is wanting, it remains the view of many people, that:

> An armed police service is becoming more and more probable. There is only so much I can ask officers to take. (Condon, 1994)

According to Bonifacio (1991), with the exception of having one's partner killed, sustaining a serious injury is the most traumatic experience in police work. A serious injury is a blow to both physical and psychological self-concepts. The self-concept is, at a sub-conscious level, a kind of physical self-esteem, a belief in a high degree of invulnerability. It is this special perception that enables an officer to place her or himself in a dangerous position and not to flee, but, on each occasion when an officer falls victim to the gun, it is a demonstration of the fragility of the concept. Because they are 'in a special position of jeopardy and ... seek to reduce their vulnerability' (Sargent *et al.*, 1995), police officers will inevitably call for more protection (Southgate, 1991).[10] The critical question is not whether, or when, such calls occur and whether, or when, they will be acted upon, it is about who will make the decision and the extent to which the police themselves are prepared for the consequences.

Fortunately, ACPO currently takes the view that the general arming of police officers is to be avoided, that firearms capability remains best confined to a combination of tactical units and ARVs, and that deployments should be made only in response to particular and specific events. In support of these views, Sharples (1994) suggested that increased availability of firearms to police could result in:

- higher numbers of injuries or deaths;
- increased levels of suicide by police;
- a reduction in recruiting.

Sharples also asserts that there is ample evidence to suggest that the public does not want an armed police service, and, over the last two years, the debate appears to have been restricted if not abandoned.

For the time being, such a stance is to be applauded. We must not allow over-hasty decisions to be made that will remove from us for ever that flavour to British policing that is, even in a European context, a unique outcome of Peel's attempt to create a 'policing of the people, by the people, for the people'. It may well be that, despite the concentration in this chapter upon things American, police forces in continental Europe and elsewhere have much to offer us in terms of insights about the deployment and use of armed police. For example, a comprehensive examination of the apparent restraint with which Japanese police officers use their weapons might be worthwhile (McKenzie, 1984). Similarly, the open publication of research papers on police training in firearms use, as in The Netherlands (see, for example, Vrij *et al.*, 1994) and Germany, could be of considerable benefit in enhancing the quality of the debate.

The police remain, by and large, unenthusiastic about routine arming, as does a substantial proportion of the public. A survey of 1,000 members of the public, published contemporaneously with the Police Federation (1995) survey, showed that '... only about one in four people supported routine arming ...' (Bennetto, 1995). Nevertheless, there remains a feeling that, at some stage, perhaps in the early twenty-first century, such an outcome will become inevitable. On the assumption that this is so, might it not be prudent to address some or all of the areas of selection, training, reporting and so on addressed in this chapter?

Finally, however, the most significant problem remains. The police are sometimes rather poor at providing for the public what they want, particularly when the decision involved may be said to be one of a professional, operational kind; the disparity between the public and police responses to the survey undertaken for the *Operational Policing Review* (JCC, 1990) is proof enough of that. For as long as the police service remains able to make 'operational' decisions, albeit that they may have substantial 'policy' elements, without the need to defer to *any* public body, the worry remains that, click-by-click of the ratchet, the British police service will become a fully armed body, but through the back door.

If Wells (1993) is correct in his assertion that such an event would,

> ... at a stroke, increase the perception that we had moved irrevocably towards an armed culture, so urging members of the public – including first criminal members of the public – to arm themselves.

it cannot be right that such a decision may be made by stealth and in the absence of any public, and in particular of any Parliamentary, debate. The changes in the relationship between the police and the public would be immense. They must be the subject of a decision-making process which transcends the policy/operations dichotomy of the police accountability debate and which, if only in this connection, denies the full majesty of 'constabulary independence'. Such a decision cannot be one of tacit or assumed approval. It must be a consequence of an open and clear public and/or parliamentary mandate. Similarly, it is high time that the 'rules of engagement' for both firearms use and the deployment of lower-level weapons be brought into the open.

Notes

1 (*R* v *Metropolitan Police, ex parte Blackburn*, [1968] 2 QB 118; *R* v *Metropolitan Police, ex parte Blackburn* [1979] *Times* 1 December; *Fisher* v *Oldham Corporation* [1930] 2 KB 264; *R* v *Chief Constable of Devon and Cornwall, ex parte Central Electricity Generating Board* [1981] 3 All ER 835; *R* v *Secretary of State for the Home Department, ex parte Northumbria Police Authority* (CA, 18 November 1987, unreported)).

2 The Gallup poll revealed that although the general public supported the arming of the police they did so more than did the police themselves. Sixty-seven per cent of the public respondents thought the police should carry guns whilst only 46 per cent of police wanted so to do. When items were analysed by the police force to which respondents belonged, it was found that whilst 63 per cent of Metropolitan officers wanted to be routinely armed, only a small minority of constabulary officers did (McMahon, 1994; Connett, 1994).

3 The evidence from the Gallup poll of police officers (McMahon, 1994; Connett, 1994) suggests that the major support for the notion of routine arming comes not just from major city officers (including the Metropolitan Police, see note 2 *supra*) but also from younger officers with limited service. Young officers become older officers, their place is taken by those who are, shaped by the police culture, filled with fear and apprehension about the 'danger out there' and the need for protection. How long can chief officers stand up against what will, in this, albeit speculative scenario, become an irresistible force for change?

4 A similar conclusion was reached by Moxey and McKenzie (1993) when they pointed to the 'unacceptable behavioural dynamics of officers' which apparently led 7 per cent of the officers in a single police division to be involved in 50 per cent of assaults on police. The same group of officers accounted for more than 50 per cent of the complaints on that division.

5 It must be acknowledged that several forces have recently introduced a truncated version of the continuum, to be taught to officers trained to use the new long-handled baton. In general, however, the verbal descriptions of the levels are excessively brief by contrast to those discussed here. More surprisingly, however, many talk only of *escalating* force and fail to consider the need to define 'disengagement' as an option.

6 Sixty per cent of respondents in the 1995 Police Federation survey expressed dissatisfaction with their self-defence training.

7 In the first of the trials of police officers involved in the assaults upon Rodney King in Los Angeles, the defence strategy was, using the video film of the incident, to account for police behaviour in a fine-grained, frame-by-frame manner. Such an analysis enabled defence witnesses, by indicating to the jury discrete behaviours emitted by King, to establish the legitimacy of the application of particular forceful responses by the officers. It was a use of the continuum of force. It was successful. (See Skolnick and Fyfe (1993) for a full account and discussion of these events.)

8 McKenzie and Gallagher (1989: Appendix IV, p. 195) cite the full Use of Force instructions issued to the Tallahassee Police Department, Florida.

9 In passing, one problem with such legislation, if it is introduced, is that the Official Secrets Act of 1911 is unlikely to be repealed or even modified.

10 In a similar way, Eisenberg (1975) commented that danger, fear of serious injury, the likelihood of disability and the apprehension of death can add to the hazards of police work. Police officers, themselves, suffer from a degree of fear of crime (Jermier *et al.*, 1989).

References

ACPO (1983) *Report of the Working Party on the Selection and Training of Authorised Firearms Officers.* London: Association of Chief Police Officers.

Albrecht, S. (1992) *Street work: The Way to Officer Safety and Survival.* Boulder, CO: Paladin Press.

Bayley, D.H. (1977) *The Police and Society.* London: Sage

Bennetto, J. (1994) 'Police Seek Wider Use of Armed Patrols', *Independent,* 8 July.

Bennetto, J. (1995) 'Police Reject Guns on Beat', *Independent,* 16 May.

Bonifacio, P. (1991) *The Psychological Effects of Police Work: A Psychodynamic Approach.* New York: Plenum Press.

Clede, W. and Parsons, K. (1987) *Police Non-lethal Force Manual: your choices this side of deadly.* Harrisburg, PA: Stackpole Books.

Condon, Sir P. (1994) Interview. *Panorama.* BBC Television. 21 June.

Connett, D. (1994) 'The Police Federation's Annual Conference: Arming Officers is Popular with the Public'. *Independent,* 18 May.

Dunham, R. and Alpert, G. (eds) (1989) *Critical Issues in Policing: Contemporary Readings.* Prospect Heights, IL: Waveland Press.

Eisenberg, T. (1975) 'Job Stress and the Police Officer: Identifying Stress Reduction Techniques' in Kroes and Hurrell (1975).

Fyfe, J. (1989) 'The Split Second Syndrome and Other Determinants of Police Violence' in Dunham and Alpert (1989).

Geller, W. and Scott, M. (1992) *Deadly Force: What We Know.* Washington, DC: Police Executive Research Forum.

Giffard, J. (1998) 'Right of Reply', *Independent.* 2 September 1998, 5.

Green, J.G. (1995) 'Officer Needs Assistance: Suicide in the New York City Police Department', *CJ Update,* XXIII (2) (Winter, 1995), 2.

JCC (1990) *Operational Policing Review.* Surbiton, Surrey: Joint Consultative Committee.

Jermier, J.M., Gaines, J. and McIntosh, N.J. (1989) 'Reactions to Physically Dangerous Work: A Conceptual and Empirical Analysis', *Journal of Organisational Behaviour,* 10, 15–33.

Johnston, P. (1998) 'Police "using CS Sprays too often"', *Electronic Telegraph.* UK News, 26 June.

Kleinig, J. and Leland Smith, M. (eds) (1997) *Teaching Criminal Justice Ethics: Strategic Issues.* Cincinnati: Anderson.

Kroes, W. and Hurrell, J. (eds) (1975) *Job Stress and the Police Officer.* Washington, DC: Government Printing Office.

Leppard, D. (1994) 'Police Set to Use Machine Guns to Fight UK Crime', *Sunday Times.* 15 May.

Lustgarten, L. (1986) *The Governance of Police.* London: Sweet and Maxwell.

McKenzie, I.K. (1984) 'Policing in Japan', *Police Review,* 92, 4791.

McKenzie, I.K. (1994) 'Get Yourselves Ready for 2001', *Policing,* 10 (2), 99–110.

McKenzie I.K. and Gallagher, G.P. (1989) *Behind the Uniform: Policing in Britain and America.* Hemel Hempstead: Harvester Wheatsheaf.

McMahon, B. (1994) 'Police Leader: We Are Cannon Fodder', *Evening News.* London: 17 May.

Midgley, D. (1995) 'Gun Law: What Happens When the Police Break It?' *Today.* 2 March.

Morrison, S. and O'Donnell, I. (1994) *Armed Robbery: A Study in London.* Occasional Paper, No. 15. Oxford: Centre for Criminological Research.

Moxey, M. and McKenzie, I.K. (1993) 'Assaults on Police', *Policing,* 9, 172–186.

O'Neil, S. (1998) 'Police Gas Man Who Forgot Keys', *Electronic Telegraph.* UK News, 28 August.

Parsons, K. (1980) *Techniques of Vigilance.* Cincinatti, OH: Charles E. Tuttle.

PCA (1998) *Police Complaints Authority: Annual Report.* London: HMSO.

Police Federation of England and Wales (1995) *Survey of Members. Section 3: Personal Protection and Firearms.* Surbiton, Surrey: Police Federation.

Pook, S. (1998) 'Jury Rebuked after Clearing PC Who Sprayed Gas at Pensioner', *Electronic Telegraph.* UK News, 10 June.

PSI (1983) *Police and People in London: Vol. 4.* London: Policy Studies Institute.

Reiner, R. (1985) *The Politics of the Police.* Brighton: Wheatsheaf.

Reiner, R. (1992) *The Politics of the Police.* 2nd edn. Hemel Hempstead: Harvester Wheatsheaf.

Reiter, L. (1994) 'Developing Credible Complaints Systems'. Paper presented to conference entitled 'Preparing Policing for the 21st Century: The American Experience', University of Portsmouth, 6–8 April.

Robin, G.D. (1980) *Introduction to the Criminal Justice System.* New York: Harper and Row.

Rosewell, R. (1994) 'Bite the Bullet and Arm the Police', *Mail on Sunday,* 22 February, 28.

Sargent, S., Brown, J. and Gourlay, R. (1995) 'Who Wants to Carry a Gun?', *Policing,* 10 (4).

Sharples, J. (1994) 'Firing Back', *Police Review,* 13 May, 18–19.

Skolnick, J. H., and Fyfe, J. (1993) *Above the Law: Police and the Excessive use of Force.* New York: Free Press.

Southgate, P. (1991) *The Management and Deployment of Armed Police Response Vehicles.* London: Home Office Research and Planning Unit.

Stokes, P. (1998) 'Police CS Spray Subdues Man, 73', *Electronic Telegraph.* UK News, 5 December.

Vincent, D. (1998) *The Culture of Secrecy in Britain 1832–1996.* Oxford: Oxford University Press.

Vrij, A., van der Steen, J. and Koppelaar, L. (1994) 'Aggression of Police Officers as a Function of Temperature: An Experiment with the Fire Arms Training System', *Journal of Community and Applied Social Psychology,* 4, 365–70.

Waddington, P.A.J. (1994) 'British is Best', *Police Review,* 14 January, 18–19.

Wells, R. (1993) *Annual Report of the Chief Constable, 1993.* Sheffield: South Yorkshire Police.

Wells, R. (1994) Interview. *Panorama.* BBC Television. 21 June.

Winston, K. I. (1997) 'Teaching with Cases' in Kleinig and Leland Smith (1997).

Chapter 12

Reflections on investigative interviewing

JULIE CHERRYMAN AND RAY BULL

Introduction

During the last 15 years, with the publicity surrounding cases such as 'The Guildford Four' and 'The Birmingham Six', and the more recent Nikki Allen and Rachel Nickell murder cases, there have repeatedly been calls for more acceptable, less oppressive police investigative interviewing techniques. However, only recently has research been used in a positive manner to help improve investigative interviewing.

In this chapter it is our intention to concentrate mainly on the interviewing of suspects (an interview being 'a conversation with a purpose' (Hodgson, 1987)). However, we will also refer to the interviewing of witnesses and victims, not least because there has been more research published on these latter two topics.

Baldwin (1994) noted that:

> The interviewing of suspects is regarded by most informed observers as a critical – perhaps the most critical – stage in the processing of almost all criminal cases. Police investigators see such interviews in the same light themselves, and there are very few criminal cases indeed of any seriousness in which the suspect is not interrogated by police officers. (p. 66)

This chapter is organised into sections similar to the sequential phases of an investigative interview. Thus, the first part focuses on planning and preparation (including the interviewing of vulnerable interviewees). This is followed by a focus on what occurs within an investigative interview, for example the caution, the right to silence and confessions. What happens at the end of the interview is then examined, followed by comment on the interview as a whole. The chapter concludes with the issue of training.

In the relevant literature (e.g. Williamson, 1994) reference has often been made to the oppressive nature of investigative interviewing. However, in England and Wales the advent of the Police and Criminal Evidence Act 1984 (PACE) has probably resulted in a reduction in the use of grossly oppressive interviewing (Williamson, 1993). Therefore, the pre-1984 literature is now not so apposite and will not be much referred to here.

A few years ago all police officers in England and Wales were issued with two booklets, *A Guide To Interviewing* and *The Interviewer's Rule Book* (The Central Planning and Training Unit, 1992a and 1992b). These advocated the model known as 'PEACE' (a mnemonic for: planning and preparation, engage and explain, account, closure, and evaluation), and they sought to assist police officers in their attempts to avoid the poor performance some-times found in investigative interviewing (Fisher *et al.*, 1987).

Planning and preparation before the interview

Baldwin (1992) noted that preparation is a prerequisite of good interviewing but that almost a third of police officers in his study complained of insuffi-cient time to prepare adequately for their interviews. 'Lack of time' is often referred to by police officers as being an important factor affecting the qual-ity of their interviews (Bull and Cherryman, 1996).

Morgan and Stephenson (1994) reiterated Maguire's (1994) point:

> ... with a few exceptions (such as regional crime squads and special units), the organisation and culture of a typical criminal investigation department is not geared to routine, methodical investigations, either before or after arrest. For the most part, CID work is unpredictable, heavily bureaucratic and under-resourced. Officers are under continual pressures from mounting case loads, administrative changes, and senior colleagues, as well as from politicians and the media to pro-duce better results. In response to this 'chaotic' environment, Maguire found that police tactics tend to be reactive and highly individualistic, relying on the largely unsupervised initiatives of relatively junior officers to get results. (p. 9)

Bull and Cherryman (1996) found that many officers were of the opinion that time to plan and prepare is a strong determinant of the quality of inves-tigative interviews. (However, it is not known to what extent this really is the case or whether police officers merely use lack of time as an excuse.) It could be argued that if an interview is properly prepared then investigations would take less time in the long run.

It is likely that planning and preparation are of considerable importance for the quality of investigative interviews, yet studies to determine the sorts of things which constitute effective planning and preparation have not been sys-tematically carried out. Köhnken (1995) described planning as being one way in which the interviewer can reduce the cognitive load and, therefore, free more cognitive capacity for information processing in the interview. The PEACE police training package and its accompanying booklet, *A guide to interviewing* (Central Planning and Training Unit, 1992a), emphasised the importance of good planning and preparation. They described planning as '... the mental process of getting ready to interview' and preparation as 'con-sidering what needs to be made ready prior to interview. It includes such things as the location, the environment and the administration.' The booklet contains a list of issues which should be included in the planning of inter-views:

- understanding the purpose of the interview;
- defining the objectives of the interview;
- understanding and recognising the points to prove;
- analysing what evidence is already available;
- assessing what evidence is needed and where it can be obtained, whether from an interview or otherwise;

- understanding PACE and Codes of Practice;
- designing flexible approaches. (p. 1)

McGurk *et al.* (1993) offered some explanation of what might occur in planning and preparation:

> Planning for interview: reading relevant statements, asking to see the custody record, considering the requirements of PACE, collecting exhibits and taking account of the emotional state of the witness/suspect. (p. 11)

Shepherd (1994) has offered a system of information recording, to enhance the planning and preparation stage, called SE3R (Skim, Extract, Read, Review, Recall).

People present at the interview

The 1984 Police and Criminal Evidence Act (PACE) requires interviews with suspects be audio tape recorded, that the suspect be asked if he/she wishes a legal representative (solicitor) to be present, and that in 'the case of persons who are mentally disordered or handicapped' an 'appropriate adult' be present. Very little published research exists on the effects of the presence of suspects' legal representatives or of appropriate adults on investigative interviews.

A relatively low number of suspects (around 25 per cent) seem to request legal advice prior to their investigative interview (Brown, 1989; Dixon, 1990; Sanders *et al.*, 1989). According to McConville *et al.* (1994), this is due to 'the failure of the suspects to invoke the right and the success of the police in minimising the occasions on which suspects request the services of a lawyer'.

Vulnerable interviewees

Gudjonsson (1992, 1993) discussed how the vulnerable adult may be more susceptible to offering a false confession. The onus for identifying when an appropriate adult is necessary lies with the police, who then have to provide this person. Gudjonsson (1993), and Irving and McKenzie (1993), pointed out that it is not an easy task for police officers to determine which adults fall into the category of 'vulnerable' (Bull *et al.*, 1983).

Bull and Cullen (1992, 1993) produced a booklet to inform Scottish Procurators Fiscal (prosecutors), and any other interested parties, about the complexities involved in the effective interviewing of 'mentally handicapped' witnesses (i.e. those with learning disabilities).

Jenkins (1993), a forensic medical examiner (police surgeon), noted some of the problems and difficulties which face the forensic medical examiner in this context. He made the recommendation that all such clinicians should 'attend a course and obtain a certificate to prove their efficiency in detecting abnormal mental health and assessing fitness for interview'. Gudjonsson (1994) concluded that:

> Police officers and forensic medical examiners should be provided with basic training in how to identify vulnerable interviewees. In addition, police officers should be provided with training in how to interview people to maximise the relevance,

completeness and reliability of the information obtained. Special training is required for interviewing those who are at risk; once identified as being at risk the police should exercise special caution when interviewing them (e.g. phrasing questions simply, avoiding leading questions, and ensuring that they are not placing them under undue pressure), because it increases the likelihood that information obtained during the interviewing is reliable and will not be ruled inadmissible when the case goes to trial. (p. 103)

Torpy (1994) described nine cases involving defendants of limited cognitive ability. He presented written and verbal evidence to courts with regard to the defendants' degree of intellectual impairment, ability to read and to comprehend. Torpy noted that:

> In all cases there was a major attempt to obtain a confession, sometimes without the protection of PACE and typically without any recognition of the degree of dysfunction and intellectual difficulties. Some interrogations lasted over two days and involved six to ten hours of questioning. (p. 21)

Gudjonsson and MacKeith (1994) detail a single case of a false confession of a 'mentally handicapped' man. They provide a psychological framework to explain how the investigation resulted in a false confession to double murder. Milne and Bull (1996) and Milne *et al.* (1999) have recently conducted two studies on how best to interview witnesses who have a learning disability. (See also Bull, 1995a.)

In the interview

The caution (which will be discussed below) has to be read at the beginning of an interview (PACE, Code C, 10.5 and 11.2). Within the caution is the declaration that the individual has the right to remain silent.

The right to silence

Moston and Stephenson (1993) explain how, when there is either strong or weak evidence against an individual, the suspect's silence seems not to make a great deal of difference to whether the suspect will be charged. However, where there is evidence against a suspect which is 'moderately strong' the suspect's silence does seem to have a bearing on whether the suspect will be charged or not.

The removal of the 'right to silence' has been hotly debated (Morgan and Stephenson, 1994). Leng (1994) outlined points for and against the abolition of the right to silence, summarised below.

Arguments in favour of abolishing the right to silence

- Firstly, it is unprincipled as individuals should help the police.
- Secondly, it is pointless: why should we give the suspect a chance to escape justice?
- Thirdly, it is illogical: if the only reason for a suspect to remain silent is guilt, why should the judge and jury not be told about this?

197

- Fourthly, it may pervert the course of justice – depriving the jury of cogent evidence.
- Fifthly, the exercise of the right to silence may obstruct the investigation, that is, evidence is denied from the best source (the suspect).

Arguments against abolishing the right to silence

- Firstly, the right of silence provides safeguards and protects the individual from self-incrimination.
- Secondly, the onus lies upon the state to prove guilt.
- Thirdly, if the right of silence were abolished, would this usurp the function of the trial?
- Fourthly, suspects may be 'at risk' in an interview and the right of silence may help the suspect to avoid this risk.

Maguire (1994) added to the debate saying that the right to silence is a fundamental part of an adversarial system and that to abolish it would be a retrograde step. He pointed out that, by abolishing the right to silence, there may be a possibility that the police may be encouraged to view confessions as central to police work. Evans (1994) noted that juveniles do not exercise their right to silence and that they are given little support from anyone, even in oppressive interviews.

A majority of the members of the Royal Commission on Criminal Justice (1993) were of the view that a change in the right to silence law could possibly lead to increases in false confessions from vulnerable persons (Morgan and Stephenson, 1994). However, in 1994 the Home Secretary, as part of the Criminal Justice and Public Order Bill (England and Wales), proposed a new police caution which noted that adverse comments may be drawn in court if suspects remain silent during police questioning. His proposed new caution was:

> You do not have to say anything. But if you do not mention now something which you later use in your defence, the court may decide that your failure to mention it now strengthens the case against you. A record will be made of anything you say and it may be given in evidence if you are brought to trial.

Gudjonsson and Clare (1994) empirically tested how easily understood this proposed new caution was and found that difficulties existed in understanding it, particularly for people with mild learning difficulties and people with mental health problems. Possibly in the light of this, a modified new caution was proposed early in 1995 by the Home Secretary:

> You do not have to say anything. But it may harm your defence if you do not mention when questioned something which you later rely on in court. Anything you do say may be given in evidence.

Some police interrogation techniques (especially in the USA) seem to have been based on breaking down the suspect's resistance (Gudjonsson, 1992). Gudjonsson gives a comprehensive account of the Miranda[1] rights. He cited Stutz (1989) in describing the main reasoning behind Miranda as being to deter police misconduct. As late as 1987, MacDonald and Michaud, in their book on confessions, describe ways in which police officers in the USA might minimise the effects of the Miranda rights, make the suspect talk, and confess. In 1994 Lieutenant Bill Walsh of the Dallas Police Department pointed out that there is a difference between investigation and interrogation, with the first goal of interrogation being to manipulate the suspect.

Moston (1990) studied tape recorded interviews in 133 cases in which suspects exercised the right to silence. Outlining the different ways officers tackled such interviews, Moston concluded that officers often lacked the skills necessary to negotiate with suspects. If a confession or an admission was not achieved, the interviewers often promptly ended the interview, possibly blaming the 'failure' on suspect resistance. Moston, Stephenson and Williamson (1990) claim that interviewers could be taught how to react when suspects exercise their right to silence. (A legal adviser may advise the suspect to remain silent during interview despite the fact that it may not always be in the suspect's own best interests to remain silent.)

The main part of the interview

Rapport

Once the caution has been given, the main part of the interview can now take place. Rapport building is perceived as being an important factor in the 'success' of an interview (Köhnken, 1995) and is advocated in many police training courses on interviewing. However, it seems rare to find evidence of rapport building at the beginning of tape recorded interviews with suspects (Moston and Engleberg, 1993).

The cognitive interview

The cognitive interview (CI) is a type of interview which is mainly used for the interviewing of co-operative witnesses. The cognitive interview has often been found to elicit much more correct information, as compared to a control group (see Köhnken et al., 1999; Milne and Bull, 1999). However, a recent field study (Memon et al., 1995; Memon et al., 1994) found that the CI did not elicit increased correct recall from witnesses, a factor which was ascribed to the probable ineffectiveness of the training of the police officers involved.

There is no known research about the effectiveness of CI when interviewing suspects. However, it is generally accepted that CI is a useful tool to aid memory (but only where the interviewee is a willing participant). Interviews with suspects who have made a confession or an admission, and those with suspects who, actually, were not involved in the crime, may benefit from the use of CI, especially to elicit corroborative police information.

Shepherd (1991) helped develop an investigative interview training package which was made available to various police forces by the Merseyside Police. It included within it a technique called 'conversation management' (CM). Conversation management was designed (see Milne and Bull, 1999)

199

to allow a free flow of information between the interviewer and the interviewee (whether this be a suspect or witness or victim). George (1991) conducted a field study to compare the effectiveness on witness recall of police training in CI, CM and both CM and CI together, with a control group of 'untrained' police officers. Officers trained in CI alone outperformed all the other groups, including the group where the police officers were trained in CM and CI. Those officers trained in CM alone showed only a small improvement over the untrained officers.

Interviewing children

Much has recently been published (e.g. Ceci and Bruck, 1995; Poole and Lamb, 1998) on how best to interview child witnesses (though very little on the interviewing of children who are suspected of committing crime). This literature often advocates a phased approach (Bull, 1992, 1994, 1995b) involving the four interview phases (i) rapport, (ii) free recall, (iii) questioning, (iv) closure. In this 'child' literature, advice is given concerning techniques to be used in those parts of the interview (i.e. free recall and questioning) which attempt to obtain an account from the interviewee. Very little research on the usefulness of this approach with suspects has been conducted. Detail on the techniques which could be used in the main part of an interview with a suspect seem somewhat overlooked in the booklets given to all police officers in England and Wales (Central Planning and Training Unit, 1992a, 1992b).

Confessions

Moston *et al.* (1992), who sampled 1,067 tape recorded interviews, found that 42 per cent of suspects made an admission or a confession. Irving and McKenzie (1989) found in their observational studies that 68 per cent and 65 per cent, respectively, made admissions or confessions. Higher confession rates have been reported by Baldwin and McConville (1980) and Zander (1979) using Crown Court files (which may not have been representative of the whole range of crimes). The research by Moston *et al.* (1992) was concerned with the possible associations between the characteristics of a suspect, of the case and of a suspect's decision to admit or deny having committed an offence. They looked at strength of evidence, type of individual, age, sex, experience and temperament, type of offence, severity of offence, and legal advice with regards to the possible effect(s) that these have on whether the suspect makes an admission or confession. They reflect:

> The police interviewer may also be affected by the very same characteristics ... do case characteristics have a bearing on interview styles, or does some other variable such as personal preference play a more important role? It is quite possible that an interviewer might have a favoured style of questioning that is employed in all interviews, regardless of any variations in cases. (p. 38)

They advocate the use of some persuasive questioning as being legitimate and necessary in certain circumstances, but warn that in these cases the police must show that they have not behaved oppressively.

The topic of oppression is a major area of debate since PACE (Feldman, 1990). There is now emphasis in police forces on 'ethical interviewing' (Williamson, 1993) but police officers are still very much under pressure to keep criminals off the streets. Need these two be opposed? Certainly, if the courts are going to rule that persuasive police interviewing is oppressive, then interview evidence based on persuasion may be ruled inadmissible. There does seem to be a major problem with trying to determine exactly what is oppressive. In two different circumstances the same police behaviour could be ruled oppressive in the one but not in the other. That is, it could be argued that characteristics of the suspect and of the case, environmental factors (and other things) should influence the decision as to whether or not police behaviour is oppressive. Before self-incriminating evidence can be accepted against the defendant, courts in many countries must be sure of the voluntary nature of the statement. Gudjonsson (1992) listed the types of factors that may be appropriate in deciding whether the information has been given voluntarily. These include the characteristics of the suspect,[2] the conditions of the detention,[3] and the nature of the interrogation.[4] Research on these issues would allow a better description of what is and what is not oppressive. This would be very useful since many police officers do not feel fully aware of exactly what they can and cannot do in an interview despite the fact that, after each interview with a suspect, they sign to say that the interview was conducted within the rules of PACE.

In 1993 Stockdale noted that some officers viewed trying to gain an admission as a basic aim of the interview with a suspect. In 1997 Plimmer (an experienced detective) still found this to be the case. Moston *et al.* (1990) argued that a preoccupation with obtaining confessions reduced the effectiveness of the interview because officers then ignored opportunities for securing good corroborative evidence against the suspect. However, Baldwin (1992) noted, as did Evans (1993) and Pearse and Gudjonsson (1996), that, though few suspects were persuaded at interview to admit guilt or participation in criminal offences, much of police interview training focused on this aim.

Skolnick and Leo (1992) noted three sometimes conflicting principles which underlie the confession laws in the USA:

[F]irst, the truth-finding rationale, which serves the goal of *reliability* (convicting an innocent person is worse than letting a guilty one go free); second, the substantive due process or *fairness* rationale, which promotes the goal of the system's integrity; and third, the related *deterrence* principle, which proscribes offensive or lawless police conduct. (p. 5)

Two techniques that might be used by officers are exaggerating to the suspect the strength of evidence (maximising) and underestimating the seriousness of the crime (minimising). What might the effects be of such interviewing behaviour? Kassin and McNall (1991) empirically tested the effects of maximising and minimising on a group of undergraduates and found that these ploys 'may well communicate implicit promises and threats to unwary criminal suspects'. In a follow-up experiment they found that mock juries disallowed evidence resulting from threats of punishment, but that conviction rate was significantly increased after minimisation or promises.

Leo (1992) described how the nature of police interrogation in America has changed from coercive (with use of force) to being deceptive (with sophisticated psychological tricks and ploys). He concluded that:

> the effect of permitting this trickery and deceit during interrogation may be:
> - to officially sanction the manipulation and exploitation of human relationships;
> - to authoritatively encourage police to lie in other contexts;
> - to undermine public confidence and social trust;
> and, in some instances,
> - to provoke false confessions. (p. 54)

Of course, the use of such interrogation practices may vary to some extent from one country to another. (For more on these techniques see Memon *et al.*, 1998.)

At the end of the interview

The end of an interview is an important stage. The National Crime Faculty's (1996) publication, *Investigative Interviewing: A Practical Guide,* gives a comprehensive account of the procedure which should be followed at that time.

After the interview, the interviewers have to evaluate the information which has been gained. They either make a full transcript of the interview or a summary of what is considered to be the relevant parts of the interview. This second alternative is not an easy task. Baldwin and Bedward's (1991) paper was concerned with the problems that confront police officers when seeking to make an accurate summary of an interview with a suspect. They listened to 200 audio tape recorded interviews and concluded that greater effort will be needed to achieve an acceptable standard of summary of the interview.

Hirst (1993) when reviewing the Royal Commission Research Papers noted that half of the summaries of interviews (from paper No. 2) were misleading or lacked detail. She noted:

> The studies argue that the process of summarisation is a selection process. Notwithstanding individual variations between officers with skills at summarising, the prosecutorial role of the police in the criminal justice system will mean that they [the police] cannot be expected to take a defence or even a neutral stance in preparing summaries. (p. 17)

An interesting, unresearched question involves the extent to which problems with summaries could indicate bias *during*, not merely after, the interview. This is surely a topic deserving of research particularly as Mortimer (1994a and 1994b) found that interviewing officers' beliefs influence their conduct of interviews.

The investigative interview as a whole

Williamson (1994), himself a senior police officer, made three reflections on current police practice:

(a) Unethical behaviour by interrogators has undermined public confidence and left the police service with a serious skills deficit in its ability to obtain evidence through questioning.

(b) The principles of investigative interviewing designed to create a new approach to police questioning have not been sufficiently understood by the service.

(c) Currently, and in particular after any removal of the right of silence, the judges will apply strict criteria before admitting evidence obtained through questioning. They will be unlikely to admit anything which is not consistent with the principles and training on investigative interviewing.   (p. 107)

Williamson continued:

... it does not take much skill to beat a confession out of a suspect detained in police custody. The police in this country would correctly deny that such things happen but unfortunately a considerable proportion of the general public thinks that it happens regularly.   (p. 107)

Investigative interviewing places high demands upon the cognitive resources of the interviewer (Köhnken, 1995), and as we all suffer from limited cognitive capacity, any cognitive effort which is being used to conduct the interview will not be available for concomitantly processing information gained within the interview. Köhnken stated the following general rule:

any procedure or technique that reduces the cognitive load on the interviewer increases the likelihood that more information will be processed by the interviewer.   (p. 221)

He noted three particularly important ways of reducing the cognitive demands on the interviewer: (i) by minimising the amount of notetaking during an interview, (ii) careful planning of the interview, and (iii) thorough interview training and extensive interview practice. These issues are presently being addressed in policing in England and Wales.

Training

Baldwin (1992) contended that there is something extra which a skilled interviewer brings to the situation:

In short, the best interviewers appear to bring to interviews some natural social skills which they adapt as the circumstances demand ... they had generally prepared carefully beforehand, they put the allegations clearly and calmly and made no assumptions about what the response to the allegations should be ... they listened to what the suspects had to say, challenging denials that were made when they did not square with the available evidence and without harrying or bullying, retained a firm control of what was taking place. A good interviewer therefore has well-developed communicative and social skills, a calm disposition and temperament, patience, subtlety, an ability to respond quickly and flexibly, legal knowledge and some imagination. (p. 13)

Baldwin stated that the competence of an investigator generally seemed apparent from the outset. He noted how the lack of care taken with the initial announcements at the start of the interview tended to spill over into the interviewing concerning the incident in question. He found that 36 per cent (of 600 interviews) were either 'not very well conducted' or 'poorly conducted'. He noted that these less than satisfactory interviews included such things as ineptitude, assuming guilt, poor interview technique and unfair questioning or unprofessional conduct. McGurk *et al.* (1993) offered a useful summary of these criticisms and used a set of performance indicators to assess the standard of police investigative interviews. These indicators were arrived at by reviewing the literature on police interviews and by interviewing small groups of relevant people (police managers, police officers, Crown Prosecution Service Solicitors, prisoners from Maidstone prison), and they cover the main points of the widely used PEACE training package (briefly described above and more fully described in Milne and Bull, 1999). However, though these are useful criteria, how do the police themselves perceive the objectives of investigative interviewing?

Stockdale (1993), from her sample of 208 police officers (of all ranks), gathered the following objectives: to elicit the truth, to obtain the full facts, to find out as much as possible about the incident/alleged offence, to prove an alleged offence/points of law (and test the statutory defence if a criminal offence), to establish someone's guilt or innocence, to find out the other side of the story and reasons for their actions, and to gain an admission. Interviews were often seen by officers as the most important part of the job, and officers thought of interviews as often being the only way of getting the information required. McGurk *et al.* (1994), when conducting a job and training needs analysis for detectives, found that interviewing witnesses and interviewing prisoners both were in the top four of the most frequently carried out tasks. They also found that taking statements, interviewing witnesses and interviewing prisoners were perceived by the police as being the top three most important tasks, with interviewing prisoners being rated as the most important task.

Stockdale (1993) found many police officers to agree that there was considerable room for improvement in the standard of investigative interviewing. Many officers believed that they themselves could interview well, or were at least unwilling to admit that they might be deficient in this area. Bull and Cherryman (1996) found that no police officers (taken from a group of 93 police officers who were experienced at specialist investigative interviewing) rated themselves as 'poor' but 6 per cent did rate themselves as 'less skilled'. In contrast, 16 per cent rated themselves as 'highly skilled' and 77 per cent rated themselves as 'skilled', but are police officers able to evaluate their own ability? Baldwin (1992) reported how the officer who emerged as the poorest interviewer prided himself on his interviewing ability.

The effectiveness of training of investigative interviewing was experimentally tested by McGurk *et al.* (1993). They found that a newly devised training course seemed to improve officers' investigative interviewing. Further, Stockdale (1993) recommends that training of supervisors and managers must occur to ensure effective quality control of investigative interviews.

There is the possibility that the police culture may be preventing individual officers from publicly acknowledging that they may be deficient in this (or any other) area. Useful criteria for skilled interviewing have been set out, but it is not known to what extent the more skilled/advanced interviewing techniques can be taught. Baldwin (1992) reported how several very good interviewers had received no training and several officers who were rated only as moderate had extensive experience of training. He noted that the correlation between training and performance as an interviewer was 'rather low'. Baldwin further suggested that, whatever training is given, there is probably a hard core of officers who are unlikely to become competent interviewers. He argued that competition between forces to provide courses with higher levels of sophistication in interviewing skills may be counter-productive but that 'There is certainly a place for specialist training but it should be reserved for that minority of interviewers with proven abilities' (p. 29).

Differences among police officers

Some of the most recent research on police investigative interviewing has examined whether different officers display different interviewing styles. Sear and Stephenson (1997) examined whether officers' personality scores in terms of agreeableness, conscientiousness, dominance, neuroticism, and openness related to their interviewing behaviour. They found few relationships, partly, they suggested, because most officers displayed a similar 'cold, calculating and dominating approach to others' (p. 32). Even officers with the higher openness personality scores did not display openness in their interviewing.

Williamson (1993) did find consensus among officers in their interviewing styles. He categorised four styles, these being: dominant, collusive, counselling and business-like. He found two-thirds of officers to identify with one of these styles, with the remainder not identifying with only one style of interviewing suspects. More research is needed on the similarities/differences among interviewers, particularly on the extent to which interviewers are able to vary the style they adopt as a function of the circumstances.

Recently we have noted that while 'experts' agreed among themselves concerning the skills demonstrated in a reasonably large set of police investigative interviews with suspects (Bull and Cherryman, 1996; Cherryman and Bull, 1996), other police officers' evaluations of a sample of the same interviews did not agree with the 'experts' but appeared to be driven by whether or not a confession occurred (Cherryman *et al.*, 1998a). However, the evaluations of experienced officers who supervised and/or trained police investigative interviewing were not affected by whether there was a confession, but did not concur with each other (Cherryman *et al.*, 1998b).

Conclusion

McKenzie (1994) noted that 'The [1981] Royal Commission on Criminal Procedure suggested that the development of the "Skills of interviewing" by police officers should be placed on a "more systematic basis", and in so doing placed the onus on the police to put their own house in order' (p. 244). The recent efforts of police forces in England/Wales to do this are to be welcomed.

At last a sufficient body of knowledge now exists on investigative interviewing, including specialist or advanced interviewing (Bull, 1999; Milne and Bull, 1999), to inform the design of training courses. It cannot afford to be brief (see Memon *et al.*, 1995). Therefore, at a time of economic restraint, is it feasible to attempt effective investigative interview training for all police officers, or should extensive training (especially for specialist work) be restricted to only a proportion of officers?

Notes

1 The Miranda warnings come from a much publicised case in the USA, *Miranda* v *Arizona* (383 US 436, 1966) where there was a realisation that interrogation techniques may create, in and of themselves, enough pressure for an innocent suspect to confess.
2 Mental state, age, learning disability, physical illness, intoxication, etc.
3 Caution being complied with, access to a solicitor, length of detention prior to interview, period of time alone.
4 Threats, oppressive interviewing style, inducements, promises, etc.

References

Baldwin, J. (1992) *Video Taping of Police Interviews with Suspects – an Evaluation.* Police Research Series: Paper No. 1. London: Home Office.

Baldwin, J. (1993) 'Police Interview Techniques: Establishing Truth or Proof?', *British Journal of Criminology,* 33, 325–51.

Baldwin, J. (1994) 'Police Interrogation: What Are the Rules of the Game?' in Morgan and Stephenson (1994).

Baldwin, J. and Bedward, J. (1991) 'Summarising of Tape Recordings of Police Interviews', *Criminal Law Review,* 671–9.

Baldwin, J. and McConville, M. (1980) *Confessions in Crown Court Trials.* Royal Commission on Criminal Procedure, Research Study No. 5. London: HMSO.

Brown, D. (1989) *PACE and the Right to Legal Advice.* Home Office Research Unit Bulletin 26. London: Home Office.

Bull, R. (1992) 'Obtaining Evidence Expertly: The Reliability of Interviews with Child Witnesses', *Expert Evidence,* 1, 3–36.

Bull, R. (1994) 'How to Interview Child Witnesses', *Solicitor's Journal,* 138, 332–3.

Bull, R. (1995a) 'Interviewing People with Communicative Disabilities' in Bull and Carson (1995).

Bull, R. (1995b) 'Investigative Techniques for the Questioning of Child Witnesses, Especially Those Who Are Very Young and Those with Learning Disability' in Zaragoza *et al.* (1995).

Bull, R. (1999) 'Police Investigative Interviewing' in Memon and Bull (1999).

Bull, R., Bustin, R., Evans, P. and Gahagan, D. (1983) *Psychology for Police Officers.* Chichester: Wiley.

Bull, R. and Carson, D. (eds) (1995) *Handbook of Psychology in Legal Contexts.* Chichester: Wiley.

Bull, R. and Cherryman, J. (1996) *Helping to Identify Skills Gaps in Specialist Investigative Interviewing: Enhancement of Professional Skills.* London: Home Office Police Department.

Bull, R. and Cullen, C. (1992) *Witnesses Who Have Mental Handicaps.* Document prepared for The Crown Office, Edinburgh.

Bull, R. and Cullen, C. (1993) 'Interviewing the Mentally Handicapped', *Policing,* 6, 82–4.

Ceci, S. and Bruck, M. (1995) *Jeopardy in the Courtroom: A Scientific Analysis of Children's Testimony.* Washington, DC: American Psychological Association.

Central Planning and Training Unit (1992a) *A Guide to Interviewing.* Harrogate.

Central Planning and Training Unit (1992b) *The Interviewer's Rule Book.* Harrogate.

Cherryman, J. and Bull, R. (1996) 'Specialist Investigative Interviewing: An Analysis of Audio Tape Recorded Interviews with Suspects'. Paper presented at the Biennial Convention of the American Psychology and Law Society, Hilton Head Island, SC, USA.

Cherryman, J., Bull, R. and Vrij, A. (1998a) 'British Police Officers' Evaluations of Investigative Interview with Suspects'. Poster Presentation at the 24th International Congress of Applied Psychology and Law, San Francisco, USA.

Cherryman, J., Bull, R. and Vrij, A. (1998b) 'Investigative Interviewing: British Police Officer's Evaluations of Real Life Interviews with Suspects'. Paper Presented at the European Conference on Psychology and Law, Krakow, Poland.

Clark, N.K. and Stephenson, G.M. (eds) (1994) *Rights and Risks: The Application of Forensic Psychology.* Leicester: British Psychological Society.

Clark, N.K. and Stephenson, G.M. (1996) *Investigative Interviewing and Decision Making.* Leicester: BPS.

Dixon, D. (1990) 'Juvenile Suspects and the Police and Criminal Evidence Act' in Freestone (1990).

Evans, R. (1993) *The Conduct of Police Interviews with Juveniles.* London: HMSO.

Evans, R. (1994) 'Police Interviews with Juveniles' in Morgan and Stephenson (1994).

Feldman, D. (1990) 'Regulating Treatment of Suspects in Police Stations', *Criminal Law Review,* 452–71.

Fisher, R. Geiselman, R.E. and Raymond, D. (1987) 'Police Interview Techniques', *Journal of Police Science and Administration,* 15, 177–85.

Freestone, D. (ed.) (1990) *Children and the Law.* Hull: Hull University Press.

George, R. (1991) *A Field Evaluation of the Cognitive Interview.* Unpublished Master's Thesis, Polytechnic of East London.

Gudjonsson, G. (1992) *The Psychology of Interrogations, Confessions and Testimony.* Chichester: Wiley.

Gudjonsson, G. (1993) 'Confession Evidence, Psychological Vulnerability and Expert Testimony', *Journal of Community and Applied Social Psychology,* 3, 117–29.

Gudjonsson, G. (1994) 'Psychological Vulnerability: Suspects at Risk' in Morgan and Stephenson (1994).

Gudjonsson, G. and Clare, I.C.H. (1994) 'The Proposed New Police Caution (England and Wales): How Easy Is It to Understand?', *Expert Evidence,* 3, 109–12.

Gudjonsson, G. and MacKeith, J. (1994) 'Learning Disability and the Police and Criminal Evidence Act 1984. Protection During Investigative Interviewing: A Video-Recorded False Confession to Double Murder', *Journal of Forensic Psychiatry*, 5, 35–49.

Hirst, J. (1993) *Royal Commission Research Papers: A Policing Perspective*. Police research series: Paper No. 6. London: Home Office.

Hodgson, P. (1987) *A Practical Guide to Successful Interviewing*. Maindenhead: McGraw-Hill.

Irving, B. and McKenzie, I. (1989) *Police Interrogation: The Effects of the Police and Criminal Evidence Act*. London: The Police Foundation.

Irving, B. and McKenzie, I. (1993) *A Brief Review of Relevant Police Training* in Research Study No. 21 for the Royal Commission on Criminal Justice. London: HMSO.

Jenkins, D. (1993) 'The Custodial Interrogation – Fitness to be Interviewed', *Criminal Lawyer*, 38, 1–3.

Kassin, S. and McNall, K. (1991) 'Police Interrogations and Confessions: Communicating Promises and Threats by Pragmatic Implication', *Law and Human Behaviour*, 15, 233–51.

Köhnken, G. (1995) 'Interviewing Adults' in Bull and Carson (1995).

Köhnken, G., Milne, R., Memon, A. and Bull, R. (1999) 'The Cognitive Interview: A Meta-Analysis', *Psychology, Crime and Law*, 5: 3–27.

Leng, R. (1994) 'The Right-to-Silence Debate' in Morgan and Stephenson (1994).

Leo, R. A. (1992) 'From Coercion to Deception: The Changing Nature of Police Interrogation in America', *Crime, Law and Social Change*, 18, 35–59.

MacDonald, J. and Michaud, D. (1987) *The Confession and Criminal Profiles for Police Officers*. Denver: Apache Press.

McConville, M. (1993) *Corroboration and Confessions: The Impact of a Rule Requiring that No Conviction Can Be Sustained on the Basis of Confession Evidence Alone*. Royal Commission on Criminal Justice. London: HMSO.

McConville, M., Hodgson, J., Bridges, L. and Pavlovic, A. (1994) *Standing Accused*. Oxford: Clarendon Press.

McGurk, B., Carr, J. and McGurk, D. (1993) *Investigative Interviewing Courses for Police Officers: An evaluation*. Police Research Series, Paper No. 4. London: Home Office.

McGurk, B., Platton, T. and Gibson, R. L. (1994) 'Detectives: A Job and Training Needs Analysis' in Clark and Stephenson (1994).

McKenzie, I. (1994) 'Regulating Custodial Interviews: A Comparative Study', *International Journal of the Sociology of Law*, 22, 239–59.

Maguire, M. (1994) 'The Wrong Message at the Wrong Time? The Present State of Investigative Practice' in Morgan and Stephenson (1994).

Memon, A. and Bull, R. (1991) 'The Cognitive Interview: Its Origins, Empirical Support, Evaluation and Practical Implications', *Journal of Community and Applied Social Psychology*, 1, 1–18.

Memon, A. and Bull, R. (eds) (1999) *Handbook of the Psychology of Interviewing*. Chichester: Wiley.

Memon, A., Bull, R. and Smith, M. (1995) 'Improving the Quality of Police Interviews: Can Training in Use of Cognitive Techniques Help?', *Policing and Society*, 5, 53–68.

Memon, A., Holley, A., Milne, R., Köhnken, G. and Bull, R. (1994) 'Toward Understanding the Effects of Interviewer Training in Evaluating the Cognitive Interview', *Applied Cognitive Psychology*, 8, 641–59.

Memon, A., Vrij, A. and Bull, R. (1998) *Psychology and Law: Truthfulness, Accuracy and Credibility*. Maidenhead: McGraw-Hill.

Milne, R. and Bull, R. (1996) 'Interviewing Children with Mild Learning Disability with the Cognitive Interview' in Clark and Stephenson (1996).

Milne, R. and Bull, R. (1999) *Investigative Interviewing: Psychology and Practice*. Chichester: Wiley.

Milne, R., Clare, I. and Bull, R. (1999) 'The Use of the Cognitive Interview for Adults with Mild Learning Disability', *Psychology, Crime and Law*, 5: 81–99.

Morgan, D. and Stephenson, G. (eds) (1994) *Suspicion and Silence: The Right to Silence in Criminal Investigations*. London: Blackstone.

Mortimer, A. (1994a) 'Asking the Right Questions', *Policing*, 9, 111–24.

Mortimer, A. (1994b) 'Police Investigative Interviewing: Pre-Interview Thinking and Written Interview Behaviour'. Paper presented at the 4th European conference on Psychology and Law, Barcelona.

Moston, S. (1990) 'The Ever So Gentle Art of Interrogation'. Paper presented at the Annual Conference of the British Psychological Society, Swansea.

Moston, S. and Engleberg, T. (1993) 'Police Questioning Techniques in Tape Recorded Interviews with Criminal Suspects', *Policing and Society*, 3, 223–37.

Moston, S. and Stephenson, G.M. (1990) 'Predictors of Suspect and Interviewer Behaviour during Police Questioning'. Paper presented at 2nd European Conference on Law and Psychology, Nürnburg.

Moston, S. and Stephenson, G.M. (1993) *Police Interrogation and Suspect Behaviour*. Leicester: British Psychological Society.

Moston, S. Stephenson, G. and Williamson, T. (1990) *Police Interrogation Styles and Suspect Behaviour*. Summary Report to Police Requirements Unit. London: Home Office.

Moston, S. Stephenson, G. and Williamson, T. (1992) 'The Effects of Case Characteristics on Suspect Behaviour during Police Questioning', *British Journal of Criminology*, 32, 23–40.

National Crime Faculty (1996) *Investigative Interviewing: A Practical Guide*. Bramshill: National Crime Faculty.

Pearse, J. and Gudjonsson, G. (1996) 'Police Interviewing Techniques at Two South London Police Stations', *Psychology, Crime and Law*, 3, 63–74.

Plimmer, J. (1997) 'Confession Rate', *Police Review*, 7 February, 16–18.

Poole, D. and Lamb, M. (1998) *Investigative Interviews of Children: A Guide for Helping Professionals*. Washington, DC: American Psychological Association.

Sanders, A., Bridges, L., Mulvaney, A. and Crozier, C. (1989) *Advice and Assistance at Police Stations and the 24 Hour Duty Solicitor Scheme*. London: Lord Chancellor's Department.

Sear, L. and Stephenson, G. (1997) 'Interviewing Skills and Individual Characteristics of Police Interrogators' in Stephenson and Clark (1997).

Shepherd, E. (1991) Resistance in Interviews: The Contribution of Police Perceptions and Behaviour'. Paper presented at the British Psychological Society Division of Criminological and Legal Psychology Conference, Canterbury.

Shepherd, E. (1992) 'Ethical Interviewing', *Policing*, 7, 42–60.

Shepherd, E. (1994) *Becoming skilled: Police Station Skills for Legal Advisors*. London: The Law Society.

Skolnick, J. and Leo, R. (1992) 'The Ethics of Deceptive Interrogation', *Criminal Justice Ethics*, Winter/Spring, 3–12.

Stephenson, G. and Clark, N. (eds) (1997) *Procedures in Criminal Justice.* Leicester: British Psychological Society.

Stockdale, J. (1993) *Management and Supervision of Police Interviews.* Police Research Group Paper 5. London: Home Office.

Stutz, W. (1989) 'The American Exclusionary Rule and Defendants' Charging Rights', *Criminal Law Review,* 117–28.

Torpy, D. (1994) 'You Must Confess' in Clark and Stephenson (1994).

Walsh, B. (1994) 'Interrogation an Important Tool for Law Enforcement', *National Resource Center on Child Sexual Abuse Newsletter,* 3, 3–4.

Williamson, T. (1993) 'From Interrogation to Investigative Policing: Strategic Trends in Police Questioning', *Journal of Community and Applied Social Psychology,* 3, 89–99.

Williamson, T. (1994) 'Reflections on Current Police Practice' in Morgan and Stephenson (1994).

Zander, M. (1979) 'The Investigation of Crime: A Study of Cases Tried at the Old Bailey', *Criminal Law Review,* 203–19.

Zaragoza, M. *et al.* (eds) (1995) *Memory and Testimony in the Child Witness.* Thousand Oaks, CA: Sage.

Part III
ACCOUNTABILITY, ORGANISATION AND MANAGEMENT

Chapter 13

New directions in accountability

BARRY LOVEDAY

Introduction

The issue of police accountability has in recent years become less of a politically contested issue than it was in the 1980s. For a variety of reasons the debate over policing has tended to focus largely on improving, *inter alia*, police effectiveness, police management and related questions rather more than consideration of how the police service should be made accountable for what it does. There have been, of course, some exceptions. A number of commentators have continued to explore the development of new structures of accountability and the complexities which surround this subject (Loader, 1999; Jones and Newburn, 1994; Waddington, 1999). It is, however, fair to say that in large part, performance management and measurement within police forces have assumed a significance that only reflects a more general trend within all public services, which are now overwhelmingly concerned with service delivery. This emphasis was, of course, a reflection of the earlier Conservative government's priorities. Yet, this can only be expected to continue, given 'New' Labour's complete agreement with this approach and its adherence to performance measurement in the public sector. Such indeed is the salience accorded to 'performance management' that it must now be viewed as a primary mechanism in terms of making the police accountable for what they do (see Waters, Chapter 16).

While performance management has assumed, in terms of accountability, a high significance, it is also the case that over recent years other developments have helped to reshape the structure of formal accountability of the police. Related closely to the issue of performance has been, of course, the influence exercised by the Audit Commission, the reports from which, particularly in the 1990s, proved to be so decisive in the reorganisation of police forces in terms of their internal organisation and structure (e.g. Audit Commission, 1993, 1996). Closely linked to the rise of the Audit Commission has been the expanded role now accorded to Her Majesty's Inspectorate of Constabulary (HMIC). A decision to enable the HMIC to publish both annual reports on police forces and undertake 'thematic' reviews has given this body a new influence based on greater publicity which has for example served, in a not too dissimilar way, to highlight the work of the Prison Inspectorate in recent years. This, along with the extension of the Inspectorate's responsibilities to include the London Metropolitan Police Service, has arguably given the HMIC both a new 'political' edge and influence that even the most recalcitrant chief constable may find difficult to elude. Additionally, the Metropolitan Police Service will be made statutorily answerable to a new London police committee which will be linked to new forms of government for London, most notably to its elected Mayor.

The role of HMIC is, of course, very closely linked to the expanded responsibilities of the Home Secretary. Following the Police Act of 1964 it was at times difficult to ascertain the extent to which the Home Secretary was able to influence policing policy, given the lack of transparency that ultimately characterised the 'tripartite relationship' of chief constable, Home Secretary and Police Authority established by this statute. As was to be argued later, it appeared that very often the Home Secretary, made responsible for the 'efficiency' of police forces (among much else), was able to exercise 'power without responsibility' as he (*sic*) would often refuse to answer in the House of Commons questions on 'local policing' matters which his office had clearly influenced (Reiner, 1992; Reiner and Spencer, 1993). Since the introduction of the Police and Magistrates' Courts Act (1994), this matter has, however, become somewhat clearer. Under this Act the Home Secretary is now given explicit responsibility for determining what are described as 'national key objectives' which all police forces in England and Wales must be expected to pursue (see Waters, Chapter 16 in this volume).

Nor can, in relation to accountability, new police discipline and complaints mechanisms be overlooked. Following an influential report from the Select Committee on Home Affairs, the Home Secretary was to announce significant changes to police discipline regulations, particularly in relation to standards of proof required to sustain a complaint against a police officer. The issue of complaints procedures was also to be addressed in Northern Ireland where following the passing of the Police (Northern Ireland) Act in 1998 the Office of Ombudsman was to replace the Northern Ireland Independent Commission for Complaints. One very noticeable feature of this legislation was to be the creation of a civilian investigative body whose members would be given all the powers of a constable, particularly in relation to search and seizure of evidence (Loveday, 1999).

These and other developments might suggest that the degree of accountability required of the police service is now of such an order that the debate could be effectively brought to a close. Greater intervention in police management and service delivery, largely at a national rather than a local level has, it could be argued, served to make the police service answerable for their actions to a degree not countenanced by the police service only two decades ago. To what extent, however, have these developments provided an effective mechanism which makes the police service accountable to the people? To what extent does the current emphasis on performance, quality of service *et al.* provide both a new and effective form of police governance?

Accountability: the local dimension

The Conservative governments' commitment to making public services more 'business-like' in their management was, of course, to extend to local police forces and police authorities. Under the Police and Magistrates' Courts Act 1994 the traditional role of the police authority as a largely elected adjunct to the County Council was to be significantly diluted as a consequence of the then government's espoused aim to improve the efficiency of police forces. In what proved to be a spurious claim, the same government radically reduced the membership of local police authorities, from around 30 members to 16, while requiring the new authorities, along with the Home Secretary, to jointly select 'independent' nominations to make these bodies more 'representative of the community'. It is sufficient to note that while the Conservative Home Secretary, Michael Howard, was to claim to seek wider social representation, ultimately those independents who were to be selected were drawn overwhelmingly from professional and/or business backgrounds (Loveday, 1995). Outside of the Metropolitan Areas, where Joint Boards already pertained, the change in membership of the police authority was to be matched by the effective secession of the authority from the local County Council, as the 'reformed' authorities were made, within the 1994 Act, independent of the local authority. They have become free-standing corporate bodies and enjoy effective autonomy in terms of funding. The resulting 'democratic deficit' provided only further evidence of the Conservative campaign against local authority provision. It was, however, to be justified in terms of improved efficiency in both the delivery and management of police services.

Monitoring performance

The commitment to better management of service was to be also reflected in terms of the responsibilities given to the 'new' police authorities. While they continue to have a statutory responsibility for recording complaints against the police, the primary duties which now fall to them consist of local community consultation and 'monitoring' police performance. They also have a responsibility for setting the annual budget and for drawing up the Local Policing Plan each year. Within the latter, the police authority is able to identify local policing objectives and targets for the police force on an annual basis. The same policing plan will also accommodate those national key objectives identified for the forthcoming year by the Home Secretary. These responsibilities contrast rather strongly with those which police authorities have had to relinquish and which gave them a 'hands-on' responsibility for the provision of police support services. It does, however, serve to highlight the new form of managerial rather than electoral accountability which now characterises their operation. The primary function of the police authority is to help set objectives and thereafter to monitor police performance. In doing so, the police authority is also required to provide an annual report to the Home Secretary identifying police performance in relation to set targets.

Just how successful police authorities have proved to be in discharging these responsibilities remains a matter of debate. Early evidence from one police force suggested that elected members and some magistrates found it difficult to respond to the new emphasis placed on managerial performance measures which reflected the now rather etiolated role given to the police authority. Nor was the police authority able to make a real judgement of police efficiency through league tables or other performance indicators as it had no source of information or analysis that was independent of the police. Indeed, one of the interesting features of current arrangements remains the complete dependence of the police authority on information provided by the police force for which they have ostensible oversight (Loveday, 1998). Nor has the police authority any ready means of penalising either the police force or its most senior representative for underperformance. As the chief officer retains operational independence and may as a consequence ignore the Local Policing Plan at any time, for operational reasons, it becomes difficult for the police authority to exercise any real influence over what the police either do or fail to do. Moreover, while most chief officers are now on 'fixed contracts', these are best described as 'soft contracts' designed very largely, it would seem, to protect pension rights rather than being linked to performance outputs (Baker, 1996). Any likelihood of police authorities seeking to develop a more independent role may be made more difficult as police chiefs, with the clear encouragement of HMIC, have increasingly sought to envelop the Local Policing Plan within five-year Strategic Plans for the police force. These Strategic Plans are essentially police-led and directed, as minimal police authority input commensurate with the legislation is encouraged (Loveday, 1998).

Community consultation

One further responsibility of the police authority encompasses community liaison and consultation. Established under the Police and Criminal Evidence Act in 1984, police/community consultative groups now operate under the Police Act 1996. It was the existence of these fora which the Conservative government was to use, in part, as a defence for the radical reduction in elected members on local police authorities. First identified as a more useful way of engaging the community than electoral mechanisms by Kenneth Baker when Home Secretary in 1991, it was always seen by that government as one effective way of undermining local authority responsibilities against which both the Thatcher and Major governments waged open war. As has been demonstrated by both independent research and HMIC inspection, however, the laudable aims and intentions which lay behind their creation in the Scarman Report (1981) has proved difficult, if not impossible to implement (Morgan and Maggs, 1985; Stratta, 1990; Loveday, 1998).

Evidence from both official reports and research suggests that these fora have failed to engage the local community to any great extent and, in terms of their membership, appear to reflect a social class that can usually be expected to have least contact with the police in any capacity. Largely white, male, middle-class and middle-aged, they may continue to view these fora as being largely 'educative', where the local police seek to explain current police priorities and (the inadequacy of) resources. Some commentators have more recently attempted to defend the reform of local police governance by reference to the statutory requirement placed on police authorities under the 1996 Police Act, to consult with all community liaison groups prior to agreeing to the Local Policing Plan (Morgan and Newburn, 1997). It is likely, however, that little was expected from this consultative mechanism by the government which undertook these reforms, other than undermining local government provision (Loveday, 1991). The emphasis given to police consultative arrangements may have reflected a quite different and partisan political agenda and is one which may have eluded those commentators who, later, were so readily to defend these 'reforms'.

Public participation remains extremely limited and public interest may not have been readily sustained, if only because of the very limited amount of information released to consultation groups by police representatives. It would appear that, while the police may view the consultative process as one that is largely educative, this will be based on very limited amounts of information which may impede those attending from making any informed judgement about current (or past) policing activity. Poor attendance can, therefore, be expected to follow on from poor communication. One example, drawn at random from recent HMIC reports, may serve to identify the nature of the problem. As was noted under Community Consultative Arrangements in an inspection of one force:

> In all areas meetings are held at least quarterly within divisions and in addition to members of the authority and police officers, over thirty members of the public have [on average] attended over the last twelve months ... Although discussion takes place about the following years' force level and divisional policing plans, there is limited awareness of their content amongst even those members of the public who are most interested in policing. This is partly due to little written information being provided by the police about divisional performance ... PCCG discussions about policing plans ... usually take place without any written information about past divisional performance or options for future priorities, making it difficult for members of the public to contribute constructively.
>
> (HMIC South Wales Police, 1997/8: 7.6/7)

While in this example HMIC was to recommend that new ways needed to be found to provide information to PCCGs, it is difficult to accept that these bodies could be expected to provide any meaningful contribution to the local police planning process in which they are now statutorily involved. The very limited value of PCCGs has been recognised by the Home Office, whose research arm has identified a number of alternative strategies that might be usefully employed to identify 'community views' (Police Research Group, 1996). The 'black hole' in terms of local consultation that now exists within the 'reformed' structure of local police governance remains a matter of concern, if only because it effectively undermines the planning process which supposedly characterises the generation of current policing strategies. Thus, the police authority has neither the information nor independence to critically evaluate police proposals. Neither is it very frequently in receipt of informed views and priorities from the community by way of community consultation. One consequence of this unfortunate conjunction is that the police force itself becomes the primary formulator of policing strategies, a feature which may have been reinforced by changes in police force budgetary responsibilities from police authority to chief constable required under the 1996 Police Act.

The chief officer

One overall 'winner' from the 1996 Police Act has been the chief constable. With the requirement within the Act to devolve the budget from the Police Authority to the chief officer, the latter now has effective control over all expenditures. As such, the chief officer has become both the purchaser and provider of services. One consequence of this has been the recruitment of support staff (finance and accountancy personnel) to enable the chief officer to manage the force. As budget holders, chief officers now have an immediate responsibility for all police manpower decisions and it is for the chief officer to decide as to the manpower level deemed to be appropriate. Additionally as budget holder, this officer has a responsibility for the provision of support services, police buildings, civilian staff, police vehicles, etc. which were once those of the police authority. As a result of devolved budgeting, therefore, it is now the case that the chief officer has both financial and operational control of the police force. Although devolved budgeting was in fact predicated on further devolution of the budget from the chief officer to Local Command Units, this has yet to be accomplished in many forces and as a result most resource decisions continue to be taken at police headquarters (Loveday, 1998).

One consequence of statutory reform has therefore been a significant enhancement of the 'power balance' of the chief constable and the police force overall, in relation to the police authority. This position has additionally been further strengthened by the continuing development of the Association of Chief Police Officers (ACPO) whose permanent secretariat, based in London, now provides a degree of policy co-ordination for ACPO members never before experienced. Such co-ordination of approach to both the Home Office and to police authorities may also substantially enhance the overall influence of both the Association and individual chief officers (Cope et al., 1997). One reflection of such co-ordination may perhaps be seen in the creation within many police headquarters of 'Command or Business Teams' by the chief officer, itself a reflection of the new 'managerial' and 'business' approach to which they are committed. They will also now usually include senior civilian support personnel, who report directly to the chief officer, not the police authority. It is these teams, which are the primary motors of the planning cycle referred to earlier, which highlight the reality of such planning which is largely police initiated and police led. This is unlikely to change to any significant degree as police authority dependence on police data becomes inevitable, since this body has no independent source of information, little in terms of resources and very limited numbers of support staff.

The limited influence which the police authority can exercise may however be changing with the arrival of the Association of Police Authorities (APA). This new association has replaced the bifurcated structure based on the two local authority associations which were to subsequently amalgamate within the single Local Authority Association. Yet, as minutes from its annual workshop appear to demonstrate, the position of the police authority remains problematic. As was to be argued by members of one recent APA workshop, 'policing plans had a limited effect as a means of enforcing changes on a chief constable' and, 'If people perceive the chief constable to be the more powerful in the relationship they are right' (Association of Police Authorities, 1998). Elsewhere an APA working party was to consider on the basis of experience to date whether the police authority should commission independent research. The conclusion that it should do so was, however, more than balanced by the observation that 'police forces were not in favour of police authorities conducting independent research' (Association of Police Authorities, 1998). Additional matters of concern which served to substantiate claims of police authority dependence on the police force related to 'reliance on seminars in police authorities' which appeared to give 'the police undue influence in moulding opinion among members', as the police provided the main source of information when these were held (Association of Police Authorities, 1998).

On this basis it would appear that the evident imbalance between chief officers and the police authority may now be compounded by the performance monitoring which falls to the police authority based largely on data generated and explained by senior police officers. The apparent cul-de-sac which is currently being closely explored by the 'reformed' police authorities may come at some cost, however. First, it is not at all clear that local or strategic plans have any bearing at all on policing on the ground. Evidence from numerous inspections suggests that in many police forces this approach remains a paper exercise that in the absence of effective internal channels of communication primarily engages chief officers rather than the force as a whole (Loveday, 1999). If this is the case, it would appear that individual discretion exercised by operational officers on the ground can be expected to be as significant as ever with the attendant problems that this can be expected to generate (Choongh, 1997). Yet, the severely reduced elected element within the 'reformed police authorities' also means that channels of communication up from the community have been significantly curtailed. In this situation, the democratic deficit which characterises local police governance becomes a matter of some concern.

With just nine elected members, it is unlikely that these will be able to pick up on matters of concern to the 'communities' policed. Indeed, the term 'community' ceases to have any application at all within the larger regional police areas such as West Midlands or West Yorkshire, where over a million people may now be represented by nine elected councillors. Moreover, the removal of the police authority from real contact with the community policed can have embarrassing consequences. As the appointment by the Merseyside Police Authority in 1998 of a new chief constable was to demonstrate, the police authority did not appear able to identify issues which might raise questions of public confidence over appointments made in its name (Loveday and Brearley, 2000). If, therefore, it is argued that the police authorities are now more 'business-like', they appear to be far less aware of local concerns and political nuances which their predecessor bodies could usually be expected to detect. Indeed, as the Merseyside experience demonstrated, while the police authority could apparently deal with any number of performance measures and indicators, it appeared unable to accurately gauge the feelings of the people it ostensibly claimed to represent. In the case of Merseyside, to appear to be able to fully grasp the content of agenda items with which it was confronted.

The managerialist orientation of current mechanisms of accountability appear to have generated some less than attractive results. Effectively the operational financial and planning responsibilities within police forces are firmly in the hands of the chief officer. There appears to be, however, no real counterbalance from local police authorities or indeed PCCGs. As a consequence, it might well be argued that, far from being 'too political', current local accountability mechanisms are not 'political' enough. In opposition, the current Home Secretary, Jack Straw, introduced in 1979 a Police Bill to empower, quite significantly, local police authorities, a proposal which would seem to have gone the same way as very much else with 'New' Labour. The Home Secretary appears to have no plans to change the current structure of police authorities, inherited from the last Conservative government, and has in fact only reiterated his continued commitment to performance measurement as a critical element in bringing police forces to account (Police Foundation, 1998).

The Patten Report and policing Northern Ireland

The need for effective mechanisms of accountability has, of course, been most recently identified by the Patten Commission on policing. It is of interest here that the Commission was to recognise early on that, to secure support, the new policing arrangements would need cross a divided community. It was important for a 'reformed' Police Board to command both respect and credibility, while also having real power and responsibility (Patten, 1999: 6.1). In the light of the progressive degradation of locally accountable police authorities in England and Wales, it is of interest to learn that for the Patten Commission an 'elected majority was essential' with the remaining membership (made up by 'independents') bringing additional expertise relevant to the work of the Board (Patten, 1999: 6.11). This structure, in fact, only replicated that imposed on police authorities in England

and Wales in earlier legislation. While many of the Patten proposals are likely within the context of Northern Ireland to improve 'transparency', it is also clear that the Commission did not have the benefit of a *tabula rasa* but was required to work within the statutory parameters of the 1998 Police Act designed by the former Conservative government and implemented by New Labour. As was to be noted within the Patten Report, the Police Act 1998 contained 'labyrinthine provisions as to objectives, performance targets and policing plans' which the Commission was to find confusing 'both in the text and the oral briefings received from Government officials' (Patten, 1999: 5.11).

For the Patten Commission, the obfuscation which performance management represented required it to explore more fully the nature and forms of accountability within the police service and the public sector more generally. In doing so, the Commission was to confront the convention of police 'operational independence' which in the past has proved so difficult to negotiate effectively. The basis of police 'constabulary independence' has been both analysed and fundamentally questioned by Geoffrey Marshall, who has concluded there is little in law or past practice to sustain such a convention (Marshall, 1965, 1978; Marshall and Loveday, 1994). In relation to the term 'operational independence', the Patten Commission was to argue that the term appeared to be an extrapolation from the phrase within the 1964 Police Act which gave the chief officer the 'direction and control' of the police force. The Commission was to conclude, however, that the scrutiny of the police would be impeded by the assertion that such scrutiny be limited to matters outside the scope of police 'operational independence'. As was to be argued within the Report:

> Long consideration has led us to the view that the term 'operational independence' is itself a large part of the problem. In a democratic society all public officials must be fully accountable to the institutions of that society for the due performance of their functions and a chief of police cannot be an exception. No public official, including a chief of police, can be said to be 'independent'. Indeed, given the extraordinary powers conferred upon the police, it is essential that their exercise is subject to the closest and most effective scrutiny possible.
>
> (Patten, 1999: 6.20)

The Commission noted that the use of the term 'operational independence' did not exempt the conduct of an 'operational matter' from enquiry or review. It was to comment, however, that while this was so, the use of the term might suggest that it did, 'and the invocation of the concept by a recalcitrant chief constable could have the effect' that it was (Patten, 1999: 6.21). As a result, the Patten Commission was to recommend that in future 'operational responsibility' was the most appropriate term to encapsulate the duty which fell to the chief officer. In encouraging the application of 'explanatory accountability', the Commission was also to recommend the provision of a new power to the Police Board. This power would enable the Police Board to hold inquiries into any matter of concern to the Police Board and that all members of the police service should be required to co-operate with any inquiry (Patten, 1999: 6.23). The Commission was also to recommend that the Police Board be able to employ between 30 and 50 full-time staff to include experts in 'budgets, value for money, human rights and other key aspects of policing', which the Board would need to monitor the force. Police Board staff would also be able to conduct or participate in any such inquiries called for by the Police Board (Patten, 1999: 6.24).

One futher controversial recommendation from the Patten Commission which, with some amendments, has been accepted by the Secretary of State for Northern Ireland, concerns the creation of 'District Policing Partnership Boards'. These are to be established as a committee of the district council with a majority-elected membership which, it is intended, will encourage the decentralisation of policing within the Province. Some 'independents' with some expertise in community safety issues will also be recruited to the District boards. These 'independents' are also expected to broaden representation on the DPPBs in terms of religion, gender, age and cultural background. The proposal to give the DPPBs a revenue-raising power has been rejected and it is now unlikely that they will be able, as intended by the Commission (Patten, 1999: 6.33), to purchase 'additional services' from either the police or private sector. Nor is it envisaged that the DPPBs will replace existing police community-liaison arrangements, which are likely to be retained. The role of the DPPBs will, however, be to provide a platform and channel of communication between the local community and the police force. It will also act in an 'advisory, explanatory and consultative' capacity to the local police commander. All DPPBs' boundaries are to be made coterminous with a police district (Patten, 1999: 6.28). They will be expected to meet in public once a month and to establish procedures to 'allow for members of the public to address questions to the Board and the police' (Patten, 1999: 6.37). At the District level, moreover, the presumption will be, as elsewhere, to make public 'police codes of practice, all ethical and legal guidelines governing all aspects of police work, including such covert aspects as surveillance and the handling of informants' (Patten, 1996: 6.38). As is argued in the Report:

> The presumption should be that everything should be available for public scrutiny unless it is in the public interest, not the police interest, to hold it back.
>
> (Patten, 1996: 6.38)

Mechanisms of accountability

As has been recognised by the Patten Commission, a crucial element in establishing effective mechanisms of accountability continues to be closely linked to the creation of elected bodies that are themselves democratically accountable to the local community. Only in that way are they likely to enjoy the degree of legitimacy and authority which is required to bring the police force to account. It is primarily for these reasons that proposals for the creation of 'police commissions' recommended by some commentators (Jefferson and Grimshaw, 1984) and recently most persuasively by Loader (1999) would appear unlikely to long survive close scrutiny. As has been identified elsewhere (Loveday, 1995), nominations as an alternative (or in addition) to election, no matter how laudable the intention, ultimately raise questions of legitimacy concerning those nominated. Moreover, the creation of national, regional and local police commissions made up of elected and nominated members would appear likely to replicate the complexities of this kind of structure which characterised the earlier proposals of some commentators who argued a similar case (Jefferson and Grimshaw, 1984). It is also not at all clear that 'policing' can always be identified as a discrete issue divorced from other issues that require this service. The police function cannot be dissociated from social and economic factors which are unlikely to be within the power of a police commission either to address effectively or resolve (see Mawby, Chapter 7 in this volume). As a result, there must be a continuing need to bring police services more closely within the realm of local government rather than to encourage their further removal from this arena. This could be accomplished along with greater accountability through local direct election to police committees. Indeed, as Loader has succinctly argued:

> The requirement for representative institutions capable of rendering the police accountable remains of pivotal importance and free direct elections serve, in a democratic polity, as one of the most salient means for the production of such institutions. (Loader, 1994: 534)

The most effective provision of direct and free elections may still be based on local government and, as has been argued by one commentator, this remains the most effective form of both service provision and public participation (Jenkins, 1996). As has been clearly recognised by the Patten Commission, the police as a service can be expected to operate most successfully within a devolved structure where the police force area is congruent with local government boundaries. This may prove to be, anyway, a more attractive option than the creation of 'police commissions' which, being independent of other locally elected bodies, might in the long term be expected to exercise less influence as one product of their relative isolation from local government. It would also appear that, after two decades of centralisation, there is now a clear movement towards effective devolution to either regions or local government in terms of service responsibility. This has been demonstrated most clearly, for example, in relation to current crime and disorder strategies in England and Wales, which have been made a new, statutory responsibility of local authorities.

The Crime and Disorder Act 1998

One interesting development within the law and order field was to be the decision of New Labour to quickly implement its manifesto commitment on crime reduction strategies. In adopting the recommendations of the 1991 Morgan Report, New Labour was to give a new statutory responsibility to local authorities for the development of local crime and disorder strategies in conjunction with the local police force. Under the Act the local authority and chief police officers are made the 'responsible authorities' for initiating and implementing crime-reduction strategies with the co-operation of local probation and health services. By its introduction, the legislation ends the traditional police monopoly of responsibility for crime control within the local authority area. Under provisions within the Act this is now a responsibility shared with the local authority (Crime and Disorder Act, section 5).

In requiring the 'responsible authorities' to develop crime and disorder strategies, there is, perhaps for the first time, evidence of a more systematic approach to the problem of local crime control than ever pertained in the past. The 'responsible authorities' are now required to conduct a local crime audit and thereafter to publish a report based on the audit. They are also required to ascertain the views of 'persons or bodies' in the area (Crime and Disorder Act, section 6). Thereafter, a crime-reduction strategy will be formulated with short and long-term objectives and targets (see also Gilling in this volume, Chapter 8). Based on a three-year cycle, the local authority will be required to evaluate the effect of the strategy in terms of measuring its impact on, *inter alia*, crime rates, criminal damage and fear of crime in the local area.

In operationalising powers within the Crime and Disorder Act, much reliance is placed on inter-agency arrangements at the local level. Within the counties, the Chief Officers Group is made up of chief executives of districts and chief officers of police and probation services. At the local level, the local authority and local chief of police are expected to co-ordinate both the implementation of the crime-reduction strategy and its evaluation. As has become clear in the relatively short period of its operation, however, the Act has had some clear consequences for the police and can in the longer term be expected to impinge substantially on current mechanisms of accountability. One consequence of the introduction of local crime audits has been, for example, their adoption by the local police as the 'local policing plan' for the area. One result of the Act's requirement that this function be exercised as a local district function has been to throw into even further doubt the current value and purpose of the police authority's own Local Policing Plan. As has been demonstrated in a number of counties, the very number of local districts involved in the development of crime and disorder strategies has effectively fragmented the planning process and may well question the purpose of this function at the police authority level.

Within the context of the Crime and Disorder Act 1998, there is moreover an expectation that in provision of resources to reach crime-reduction objectives, the local district (or unitary) authority can expect to have a substantial input to both the initial district local policing plan and in the determination of policing priorities thereafter. In doing so, they might expect to exercise a more direct influence over what the police do than has probably ever pertained to police authorities both currently and in the past. In this context, any claim to 'operational independence', the traditional barrier to the joint determination of policing policy, can be expected to have far less application. This is because the the local crime strategy and its development can be expected to make the local authority an integral partner in this process which may also substantially increase the role of the local authority in local 'policing' policy over time. Additionally, as and when police budgets are devolved from police headquarters to local command units or divisions, the partnership arrangements established between the local authority and police force can be expected to be strengthened. Irrespective of that development, local authorities must be expected to exercise much greater influence over how policing priorities are determined in the area. This, again, is likely to raise questions as to the continued role of the 'local' police authority, whose immediate responsibilities would appear to be increasingly irrelevant to the local determination of operational policing activity at district level.

The significant changes to the delivery of policing at the local level and the statutory responsibilities now given to local authorities as responsible authorities under the Crime and Disorder Act may also raise new problems in terms of the accountability of both the police and other services involved in 'partnership arrangements'. To whom at county-council level, for example, is the Chief Officers Group ultimately accountable? To whom are the 'responsible authorities' at district (or unitary) level answerable for the implementation of crime-reduction strategies? While at district (or unitary) level this problem might be easily addressed by the creation of a local-authority-based 'community safety' or crime-prevention committee, there would appear to be no immediate structure that could encompass 'Chief Officer Groups' at the county level. Yet, as has been argued, it must be a clear expectation that, as current crime-reduction (and other) strategies unfold, the emphasis in terms of the determination of policing strategy may continue to be at the local level, made in close conjunction with the local authority. However, until the question of accountability in this context is ultimately resolved, it is clear that the Crime and Disorder Act may encourage the resurrection of a more 'local' dimension to policing than might have ever been intended by those responsible for the introduction of this legislation.

Accountability: the national dimension

Although there has been a new movement towards 'local' determination of policing, it is important to recognise that there have also been countervailing trends made evident in the expansion of policing responsibilities that have a clear national dimension. As such, these developments may only have further enhanced the responsibilities of the Home Secretary which have been substantially expanded under successive legislation. In addition to the operation of Regional Crime Squads which, as has been argued by Maguire and Norris (1992), cross the normal boundaries of accountability, the creation of both the National Criminal Intelligence Service and National Crime Squad have both served to clearly strengthen the national dimension to policing. This development, besides being seen as the most effective way to respond to both serious domestic and international crime (for example, the current 'drugs crisis'), may also have been encouraged by membership of the European Union. The national dimension is probably most clearly identified in the creation and operation of the National Crime Squad. Although at the time the government was eager not to make any comparison between the NCS and the FBI in the United States by stating that the NCS would be an 'adjunct' to local forces, nevertheless the creation of the NCS has led one commentator to suggest that:

> Although the initial functions of the NCS are in support of individual police forces, the development of the squad may well be seen as another step towards the eventual nationalisation of policing in the UK. (Uglow, 1997: 36)

For a variety of reasons, the mechanisms of accountability for both the NCS and NCIS have been the subject of debate. As has been identified by Uglow in terms of accountability, the governance of both the NCS and NCIS is modelled on that of local police forces which are controlled by the chief constable and accountable to the police authority. As the 'service authority' for the NCIS, its 'core' membership consists *inter alia* of 17 members made up of 'independent members' chosen by the Home Secretary, local authority members of police authorities and senior police officers. The primary function of the service authority is to 'maintain an overview of the work of the service' (Uglow, 1997: 11). This might prove to be difficult as the NCIS is given, under statute, a very wide remit in terms of intelligence gathering which is not restricted to 'serious crime' nor exclusively to the prevention and detection of crime.

Following the refusal of the then Conservative government to create a commissioner to oversee the NCIS function, particularly in terms of ensuring that unnecessary data was not collected and that standards were safeguarded (Uglow, 1997: 13), all quality-control measures remain internal to NCIS. It remains, therefore, a matter of speculation as to whether the 'service authority' as constituted can provide the degree of oversight in relation to data collection that an independent commissioner may have offered. This may prove to be a matter of concern particularly in the light of recent revelations concerning the accuracy of Criminal Records Certificates, now the responsibility of police forces (Cohen, 2000). In this context the accountability of this national police arm may be more tenuous than that which pertains to the National Crime Squad whose functions are limited to the prevention and detection of serious crime. The 1997 Police Act effectively merged long standing Regional Crime Squads into a national unit on a statutory basis and in so doing may have served to enhance their accountability. Thus, the National Crime Squad was established not merely to co-ordinate the work of existing Regional Crime Squads but to absorb them into a national structure under the control of a director general (Uglow, 1997: 39).

The creation and operation of these national police units reflect a long-term trend towards the extension of central government's influence over and responsibility for policing. This has, for example, proved to be most notable in relation to police training where a previously pronounced 'shared' responsibility between local police authorities and the Home Office has been replaced by National Police Training whose director (a member of HMIC) is based at the Police Staff College, Bramshill. Indeed, as the role and influence of the Home Secretary has been extended, it has to some degree raised fundamental questions as to the continued viability of current mechanisms of local accountability. This has arisen not just in relation to the long-term impact of the power given to the Home Secretary to set 'national key objectives' but also in relation to HM Inspectorate which reports to the Secretary of State. Under the Police and Magistrates' Courts Act 1994, it would appear that HMIC now has the unusual responsibility of overseeing and commenting upon the 'efficiency' of local police authorities in the discharge of their statutory duties, particularly in relation to the performance of the police within their annual reports (see HMIC Report, 1996/9). This development might be thought to raise some interesting issues in terms of the precise constitutional status of the police authority as a statutory body supposedly independent of central government.

Additionally, the Home Secretary has both a statutory responsibility for the 'efficiency' of police forces and also exercises a central role in the determination of complaints and discipline regulations for the police service. Most recently the Home Secretary has made clear his resolve to fundamentally change the standard of proof required to discipline errant police officers, following recommendations from the House of Commons Select Committee on Home Affairs report in 1998. In future, police officers may be found guilty of a disciplinary offence 'on the balance of probabilities' rather than on the basis of 'proof beyond reasonable doubt'. The application of standards of proof will, however, operate on a sliding scale reflecting both the seriousness of the alleged offence and the possible disciplinary outcome for the officer involved. The Home Secretary has also, following the Report of the Macpherson Inquiry into the death of Stephen Lawrence, accepted the recommendation to make the police service subject to new anti-discrimination laws. Under the Race Relations (Amendment) Act 2000, the police will be subject to provisions contained within the existing Race Relations Act from which the service was excluded during the passage of the original Act, following successful lobbying by the Police Federation at that time. As amended, the Act will also be used to combat institutionalised racism and indirect discrimination both within the police service and across the public sector (Travis, 2000b). It may also mean that in any future case where discriminatory behaviour is alleged by either a member of the public or a minority group police officer, the Commission for Racial Equality may be able to extend its power to carry out general and formal investigations into the police, possibly in conjunction with the Police Complaints Authority (Travis, 2000a). These developments only serve to emphasise the growing significance of national bodies in the 'local' government of the police.

Conclusion

Current developments within the police organisation both on a local and national basis might suggest that the nature and form of accountability of the police continues to remain a matter of concern. In terms of local accountability, this is manifested most clearly in the inability of the 'new' police authorities to effectively represent the interests of the local community and the failure of 'community consultation' in any way to redress the democratic imbalance occasioned by the removal of so many elected members under the Police and Magistrates' Courts Act 1994. Nor is the problem of the democratic deficit entirely resolved by developments initiated by the Crime and Disorder Act 1998. As yet, there are no clear mechanisms in place to make 'the responsible authorities' or the Chief Officers Group accountable for crime reduction or other local strategies they may pursue. In this context it remains unclear as to what role the police authority might be expected to play given its effective removal from local government and the fragmentation of the police planning process encouraged by the same Act.

It is the case, however, that for the foreseeable future, New Labour will continue to view police performance as an important means of making the police more 'accountable'. As the government's Strategic Plan for Criminal Justice demonstrates (Home Office, 1999), much importance continues to be attached to the police (and other criminal justice agencies) attaining a number of clearly identified objectives and targets.

For the police service, the continuing importance of performance measurement as a mechanism of accountability is probably best reflected in the application of the government's 'Best Value' initiative to local police forces. Within the Best Value programme, it is noticeable that failure on the part of an authority to achieve 'best value', or to significantly improve performance, may well lead to unilateral central government intervention, where a central department can be expected to take responsibility for the service. In this context it is interesting to discover that the police authority has been identified as the 'best value' authority, not the chief constable. This might be thought rather perverse given the little influence that body now exercises over either police operational matters or police finance. The application of 'best value', if not enhancing the role of local police authorities, could, however, encourage further central intervention into 'local policing arrangements' under the guise of improving 'police force efficiency'. Such intervention might be considered easier where the police authority was given ostensible responsibility for police performance.

One further and (potentially) most challenging development which can be expected to impinge on current mechanisms of accountability of the police relates to the Human Rights Act 1998 which applies for the first time the European Convention of Human Rights to domestic arrangements in England and Wales and comes into force in 2000. Within the Act, Article 5 deals with an individual's right to liberty and security and is concerned *inter alia* with the use of stop and search and arrest powers by the police and also suspect rights while in police detention. The provision of such protections as are offered within Article 5 will go some way towards strengthening suspects' rights now encapsulated within the Police and Criminal Evidence Act 1984. As has been argued in relation to the introduction of the Human Rights Act 1998, the provisions within Article 5 will ensure that any suspected breach of arrest and detention procedures will be subject to scrutiny by lawyers, be they attempting to persuade the Crown Prosecution Service or any other prosecuting parties to drop charges against their clients or litigating against a police force for maltreatment of a detainee during or after arrest (Bowen, 2000). In the light of this, it is perhaps of no surprise that ACPO's Human Rights Committee is proceeding with 'compliance audits' across a number of areas subject to the Act which include, *inter alia*, use by police of stop and search and police powers of arrest. While the potential ramifications of the Act appear to be causing 'consternation' among all criminal justice sector personnel (Bowen, 2000), it is clear that the police service can be expected to be the most heavily engaged in meeting its demanding requirements. As has been argued recently by a former ACPO president:

> The challenge facing leaders of the police service is to prepare police officers to be capable of articulating and safeguarding human rights in a demonstrable way when using their powers. (Bowen, 1999: 45)

The Human Rights Act 1998 will require the police service to re-orientate its priorities away from a traditional espousal of crime-control strategies to the protection of human rights. In doing so it will present a major challenge to the police while also, through the courts, making it perhaps more accountable as a service than it has ever been to date. Yet, the application of the European Convention on Human Rights to UK domestic law by way of the 1998 Human Rights Act, while welcome, cannot address the wider political problems of transparency and accountability which now characterise current arrangements. It is also less than certain that the emphasis placed on performance criteria by the government can really be seen in any regard as an appropriate method of bringing the police service to account for what it does or does not do. As has been recently argued by a number of commentators (Reiner, 1992; Choongh, 1997), much policing activity remains highly discretionary, largely unrecorded and as a result 'invisible' to those who seek to monitor 'police performance'.

It is also clear that, as now structured, local 'police authorities' are unable to fulfil the 'political' role that has been traditionally ascribed to them. That is they are unable, as a result of their significant loss of elected councillors, to provide an effective voice and channel of communication for local citizens to challenge the chief officer on specific policing decisions and related issues. Given this and the clear failure of 'police–community consultation' to engage the people, there is, it might be thought, a case for the redetermination of both the structure and function of existing mechanisms of accountability. This might begin to challenge the demonstrable inadequacies of current arrangements for the government of police.

References

Audit Commission (1993) *Helping with Enquiries.* London: HMSO.

Audit Commission (1996) *Streetwise. Effective Police patrol.* London: HMSO.

Association of Police Authorities (1998) *Speaking with Authority. APA and Home Office Conference Report.* Blackpool, November.

Baker, M. (1996) 'On what authority?', *Policing Today,* 2: 10–13.

Bowen, R. (2000) *Human Rights Act – Coming to lawyers near you. Criminal Justice Management.* Manchester: Partnership Media Group.

Butler, D. and Halsey, A.H. (eds) (1978) *Policy and Politics.* London: Macmillan.

Choongh, S. (1997) *Policing as Social Discipline.* Oxford: Clarendon Press.

Cohen N. (2000) 'Lies, Damned Lies and Jack Straw's Statistics', *Observer,* 6 February.

Cope, S., Charman, S. and Savage S. (1997) 'Police Professionalisation: The Role of ACPO'. Paper given to the Public Services Research Unit Conference, Cardiff Business School.

HMIC Primary Inspection (1996) West Midlands Police. London: Home Office.

HMIC (1999/2000) Inspection Dorset Police. London: Home Office.

HMIC Report (2000) *Policing London.* London: Home Office.

Home Office (1999) *Criminal Justice System. Strategic Plan 1999–2002.*

Jefferson, T. and Grimshaw, R. (1984) *Controlling the Constable.* London: Muller.

Jenkins, S. (1996) *Accountable to None. The Tory Nationalisation of Britain.* London: Penguin Books.

Jones, T. and Newburn, T. (1994) *Democracy and Policing.* London: PSI.

Jowell, J. and Oliver, D. (eds) (1994) *The Changing Constitution.* 3rd edn. Oxford: Clarendon.

Leach, S. and Davis, H. (eds) (1994) *Enabling or Disabling Local Government.* Buckingham: Open University Press.

Loader, I. (1994) 'Democracy, Justice and the Limits of Policing: Rethinking Police Accountability', *Social and Legal Studies,* 3, 521–44.

Loader, I. (1999) 'Governing Policing in the 21st Century', *Criminal Justice Matters,* 38, Winter.

Loveday, B. (1991) 'Police and Government in the 1990s', *Social Policy and Administration,* 25(4).

Loveday, B. (1994) 'Police Reform' in Leach and Davis (1994).

Loveday, B. (1995) 'Who are the Independent Members?', *County News.* Association of County Councils, April.

Loveday, B. (1998) 'Waving Not Drowning: Chief Constables and the New Configuration of Accountability in the Provinces', *International Journal of Police Science and Management,* 1(2).

Loveday, B. (1999) 'The impact of Performance Culture on Criminal Justice Agencies in England and Wales', *International Journal of the Sociology of Law,* 27.

Loveday, B. and Brearley, N. (2000) *Police and Public Order* [in] *Britain in 1998.* London: Institute of Contemporary History, London University.

Maguire, M. and Norris, S. (1992) *The Conduct and Supervision of Criminal Investigations.* Royal Commission on Criminal Justice. Research Study No. 5. London: HMSO.

Marshall, G. (1965) *Police and Government*. London: Methuen.

Marshall, G. (1978) 'Police Accountability Revisited' in Butler and Halsey (1978).

Marshall, G. and Loveday, B. (1994) 'The Police: Independence and Accountability' in Jowell and Oliver (1994).

Morgan, R. and Newburn, T. (1997) *The Future of Policing*. Oxford: Clarendon.

Morgan, R. and Maggs, C. (1985) *Setting the Pace*. Bath: Bath University.

Patten, C. (1999) *The Report of the Independent Commission on Policing for Northern Ireland. A New Beginning: Policing in Northern Ireland*. London: HMSO.

Police Foundation Annual Lecture (1998) The Rt. Hon. J. Straw, Merchant Taylors' Hall, London.

Police Research Group (1996) *It's Good to Talk: Lessons in Public Consultation and Feedback*. London: Home Office.

Reiner, R. (1992) *The Politics of the Police*. London: Harvester Wheatsheaf.

Reiner, R. and Spencer, S. (1993) *Accountable Policing*. London: IPPR.

Scarman, Lord (1981) *The Brixton Disorders, 10–12 April 1981. Report of an Inquiry*. Cmnd 8427. London: Home Office.

Stratta, E. (1990) 'A lack of Consultation', *Policing* (6), Autumn.

Travis, A. (2000b) 'Straw Extends Race Law', *Guardian* 27 January.

Travis, A. (2000a) 'Police to Lose Immunity from Race Law', *Guardian* 23 February.

Uglow, S. (1997) *The Police Act*. Bristol: Jordan's Publishing Company.

Waddington, P.A.J. (1999) *Policing Citizens*. London: UCL Press.

Chapter 14

Equal opportunities and the future of policing

SANDRA WALKLATE

Introduction

The introduction of the Sex Discrimination Act in 1975 and the Race Relations Act in 1976 made it unlawful to discriminate against a person, either directly or indirectly, in the field of employment on the grounds of sex, marriage or race. The process of implementing these two pieces of legislation, and the equal opportunities policies which flow from them, has been, and still is, long and tortuous in the workplace in general and the world of policework in particular. Indeed, there was active resistance to the applicability of the Sex Discrimination Act to the police, marked by the use of unofficial (and illegal) quotas in the recruitment of policewomen for a number of years following its introduction. However, in the wake of the Scarman Report (1981), any resistance to equal opportunities policies became increasingly difficult to justify. That report suggested that action needed to be taken to address the overt racist behaviour of some police officers against people from ethnic minorities and that there was a need to increase the number of police recruited from ethnic minority groups. Moreover, a cursory reading of the Macpherson Report (1999), produced in the wake of the murder of Stephen Lawrence, would suggest that, in respect of some of these issues relating to equal opportunities, little has changed in the intervening years. Such a view would, however, be mistaken.

An HMIC thematic report produced in 1995 entitled *Developing Diversity in the Police Service* argued for the development of a different style of policing. It placed central importance on equal opportunities training as a mechanism for managing cultural change within police organisations, a view which endorses that of Heidensohn (1992). She suggests that equal opportunities policies can impact upon policing in a number of different ways: in keeping the law, in achieving a representative bureaucracy, in bringing a source of innovation and change into policy, in 'feminising' policing, in undermining police tradition and 'proper policing', and in increasing opportunities for individual women and women as a whole. From a point of view, therefore, issues relating to equal opportunities raise fundamental questions about the nature of the policing task as a whole. This is certainly the view that will be taken in this chapter. As a consequence, this chapter will endeavour to address the impact that the legislation relating to discrimination has had on policing in respect of police officers' relations with each other, with members of the public, and what the future of policing might look like as equal opportunities policies are more fully embraced.

Home Office Circular 87/1989 marked a significant shift in internal policing policy with respect to equal opportunity issues in general. Home Office
Circulars have become increasingly important over the last 15 years or so in
prompting and initiating policing policy changes. These circulars do not dic-
tate local force policy but act as guidelines for the basis of local policies; in
other words local forces remain relatively autonomous in this and in other
respects. As McKenzie (1993: 160) states:

> Even in the EO [equal opportunities] area this autonomy has an impact, for Chief
> Officers may decide the nature of their initiatives and the extent of their interven-
> tion with total freedom.

Whilst little of this variation has been fully documented, local interpretation can set the overall tone of an individual force's orientation to equal
opportunities policies and practices. There are, however, some common
themes.

Home Office Circular 87/1989 clearly stated that force policies 'should
ensure the best use is made of the abilities of every member of the force' and
that they should show:

> ... that all members of the service are firmly opposed to discrimination within the
> service and in their professional dealings with members of the public.

It recommended that forces use the codes of practice issued by the Equal
Opportunities Commission and the Commission for Racial Equality as guidelines in formulating their own policies and practices. Most forces to date
have taken these guidelines as their frame of reference. This has meant that
policies have been centred on sex, race and marital status. South Yorkshire
was the first police force to include a clause addressing the issues of 'sexual
orientation' in February 1991. Its policy states:

> The South Yorkshire Police declares that it is opposed to any form of treatment
> which is less, or more, favourable, whether through direct or indirect discrimina-
> tion, in respect of all members and employees, together with all applicants seeking
> employment, on grounds of sex or sexual orientation, marital/parental status,
> colour, race, nationality, ethnic or national origins, religious beliefs, creeds; or are
> disadvantaged by conditions or requirements which cannot be shown to be
> justified.   (Quoted by Burke, 1993: 237–8)

Several other forces have since included 'sexual orientation' in their policies, though such considerations are still the exception rather than the rule.
In all, then, Home Office Circular 87/1989 provided both the central focus
for policy development on equal opportunities and offered scope for variations in those policy developments.

In some respects, therefore, it is possible to argue that some significant
inroads on equal opportunities had already been made within policing by
the early 1990s, especially if the point of comparison were other organisations both within and outside of the criminal justice arena. However, policy
formation neither necessarily reflects changing practices nor necessarily
prompts changing practices. In the context of equal opportunities in relation

to policing, there are (at least) three substantive areas in which it would be necessary to consider whether change in practice was taking place: in relation to people from ethnic minorities, to women, and to issues of sexual orientation. This chapter will examine each of these areas in turn starting with people from ethnic minorities.

Black and Asian people, policing and equal opportunities

In 1998 the Lawrence Inquiry ensured that the whole question of the policing of people from ethnic minorities was re-opened in a very public way. The work of that Inquiry focused attention on whether or not the police officers investigating the death of Steven Lawrence were incompetent or racist. In addressing the latter question, the Inquiry took evidence from different police forces. During this process the admission by David Wilmot, the chief constable of Greater Manchester, that his force was 'institutionally racist' led to considerable media coverage and debate. In the wake of this admission, several other forces made similar statements resulting in the Home Secretary addressing an ACPO conference declaring an intention to introduce recruitment targets for police forces for people from ethnic minorities (see also Williamson, this volume, Chapter 2).

The Macpherson Report (1999) defines 'institutional racism' in the following way:

> 'Institutional racism' consists of the collective failure of an organisation to provide an appropriate professional service to people because of their colour, culture or ethnic origin. It can be seen or detected in processes, attitudes and behaviour which amount to discrimination through unwitting prejudice, ignorance, thoughtlessness, and racist stereotyping which disadvantage minority ethnic people.

This is not the place to debate the efficacy or otherwise of this definition; suffice it to say that it carries with it ramifications for the whole of British society, some of which have already been translated into practice in the context of the criminal justice system especially in the setting of recruitment targets.

In 1998, 2 per cent of the total police force establishment in England and Wales consisted of police officers from ethnic minority groups. The highest ranking officer from an ethnic minority was an assistant chief constable in Lancashire. Given that over ten years earlier the Scarman Report (1981) had argued that special efforts be made to secure more recruitment from people from ethnic minority groups so that police forces could move toward being more representative of the community as a whole, the current record on recruitment does suggest that there is room for improvement. However, difficulties face such recruitment campaigns.

For example, people from ethnic minorities do not necessarily possess a positive image or positive experiences of policing, especially young black people. Moreover, those who do join the police force are likely to experience difficulties in their relationships within their own communities as well as within the police force. This latter issue was aptly illustrated in 1991 when P.C. Singh took his own chief constable to an industrial tribunal and won his case. As Holdaway (1994: 81) clearly states, this case demonstrated the persistent difficulties faced by black and Asian officers.

> During the hearing it became clear that senior officers thought the racialist joking and banter prevalent in their force was all but part and parcel of the conditions of employment for all officers, irrespective of race.

Such views, it has been argued, are embedded in police 'canteen culture' and may also be reflected in practices in relation to members of the public, though this is never a simple nor straightforward process. (See the recent discussions of 'canteen culture' developed by Hoyle, 1998 and Waddington, 1999.)

It is widely recognised, in the literature on policing at least, that people from ethnic minorities feel that they are simultaneously over-policed by their local police force and under-serviced by them when they find themselves to be the victims of crime. This is one reading of the figures on stop and search for example. Home Office figures report that in 1997–8 five times as many black people were subjected to stop and search procedures than white people. Interestingly such figures are not uniform. They vary from being three times as many stops for black people in Bedfordshire to seven times as many in Leicestershire. Such variations are not wholly explicable by reference to the percentage of black people in the population. However, neither are they wholly explicable in terms of 'institutional racism'. Part of the explanation is rooted in understanding the historical legacy of policework.

The historical purpose of policework was, and arguably still is, concerned to separate the 'roughs' from the 'respectables': policing the 'police property' (Lee, 1981). The constituency of such 'police property' has changed, a changing process in which black people, arguably, have come to feature more significantly since the early 1970s (see, for example, Hall *et al.*, 1978).

The overall consequent effect of this historical legacy is that Afro-Caribbeans are 50 per cent more likely to be stopped in their vehicles than white people and nearly four times more likely to be stopped on foot (Southgate and Crisp, 1992). More recent research conducted by Jefferson, Walker and Seneviratne (1992), however, demonstrates that such general statistical assertions become increasingly more complicated when within-area racial comparisons are made. Their work clearly demonstrates the need to separate out the experiences of Afro-Caribbean and Asian people from white people, and to consider their experience of policing in 'blacker' populated areas as compared with 'whiter' populated ones. Put simply, they found that white youths in 'blacker' areas had experiences of policing similar to those of black youths in 'whiter' areas. In other words, whilst Holdaway (1998) might argue that it is important to consider the ways in which the unreflective practices of police officers impact upon people from ethnic minorities, those unreflective practices are not articulated in simple or straightforward ways in all localities.

However, despite evidence such as this, which arguably points to the complex way in which class and race interact which each other, in the Lawrence Inquiry and the subsequent media coverage of it, the opinion has been constructed that very little in terms of actual police practice appears to have changed. This does not mean that considerable efforts have not been made on the part of police forces to institute change both in their internal and external practices. Training initiatives have been a prominent feature of these efforts.

Oakley (1994) documents the range of training initiatives that have been instituted in the field of community and race relations from the early 1980s to date. He argues that the formulation and implementation of equal opportunities polices has 'served to establish a more positive ethos' (Oakley, 1994: 102) in which such training initiatives might be taken more seriously. This, alongside the ACPO statement of 'common purposes and values', according to Oakley (1994: 103):

> ... transforms the status within policing of 'community relations', which moves from a peripheral concern to being central to the policing role.

This is a statement which usefully returns us to the question of the extent to which issues relating to equal opportunities can raise fundamental questions concerning the nature of the policing task.

To summarise: police forces still do convey a strong symbolic message with respect to issues of race, most clearly delineated by patterns of recruitment. Despite recruitment campaigns and posters that invariably feature the face of a black or Asian police officer, policing is still an overwhelmingly white occupation. Those officers of black and Asian origin who do join the police force still face the considerable day-to-day routine difficulty of managing racial banter not only from their colleagues but also from members of the public. Indeed, despite considerable efforts in training initiatives, police–public encounters are still informed by stereotypical, historically rooted, notions of who is likely to be a troublemaker.

Yet, this view needs to be balanced by the increasing concern shown by the police towards the victims of 'racially motivated' crime. This has been taken much more seriously with some forces establishing and resourcing special units to deal with the impact of such incidents. And while there are significant problems in both the reporting and the ultimate recording and prosecution of such incidents, there is nevertheless an increasing commitment to take such incidents seriously. So, despite the 'whiteness' of police forces, some inroads have been made since the early 1980s to address some of the policing concerns of those from ethnic minorities – inroads which may not be best served by the introduction of targets and the resistance that such targets will produce (Johns, 1999). Police forces are also predominantly male, so we shall consider the relationship between women and policing and equal opportunities next.

Women, policing and equal opportunities

In 1981 policewomen accounted for 8.6 per cent of the total force establishment in England and Wales. By 1993 this had risen to 13.2 per cent (HMIC Report, 1993), though this rise masks marked regional variations from 9.2 per cent in South Wales to 16.1 per cent in the West Midlands. It should be noted that even these small percentages put Britain at the higher end of the international policing scale with respect to the employment of women (Heidensohn, 1998). Both Jones (1985) and Heidensohn (1989) noted that women occupied very few senior posts. Indeed, in 1992, when Alison Halford was pursuing her sex discrimination case, as an assistant chief constable, she was then the highest-ranked serving female officer. In 1994, however, three women achieved the rank of deputy chief constable and, in 1995, Britain saw its first woman chief constable with the appointment of Pauline Clare to head the Lancashire Police.

These figures in and of themselves suggest not only that women are under-represented in policework, but also that once recruited, their road to the top is certainly a 'greasy pole'! Part of the explanation for this under-representation of women in policing (as with black and Asian people) lies in the recruitment process: few women apply to become police officers. Why they do not apply may, of course, be connected to the kind of public image that policework has, and the kinds of experience women have of policing both as members of the public and as police officers. We shall discuss the second of these issues first of all.

Kinsey's (1985) report on police officers on Merseyside indicated that 43 per cent of those officers under 30 years of age on station duty (the least prestigious job) were women. Coffey, Brown and Savage (1992) report that women were under-represented in many specialist departments and totally absent from others. Brown, Maidment and Bull (1993) found that the deployment patterns of women police officers gravitated towards 'low frequency labour intensive specialised tasks', for example supporting rape victims or victims of sexual abuse (an issue which shall be returned to). Anderson, Brown and Campbell (1993: 11) state consequently:

> ... women officers are limited in the amount and type of experience they are able to gain. This in turn affects their job satisfaction and may inhibit their promotion prospects. That fewer women than men achieve promotion in turn can reinforce male stereotypes about women's abilities.

A similar finding is endorsed in the work of Holdaway and Parker (1998). Some of these stereotypes relate to the presumed physical nature of the job and women's abilities to handle it (Heidensohn, 1994). Others relate to the presumed management problem posed by policewomen, that is, to their short average service record before leaving to have children. Neither of these stereotypes is necessarily supported empirically, nor are they insurmountable, but they do relate to the well-documented 'cult of masculinity' which it is argued pervades 'cop culture'. This is evidenced in the studies conducted by Smith and Gray (1983); Bryant, Dunkerley and Kelland (1985) and Jones

(1987). These attitudes leave many policewomen with the choice of either embracing this male culture as their own or fulfilling the more traditional expectations associated with their role: what Ehrlich-Martin (1980) has referred to as the strategies of *POLICEwomen* or *policeWOMEN*. Strategies that may, of course, be compounded or challenged by the ways in which equal opportunities policies are, or are not, put in place.

These are some of the historical and contemporary barriers to an effective and meaningful equal treatment of female officers within the police force. The question remains, is there any evidence to indicate that the experience of policewomen might be changing?

Commentators have suggested that in some respects Alison Halford's sex discrimination case, supported as it was by the Equal Opportunities Commission, alongside the high-profile media coverage that it generated, acted as a catalyst in encouraging other policewomen to speak out about their experiences. (See, for example, Gregory and Lees, 1999.) Indeed, since 1992 a number of other cases have been similarly reported in the media, though not so extensively. Whether or not the Halford case has had such a catalytic effect is a moot point. What is clear is that there is now a greater awareness of the nature and extent of sexual discrimination in the police force. For example, the report produced by Anderson, Brown and Campbell (1993) for the Police Research Group indicated that nine out of ten policewomen experience verbal sexual harassment, six in ten had offensive comments made about their appearance, three in ten were subject to unwanted touching, and one in ten had given serious thought to leaving the police force because of harassment. (See also, Brown, 1998.) Moreover, the 1996 HMIC Report (HMIC, 1996) suggested that discrimination and harassment are not only continuing but may be becoming more hidden as a result of changing practices and, as a consequence, more problematic.

The issue of the best deployment of female officers may compound experiences such as these. An examination of the deployment patterns of policewomen raises two questions: what assumptions underpin those deployment patterns with respect to the skills of female officers, and how might better use be made of these skills? These assumptions can be discerned in a number of ways; here we shall examine them by overviewing some of the developments which have taken place over the last ten years in police–public relations, the second dimension which equal opportunities policies might be expected to address. We shall pay especial attention to those areas in which the police have endeavoured to put into place an improved response to women as 'victims' of crime.

Women as 'victims' of crime and equal opportunities

It has been argued that improved service responses to women as victims of crime were put in place during the 1980s and early 1990s as much as a consequence of the increasing concern to secure public support for policing as they were a product of the concern to address women's needs (Radford and

Stanko, 1991). Whatever the underlying concern, significant policy initiatives have occurred both in the police response to women reporting rape and to 'domestic' violence. In the context of rape, the much-publicised televised handling of a rape complainant by the Thames Valley Police (BBC1, 18 January 1982), and the public outcry that followed it, precipitated Home Office Circular 25/1983. That circular outlined how incidents of rape might be handled more effectively. Consequently, many forces following the lead of the Metropolitan Police proceeded to establish 'rape suites'. To what extent these changes have resulted in substantial changes for women who have reported an incident of rape is, however, subject to some debate. As Smith (1989: 26) states:

> Most police forces have recognised the need to reconsider their own responsive-ness to rape. Nevertheless, the evidence from this study of two London boroughs suggests that it is still the classic stereotype of rape which is more likely to be offi-cially recorded as a crime.

In a later study by Grace, Lloyd and Smith (1992: 5) it is reported that:

> Alleged acquaintance attacks are the least likely to result in a conviction ... [and] are the most likely cases for women to withdraw their complaints.

This suggests that there is much work still to be done in this area and per-haps supports the view that such reforms constitute mere 'window dressing' (Radford and Stanko, 1991: 196) on the one hand, and the treatment of women as consumers of a service on the other (Walklate, 1993). The same analysis might also be offered of the recent flurry of policy activity in the area of 'domestic' violence.

Following on from what was considered to be both an innovative and a suc-cessful policy response to 'domestic' violence developed by the Metropolitan Police, Home Office Circular 60/1990 gave considerable impetus for other force areas to follow their model. This circular reminded all chief constables of the range of legal strategies under which offenders might be arrested (espousing a 'positive stance' towards arrest for 'domestic' incidents) as well as recommending the establishment of 'dedicated' units through which to support the 'victim' of such incidents.

As was hinted earlier, this circular prompted a relatively rapid, and cer-tainly imaginative, response from police forces up and down the country as they put efforts in place to take the issue of 'domestic' violence much more seriously than consigning it to the category of 'rubbish' work. This, despite the fact that both elements of this overall policy stance are fraught with diffi-culties. One aspect to those difficulties connects the substantive concerns of each of these areas of policing policy activity. They can be posed as two ques-tions: are these the kinds of policy developments which offer women, as members of the public, the kind of policing policy response they want and/or are entitled to, and who in the police force has acquired the respon-sibility, for the most part, for delivering these policies? Both of these questions return us to the issue of equal opportunities.

The use and deployment of policewomen in the re-orientation and implementation of policy initiatives in relation to rape and 'domestic' violence has been a significant feature of the respective implementation of these policies. The use and deployment of policewomen in this way rests on two assumptions. First, that women would prefer to be dealt with by a female officer. Second, that female officers are more likely to have the appropriate qualities to offer to women. It is worth commenting on each of these assumptions in greater detail before examining their relevance for equal opportunities policies.

Limited, though not totally convincing, evidence supports the view that women would prefer to have their case dealt with by a female officer. Heidensohn's (1992) study suggests that, from the policewoman's point of view, certain levels of job satisfaction be achieved when involved in work oriented towards supporting women. Moreover, her respondents felt that a certain quality of support was also maintained for the women concerned in these circumstances. Heidensohn's interviewees, however, also pointed out that they could identify police*men* who were equally capable of offering the same kind of quality support. One of the hidden problems here is, of course, that we have very little *gendered* empirical knowledge of what kind of policing the public want on which to base policy practice (Walklate, 1992).

For example, Radford's (1987) survey of women's views of policing revealed that 44 per cent of her sample thought that women officers would be more understanding in relation to violence against women, though 32 per cent thought they would not be. Many said they would prefer to speak to another woman in the context of 'domestic' violence but similarly others recognised that women officers had to be tougher than the men to succeed (Radford, 1987: 40–1). Even this evidence, then, displays some understandable ambivalence to the idea that female officers will automatically be more supportive than their male counterparts.

It may be, of course, that what women as 'victims' of crime are asking for is a *quality* of support which is commonly, and stereotypically, associated with women, though the delivery of which is not necessarily guaranteed by them. The apparent ease with which female officers have been most readily accepted as suitable for this kind of work, then, not only raises questions of whether or not this guarantees the kind of service that the public (women) want, but also raises particular and general questions for policewomen as workers in a male-dominated profession.

At a particular level it raises the question of how can policewomen take seriously, and encourage their predominantly male colleagues to take seriously, an area of work historically labelled as 'rubbish' work, i.e. not proper policework. At a more general level, it foregrounds a potential area of contradiction between espoused policy commitments, especially with respect to equal opportunities and what appears to be the current trend of deployment patterns with respect to 'domestic' violence. In other words, how might it be possible to make sense of the espoused commitment of a police force to equal opportunities alongside its deployment of policewomen in areas traditionally defined as low-status work or women's work? Indeed, some of the policy developments discussed here, from a point of view, echo and replicate the role for policewomen in a very similar way to that work done in the old Policewomen's Departments, prior to integration. The question is therefore raised, how and in what ways might equal opportunities policies impact upon such deeply embedded practices.

As Hanmer and Saunders (1991) observed, when faced with the question of guaranteeing service delivery by policewomen for other women, forces frequently fell back on the statement that they are an 'equal opportunities' employer. Such a statement, couched as it is in a concern to deploy individuals according to their merits, allows forces to advertise specialist posts, for example for a domestic violence officer, openly across the force. Individual officers put themselves forward for such postings. Hypothetically speaking, but rooted in what is already known about 'cop culture', this process allows for a number of complex mechanisms to come into play.

First, in general, fewer male officers are likely to apply for such postings than female officers. This might be as a result of their evaluation of their own skills but also has to be seen alongside the persistent effects of 'cop culture' and the associated definition of what counts as 'proper policing'. Second, women do put themselves forward for such work; perhaps seeing such specialist work as an added opportunity for promotion as well as evaluating themselves as having the appropriate skills for such work. Third, selection procedures pay due attention to the kinds of qualities considered appropriate for such work: being sympathetic, supportive, able to listen, able to communicate effectively, etc. The resultant effect of these processes is that more women enter this specialist work. At the same time, a police force is able to defend its equal opportunities policy.

As was suggested earlier, these processes certainly seem to be in play in those force areas where efforts are being made to respond seriously to Circular 60/1990. That this for the most part coincides with the (little) evidence we have of what women and local agencies would prefer from policing on this issue may be accidental but it is, nevertheless, effective. More seriously perhaps, the consequence of relying on such processes can result in the complacent belief that equal opportunity issues have been attended to, but which frequently leaves the reins of change in the hands of those who have perhaps the least interest in seeing change occur: senior policemen. The question remains as to whether such a pessimistic analysis of the cumulative effect of these processes is justified. It is at this juncture that the question of what counts as 'proper policing' re-emerges.

What counts as proper policing can be interpreted in a number of different ways, from what counts as the central policing task to what counts as the central skills associated with the completion of that task. It is clear that the increasing involvement of police forces in a more positive response towards 'domestic' violence raises issues on both these counts. First, police officers are being asked to take the policing of the private domain seriously and second they are being asked to be sensitive and supportive in their subsequent response to women in violent relationships. The work of Hoyle (1998) suggests some success on both of these counts. Given the evidence and argument presented here, however, there are (at least) two possible outcomes to these changes in the re-orientation of the policing task.

The first possible outcome to these processes results in the reproduction of police forces prior to integration; in other words, in some areas Police Women's Departments are becoming reconstituted in all but name. This outcome endorses the view of all those who believe that general policework is too dangerous for women and that using women for women's and children's issues makes best use of the qualities they have to offer (see also Holdaway and Parker, 1998). This result leaves the 'dirty work' to the men, 'ghettoises' women's issues, and leaves the rest of policework relatively untouched in both style and service delivery.

The second possible outcome is one in which both statements on equal opportunities and statements on 'domestic' violence are embraced by all members of a police force, both male and female, in order to create an atmosphere in which male and female officers can pursue their career aspirations in whatever line of work either sex of officer chooses. It has frequently been suggested that such an outcome can only become possible when women make up at least 25 per cent of a total organisation's workforce (Moss Kanter, 1977). It is clear that police forces in the UK are a long way from achieving that goal. However, what underpins this projected outcome is a certain optimism that if these two areas were seriously embraced then it would demand a fundamental re-examination of what counts as policing. In other words, it would also of necessity challenge men's conceptions of what policing is about, why they became police officers, etc.

It can be seen, therefore, at this moment in time that with respect to women as police officers and women as police customers, a serious commitment to equal opportunities policies has the potential to challenge fundamentally what counts as policework. Whether or not that challenge will actually occur, and if it does, how it will be met, is as yet not wholly clear. Some change is obviously taking place, but the extent to which this will result in a genuine re-orientation of policework is a moot point: it certainly returns us to the question of what counts as proper policework raised earlier in relation to ethnic minority issues.

Sexual orientation, policing and equal opportunities

Of the three dimensions to equal opportunities under discussion here the question of sexual orientation has been the most invisible and consequently the least debated. No one knows how many homosexual or lesbian police officers there are. Moreover, as was stated at the beginning of this chapter, the commitment by South Yorkshire police in their equal opportunities statement to issues relating to sexual orientation is, as a consequence, all the more remarkable. As Richard Wells, the chief constable of South Yorkshire Constabulary stated:

Provided that an officer's sexual conduct, as with anyone else, is within the law, I see no reason why they shouldn't be treated absolutely equally in terms of promotion or work opportunity. (1991: 105)

As forward-thinking as a statement like this is, the reality of life and work experience for gay and lesbian police officers still leaves much to be desired in living up to such a rhetorical claim. In this respect, as with female and black officers, the powerful influence of police occupational culture takes its toll.

Burke's (1993) study provides some insight into the experiences of lesbian and gay police officers and their sometimes hugely complex strategies for managing their dual identities. The price to be paid for 'coming out' is indeed high given the macho nature of cop culture and the potential insinuation that gay officers are much more suspect and open to blackmail. Indeed, whilst the testimony of some of the officers in Burke's sample accepted that statements on equal opportunities were a step in the right direction, they also indicated that such statements may do little to enhance the working life of gay officers in the face of the embedded nature of the norm of heterosexuality in the occupational subculture. Some, though, would argue that the formation of the Lesbian and Gay Police Association during 1990–1 marked the beginnings of a greater confidence amongst gay and lesbian police officers to challenge that norm of heterosexuality.

The public exposé of the existence of this organisation in the *Police Review* in 1991 led to quite a furore in both the police and the national press, illustrating perhaps more effectively than anything else the deep-rooted attitudes to homosexual and lesbian people in general alongside the contradictions the question of sexual orientation raises for policing and police officers in particular. Despite this furore the organisation survives, providing at least a basis for an alternative system of welfare and networking for homosexual and lesbian officers.

The difficulties faced by homosexual and lesbian officers are in some respects compounded when considering police relations with the gay and lesbian public, though again this aspect of police community relations is not that well documented. In this respect, the laws around sexual behaviour, particularly in public, and the discretionary implementation of the law, constitute key aspects in the policing of homosexual activities around which there has always been contention. However, some police forces, informed by equal opportunities thinking, have ensured that their policies on 'domestic' violence, for example, extend to homosexual and lesbian relationships.

Conclusion: looking to the future – equal opportunities as a source of radical change?

This chapter has argued that equal opportunities policies, if taken seriously, have the potential to impact not only upon the internal dynamics and relationships of police organisations, but also on relationships with the public.

These two aspects of policework are clearly connected. For example, if a male police officer can relate in a non-sexist manner to his female colleague, then the possibility that he might also relate to a female member of the public in that same way is greatly enhanced. The end result is not only better internal working relationships but an improved service to the public. However, in arguing that equal opportunities policies are a key dimension along which such interconnections are forged, it is also the view of this chapter that recognising such interconnections constitutes a fundamental challenge to what is understood as proper policework. This requires a fuller explanation.

There are several different ways in which it could be possible to argue that equal opportunities policies provide a mechanism for significant organisational change. In comparing the impact of equal opportunities policies on policework in the United States with the United Kingdom, McKenzie (1993) comments on the potential for change through an American-style 'litigation approach'. And whilst he suggests that such an approach is unlikely in the United Kingdom, it has to be said that increasing awareness of equal opportunities issues does seem to be contributing to the increasing number of complaints of discriminatory behaviour from female officers in particular.

Moreover, McKenzie (1993) does suggest that stronger backing to equal opportunities issues could be given through a form of 'contract compliance':

> 'Thou shalt not discriminate' can only be effective if overt and sufficient punishment for failure so to do is attached. It may even be that a form of 'contract compliance' could be applied by Her Majesty's Inspectorate of Constabulary, through the definition of inactivity on EO issues being designated as a form of inefficiency. (McKenzie, 1993: 172)

Such a stance may, of course, encourage more activity, but leaves open the questions of what kind of activity, with what kind of outcome? This leads us to a second way in which equal opportunities policies could act as a radical catalyst of change in policework: by challenging the occupational culture.

Challenging police occupational culture has been seen to be a significant barrier to real change, as opposed to policy change, along all three aspects to equal opportunities discussed in this chapter. (See also Chan, 1996.) Effecting change to that occupational culture through equal opportunities can occur in a number of ways. The removal of unlawful quotas has contributed to the recruitment of more policewomen, for example, and the more an organisation is differently peopled, the greater the likelihood that occupational values will also change. So the more effective groups like the Lesbian and Gay Police Association become, and the greater the networking amongst black and Asian officers, the more likely it is that the presence of such groups will be felt. Of course, there is always the alternative possibility that, given the nature of some aspects of 'cop culture', such groups might also experience increased marginalisation. All of this posits quite an incremental view of change but recognises the importance of understanding the *processes of change* between police officers themselves which need to take place before any real change will occur. As Holdaway (1998:16) states:

Discrimination is articulated through taken for granted ways of working, informed by the solid traditions of the police occupational culture.

Recognising this does not necessarily imply the need for positive discriminatory practices to be put in place, but it does imply looking beyond the rank and file officer as the conduit of change.

There is, however, a third way in which equal opportunities policies have the potential for radicalising the nature of policework. This returns us to the question posed earlier in reference to Heidensohn's (1992) work on policewomen. Equal opportunities policies, whether focused on issues to do with women, people from ethnic minorities, or questions of sexual orientation, raise the question of what counts as proper policing. In other words, once anti-discriminatory practices are seriously embraced within an organisation, that embrace, by definition, demands a critical examination of how that organisation delivers its central tasks and the appropriateness of those tasks. This is a fundamental question, not only for policing, but also for society at large: what do we want policing to deliver?

The reader may have noticed that this author has consistently referred to the police as a police force rather than a police service. The use of these different words connotes quite different images of the central policing task. In the 1990s police forces became more service oriented, and indeed some of the policies documented in this chapter stand as testimony to that service orientation. Yet, at the same time, there has been an increasing emphasis on the control functions of the police.

The contradictory messages conveyed by these processes have been discussed elsewhere (see, for example, Stephens, 1994) and need not distract us here. What is of significance in this context is the way in which, for example, a commitment to equal opportunities policies to women as recipients of a police service through improved responses to 'domestic' violence, raises these very same questions about the fundamental nature of the policing task. These questions are also raised in the context of community relations work with people from ethnic minorities, as demonstrated by the commitment of many police forces to take seriously the notion of racial crime. These are both areas of work traditionally considered to be fairly low profile work in policing, and yet their importance not only in securing consent for policing in general, but also now in securing the delivery of an effective and satisfactory service, has been enhanced significantly since the mid-1980s.

The question of the effective implementation and development of equal opportunities policies is therefore fundamentally implicated in a consideration of what the future of the policing task might look like. As more policework is conducted increasingly by organisations and individuals outside of 'blue-uniform policing' the historical nature of the blue-uniform task (or 'state policework' (Brogden et al., 1988)) may become more open to question. If, for example, we expect blue-uniform policing to continue its historical involvement in clearing the 'social debris' from the streets, then we must also expect that in some parts of the country that debris is going to be more ethnically mixed than in others. This is a structural problem which equal opportunities policies, however, effectively implemented, will not solve. It is a structural problem that may nevertheless be much more likely to be dealt with fairly by 'blue-uniform' policing than by other policing organisations.

It is also the case that the government-led reforms of the early 1990s have incrementally resulted in the flattening of police management structures. It is increasingly now the case that recruits joining the police force will more than likely spend their entire careers as constables. It is, therefore, only to be expected that this will impact upon the internal patterning of the hierarchy. Taking these issues together might suggest a future for policing which looks rather more like the past than perhaps might have otherwise been anticipated.

Questions such as these as yet have no clear answer to them but they are quite definitely related to the need to understand the central questions of policework: what and who is policing for? Or to return to where this discussion began, as Johns (1999:49) states:

> To summarise, the Lawrence report has raised the public profile of institutional racism, but in doing so has merely reinvigorated an aged and theoretically ambiguous notion; nor are its central recommendations to address the problem new ... Clearly there are lessons to be drawn from the experiences of other countries, and the foundations for doing so may already have been laid, but perhaps the most effective way of dealing with societal racism would be to urgently address economic inequalities and social exclusion. Old promises wreathed in shiny new paper are one thing, but to make a difference they have to be bound with a real political will.

This is beyond policework to achieve.

References

Anderson, R., Brown, J. and Campbell, E. (1993) *Aspects of Discrimination within the Police Service in England and Wales*. Home Office: Police Research Group.

Brogden, M. Jefferson, T. and Walklate, S. (1988) *Introducing Policework*. London: Unwin Hyman.

Brown, J. (1998) 'Aspects of Discriminatory Treatment of Women Police Officers in Forces in England and Wales', *British Journal of Criminology*, 38 (2), Spring, 265–82.

Brown, J., Maidment, A. and Bull, R. (1993) 'Appropriate Skill-Task Matching or Gender Bias in Deployment of Male and Female Officers?', *Policing and Society*, 3, 121–36.

Bryant, L., Dunkerley, D. and Kelland, G. (1985) 'One of the boys?', *Policing*, 1 (4), 236–44.

Burke, M.E. (1993) *Coming Out of the Blue*. London: Cassells.

Chan, J. (1996) 'Changing Police Culture'. *British Journal of Criminology*, 36, (1), 109–34.

Coffey, S., Brown, J. and Savage, S. (1992) 'Policewomen's Career Aspirations: Some Reflections on the Role and Capability of Women in Policing in Britain', *Police Studies*, 15, (1), 13–19.

Downes, D. (ed.) (1992) *Unravelling Criminal Justice*. London: Macmillan.

Ehrlich-Martin, S. (1980) *Breaking and Entering: Policewomen on Patrol*. Berkeley, CA: University of California Press.

Grace, S., Lloyd, D. and Smith, L. (1992) *Rape: From Recording to Conviction*. Home Office Research and Planning Unit Paper. London: HMSO.

Gregory, J. and Lees, S. (1999) *Policing Sexual Assault*. London: Routledge.

Hall, S., Critcher, C., Jefferson, T., Clarke, J. and Roberts, B. (1978) *Policing the Crisis: Mugging, the State and Law and Order*. London: Macmillan.

Hanmer, J. and Maynard, M. (eds) (1987) *Women, Policing and Social Control*. London: Sage.

Hanmer, J. and Saunders, S. (1991) 'Policing Violence Against Women: Implementing Policy Changes'. Paper presented to the British Criminology Conference, York, July.

Heidensohn, F. (1989) *Women in Policing in the USA*. London: The Police Federation.

Heidensohn, F. (1992) *Women in Control? The Role of Women in Law Enforcement*. Oxford: Oxford University Press.

Heidensohn, F. (1994) '"We Can Handle It Out Here". Women Officers in Britain and the USA and the Policing of Public Order', *Policing and Society*, 4, 293–303.

Heidensohn, F. (1998) 'Women in Policing', *Criminal Justice Matters*, 32, Summer.

HMIC (1993) *Equal Opportunities in the Police Service*. London: HMSO.

HMIC (1995) *Developing Diversity in the Police Service*. HMSO: London.

HMIC (1996) *Equal Opportunities in the Police Service*. London. HMSO.

Holdaway, S. (1994) 'Recruitment, Race and the Police Subculture' in Stephens and Becker (1994).

Holdaway, S. (1998) 'Rethinking Police Race Relations', *Criminal Justice Matters*, 32, Summer, 15–16.

Holdaway, S. and Parker, S. (1998) 'Policing Women Police: Uniform Patrol, Promotion and Representation in the CID', *British Journal of Criminology*, 38, (1) 40–60.

Hoyle, C. (1998) *Negotiating Domestic Violence*. Oxford: Clarendon.

Jefferson, T., Walker, M. and Seneviratne, M. (1992) 'Ethnic Minorities, Crime and Criminal Justice: A Study in a Provincial City' in Downes (1992), 138–64.

Johns, N. (1999) 'The Lawrence Report: An Old Present Newly Wrapped?', *Crime Prevention and Community Safety: An International Journal*, 1, (2), 47–50.

Jones, S. (1985) Editorial, *Policing*, 1 (4).

Jones, S. (1987) *Policewomen and Equality*. London: Macmillan.

Kinsey, R. (1985) *The Merseyside Crime and Police Surveys: Final Report*. Liverpool: Merseyside Police Authority.

Lee, J.A. (1981) 'Some Structural Aspects of Police Deviance in Relation with Minority Groups' in Shearing (1981), 49–82.

Macpherson, Sir William of Cluny (1999) *The Stephen Lawrence Inquiry*. Cm 4262-1. London: HMSO.

McKenzie, I.K. (1993) 'Equal Opportunities in Policing: A Comparative Examination of Anti-Discrimination Policy and Practice in British Policing', *International Journal of the Sociology of Law*, 21, 159–74.

Moss Kanter, R. (1977) *Men and Women of the Corporation*. New York: Basic Books.

Oakley, R. (1994) 'The Police and Black People: The Training Response' in Stephens and Becker (1994), 85–106.

Radford, J. (1987) 'Policing Male Violence, Policing Women' in Hanmer and Maynard (1987), 30–45.

247

Radford, J. and Stanko, B. (1991) 'Violence against Women and Children: The Contradictions of Crime Control under Patriarchy' in Stenson and Cowell (1991).

Scarman, Lord (1981) *The Brixton Disorders, 10–12 April 1981: Report of an Inquiry by Lord Scarman.* London: HMSO.

Shearing, C. (ed.) (1981) *Organisational Police Deviance.* Toronto: Butterworth.

Smith, A. (1989) *Concerns about Rape.* Home Office Reseach Study 106. London: HMSO.

Smith, D.J. and Gray, J. (1983) *Vol 4: The Police in London.* London: Policy Studies Institute.

Smith, D.J. and Gray, J. (1985) *Police and People in London.* Aldershot: Gower.

Southgate, P. and Crisp, D. (1992) *Public Satisfaction with Police Services.* Home Office Research and Planning Unit Paper 73. London: HMSO.

Stenson, K. and Cowell, D. (eds) (1991) *The Politics of Crime Control.* London: Sage.

Stephens, M. (1994) 'Care and control: The future of British policing', *Policing and Society,* 4, 237–51.

Stephens, M. and Becker, S. (eds) (1994) *Police Force, Police Service: Care and Control in Britain.* London: Macmillan.

Vigh, J. and Katona, G. (eds) (1993) *Social Changes, Crime and Police.* Budapest: Eotuos Lorand University Press.

Waddington, P.A.J. (1999) 'Police (Canteen) Sub-culture: An Appreciation', *British Journal of Criminology,* 39, (2), 286–307.

Walklate, S. (1992) 'Jack and Jill Join up at Sun Hill: Public Images of Police Officers', *Policing and Society,* 2, 219–32.

Walklate, S. (1993) 'Responding to Women as Consumers of a Police Service: The UK Experience 1981–1991' in Vigh and Katona (1993).

Wells, R. (1991) cited in *Police Review,* 18 January, 105.

Chapter 15

Occupational culture as a factor in the stress experiences of police officers

JENNIFER BROWN

Introduction

As well as the personal costs incurred by stressed police officers, the consequences of occupational stress within the police service have become a
significant management issue in recent times. The landmark ruling in the
decision of *Walker* v *Northumberland County Council* supported a claim that Mr
Walker suffered a stress-induced breakdown whilst employed as a social
worker. The Council was judged to have neglected its duty of care in not fore-
seeing the effects on Mr Walker's health by failing to alleviate the work
pressures that had adversely affected him previously (McKenna, 1994: 1652).
This ruling clearly has general implications for employers including the
police. More specifically the police have been implicated in judicial decisions
such as the Hillsborough football stadium case where 96 football spectators
lost their lives and over 700 were injured when overcrowding trapped fans in
a penned part of the stadium. Police officers caught up in the disaster were
originally awarded compensation for the trauma they had suffered whilst on
duty. This was later rescinded in a House of Lords judgment, in part because
it was pointed out that police officers had access to statutory schemes allowing them to retire early on health grounds, such that additional compensation would permit an unsustainable extension to the existing law
(Pickover, 1998).

Work stress has been the subject of research since the 1950s, partly because
of its impact on productivity and the financial costs incurred through sickness absenteeism and premature medical retirements as well as concerns
about the well-being of individual workers (Brown and Campbell, 1994: 2).
Stress is a psychological concept adapted from material sciences (Arnold *et
al.* 1993). Building materials are tested to discover their breaking points. A
steel bar, for example, may be subjected to increasing pressure to discover
weaknesses or the stress point at which the bar will fracture or eventually
break. Analogous psychological pressures in the workplace derive from cultural, organisational and management sources as well as the work tasks that
staff are asked to perform. Resistance to the adverse consequences require
resources or strategies to offset the negative consequences. Failure to cope,
colloquially referred to as their breaking point, may result in people experi-
encing adverse physical or psychological health.

A factor that helps to understand the ways in which police officers cope
with stress is the occupational culture within which they work, itself a subject

of considerable research effort (Smith and Gray, 1983; Reiner, 1985; Holdaway, 1989; Young, 1991; Fielding, 1988, 1994; Heidensohn, 1992 on British police; Skolnick, 1966; Westley, 1970; Reuss-Ianni, 1983 on police in the United States). These studies find that the police are characterised by a sense of mission, social isolation, secrecy, resistance to change and are overtly masculinised. Important distinctions have been also found between the informal canteen/locker room culture of the rank and file officers and the more formal organisational culture of 'management cops'.

Police officers' attitudes to their own and fellow officers' health betray polarised responses in which being stressed is received with sympathetic support or castigation for lacking the necessary moral fibre to deal with the harsh realities of policing. On the one hand, officers are supposed to play down the vicissitudes of their job and absorb any attendant distress themselves. On the other hand, policing is represented as demanding special treatment because it is said to be amongst the most stressful of occupations (Brown and Campbell, 1994: 3). These attitudes are products of paradoxes inherent within the informal police occupational culture and between this and the formal organisational culture in which there exists a tension between the requirements of a sympathetic public service and the need to exercise physical force. This polarisation is heightened when focusing on women officers given the persistence of beliefs that policing is still an inherently 'unsuitable job for a woman' (Heidensohn, 1992: 199). The present chapter discusses features of police culture, both formal and informal, and shows how these may generate or dissipate sources of stress as well as help or hinder officers dealing with its adverse consequences.

When Smith and Gray (1983) conducted their participant observation study of London's Metropolitan Police, they observed prevailing social norms within the force as corresponding to those that develop in many male-dominated groups: the need for solidarity and loyalty. They describe a particular version evident in the police where stories of fighting and violence, conversations about sexual conquests and feats of drinking combine together into 'a kind of cult of masculinity' (p. 87). These researchers showed (p. 51) how certain actions receive exaggerated positive salience: a 'good' arrest, demonstrating skill, determination and physical strength, of a 'good' villain, ending with a 'good' result in which the case is successfully prosecuted. This is distinguished from 'rubbish' work which tends to be the more service orientated aspects of policing such as domestic violence incidents. Smith and Gray were also able to demonstrate that much police work is not only uneventful and boring but also that it can be rather aimless. As a consequence, Smith and Gray (1983: 51) argued that police officers search for interest and excitement by driving fast in cars, stopping suspects for something to do and looking for potential disturbances. However, it is also true that officers are killed and injured in the line of duty. Her Majesty's Inspectorate of Constabulary (HMIC) reported that five officers were killed between 1990 and 1995 in England and Wales and nearly 5,000 seriously injured (HMIC, 1995). Thus, it is perhaps not surprising that early recognition that officers themselves may become victims of stress and need professional help came as a consequence of dramatic incidents.

In 1963 officers Ian Campbell and Karl Hettinger from the Los Angeles Police Department (LAPD) were kidnapped and driven to an onion field where Campbell was shot and killed whilst Hettinger managed to escape (Reese, 1995). The survivor suffered considerable survival guilt especially as he had surrendered his gun in the course of the abduction. The police department did not have the expertise available to help, so it invited a psychologist to provide counselling. In Britain, similarly, it was a tragedy that provided the catalyst identifying police officers as potential victims of stress. In 1985 when the Bradford City Football stadium caught fire, over 50 people died and nearly 300 were treated for their injuries in hospital. Forty police officers were included in the toll of the injured. Police officers involved in the disaster showed persistent 'out of character ' behaviour some days after the event. Duckworth and Charlesworth (1988) noted the lack of police training and expertise to recognise and manage traumatic incident exposure and the force's chief constable took 'the unprecedented step of making available professional counselling to those officers who appeared to be suffering the psychological consequences of their involvement' (Duckworth and Charlesworth, 1988: 201).

This appeal to the special demands being made on officers in their operational roles resonates more favourably with the rank and file than the seemingly prosaic motivations of chief officers responding to stress problems associated with sickness absenteeism and premature medical retirement (HMIC, 1997). Research effort that followed in the aftermath of the Bradford disaster widened the ambit of occupational stress to include management and organisational stressors (Brown and Campbell, 1990; Crowe and Stradling, 1993; Alexander *et al.* 1993, Biggam *et al.* 1997) and the 'daily hassles' of operational deployment (Hart *et al.* 1994, 1995) as well as post-traumatic stress disorder (PTSD) (Manolias and Hyatt-Williams, 1986; Alexander and Wells, 1991).

One further point worth making by way of introduction concerns the difficulties of conducting research in the area of police occupational stress which is, in itself, a feature of the police occupational culture. Brown (1996: 178) discusses some of the reasons for the police's antagonism towards research: resistance to critical analysis and an anti-intellectualism. There is a sense in which the police feel besieged by external criticism and need to confirm positive images of themselves which are unlikely to be achieved through the findings of independent research activity. This has been the experience of investigators into stress within the service (see, for example, Kraska and Paulsen, 1997; Walker 1997). Walker (1997: 3) notes:

> Few professionals would want to admit that they are unable to cope with tasks, events and experiences for which they have been trained. They are unlikely to want to divulge this to a researcher no matter what guarantees of confidentiality are offered. Successive researchers on police officers have found the gaining of access to thoughts and feelings has been difficult.

My own experience also testifies to this. My request to undertake a study of occupational stress in a sample of chief police officers was met with the following response: a perception that such research would represent a hostage to fortune in that findings indicating that chief officers were stressed would lead to damaging headlines in the tabloid press. Results showing that the chief officers were not stressed might undermine their claims for the extremes of pressure that they experienced at a time that they were negotiating pay and conditions. The research did not take place.

The operational front line

Professional socialisation is the process of training and induction into the police culture whereby the formal procedural rules and informal practices are acquired (Fielding, 1988, 1994). Formal training requires the police officer to develop appropriate skills in controlling affective responses to tragic or unpleasant circumstances (Pogrebin and Poole, 1991: 396) and maintain discipline within a quasi-military structure whereby officers accept orders and duty assignments (Symonds, 1970: 155). In terms of the former, police officers are expected to act personably not personally in dealing with distressing operational incidents. Miller (1995: 592) notes the 'tough guy' mentality whereby police, men and women, require a certain adaptive defence in response to the routine and traumatic incidents to which they are exposed. Emotional control is an important part of the officer's occupational identity both in terms of the public's expectation and demands of the informal culture. Training instils a sense that officers' authority and successful execution of duty rests with suppression of affect (Reisser and Geiger, 1984: 317). When that control is not achieved, there are failures of the demands of both the formal and informal culture, that may combine and result in adverse reactions. Newton (1989: 18) describes the following example:

> A 14 month old baby boy who had hooked his cardigan onto his cot had fallen, twisted and hanged himself. The experienced officer attending was so distressed by this incident that he allowed the body to be moved before the attendance of a doctor and supervisory officer. [The officer reported] 'The whole incident was not dealt with at an acceptable professional level of performance. I suffered feelings of anger and sorrow for about three weeks afterwards.'

This officer found it difficult to share his distress over the incident, but also was exercised by what was a procedural failure which, as an experienced officer, he found added to his difficulties when coping with the aftermath.

Stradling, Crowe and Tuohy (1993) found that, for trainee probationer constables, there are fluctuations in their self-concept especially in regard to dimensions of self-worth and vulnerability accompanying the process of professional socialisation. With respect to their sense of self-worth, there appears to be a curvilinear relationship, in other words the recruit and the recently confirmed constables exhibit highest scores on this index, with those having served six months, one year and 18 months showing a progressive decline. The work of Janoff-Bulman (1989) may provide an explanation. Janoff-

Bulman argues that individuals operate on the basis of unquestioned, but fundamentally benign, assumptions about the world. These may be shattered by the experience of a traumatic event. The cognitive task confronting someone who has experienced such an event is to assimilate and integrate the new negative experience. For the neophyte police officer, this has to be set against a training experience that is trying to instil control over events and emotions. Notions of a just world protect individuals from negative consequences and enhance feelings of security. Naïve police recruits are excited about becoming police officers and have yet to face the tough and sometimes messy actualities of policing tasks. As these become a reality, the threats to the identity of inexperienced officers may be in excess of their coping abilities. As the officer becomes more experienced, some habituation takes place as he or she finds support from the coping devices offered by the occupational culture.

Fielding (1988: 45) notes that these devices allow the officer to discharge emotion without any loss of professional status and includes the use of off-colour humour which permits a collective empathising with each other's feelings. Mitchell and Munro (1996) illustrate this with reference to the training of Scottish probationer constables in learning to deal with sudden deaths. The *in situ* advice was most likely to be 'distancing and detachment' (p. 50) manifest by avoidance strategies or the use of humour. Joyce (1989: 380) argues that there is a vicious cycle set up when confronting death whereby 'younger officers [learn] to bottle up their fear, sorrow and revulsion and to replace these with a show of bravado and practical competence'. An example of this is provided by Young (1995: 155) describing his own reactions as a young police officer:

> I was approached by a man hurrying from under the Tyne bridge. 'Officer come quick', he said 'a man's been knocked down.' I went with this breathlessly tense man. It was about 8 pm. I looked along the Quayside but saw no traffic as we tentatively examined the bloody mess lying splattered across the road. 'Where's the vehicle?' the shocked witness asked me. 'There isn't one,' I told him 'he came from up there,' and I pointed to the bridge directly above us. And I added 'He's just found out that man can't fly ...' As I took a statement from the man, I knew he was sickened almost to silence, whilst my flippant retort had set the tone for dealing with an appalling sudden death, and allowed me (just) to get through it all.

Another significant feature of the informal culture of the police is group solidarity and support. There seems to be some contradictory findings in the research literature. Alexander and Walker (1994) indicated from their Scottish police officer sample that talking things through with friends or colleagues was a strategy employed by officers. Yet, according to Stephens, Long and Miller (1997: 305) the sharing of emotional experiences is an aspect of support that is not always found in police culture. They report research findings from samples of Australian and British police officers that displays of emotion were perceived as personally weak and occupationally hazardous. Fear of not performing well in the eyes of peers lead to blocked feelings in stressful situations. They conclude that these attitudes actually hinder the

253

therapeutic responses appropriate for recovery from the possible adverse consequences of exposure to traumatic episodes. Brown and Grover (1998: 183) suggest that under conditions of low stressor exposure, social support did not necessarily buffer the police officer from potential adverse effects. It may be that the solicitousness of family or colleagues is a hindrance rather than a help. However, under conditions of high-stressor exposure, social support did seem to be important in modifying possible ill health. Stephens, Long and Miller (1997: 312), in their study of trauma amongst New Zealand police officers, also found the helpfulness of social support is variable. Support from peers in talking about negative aspects of police work was associated with beneficial outcomes, but other aspects of social interactions between colleagues was actually burdensome and resulted in poorer health outcomes.

Richmond, Wodak, Kehoe and Heather (1998) looked at the role of excessive alcohol consumption as a coping response in New South Wales police officers. They found about half the police officer respondents drank excessively. Furthermore, around two-fifths of men and one-third of women reported binge drinking. They propose that the after-hours culture involves discharging stress about violent encounters or conflicts with management which, combined with a strong pressure to conformity, induced heavy social drinking. Women officers, in particular, reported pressures to emulate their male colleagues by drinking heavily.

Gender, policing and stress

The camaraderie and social support gained through after-hours socialising are devices more likely to be enjoyed by policemen than women. Smith and Gray (1983: 91) argue that the cult of masculinity has a strong influence on policemen's behaviour towards women, that they do not accept women as equal members of the team because of an over-emphasis on physical strength and that these prejudices are worst in the CID. There is still a perception that women officers are best suited to deal with the 'emotional labour' of police work which pushes them into the marginalised social services policing (Fielding and Fielding, 1992: 206). Fielding (1988) found a grudging acceptance of women probationers by their fellow officers as training proceeded:

> The WPC [woman police constable] belongs to the feminine world of emotion, sensitivity and academic niceties like paperwork, the PC is the man of action and strength. (p. 163).

For women, policing is sexually atypical employment. Breakwell (1986: 71) argues that by adopting atypical employment, women fail to conform to gender expectations in job choice and risk suspicion being cast on their femininity. Moreover, if a woman happens to have a partner and/or children, she is even more vulnerable. This is illustrated with reference to the death of the journalist, Veronica Guerin. *Scotland on Sunday* on 22 June 1998 published the following in a leader:

[A] year after her death, people are again asking if Guerin cared too much for the glow of journalistic glory. The barely concealed implication is that Guerin jettisoned her family to further a career. It is not an accusation which would be levelled at a man who died in similar circumstances.

Women police officers are similarly susceptible. At its most tragic, injury and death of women officers have invoked headlines such as 'frail blue line' after the stabbing of constable Lesley Harrison (Heidensohn, 1992) and 'was this killing ... too terrible a price to pay for equality' after the murder of constable Nina Mackay (Brown and Grover, 1998). At a more mundane level, women who are parents have aspersions cast on either their professionalism or their fitness as mothers, or both. The following is an account from an Australian police woman (Austin, 1996):

I have had some interesting experiences in policing since becoming a mother. After returning to part-time work after the birth of my first child, I went to an incident where a young chap had gone berserk and smashed up his parents' house and seriously assaulted his father. I and a junior male officer stepped forward to take hold of him, at which he began struggling. Other police arrived and a well built young officer said, 'Wendy, I'll take him,' manouvred me out the way to physically get him into the back of the police truck. The other officers all left, taking the offender back to the police station. A senior male constable remarked to me after we had got the chap into the back of the truck, 'I didn't think you did that sort of thing anymore.' I was puzzled for a while and then realized that he was referring to my status as a mother. However, it didn't stop them from leaving me with the victims, organizing medical care, obtaining of statements, charging the offender and all the other cleaning up that mothers are so good at.

The unfit-mother accusation can be found among policemen in Britain from the research by Holdaway and Parker (1998) who report that a third of policemen agreed with the statements 'on the average, a woman who stays at home all the time with her children is a better mother than a woman who works outside the home at least half the time' (compared to 6 per cent of women), 'women officers who leave to have children should not expect a job waiting for them if they come back to work' (compared to 8 per cent of women), and 19 per cent of men agreed with the statement that 'women officers who want to be mothers should not expect a serious career' (compared with 4 per cent of women).

As has been discussed above, aspects of the police occupational culture, its solidarity and camaraderie are important features in supporting officers. Women's exclusions from these can result in an accentuation of adverse impacts of exposure to both routine and traumatic operational stressors. An illustration of this can be provided by the experience of a young WPC, whom I interviewed, who was attacked while she was checking a shop door at two o'clock in the morning. The armed intruder eventually ran off but not before pushing her to the ground and badly frightening her. (He was later thought to have been a rape suspect.) This is her description of what then happened:

WPC: The acting inspector came out; he loathed the female in distress bit and had no sympathy. They called an ambulance, as I realised I had hurt my finger. When the sergeant arrived I just burst into tears. I was taken to hospital and treated for the cut finger and bruises. Then I went back to the station. I had to give a statement at the station and was told 'As a WPC you know all about this,' and they just left me to it.

JB: Then what happened?

WPC: The next day when I went in the DI called into the CID office and pointed to the DC and said 'As you know we are very busy with a rape case – you can look into this for a week and if you get no result that will be it.' Then he said to me 'I want to speak to you … In my office.'

He had got my statement and said 'This is not very good, in fact it's a load of rubbish. Call yourself a police officer. What can we go on with this? Just one question. Why didn't you catch him? Think about your basic training.' I just had a panic attack and got myself signed off sick. The office gossip was, how come she's off for a week for a cut finger?

JB: How did you feel about all of this?

WPC: I felt a sense of failure. I should have done this or that. The police role should have kicked in. I was terrified. I thought I would never be able to go out into the dark again. In my private life I take more precautions. I can't sleep with a window open. As a potential witness I felt useless. I was incredibly small and vulnerable and insignificant. I felt defensive and pathetic. I was made to feel that I had greatly inconvenienced them [the CID]. I should stop causing them problems and stop being a child causing trouble.

JB: How do you feel about it all now?

WPC: I was let down by the police. Surely there must be an 'us and them' situation. What about the us? I am bitter about people who did not believe me or who minimalised what happened to me. It affected my career. Every so often it rears its ugly head. It comes up on my appraisal to haunt me. My superintendent wrote on one of my applications: as you are aware, WPC F has had a series of attachments and avoided working shifts. On my appraisals I have had this incident continually referred to even if only to say it is not causing her a problem as she has put the experience behind her and is dealing with the problem. This was some time after it had happened. It has blighted my career. I am that bloody police woman who was attacked. There have been jokes and remarks. The camaraderie is fine but woe betide you if the uniform is turned against you.

The experience of this officer, as a victim, went unrecognised and the focus of reactions to her experience was her professional failure. These were seen as shortcomings that not only appeared to neutralise support, but followed her for several years impeding her career progression.

Whilst the number of women officers has risen steadily since the passing of equality legislation, they still represent only about 14 per cent of the complement of officers in Australia, United Kingdom and United States (Brown, 1998a). Research, drawing on the theoretical work of Rosabeth Kanter, details the impact on police women of their relatively small numerical representation (Ott, 1989; Martin, 1989; Brown, 1998b). Kanter's thesis proposes that distortions in the gender balance of organisations has an impact on opportunities for advancement. To prosper, organisations require reduction of uncertainties and good communications. In order to maximise these features, there is a tendency to appoint similar individuals to senior positions. Thus, in organisations which have been historically male-dominated, managers will be appointed who share common features. This sustains male hierarchies by a process excluding those who are different, such as women, from upward mobility and sets up a cycle of lowered motivation and discouragement which inhibits performance, reduces organisational recognition and limits chances of advancement. Critical to this argument are the relative proportions of men and women in the workplace. Kanter (1977) suggests that the person in the minority becomes a highly visible 'token' attracting a disproportionate share of attention. Tokens are susceptible to exaggeration of difference because the small numbers encourage the application of social stereotyping. These processes lead to job performance pressures in terms of lack of privacy within the organisation where competence is taken as a measure of the general ability of the person's social category rather than his or her individual achievement. Tokens try and cope by working harder and overachieving or attempting to limit their visibility and avoid risks or controversy. Tokens become 'mistake-avoidance sensitive', have an exaggerated fear of failure at important tasks or key events, and worry about retaliation by envious dominant group members.

Dominants in organisations, on the other hand, continually assert or reclaim the group solidarity and exaggerate occupational symbols and values that differentiate them from the tokens. Kanter shows how men in the majority dramatise their feats of drinking and sexual prowess with exaggerated displays of aggression and potency. Research by Smith and Gray (1983) and later research by Brown (1998b) and Holdaway and Parker (1998) show that policewomen are subjected to sexual harassment by their male colleagues. Parker, Holdaway and Griffin (1998) link this experience of harassment to work-performance stress in women officers. They propose that both male and female police officers can experience work-performance anxiety and that excessive levels can lead to poor mental health. Because of sceptical and even hostile attitudes about their capabilities, women in policing will experience higher levels of work-performance anxiety. The mechanism through which this is mediated is sexual harassment. Thus, name calling and suggestive jokes draw attention to gender, making women more conscientious in proving that they can carry out all policing tasks. Harassment is 'designed' to de-professionalise the woman officer. Results from their study did indeed show that at excessive levels work-performance anxiety is potentially damaging for both men and women officers. One of the contributing features for women was the exposure to harassment. However Parker, Holdaway and Griffin (1998) also found that after controlling for the effect on performance anxiety, harassing behaviours were associated with positive mental health for policemen. They conclude that as gender 'dominants' sexual harassment for men becomes part of a healthy joking culture whereas for women 'tokens' such behaviours serve to heighten pressures relating to job performance.

Managers and management

Heidensohn (1996: 6) observes that policing agendas are set by several sources in democratic societies, not just by the police themselves. In particular:

> A notable feature of several Western democratic societies in recent times is the way in which new priorities have been set for police organisations. New approaches such as community or problem oriented policing have been tried out, as have more domestic or softer priorities.

These new approaches owe much to developments in Britain where the Conservative government of Margaret Thatcher began a revolution in public-sector organisations by introducing private-sector management techniques. For a discussion of this process in policing, see Leishman, Cope and Starie (1996). Further initiatives included the Citizen's Charter where the police were obliged to set clear commitments for their levels of service provision. These trends can be found in other countries, such as Germany, where Koch (1998: 178) describes the 'Neues Steuerungmodell' as the equivalent version of new public-sector management in which the police are more financially accountable and victim-sensitive. These options have led to a revitalisation of styles of policing.

These developments coincided with what Fielding (1994) notes was a crisis in the legitimacy of policing located in decline in support for the contract of policing by consent, collapse of police evidence in high-profile trials, documentaries on the dispensation of street justice, declines in crime clear-up and the coming to light of corruption amongst serving police officers. Anxious to restore the loss of public confidence in Britain's police, some of the newly appointed chief constables increasingly emphasised the caring nature of the police's contemporary role. Many police forces dropped the word 'force' and assumed a 'service' orientation (Stephens and Becker, 1994). These trends were formalised into the ACPO Quality of Service imitative whose aims were laid out in a document entitled 'Setting the Standards for Policing: Meeting Community Expectations' in which equal opportunities is afforded a central place (see Waters, 1996, and Chapter 16). The document explicitly stated there to be a direct correlation between attitudes within the organisation to minority officers, (gender and racial) and officers' attitudes to members of the public.

These reforms have created work pressures for both the managers and managed. Brown and Cooper (1992: 2151) reported results from a survey of senior police managers in the United Kingdom at a time of organisational change. Officers of the rank of superintendent and chief superintendent reported problems related to poor morale and organisational uncertainty. In particular, one superintendent indicated:

> [A]n organisation that is in a constant state of flux can only invoke in its employees

feelings of instability and uncertainty. We [the superintendents] exist on adrenalin, anti-depressants and tranquillisers. We are asked to achieve the unachievable and then criticised because of our inadequacies.

In a 'can do' culture it is very difficult to admit that, as a senior officer, you cannot accomplish what is asked of you. Inadequate resourcing, staff short-age and time pressures are amongst the most often cited stressors by senior police managers (Kirkcaldy *et al.*, 1998).

There are also pressures on the rank and file police officers to deliver on the police reform programme. The thrust of the British government's poli-cies for the police, especially those enacted through the Police and Magistrates' Courts Act 1994, identifies crime fighting as the key policing activity (Loveday, 1996). The Metropolitan Police's Operations 'Bumblebee' and 'Eagle Eye' epitomised these centrally driven directives by targeting bur-glary and street robbery and emphasised arrests as a key performance indicator. As shown by Brown and Neville (1996):

[A]rrest is a significant performance indicator that both fulfils the competitive nature of the informal culture and satisfies the Audit Commission and Home Office for tangible results.

They conclude (p. 300) that efforts to reform the working practices of the British police through an accountable 'performance' culture simply maps on to many of the competitive and masculinised features of the informal rule-bending and breaking of the canteen/locker room culture. Holdaway (1996: 81) vividly describes the potency of the rank and file informal culture in which excitement and action predominate, subverting the more discerning approach to policework advocated by police managers, for example the abil-ity to influence operational police styles away from masculine stereotype, which according to Fielding (1994: 55) 'is unlikely to find much room for expression within the social service aspects of policing'. In the spirit of a more community focus to policing, one force introduced a method called 'total geographic policing'. Brown and Fielding (1993: 338) report:

Difficulties were expressed that this practice means officers lose contact with their fellow officers and the camaraderie of the shift. This loss of contact was associated with the stress experienced by officers working in this way.

Conclusions

Whilst there may be no strong empirical evidence that police officers are more or less stressed than other occupational groups (Brown and Campbell, 1994: 169), the particularities of the police occupational culture create a working climate and foster patterns of behaviour that are supportive of but can inhibit or exacerbate individuals' adverse reactions to stressor exposure. The nature of the policing task is such that officers can be placed in danger-ous situations or face violent confrontations. The strong masculine ethos of the police places great emphasis on mutual support and solidarity amongst rank and file officers. This may work powerfully in favour of those who belong to the majority social categories of white male. However, for those who are different, or 'other' such as from the ethnic minorities or women, the informal culture places additional burdens on officers and excludes them from the informal support systems.

Having a strong ethos of controlling emotions also creates difficulties for officers when facing tragic or distressing events. Use of off-duty drinking or off-colour humour may help to dissipate the negative emotions in the short term, but even officers within the normative majority can find it difficult to deal effectively with the fallout of fear, anxiety, sadness, anger that may ensue through their operational exposure to the difficult or the dangerous. Negative attitudes towards the expression of emotion have been associated with symptoms of psychological distress (Mitchell-Gibbs, 1995). However, police officers have a reputation for shunning psychological services (Miller, 1995: 596) because counsellors are perceived as 'bleeding hearts', and officers fear that therapy will be an infantilising or humiliating experience, or more commonly that to seek help implies weakness, cowardice or inability to do the job.

Acceptance that officers themselves, in some instances, may become stress victims as a result of their involvement in operational duties seem easier to recognise than the greater probability that officers become stressed as a consequence of organisational mismanagement (Alexander *et al.*, 1993; Brown and Campbell, 1994). This has implications for the success of management or clinical interventions to alleviate or modify sources and impacts of stressor exposure. On the one hand, there needs to be a greater tolerance that seeking professional counselling is acceptable, but on the other hand it should not be seen as an occupational 'perk' to achieve a preferential earlier medical retirement settlement.

References

Alexander, D.A. and Walker, L. (1994) 'A Study of Methods Used by Scottish Police Officers to Cope with Work Induced Stress', *Stress Medicine,* 10, 131–8.

Alexander, D.A. Walker, L., Innes, G. and Irving, B.L. (1993) *Police Stress at Work.* London: The Police Foundation.

Alexander, D.A. and Wells, A. (1991) 'Reactions of Police Officers to Body-Handling after a Major Disaster: A Before and After Comparison', *British Journal of Psychiatry,* 159, 547–55.

Arnold, J., Robertson, I.T. and Cooper, A. (1993) *Work Psychology: Understanding Human Behaviour in the Workplace.* London: Pitman.

Association of Chief Police Officers (1984) *Stress in the Police Service.* London: Home Office.

Austin, W. (1996) 'The Socialization of Women Police: Male Officer Hostility to Female Police Officers'. Paper presented to the First Australian Women Police Conference, Sydney, 29–31 July.

Biggam, F., Power, K.G., Macdonald, R., Carcary, W. and Moodies, E. (1997) 'Self-Perceived Occupational Stress and Distress in a Scottish Police Force', *Work & Stress,* 11, 118–33.

Breakwell, G. (1986) *Coping with Threatened Identities*. London: Methuen.

Brown, J.M. (1996) 'Police research; some critical issues' in Leishman *et al*. (1996).

Brown, J.M. (1998a) 'Aspects of Discriminatory Treatment of Women Officers Serving in Forces in England and Wales', *British Journal of Criminology*, 38, 265–83.

Brown, J.M. (1998b) 'Comparing Charges: The Experience of Women Police Officers Serving in Australia, British Isles and United States of America', *International Journal of Police Science and Management*, 1, 227–40.

Brown, J.M. and Campbell, E.A. (1990) 'Sources of Occupational Stress in the Police', *Work and Stress*, 4, 305–18.

Brown, J.M. and Campbell, E.A. (1994) *Stress and Policing; Sources and Strategies*. Chichester: Wiley.

Brown, J.M. and Cooper, C.L. (1992) 'Tough at the top', *Police Review*, 20 November, 2120–51.

Brown. J.M. and Fielding, J. (1993) 'Qualitative Differences in Men and Women Police Officers' Experience of Occupational Stress', *Work and Stress*, 7, 327–40.

Brown, J.M. and Grover, J. (1998) 'The Role of Moderating Variables between Stressor Exposure and Being Distressed in a Sample of Serving Police Officers', *Personality and Individual Differences*, 24, 181–5.

Brown, J.M. and Neville, M. (1996) 'Arrest Rate as a Measure of Police Men and Women's Productivity and Competence', *Police Journal*, LXIX (4), 299–307.

Crowe, G. and Stradling, S. (1993) 'Dimensions of Perceived Stress in a British Police Force', *Policing and Society*, 3, 137–50.

Duckworth, D. and Charlesworth, A. (1988) '*The Human Side of Disaster*', *Policing*, 4, 194–210.

Dunham, R.G. and Alpert, G.P. (eds) (1989) *Minorities in Policing*. Prospect Heights, IL: Waveland.

Fielding, N. (1988) *Joining Forces; Police Socialization and Occupational Competence*. London: Routledge.

Fielding, N. (1994) 'Cop Canteen Culture' in Newburn and Stanko (1994).

Fielding, N. and Fielding, J. (1992) 'A Comparative Minority: Female Recruits to a British Constabulary Force', *Policing and Society*, 2, 205–18.

Hart, P., Wearing, A. and Headey, B. (1994) 'Work Experience; Construct Validation of the Police Daily Hassles and Uplift Scales', *Criminal Justice and Behaviour*, 21, 283–311.

Hart, P., Wearing, A. and Headey, B. (1995) 'Police Stress and Well-Being; Integrating Personality, Coping and Daily Work Experience', *Journal of Occupational and Organizational Psychology*, 68, 133–56.

Heidensohn, F. (1992) *Women in Control*. Oxford: Clarendon.

Heidensohn, F. (1996) 'Comparing Charges: Comparative Studies of Policing and Gender'. Paper presented to the Annual Meeting of the American Society of Criminology, 22 November.

Her Majesty's Inspectorate of Constabulary (1995) *Facing Violence: The Response of Provincial Forces*. London: Home Office.

Her Majesty's Inspectorate of Constabulary (1997) *Lost Time: Management of Sickness Absence and Medical Retirement in the Police Service*. London: Home Office.

Holdaway, S. (1989) 'Discovering Structure: Studies of the British Police Occupational Culture' in Weatheritt (1989).

Holdaway, S. (1996) *The Racialisation of British Policing*. London: Macmillan.

Holdaway, S. and Parker, S. (1998) 'Policing Women police; Uniform, Patrol, Promotion and Representation in CID', *British Journal of Criminology*, 38, 40–60.

Janoff-Bulman, R. (1989) 'Assumptive Worlds and the Stress of Traumatic Events: Applications of the Schema Construct', *Social Cognition*, 7, 113–36.

Joyce, D. (1989) 'Why Do Police Officers Laugh at Death?', *The Psychologist*, 9, 551–4.

Kanter, R.M. (1977) 'Some Effects of Proportions on Group Life; Skewed Sex Ratios and Responses to Token Women', *American Journal of Sociology*, 82, 965–90.

Kirkcaldy, B., Brown, J. and Cooper, C.L. (1998) 'The Demographics of Occupational Stress among Police Superintendents', *Journal of Managerial Psychology*, 13, 90–101.

Kirke, M.I. and Scrivner, E.M. (eds) (1995) *Police Psychology into the 21st Century*. Hillsdale: Lawrence Erlbaum.

Koch, U. (1998) 'Policing in the Context of Changing State Functions: Examples from Germany' in *Pagan*.

Kraska, P.B. and Paulsen, D.J. (1997) 'Grounded Research into US Paramilitary Policing; Forging the Iron Fist inside the Velvet Glove', *Policing and Society*, 7, 253–70.

Lazarus, R.S. (1966) *Psychological Stress and the Coping Process*. New York: McGraw-Hill.

Leishman, F., Cope, S. and Starie, P. (1996) 'Reinventing and Reconstructing: Towards a New Policing Order' in Leishman *et al.* (1996).

Leishman, F., Loveday, B. and Savage, S. (eds) (1996) *Core Issues in Policing*. 1st edn. Harlow: Longman.

Loveday, B. (1996) 'Crime at the Core?' in Leishman *et al. ibid.*

McKenna, B. (1994) 'Stress Injuries at Work', *New Law Journal*, 2 December, 1652, 1655.

Manolias, M. and Hyatt-Williams, A. (1986) *Post-Shooting Experiences in Firearms Officers*. London: Home Office, Joint Working Party on Organisational Health and Welfare.

Martin, S.E. (1989) 'Female Officers on the Move? A Status Report on Women in Policing' in Dunham and Alpert (1989).

Miller, L. (1995) 'Tough Guys: Psychotherapeutic Strategies with Law Enforcement and Emergency Services Personnel, *Psychotherapy*, 32, 592–600.

Mitchell, M. and Munro, A. (1996) 'The Influence of the Occupational Culture on How Police Probationers Learn to Deal with Incidents of Sudden Death', *Issues in Legal and Criminological Psychology*, 25, 47–53.

Mitchell-Gibbs, J. (1995) *Psychological Aspects of Traumatic Stress in British Police Officers*. BSc dissertation submitted to the University of Essex.

Newburn, T. and Stanko, E. (eds) (1994) *Just Boys Doing the Business: Men, Masculinities and Crime*. London: Routledge.

Newton, R. (1989) *The Incidence of Stress Reactions in Individual Operational Police Officers in Line of Duty Crisis: A Study and Literature Review of 'Unexpected Reactions'*. London: Home Office, Science and Technical Group.

Ott, E. Marlies (1989) 'Effects of the Male–Female Ratio at Work', *Psychology of Women Quarterly*, 13, 41–57.

Pagan, M. (ed.) (1998) *Policing in Central and Eastern Europe: Organisational, Managerial and Human Resource Aspects*. Ljubljana: Ljubljana College of Police and Security Studies.

Parker, S.K., Holdaway, S. and Griffin, M. (1998) 'Why Does Harassment Cause Distress? The Mediating Role of Work Performance Anxiety'. Paper presented to the First International Conference Institute of Work Psychology, University of Sheffield, July.

Pickover, D. (1998) 'Damage Limitation', *Police Review,* 11 December.

Pogrebin, M.R. and Poole, E.D. (1991) 'Police and Tragic Events: The Management of Emotions', *Journal of Criminal Justice,* 19, 395–403.

Reese, J.T. (1995) 'A History of Police Psychological Services' in Kirke and Scrivner (1995).

Reiner, R. (1985) *The Politics of the Police.* London: Wheatsheaf.

Reiser, M. (1982) *Police Psychology.* New York: Lehu Publishing.

Reisser, M. and Geiger, S. (1984) 'Police Officer as Victim', *Professional Psychology: Research and Practice,* 15, 315–23.

Reuss-Ianni, E. (1983) *The Two Cultures of Policing: Street Cops and Management Cops.* New York: Transaction Books.

Richmond, R., Wodak, A., Kehoe, L. and Heather, N. (1998) 'How Healthy Are the Police? A Survey of Life-Style Factors', *Addiction,* 93, 1729–37.

Skolnick, J. (1966) *Justice without Trial.* New York: Wiley.

Smith, D. and Gray, J. (1983) *Police and People of London. The PSI Report.* London: Policy Studies Institute.

Stephens, M. and Becker, S. (1994) *Police Force, Police Service.* London: Macmillan.

Stephens, C., Long, N. and Miller, I. (1997) 'The Impact of Trauma and Social Support on Posttraumatic Stress Disorder: A Study of New Zealand Police Officers', *Journal of Criminal Justice,* 25, 303–14.

Stradling, S., Crowe, G. and Tuohy, A. (1993) 'Changes in Self-Concept during Occupational Socialization of New Recruits to the Police', *Journal of Community & Applied Social Psychology,* 3, 131–47.

Symonds, M. (1970) 'Emotional Hazards of Police Work', *American Journal of Psychoanalysis,* 30, 155–60.

Walker, M. (1997) 'Conceptual and Methodological Issues in the Investigation of Occupational Stress: A Case Study of Police Officers Deployed on Body Recovery at the Site of the Lockerbie Air Crash, *Policing and Society,* 7, 1–17.

Waters, I. (1996) 'Quality of Service: Politics or Paradigm Shift?' in Leishman *et al. op. cit.*

Weatheritt, M. (ed.) (1989) *Police Research Some Future Prospects.* Aldershot: Avebury.

Westley, W. (1970) *Violence and the Police: A Sociological Study of Law, Custom and Morality.* Cambridge, MA: MIT Press.

Worden, Pollitz, A. (1993) The Attitudes of Women and Men in Policing: Testing Conventional and Contemporary Wisdom', *Criminology,* 31, 203–41.

Young, M. (1991) *Inside Job.* Oxford: Clarendon.

Young, M. (1995) 'Black Humour – Making Light of Death', *Policing and Society,* 5, 151–67.

Chapter 16

Quality and performance monitoring

IAN WATERS

Introduction and background

The focus on quality and performance in the English and Welsh police has in many ways intensified since the 1990 launch of the ACPO Strategic Policy Document (SPD), *Setting the Standards for Policing: Meeting Community Expectation*. As discussed elsewhere (see Waters, 1996), the SPD signalled the launch of the national Quality of Service (QOS) programme in the police. The document itself contained the Statement of Common Purpose and Values (SCPV) which emphasises the need for the police to act with 'integrity, common sense and sound judgement', and to 'respond to well-founded criticism with a willingness to change' (ACPO, 1990). The statement was broadly accepted in the forces of England and Wales and regarded as a cornerstone of the QOS initiative.

It is important to recall that the 1990 Operational Policing Review (OPR) (Joint Consultative Committee, 1990) lay at the foundation of the national quality programme. The OPR highlighted the gap in public and police expectations about the ideal style and objectives of policing: this finding, plus an apparent decline in public confidence in the police (as evidenced by the British Crime Survey of 1988), prompted ACPO to review the strategic direction of the police and the ways in which it could embrace a 'quality' approach to enhance its public standing and service provision. As officer respondents testified, there was a clear effort to promulgate a more 'service-oriented' approach: the aim was to de-emphasise the more forceful aspects of policing, and to inculcate a more responsive model (or image) of policing. As developed elsewhere (see Brown and Waters, 1996), recent years have witnessed an oscillation between protective/service models of policing, and order/enforcement models. The quality approach represented one of the periodic swings back toward a more caring or community-oriented emphasis.

The advent of quality in the police paralleled the growth of consumerism and managerialism within the public sector as a whole. As Potter (1994: 250) indicates, the representation of consumer interests has been one of the key elements in the growth of public-sector commodification. Leishman, Cope and Starie (1996: 11) analyse the rise of 'New Public Management' (NPM), with its emphasis on market forces, reorganising public-sector management to resemble a more business-oriented approach, the promotion of greater efficiency, developing performance indicators, and making public agencies more consumer-responsive. As they state (*ibid.*: 12), NPM has had a marked impact on nearly all public-sector organisations, and the police service has been increasingly obliged to embrace NPM. Farnham and Horton (1993: 241) note the cultural shift from the traditional public-service ethos (based on 'need, equity, fairness and altruism') to that of 'public business':

> All public services are now perceived as businesses with mission statements identifying their goals and objectives, which can either be quantified or measured ... This is not always easy to do, for example, in areas like the police and prison services.
>
> (*ibid.*: 242).

Farnham and Horton recall (p. 242) that up until 1987 there was greater managerial emphasis on reducing costs of services and controlling 'inputs', but that after 1987 the emphasis on 'quality' and 'consumer' demands came to the fore. One motivation for the police to adopt quality reforms was the decline in its standing with both the government and the public. The mounting pressure on the police in the early 1990s is epitomised by a *Sunday Times* article of 17 May 1992 (p. 12) by Michael Prescott, who talked of the perception of 'laziness, incompetence and rudeness' in the police, who were 'now revealed as practitioners of all that is anathema to Thatcherism, and ... derided as the last great unreconstructed national industry'. In 1990, the Chief Inspector of Constabulary addressed the Senior Command Course at Bramshill, and emphasised the need for constant change within the police (Woodcock, 1990: 5). In his closing comments, Sir John Woodcock talked of quality:

> I am still convinced that the vast majority of the law abiding public feel warmly about the police. It is in the interests of the service to ensure this situation remains. Not only has the 'marketing' to be done but more fundamentally, the 'quality of the service' to the customer must be raised. Quality is essential – nothing less will do. This must be the message that all police officers work towards. (*ibid.*: 32)

Reiner (1992: 104) suggests that the police had lost the confidence of what he calls the articulate 'talking classes', and Morgan and Newburn (1997: 49) note how the 'accord' between the police and the Thatcher government had waned in the latter half of the 1980s. Police leaders realised that confidence (both public and governmental) had declined to an uncomfortable level, and accepted that something had to be done. One Assistant Chief Constable (ACC) interviewed commented on the development of quality reforms in the police:

> I think it was clear that if we were to go forward into the 90s ... we had to have a look at our organisation. ... we then recognised that and then we initiated it ...
>
> (Interview, November 1993)

While the then chief constable of Leicestershire (Hirst, 1991a: 189) suggested that the national QOS initiative was designed to 'bridge the gap between service delivery and public expectation', Weatheritt (1993: 36) also notes that the service 'wanted to restore its credibility and part of doing that was being seen to take the initiative'. Reiner (1992: 266) notes that consumerism became a critical element in public-sector reform and that police leaders 'rapidly latched on to this new language as a way of founding a new ethic of service to revive their flagging status', and as a means of avoiding imposed forms of accountability. As it happens, the 'quality' ethic, and con-comitant initiatives, failed politically in that the Conservative government unleashed significant police reforms from 1993 onwards. Reiner (1997: 1036) notes that the 'self-engineered change' brought about by police lead-ers failed to satisfy central government.

While quality remained high on the police agenda in the late 1990s, other reforms and initiatives of the decade have significantly affected the progress and development of the QOS programme. There has been an ever-growing emphasis on the measurement and monitoring of performance and the application of business techniques: this has, of course, echoed the reforms introduced by the previous Conservative government, as well as the more recent policies of the Labour government, which have again focused on con-cerns of cost and input. Various agencies have become embroiled in the debate about police performance and quality, including the Audit Commission, the HMIC, the Association of Police Authorities (APA), the Home Office and, of course, ACPO. In referring to the influence of each of these agencies, this chapter charts the development of the QOS programme in the police, and identifies the extent to which issues of performance have become increasingly prevalent, particularly with the current emphases on 'Best Value' and efficiency savings in the police.

Quality in the police

Numerous public sector organisations have adopted the tenets of 'quality' in their response to the reform agenda of the 1980s and 1990s. As Lawton and Rose (1994) indicate, quality is rooted in the private sector, and its origins can be traced back to the rebuilding of the Japanese economy after the Second World War. Many authors (including Dale and Oakland, 1994) have identified the importance of 'quality management' and customer care in the business world, and their importance for organisational and competitive sur-vival. The police have adopted many aspects of a business-oriented quality, but within their own QOS programme they have also embraced the public-service ethos referred to by Farnham and Horton (1993). Forces abroad (such as in New Zealand and Hong Kong) have also developed ongoing quality programmes in the 1990s: the Hong Kong police have their own 'service quality wing' overseeing initiatives to promulgate a consumer-oriented approach in service delivery (as well as guiding internal reforms), and the New Zealand police have launched their own 'quality policing' programme. The SCPV is a prime example of the more traditional, public-oriented emphasis in the UK, although the definitions and aims of 'quality policing' can be multifarious (see Waters, 1999).

Prior to the national initiative, launched at Bramshill Police Staff College in October 1990, various police forces had entertained the concept of quality or had instigated their own reform programmes. An early example is Kent Constabulary's 'The Way Ahead' programme (1989) which (amongst other things) was designed to identify the views and priorities of the public. Thames Valley Police, which has been at the forefront of reform and quality developments, launched its 'Make Contact' programme in 1986, and subsequently its 'Make Quality Contact' and 'Service in Action' programmes in the early 1990s, both of which took forward the quality philosophy in terms of service delivery and strategic development.

Probably the best known organisational and quality reform package was the Metropolitan Police's 'Plus' programme, which greatly influenced the subsequent development of the national QOS initiative. The corporate identity consultants, Wolff Olins, had pinpointed the need for the force to develop a 'clear collective vision', which would entail the improvement of management systems, behaviour, communication, attitudes and visual identity (Wolff Olins, 1988: 16). From this was born the massive 'Plus' programme which, as the Commissioner indicated in his report for 1989, was designed to:

> ... tackle and change, where necessary, the culture of the organisation; it is about changing the emphasis from a 'force' to 'service' ethos; it is about ensuring that those police and civil staff who provide help and assistance to our public are well supported and thereby able to give the best service possible to those who need it ...
> (Metropolitan Police, 1990: xii)

As McLaughlin (1992: 478) states, Plus was the prototypical mission statement for policing in the 1990s. Walker (1994: 55) notes the 'major programme of change' undertaken under the banner of Plus, and King Taylor (1992) includes Plus as a case study in her analysis of 'total quality':

> Given the traditions of the Metropolitan Police, the climate in which it operates and its culture, one can only be impressed that its service excellence programme, known as Plus, ever took off at all.

In addition to the impetus afforded by Plus, the 1990 OPR was the immediate precursor to the national initiative. The concerns which led to the OPR were stated as follows: 'traditional' policing was threatened; the traditional service role of the police was being undermined by the focus on economy, efficiency and effectiveness; and the effect of balancing the competing needs of 'value-for-money' and maintaining high standards of policing service could be to adversely affect the quality of life for citizens (Joint Consultative Committee 1990: 2). It is important to recall these concerns given the current emphasis on 'Best Value' and efficiency savings. Amongst the clearly political aims of the OPR, one was to emphasise that the police had attempted to improve their efforts toward economy and efficiency, and to 'add evidence to the police position in the competition for resources' (*ibid.*: 2). It was feared that 'if the current demand trends continued, the whole concept of policing by consent ... would be lost to the accountants' balance sheet' (OPR, 1990: 1). Some recent police respondents expressed similar fears, and one ACPO member was acutely aware that the current scenario in some ways paralleled the concerns in the late 1980s:

> There's a danger that we'll be back where we were before 1990, that all we're concerned with is, 'Let's look at performance data and see where we're going'... we try to maintain the position that we are primarily concerned with a high quality police force ...
>
> (Interview, November 1998)

Of the OPR's wide-ranging recommendations, one was to re-emphasise the service's commitment to 'the highest values', as well as to review the policing style in all forces. Following the OPR, the QOS sub-committee of the ACPO General Purposes Committee was set up in 1990, and included representatives from HMIC and the Home Office. As well as the SCPV, the major thrust of the QOS initiative in the early stages was the SPD itself. While the SPD stressed that the service had made great progress in implementing a more 'responsive, sensitive and impartial' service since the Scarman report of 1981, it acknowledged that the police were not providing a consistently acceptable standard of fairness, courtesy or sensitivity in its service to the public (ACPO 1990: 6). It was stressed that there should be clear mechanisms to monitor public satisfaction, and clearly identified standards of behaviour within the police, with particular reference to equal opportunities and members of the public.

Progress along these lines has differed markedly between forces, but HMIC respondents and senior officers were generally keen to point out that the quality philosophy has successfully embedded in the 1990s. Hirst's address to the 1991 QOS conference at Bramshill outlined steps which had progressed the initiative, including publication of advice to forces on customer surveys, discussion with HMIC and the Audit Commission on service delivery and performance assessment, and the designation of 'quality assurance' officers in all forces (ACPO, 1992: 16). It was added:

> ... perhaps the greatest achievement had been to underline and impress on all concerned the fact that the change in progress was a change in policing culture.
>
> (*ibid.*: 16).

Internal quality and culture

The occupational and organisational culture of the police has often been perceived in a rather negative light. In the 1980s, Brogden, Jefferson and Walklate (1988) identified aspects of the occupational sub-culture traditionally associated with the police, such as autonomy and secrecy. Reiner (1992) discusses 'cop culture' and pinpoints its facets of cynicism, pessimism and conservatism. More recently, Holdaway (1996) has assessed the problems of racialised relations within the police, and, of course, the Stephen Lawrence Inquiry (Macpherson, 1999) highlighted 'professional incompetence, institutional racism and a failure of leadership by senior officers' (*ibid.*: para 46.1) in the Metropolitan Police Service (MPS). One of the ACCs interviewed during the current research commented that there are 'dangerous things' amongst the lower ranks, such as bullying and prejudice.

While early aspects of the QOS programme focused on the provision of service to the public, the 'Getting Things Right' (GTR) initiative was primarily aimed at improving organisational management, working practices and culture. GTR was broken down into six 'internal service areas': leading and managing people; communication; internal organisation; managing resources; systems and procedures; and strategy for action. The aim has been to inculcate a culture 'in which quality support and service are given to all staff and, through them, to our customers in the community' (ACPO, 1995: 1). Under the key service area of 'Leading and Managing People', it was noted that there should be greater emphasis on 'visible, committed and supportive leadership', teamwork, trust and openness, giving authority to staff, recognition and reward of staff, and generally valuing people within the organisation: 'Investment in internal customer care is repaid many times over by improved quality of service' (*ibid.*: 14–15). While there have been mixed views in the police about the impact of GTR, ACPO claimed in 1995 that most forces were adopting some or all of the principles within the GTR framework, and concluded from their survey of forces that:

> a considerable amount of work has been done by individual forces in an effort to promote quality issues and encourage staff to deliver a high quality service to all customers, internal and external to the organisation. (ACPO, 1995)

Although some officers interviewed were concerned that there has been too much 'navel-gazing' with regard to culture and working practices, others have welcomed change within the organisation. One superintendent accepted the need for constant change in the police, and acknowledged the importance of 'internal' quality:

> ... we put a lot of effort into internal marketing and communication, making people aware of what the changes are, what's important, what their performance is, and that helps morale as well. Knowing what your job is, clear feedback on what is good and what isn't so good, I think improves morale and quality service you give.
> (Interview, December 1998)

Customer surveys

An important element of the ACPO initiative in the early to mid-1990s was the application of performance indicators directly related to customer satisfaction, as indicated below:

- percentage of callers satisfied with response to 999 calls;
- percentage of customers satisfied with service at station inquiry counters;
- percentage of victims satisfied with initial response to a report of violent crime;
- percentage of victims satisfied with initial response to a report of domestic burglary;
- percentage of victims satisfied with police performance at the scene of a road-traffic accident;
- percentage of public satisfied with perceived levels of foot and mobile patrols.

It was felt very strongly by police leaders that these qualitative indicators were important to balance the more quantitative PIs (performance indicators) of HMIC and the Audit Commission. The first set of national PIs was issued in 1993 (see Home Office Circular 17/93), and the six ACPO indicators formed part of that suite. Although ACPO issued guidance on conducting surveys to provide data for their PIs, this process has never been standardised and forces have employed different methodologies to ascertain customer satisfaction. The original ACPO indicators have now been incorporated into the Audit Commission's set of performance data, and the 1996/7 Commission report included these for the first time (Audit Commission 1998a: 4). As the Chief Inspector of Constabulary reports for the period 1997/8:

> The degree of public satisfaction is a particularly important element against which to assess service delivery ... The overall figures continued to show that a reassuringly high level of public satisfaction was achieved in the areas surveyed.
>
> (HMCIC, 1998: 68)

The variety of methodologies employed to survey customer satisfaction makes it difficult to compare results from forces, and figures must be interpreted with some caution. Nevertheless, average satisfaction figures (1997–8) for the service functions in England and Wales are shown below:

Table 16.1 Levels of satisfaction with police service

Service function	Average % satisfaction
999 calls	85
Station enquiries	90
Response to violent crime	83
Initial response to burglary	92
Service at road accidents	92
Satisfaction with patrol	41

(Audit Commission, 1999: 50)

As can be seen, there is clearly much less satisfaction with perceived levels of foot and mobile patrols, but as the Audit Commission (1996) emphasises, public expectations of patrols are probably unrealistically high given current resource demands.

The changing face of quality

As argued elsewhere (see Waters, 1996), the QOS programme has straddled two broad schools of thought. On the one hand, it has encapsulated elements of the traditional public service ethic (Farnham and Horton 1993: 253), with an emphasis on equity, probity and professionalism. On the other hand, it has focused on key aspects of NPM, such as consumerisation and performance measurement. Loveday (1995: 288) discusses the application of a social-market approach within the public sector generally and the police in particular. On occasions there has been some tension between the 'public sector' and 'business' models of quality, but in the closing years of the 1990s, the latter has clearly predominated. As one ACPO representative phrased it during interview, the 'nice, cuddly' brand of quality has been replaced by a tougher business orientation. Another stated toward the end of 1998:

> ... it's all very sort of hard-edged management stuff ... it's not giving the police service a sort of softer, more community-friendly image or something like that ... Quality in this context, and standards, are really about efficiency and effectiveness, and do we deliver? It's not about a sort of PR exercise in any sense...
>
> (Interview, October 1998)

The changing work and structure of ACPO groups dealing with quality and performance are indicative of the developing emphases. The 1996 ACPO Annual Report described the work of the QOS committee in 1995/6 and concluded that 'performance management continued to represent the "growth area" ... There has also been a recognition that quality of service, although still important, forms a part of performance management ...' (p. 37). In the 1990s (as witnessed by the Comprehensive Spending Review and Best Value) there was a growing concern about the use of resources and VFM (value for money). The Association of Chief Police Officers noted that 'the performance of forces has to be seen against increasing demand and limited finances' (*ibid.*: 37), and that the ACPO Finance and QOS committees would have a joint working group to consider resource allocation and policing plans.

In October 1996, the QOS committee transformed into the Performance Management Committee (PMC) in recognition of the changing nature of its work. In the 1997 Annual Report of ACPO, the PMC's tasks for 1996/7 were listed as: continuing the publication of the national factsheets (see, for example, ACPO, 1994), to consider how far benchmarking would be used as a means of improving police performance, and to monitor and refine the operation of PIs (ACPO, 1997: 45). It was added:

> The consequences of limited funds mean that the work of the Committee is crucial in ensuring that the service is developing performance management systems to make the most of stretched resources and deliver the quality and range of services sought by the public.
>
> (*ibid.*: 45)

It was also noted how the PMC had led ACPO's response to the proposed 1997/8 Key National Objectives and while ACPO 'welcomed stability [it] highlighted concerns about the narrowness of the Objectives and the PIs associated with them' (*ibid.*: 46). At the time of writing, the PMC is divided into three sub-committees. The first of these is known as the 'Harmonisation of Business Processes Sub-committee', and according to ACPO (1998b: 16) the aim is to 'map the volume processes of the police service to provide a framework within which forces can benchmark their activities'. The service will utilise process mapping software so that 'forces will identify differences in the translation of inputs into outcomes to enable efficiency savings to be identified' (*ibid.*: 16).

The 'Performance Measurement Technical Sub-committee' has led ACPO's contribution to the development of performance indicators, and acted as a point of liaison with the Home Office, HMIC and the Audit Commission on this contentious area. The third sub-committee, concerned with 'Standards and Quality' has 'worked to define what policing standards are required to ensure the delivery of the best possible service to the public' (*ibid.*: 17). This sub-committee perhaps represents the closest link to the previous 'Quality of Service' committee. In May 1998 this sub-committee published 'Quality in the Police Service', a document which aimed to provide a working definition of policing quality. Despite the *Zeitgeist* of managerialism and business concepts, the sub-committee maintains that its definition of police quality:

> differs from those commonly used in a business environment. It is recognised that such a definition needs to take account of the complexity of policing, in an environment where resources are constrained, demand is rising and where demands are often competing ... it is acknowledged that for numerous reasons the Service could never meet all the expectations of the public. (ACPO, 1998a: 1)

It is also suggested that the term 'customer' is not entirely appropriate in discussing policing, in that the particular needs of an individual may be unreasonable or beyond the scope of the police. At the heart of this new definition of quality is an equation, whereby:

$$\text{Service required} = \text{Service delivered.}$$

Quality, it is suggested, is achieved when this equation remains balanced. Following logically from this, an increase in requirement for services will need to be matched with an increase in service delivery. A reduction in budget, leading to a loss of service, will need to be matched by a reduction in expectation, so as to preclude the perception that quality has dropped. In addition, service requirement includes both *expectation* and *need* and service delivery incorporates:

- equality of service delivery;
- access to services;
- service levels;
- the volume of service;
- the type of service.

Some members of the police are less than enthusiastic about this model, and one superintendent (interview, November 1998) emphasised the difficulty in defining 'need', and noted the frequent discrepancy between police and public perceptions of service requirement.

One member of the PMC reflected on its current activities and the breadth of ongoing reforms:

> This is obviously not a static agenda for a number of very good reasons. One is that the Service and the Home Office are still feeling their way in a performance type regime... the new government has certainly set a whole new agenda, given it all a

much higher priority, and introduced some new concepts. And I think try to encourage much greater inter-agency working ...   (Interview, October 1998)

The 1998 ACPO Annual Report identified objectives for the PMC in the forthcoming year which included: to help develop the ACPO response to the government's emphasis on 'outcomes' with reference to the Comprehensive Spending Review; to continue to refine the concept of quality in line with work on policing standards and PIs; to assist the development of the police response to 'Best Value'; and the development of 'benchmarking' (ACPO, 1998b: 18).

In addition to the work of ACPO, the concept and language of quality has been utilised by individual forces in the latter half of the 1990s. For example, Beckley and Hirons (1996) identify how West Mercia Constabulary introduced a system of National Vocational Qualifications (NVQs) in customer service, and Leicestershire Constabulary facilitates members of the public to register 'quality of service complaints' with a special leaflet and form. The Cleveland Police have written of their 'Quality Strategy' (Cleveland Police Authority, 1997: 12) which has entailed attempts to 'listen and respond to the wishes and expectations of our customers' (including a large public-opinion survey), as well as staff undertaking NVQs in customer care. Some forces have quality of service departments or units to oversee relevant policies and initiatives, although in several forces 'quality' is subsumed in performance review departments. The performance review unit of Avon and Somerset Constabulary, for example, recently used survey results to assess the change in public satisfaction and opinion since 1993/4 (Avon and Somerset Constabulary, 1998). Most forces have clearly identified and published service standards: the Essex Police, for example, have been publishing their 'Service Delivery Standards' since 1993 (Essex Police, 1996). In their Policing Plan for 1997/8, the Metropolitan Police included police service charter standards which emphasised the need to 'leave our customers with a good impression of the service received' (Metropoplitan Police Service, 1997: ii), as well the need to pursue fair and ethical approaches, to uphold integrity and to improve communication with minority communities (*ibid.*: 10). The Stephen Lawrence Inquiry has, of course, re-emphasised such objectives.

A number of forces (including South Yorkshire and Hertfordshire) have adopted the tenets of the European Foundation for Quality Management (EFQM) which as Bland (1997: 11) points out is concerned with promoting the principles of 'total quality management' and assessing organisational performance (see also Foley, 1994). Her Majesty's Inspectorate of Constabulary (1998) discusses the application of business models (including EFQM) but does acknowledge that these can 'strike terror in the hearts of practical coppers' (*ibid.*: 152). The HMIC identifies the framework and benefits of a 'business excellence' model (including a commitment to continuous improvement, empowerment of staff and benchmarking), but warns of the difficulties in swiftly identifying improvements in quality and performance as a direct result of applying such an approach (*ibid.*: 154).

Performance monitoring

As Weatheritt (1993: 24) indicates, the issues surrounding the debate about performance measurement are both technical and political. The technicalities of accurately monitoring policing activity are extremely complex: one must measure policing 'input' (such as time spent on patrol), 'output' (such as number of arrests) and 'outcome' (which could include community safety or a reduction in the fear of crime). Crime and incident recording are not yet fully standardised across the 43 English and Welsh Home Office forces, and the aims of a policing strategy can be complex and sometimes contradictory.

In 1993, Eric Caines (a key member of the Sheehy Inquiry into police pay and responsibilities) argued:

> The entire system of accountability must be tightened. The performance of chief constables and their forces needs to be measured and exposed to public gaze ... There needs to be a strong national framework of objectives, which reshaped police authorities would adapt to their local situations ...
>
> (*The Times*, 9 September 1993: 20)

The Police and Magistrates' Courts Act 1994 (PMCA) instigated a framework of objectives and accountability which caused disquiet for many senior officers. Sir John Smith criticised the government's police reforms and implied that the mooted combination of national objectives, performance-related pay and fixed-term contracts could threaten the 'prized integrity of policing' (Smith, 1994: 7). As Loveday (1996: 73) indicates, the official perception of the Conservative administration was that the police service had 'lost its way' and required a much clearer steer in its objectives. As a result, the PMCA ratified the authority of the Home Secretary to set national key objectives (KOs), underpinned by key performance indicators (KPIs). This can be regarded as another step in the drift of centralisation of power over the police which Leishman, Cope and Starie (1996: 21) discuss. As Brown (1998: 65) outlines, the PMCA (subsequently consolidated by the Police Act 1996) has also required the publication of a costed policing plan by each police authority, to include a statement of the authority's policing priorities and an indication of how financial resources are to be used. Importantly, the police authority has had to take heed of the Home Secretary's objectives and performance targets, and provide details of its own localised objectives and targets (*ibid.*: 65).

While these developments have been regarded by some critics as another step in the trend of centralisation, the politicised debate about performance monitoring abated somewhat in the late 1990s. Savage (1998: 4) suggests the potential for increased centralised influence from the national objectives has not yet transpired in that the objectives have been relatively uncontentious. In 1996, the Chief Inspector of Constabulary welcomed the 'continued consistency in the setting of objectives' (HMCIC, 1996: 73), and remarked that there was now a 'comprehensive series of measures' to monitor police performance, with the 'performance culture much more deeply rooted in service provision' (*ibid.*: 70). The Chief Inspector did note, however, the difficulty of measuring and comparing police performance, and of 'presenting the many facets of service delivery in a meaningful way' (*ibid.*: 71). In his report for 1997/8, the Chief Inspector noted (1998: 7) the increasing need for HMIC to effectively compare force performance, and the introduction in July 1997 of a new comparative model. In commenting on police performance on the Home Secretary's key objectives for the period of inspection, it was stated:

> Overall, the data presented for 1997/98 show an extremely healthy picture of police performance, with a number of notable success stories in individual forces … no force has returned a universally poor performance.   (*ibid.*: 43–4)

The KOs for 1997/8 were: to maintain, and if possible increase the number of detections for violent crime; to increase the number of detections for burglaries of people's homes; to target and prevent crimes which are a particular problem (including drug-related criminality), in partnership with the public and local agencies; to provide high-visibility policing so as to reassure the public; and to respond promptly to emergency calls from the public.

As well as HMIC, the Audit Commission (AC) are key players in monitoring policing, and have been become increasingly influential through the 1990s. At the beginning of the decade, Love (1991) highlighted the growing impact of the AC on central policing issues, a trend which perhaps reached its operational zenith with the publication of 'Helping with Enquiries: Tackling Crime Effectively' (1993), and 'Streetwise: Effective Police Patrol' (1996). Under the Local Government Act 1992, the Audit Commission became empowered to determine sets of indicators for local authorities; these have allowed performance comparisons with particular reference to cost and the three 'Es'. Police leaders, such as Butler (1992b), have raised questions about the Citizen's Charter, the development of PIs, and the role of the Audit Commission. In 1995, Paul Whitehouse (then chairman of the QOS committee) expressed concerns about the Audit Commission's first national (and comparative) report on police performance, and warned against the use of data to directly compare forces and added:

> Performance indicators constitute a tool for good management but they are only indicators and a means to an end, not an end in themselves … It would be a grave mistake for the Service to allow them to dictate policing strategies entirely … They do not provide answers or constitute in themselves a measure of success.
> (ACPO QOS Committee, ACPO, 1995)

In their police report for 1997/98, the AC themselves state that the PIs 'on their own do not give the full picture of performance', but nevertheless affirm that their reports should contribute to the debate about the most efficient and effective way to deliver policing services (Audit Commission, 1999: 4). While they note that in the past year there had been some overall improvements in police performance (such as response to emergencies), the Audit Commission tend to be critical of the variation between forces:

> The gap between the best and worst performers in clearing up crime, for example,

has widened steadily over the past three years ... This is worrying, especially as some of those whose performance is deteriorating are spending more each year.

(ibid.: 2).

VFM and 'best value'

The modern emphasis on value for money (VFM) in the police originated with the publication of HO Circular 114 of 1983 (Berry, 1998: 7). Since then there has been a growing emphasis on VFM in the police. In 1989, the then Commissioner of the Metropolitan Police acknowledged the ascendancy of VFM, but stressed that 'in policing terms, value for money must be judged on a mix of the quantifiable and the qualitative – and the latter is absolutely vital' (Imbert, 1989: 264). In his key circular to the police the Home Secretary stated in 1998:

> The Government is committed to delivery of efficient, effective and high quality public services. That is why the new duty of Best Value, to be introduced in April 2000, will require local authorities, including police authorities, to demonstrate the increasing efficiency, effectiveness and quality of their services.
>
> (Home Office, 1998: 1)

As is also indicated in this circular, forces are additionally obliged to set a target for 2 per cent efficiency gains year-on-year from 1999–2000. Policing plans will need to include a 'statement of planned efficiency gains – defined as a combination of increasing output ... at the existing level of resources and cash savings for a constant or higher level of output – and how those will be reinvested to meet policing needs' *(ibid.:* 6). This particular initiative emerged out of the Comprehensive Spending Review, and pre-dates the more recent 'Best Value' (BV) initiative; as one member of the police 'value-for-money' team in the Home Office Police Resources Unit indicated, these 2 per cent efficiency savings demand some of the planning processes which will be required for Best Value, and indeed will run in tandem with the latter. There was considerable concern among police respondents about the efficiency savings, which were described as a rather blunt instrument to cut the cost of policing. However, the Home Secretary has made it clear that the 'commitment to efficiency should not be interpreted as a green light for crude cuts in staffing, matched by cuts in outputs ...' (Home Office, 1998: 6).

As Jenkins (1998: 17) points out, under BV police authorities will have the statutory responsibility to consult with the public in determining policing priorities. The responsibility of each chief constable is to demonstrate that the force has provided the best value possible. The Audit Commission (1998b) have issued guidance to assist local authorities in their preparation for BV, and as they indicate, police authorities will be required to secure year-on-year improvements in services, and note that the 'Home Secretary will have powers to tackle serious or persistent failure' *(ibid.:* 8). At the 1998 ACPO Summer Conference, Ruth Henig (chair of the APA) voiced concern about the potential for such government intervention, and was cited as saying: 'we in the APA are vigorously opposed to any extension of Home Office powers'

(*Police Review*, 24 July 1998, p. 15). Her Majesty's Inspectorate of Constabulary will bear the primary responsibility for monitoring Best Value, although the APA has again expressed concern that the independence of PAs will be threatened as a result (see *Police Review*, 5 February 1999, p. 8).

One ACPO representative (interviewed in late October 1998) stressed that most police leaders were now adopting a much more pragmatic and 'business-like' approach to performance management but noted the 'fluid' nature of current reforms:

> Now, the whole question of performance, efficiency, effectiveness, value-for-money, best value, all of that is now very central to the agenda of the police service ... It is, I have to say, a very transitional phase we're in just at the moment between the sort of systems that were set up in the early, mid-1990s, and now ... new concepts like 'Best Value', which is not just value for money ... it is about quality, as much as the purely financial aspects ...

ACPO indicate in their 1998 Annual Report (p. 15) that they 'developed the case for a 6.1 per cent increase in budget for the coming 1999/2000 financial year to meet known demands ... In this context, the 2.7 per cent cash increase announced for 1999/2000 represents a tough settlement.' As is also noted, the government's introduction of Best Value took on extra significance, but its emphasis on the three 'Es' 'has been broadly welcomed by the Association' (p. 15). This view was echoed by the ACPO representative last cited:

> We welcome efficiency plans. And we feel that a lot of the good work that police forces have done in the past has not altogether been appreciated, partly because we haven't been good at explaining it ourselves ... but also there hasn't been a framework or mechanism for it, for explaining, you know efficiency and so forth, and efficiency plans and Best Value will give that opportunity ...
>
> (Interview, October 1998)

Forces will also be required to cost their policing activities and as the Chief Inspector of Constabulary indicates (HMIC, 1998: 118) at least six forces were developing costing techniques during the inspection for 'What Price Policing?'. This major report presents a comprehensive overview of VFM and the three Es, as well as case studies of particular forces. In the preface, the Chief Inspector of Constabulary (David O'Dowd) reflects upon VFM:

> Achieving improved value for money is perhaps the most important yet difficult challenge faced by the service. Value for money is not an isolated abstract concept but in a well-run organisation something that is the concern of all staff, and touches on each and every aspect of service delivery.   (p. 1)

One Inspector responsible for BV in his force felt that the HMIC report was useful in that it provided a steer for the service, but provided inadequate detail or guidance for specific VFM strategies. It was added:

> ... there's now a need for probably more clarity, because otherwise forces spend a lot of people's money trying to develop different systems ... and as a value-for-money initiative it might be worthwhile them actually giving clearer guidance.
>
> (Interview, November 1998)

A respondent in a difference force, responsible for developing 'quality', reflected on BV:

> I think the feeling is that it is a subject that is only just beginning to develop ... and everyone's looking to know where they've got to get to, but as yet we haven't gone through that evolutionary process. And nobody has got the perfect model ...
>
> (Interview, December 1998)

HMIC (*ibid.*) note that:

- the application of VFM practice will be increasingly central to core policing services (p. 16);
- despite the setting of performance targets in forces, the supporting information technology often fails to supply accurate performance information (p. 27);
- a 'performance culture' is nevertheless developing within the police, with an expectation of internal and external levels of service which meet reasonable VFM expectations (p. 31).

Importantly, it is stressed that 'quality' is an important ingredient in the VFM equation:

> If the quality of a service is improved at no extra cost, there has been an improvement in VFM terms – a factor not always fully recognised ... However, there has been some tendency to hide between the quality argument on the assumption that pressure to improve performance will always be detrimental to quality. (*ibid.*: 85)

Senior HO officials agreed, as did other respondents, that the HMIC report had been very influential and had not 'pulled any punches'. Some senior officers, however, were less than enthusiastic and suggested that some of the conclusions and examples presented in the report were overly simplistic or problematic.

Aims and objectives, and ministerial priorities

As Home Office officials stated during interview, the Police Resources Unit (PRU) of the Police Policy Directorate has led the agenda on BV. As part of the current reforms, the PRU has also been instrumental in recalibrating the 'overall aims and objectives of the police'. This exercise formed part of the 1998 Comprehensive Spending Review (CSR), and the aim was to encapsulate all of the policing functions within one schematic and conceptual framework. This work was conducted with the involvement of ACPO and APA, and in mid-1998 the resulting diagrammatic representation was distributed to forces. Included was a 'statement of purpose' for the police:

> To help secure a safe and just society in which the rights and responsibilities of individuals, families and communities are properly balanced.

The three core aims of the police are to:

- promote safety and reduce disorder;

- reduce crime and the fear of crime;
- contribute to delivering justice in a way which secures and maintains public confidence in the rule of law.

Subsumed in these aims are eleven specific objectives:

- keep order (and restore it where necessary) and reduce anti-social behaviour;
- reconcile conflicting rights and freedoms of the public;
- improve safety and reassurance of public, especially those at risk of harm;
- contribute to improving road safety and the reduction of casualties;
- disrupt organised and international crime;
- prevent terrorism;
- reduce crime through investigation, detection and addressing the causes of crime;
- reduce the fear of crime;
- provide high-quality, timely, evidence contributing to fairly conducted prosecutions;
- deal with suspects fairly;
- help to meet the needs of victims and witnesses.

The current work on developing the set of PIs for 2000/2001 incorporates these new objectives, but one ACPO member was concerned about this process:

> Now the question is, what are they going to do with these ... and is it going to be some sort of sterile straitjacket in which they're going to have a range of performance indicators that mean ..., instead of having 30, I'm [now] going to have 300 ... I'm afraid that they cannot encapsulate the totality of policing in the sense of its contribution to the social fabric of this country, in 11 boxes. They can't do it.
>
> (Interview, November 1998)

This respondent felt that the CSR had resulted in 'a very mechanistic approach by the Treasury to defining policing', while one superintendent felt there was 'nothing new' in this formulation:

> At first sight, it looks quite complex, but when you actually dissect it and look at what it means for policing, it actually isn't that different from what we do already.
>
> (Interview, November 1998)

Another divisional commander commented positively:

> I think it's to be welcomed ... up to this point the performance indicators were very crude and quantitative, and not set in a proper framework ... at least we're starting to shape it ... it brings out the key points for us – integrity, community and race issues, so all the key guiding principles are in there ... (Interview, December 1998)

The Home Secretary's key objectives for policing for 1998/9 were: to deal speedily and effectively with young offenders and to work with other agencies to reduce re-offending; to target and reduce local problems of crime and disorder in partnership with local authorities, other local agencies and the public; to target drug-related crime in partnership with other local agencies; to maintain and, if possible, increase the number of detections for violent crime; to increase the number of detections for burglaries of people's homes; to respond promptly to emergency calls from the public. It was clear from these that the Home Secretary was instigating a shift toward crime reduction and prevention. The government has now replaced the key objectives with the new 'Ministerial Priorities' and it is obvious from the priorities for 1999/2000 that the shift towards reduction and prevention has been consolidated:

1 to deal speedily and effectively with young offenders and to work with other agencies to reduce offending and re-offending;
2 to identify and reduce local problems of crime and disorder in partnership with local authorities, other local agencies and the public;
3 to target and reduce drug-related crime in partnership with other local agencies, via the local Drug Action Teams, in line with the government's strategy of 'Tackling Drugs to Build a Better Britain'.

One superintendent was asked how these priorities would impact:

Certainly as an Area Commander, I feel that there is enough scope within what the Home Office are wanting us to do, for me to tailor that to local needs, and for me to deliver a policing service ... that meets the needs of the community here ... and I'm not being forced to do things because they are identified nationally ...
(Interview, November 1998)

Home Office research and involvement

The Home Office has been involved in the police approach to quality since the early days of the programme. The 'F2' division of the Police Department (as it was then) had been active contributors to the original QOS Committee, and helped develop the formative debate about performance indicators in the early 1990s. In 1993, the national QOS video was released by the Home Office Public Relations Branch, and the leaflet accompanying the video stated:

... we all know when we receive a quality service. Courtesy and politeness count, but so does meeting the needs of the customer for a professional service ... Nearly every organisation is now turning to quality of service as a way of improving its performance ... Quality of service is not a quick fix – it has to be carried forward throughout an organisation ...
(Home Office, 1993b)

In more recent years, the Home Office has promulgated the principles of quality in other ways. In 1996, the PRG (now known as the Police and Reducing Crime Unit) sponsored a conference on quality in the police service in conjunction with the Henry Fielding Centre of the University of Manchester (see Waters, 1998), and has also produced several reports which arise from the ongoing 'quality of service research programme'. For example, the Police Research Series Paper, No. 22 (Elliott and Nicholls, 1996) entitled *It's Good to Talk: Lessons in Public Consultation and Feedback*, analyses the aims and performance of consultation mechanisms. As Elliott and Nicholls point out (p. 62), under PACE 1984 and the Police Act 1996, each police authority must review its consultation arrangements 'from time to time'. One force respondent responsible for QOS monitoring felt that the current reforms had re-energised the emphasis on 'quality' and monitoring the views of the public:

> We are actually conducting a project which is to review the methodology of what we do, to ensure that we're in line with best practice in what is currently happening in other parts of the service and indeed externally and seeing how that fits into the wider consultation processes that are now coming on board with Best Value, Crime and Disorder. (Interview, December 1998)

Public consultation forms part of the statutory requirements of the CDA (1998) under section 6 of the Act, which requires local authorities and the police to devise and implement strategies for reducing crime and disorder. The respondent above felt that issues such as quality and eliciting feedback from the public had 'gone off the boil' in her force, but that it was time to take stock of the use and importance of QOS surveys and consultation.

There was evidence of confusion amongst some respondents as to how consultation and the consolidation of policing priorities should be taken forward. For example, one divisional commander believed that there was little (if any) guidance from the Home Office on the inter-relationship between Policing Plans, Best Value and the 1998 Crime and Disorder Act (CDA), and how the potential replication of public consultation and plans could prove confusing to both police and citizens. This respondent felt the CDA was of paramount concern at the moment:

> This is the key thing for me. We need now to have some clear steer centrally on how policing plans will sit alongside crime and disorder strategies, because we can't work to both. (Interview, November 1998)

Paper 24, by Nick Bland (1997) in the PRG Police Research Series, *Measuring Public Expectations of Policing: An Evaluation of Gap Analysis*, focused on a technique to measure customer expectations and perceptions of service (*ibid.*: iii). The quality 'gap' is the difference between the service expected and received, and can be either negative or positive, depending on whether the customer receives a poorer or better service than expected. Police leaders have certainly exhibited much greater awareness of the difference between customer expectations and service delivered and such principles are clearly echoed in the model of quality published by the PMC in 1998 (see earlier section of this chapter). Bland identified Avon and Somerset, Surrey and Dyfed-Powys as three forces which have employed variations of the gap approach. Avon and Somerset, for example, employed elements of gap analysis in a 1995 study conducted by the force Performance Review Unit (Avon and Somerset Constabulary, 1995).

Other PRG/PRCU publications have included Bradley's (1998) report,

Public Expectations and Perceptions of Policing, which concluded that 'the police service should adopt a different approach to policing different groups in the community, taking into account the different expectations and views of the police service held by each separate group' (*ibid.*: 14). Chatterton, Langmead Jones, and Radcliffe (1997) concluded that at a national level considerable effort had been devoted by forces to conducting their QOS surveys, but found that 'few specific examples of decisions or actions were identified as having been taken in response to QS survey findings', and that few forces had clarified the role and use of such surveys. The PRG have also focused on the development of performance indicators for crime prevention (see Tilley, 1995), and for anti-drugs strategies (see Chatterton, *et al.* 1995).

Conclusions

It is generally agreed that the development of a quality approach in an organisation can be a difficult and lengthy process (see Dale and Oakland, 1994; Morgan and Murgatroyd, 1994). Since the launch of the police QOS programme, some forces and chief officers have embraced the quality and service philosophy more enthusiastically and successfully than others. In addition, as Bourne (1998) indicates, a substantial shift in attitude and organisation is required for the police to successfully adopt a 'performance culture'. Since the mid-1990s this shift has been increasingly evident, and will continue to predominate given the regime of inspection to which the police are now subject.

At the 1996 Manchester QOS conference noted above, it was obvious that there were markedly varying levels of awareness about quality and its application. Given the history, traditions and culture of the police it is not surprising that 'quality' and 'service' are sometimes greeted with cynicism by a workforce which has witnessed a number of reforms and management fads in recent years. Nevertheless, the current research revealed that many of the quality principles (both managerialist and 'public service') have become embedded in the discourse and practices of policing. Although the Conservative government reforms of the mid-1990s deflected some energy away from the impetus and original direction of the police initiative, many of the key principles and aims of quality service have remained.

Politically, of course, the police in England and Wales have been obliged to respond to the changes, or mooted changes, to policy and legislation in the 1990s. Part of this response has entailed a narrowing or focusing of the ACPO quality committee, which was transformed into the Performance Management Committee in 1996. The work of the Committee has moved away from what can be termed the 'professional ethics' model, to one underpinned by a clear 'business' or managerialist rationale. This is typified by the current work on harmonisation of business processes, and the continued emphasis on performance indicators. This trend is set to continue given the Labour government's emphasis on 'Best Value' which, as the Audit Commission (1998b) point out, represents perhaps the greatest challenge to local government service delivery in many years. Her Majesty's Inspectorate of Constabulary (1998) have indicated that the adoption of business excellence/EFQM models is on the increase in the police, and this type of approach is bound to dominate in the foreseeable future. Some respondents were concerned, however, that the 'heart and soul' of policing was in danger of being eroded by an excessive emphasis on VFM, efficiency and business approaches.

Loveday (1999) discusses the parameters of police accountability in England and Wales, the ongoing centralisation of public services from the 1980s onward, and the growth of Home Office power. He also suggests (*ibid.*: 149) that whether or not the encroachment of central government upon local accountability will be sustained or reversed by New Labour must remain a matter for conjecture. However, given the strictures of efficiency savings, Best Value, new and developing performance indicators, and the powers of HMIC and the Audit Commission to police the police, we might conclude here that accountability to the centre is set to increase. Nevertheless, this assertion must not be interpreted simplistically, given the requirements under Best Value to consult with local communities on policing priorities and service expectations. To a large extent the analysis that 'steering the police is increasingly centralised, whereas rowing the police is increasingly decentralised' (Leishman *et al.*, 1996a: 21) still holds true. Kamenka (1989) and Dandeker (1990) wrote of the growth and power of bureaucracy and bureaucratic surveillance. Navari (1991: 162) referred to the state as the 'authoritative allocator of value' and the government as the 'only authoritative standard setter', which must monitor, intervene and enforce. At the start of the twenty-first century, it is clear that state bureaucratic surveillance of the police, and the propensity of the state to intervene, are set to increase.

References

ACPO (1990) Strategic Policy Document, *Setting the Standards for Policing: Meeting Community Expectation*. London.

ACPO (1992) *Report of Proceedings of 1991 QOS Conference at Bramshill Police Staff College*. London.

ACPO (1994) 'Your Police: A Service to Value', second ACPO Factsheet, July.

ACPO (1995) *Survey of Impact of Getting Things Right*. London.

ACPO (1996) *Annual Report 1996*. London.

ACPO (1997) *Annual Report 1997*. London.

ACPO (1998a) *Quality in the Police Service*. London.

ACPO (1998b) *Annual Report*. London.

ACPO Quality of Service Sub-committee (1991) *Key Operational Service Areas*. London.

ACPO Quality of Service Committee (1993) *Getting Things Right*. London.

ACPO Quality of Service Committee (1995) '*Publication of the Audit Commission Citizen's Charter Performance Indicators*' (letter dated 6 April 1995).

Audit Commission (1993) *Helping with Enquiries: Tackling Crime Effectively*. London.

Audit Commission (1994) *Cheques and Balances: A Management Handbook on Police Planning and Financial Delegation.* London.

Audit Commission (1996) *Streetwise: Effective Police Patrol.* London.

Audit Commission (1998a) *Local Authority Performance Indicators: Police Services.* London.

Audit Commission (1998b) *Better by Far: Preparing for Best Value.* London.

Audit Commission (1999) *Local Authority Performance Indicators: Police and Fire Services 1997/98.* London.

Avon and Somerset Constabulary (1995) *Public Attitudes 1994/95.* Report by Performance Review Unit. Bristol: Avon and Somerset Constabulary.

Avon and Somerset Constabulary (1998) *Public Attitudes 1993/94 to 1997/98.* Report by Performance Review Unit. Bristol: Avon and Somerset Constabulary.

Bartlett, N. (1993) 'Service Level Agreements in Thames Valley', *Police,* 25 (6).

Beckley, A. and Hirons, R. (1996) 'Quality of Service: Are You Competent?', *The Police Journal,* April.

Berry, G. (1998) *Practical Police Management.* London: Police Review Publishing Co.

Bland, N. (1997) *Measuring Public Expectations of Policing: An Evaluation of Gap Analysis.* London: Home Office, Police Research Group.

Bourne, D. (1998) 'Performance or Conformance?', *Police Review,* 8 May.

Bradley, R. (1998) *Public Expectations and Perceptions of Policing.* London: Home Office, Policing and Reducing Crime Unit.

Brogden, M., Jefferson, T. and Walklate, S. (1988) *Introducing Policework.* London: Unwin.

Brown, A. (1998) *Police Governance in England and Wales.* London: Cavendish.

Brown, J. and Waters, I. (1996) 'Force Versus Service: A Paradox in the Policing of Public Order?' in Critchner and Waddington (1996).

Burgess, P. (1994) 'Service Breakdown and Service Recovery', *The Police Journal,* January.

Butler, A. (1995) 'A Means or an End? The Future Measurement of Police Performance', *Policing Today,* April.

Butler, T. (1992a) 'Developing Quality Assurance in Police Services', *Public Money and Management,* January–March.

Butler, T. (1992b) 'Police and the Citizen's Charter', *Policing,* 8 (1), Spring.

Chatterton, M., Gibson, G., Gilman, M., Godfrey, C., Sutton, M. and Wright, A. (1995) *Performance Indicators for Local Anti-Drugs Strategies: A Preliminary Analysis.* London: Police Research Group.

Chatterton, M., Langmead-Jones, P. and Radcliffe, J. (1997) *Using Quality of Service Surveys.* Police Research Group Briefing Note. Police Research Series Paper, No. 23. London: Home Office.

Chatterton, M., Varley, M. and Langmead-Jones, P. (1998) *Testing Performance Indicators for Local Anti-Drugs Strategies.* London: Home Office, Police and Crime Reducing Unit.

Cleveland Police Authority (1997) *Annual Report 1996–1997,* Cleveland: Cleveland Police Authority.

Critchner, C. and Waddington, D. (eds) (1996) *Policing Public Order: Theoretical and Practical Issues.* Aldershot: Avebury.

Dale, B. and Oakland, J. (1994) *Quality Improvement Through Standards.* Cheltenham: Stanley Thornes.

Dandeker, C. (1990) *Surveillance, Power and Modernity.* Cambridge: Polity.

Elliott, R. and Nicholls, J. (1996) *It's Good to Talk: Lessons in Public Consultation and Feedback.* London: Home Office, Police Research Group.

Essex Police (1996) Charter Mark Application.

Farnham, D. and Horton, S. (1993) 'The Political Economy of Public Sector Change' in Farnham, D. and Horton, S. (eds) *Managing the New Public Services.* Basingstoke: Macmillan.

Fielding, N. (1996) 'Enforcement, Service and Community Models of Policing' in Saulsbury *et al.* (1996).

Foley, E.C. (1994) *Winning European Quality: Interpreting the Requirements for The European Quality Award.* Brussels: European Foundation for Quality Management.

Her Majesty's Chief Inspector of Constabulary (1992) *Annual Report for 1991.* London: HMSO.

Her Majesty's Chief Inspector of Constabulary (1995) *Annual Report for 1994/95.* London: HMSO.

Her Majesty's Chief Inspector of Constabulary (1996) *Annual Report for 1995/96.* London: The Stationery Office.

Her Majesty's Chief Inspector of Constabulary (1997) *Annual Report for 1996/97.* London: The Stationery Office.

Her Majesty's Chief Inspector of Constabulary (1998) *Annual Report for 1997/98.* London: The Stationery Office.

Her Majesty's Chief Inspector of Constabulary (1995) *Obtaining Value for Money in the Police Service: A Good Practice Guide.* London: HMSO.

Her Majesty's Chief Inspector of Constabulary (1998) *What Price Policing? A study of Efficiency and Value for Money in the Police Service.* London: HMSO.

Hirst, M.(1991a) 'The Way Ahead: What Has the Service Learned from the Operational Policing Review and October Strategy Seminar?', *Policing,* 7 (1).

Hirst, M (1991b) 'What Do We Mean by "Quality"?', *Policing,* 7 (3).

Holdaway, S. (1996) *The Racialisation of British Policing.* London: Macmillan.

Home Office (1993a) 'Performance Indicators for Police', Circular 17/1993, London.

Home Office (1993b) 'If the Job's Worth Doing ...' (National Police QOS Video). London.

Home Office (1993c) *Police Reform: A Police Service for the Twenty-first Century.* CM 2281. London: HMSO.

Home Office (1995) *Review of Police Core and Ancillary Tasks.* London: HMSO.

Home Office (1998) *Ministerial Priorities, Key Performance Indicators and Efficiency Planning for 1999/2000.* London: HMSO.

Imbert, Sir Peter (1989) 'Towards a cost-effective service to police the 1990s', *Police Journal,* 62, October.

Jenkins, C. (1998) 'Value Judgment', *Police Review,* 18 September.

Joint Consultative Committee (1990) *Operational Policing Review.* Surbiton: Police Federation of England and Wales.

Jones, T. and Newburn, T. (1997) *Policing After the Act.* Policy Studies Institute, London.

Kamenka, E. (1989) *Bureaucracy: New Perspectives on the Past.* Oxford: Basil Blackwell.

King Taylor, L. (1992) *Quality: Total Customer Service.* London: Century Business.

Lawton, A. and Rose, A. (1994) *Organisation and Management in the Public Sector.* 2nd edn. London: Pitman.

Leishman F., Cope S. and Starie P. (1996) 'Reinventing and Restructuring: Towards a New Policing Order' in Leishman *et al.* (1996).

Leishman, F. Loveday, B. and Savage, S.P. (eds) (1996) *Core Issues in Policing.* 1st edn. Harlow: Longman.

Leishman, F. and Savage, S.P. (1993) 'The Police Service' in Farnham, D. and Horton, S. (eds) *Managing the New Public Services.* Basingstoke: Macmillan.

Love, S. (1991) 'What is the Audit Commission up to?', *Policing,* 7 (2).

Loveday, B. (1995) 'Contemporary Challenges to Police Management in England and Wales: Developing Strategies for Effective Service Delivery', *Policing and Society,* 5.

Loveday, B. (1996) 'Crime at the Core?' in Leishman *et al.* (1996).

Loveday, B. (1999) 'Government and Accountability of the Police' in Mawby (1999).

Macpherson, Sir William (1999) *The Stephen Lawrence Inquiry.* Cm 4262–I. London: The Stationery Office.

Maguire, M., Morgan, R. and Reiner, R. (eds) (1994) *The Oxford Handbook of Criminology.* 1st edn. Oxford: Clarendon Press.

Maguire, M., Morgan, R. and Reiner, R. (eds) (1997) *The Oxford Handbook of Criminology.* 2nd edn. Oxford: Clarendon Press.

Marlow, A. (1995) 'What Policing is all About', *Policing,* 11 (2).

Mawby, R.I. (ed.) (1999). *Policing Across the World: Issues for the Twenty-first Century.* London: UCL Press.

McKevitt, D. and Lawton, A. (eds) (1994) *Public Sector Management: Theory, Critique and Practice.* London. Sage.

McLaughlin, E. (1992) 'The Democratic Deficit: European Union and the Accountability of the British Police', *British Journal of Criminology,* 32, (4).

Metropolitan Police (1990) *A report of the Commissioner of Police of the Metropolis (for 1989).* London: HMSO.

Metropolitan Police Service (1997) *Policing Plan 1997/98.* London.

Moore, A. (1995) 'Standards of Service', *Police Review,* 21 July.

Morgan, C. and Murgatroyd, S. (1994) *Total Quality Management in the Public Sector: An International Perspective.* Buckingham: Open University.

Morgan, R. and Newburn, T. (1997) *The Future of Policing.* Oxford: Clarendon Press.

Navari, C. (1991) *The Condition of States.* Buckingham: Open University.

O'Byrne M. (1997) 'An Improved Service', *Policing Today,* June.

Peratec Limited (1994) *Total Quality Management: The Key to Business Improvement.* London: Chapman and Hall.

Police Foundation and Policy Studies Institute (1994) *Discussion Document for the 'Independent Committee of Inquiry into the Role and Responsibilities of the Police'.* London.

Police Foundation and Policy Studies Institute (1996) *Independent Committee of Inquiry into the Role and Responsibilities of the Police.* London.

Potter, J. (1994) 'Consumerism and the Public Sector: How Well Does the Coat Fit?' in McKevitt and Lawton (1994).

Reiner, R. (1992) *The Politics of the Police.* Hemel Hempstead: Harvester Wheatsheaf.

Reiner, R. (1994) 'Policing and the Police' in Maguire *et al.* (1994) (1st edn).

Reiner, R. (1997) 'Policing and the Police' in Maguire *et al.* (1997) (2nd edn).

Reiner, R. and Spencer, S. (eds) (1993) *Accountable Policing: Effectiveness, Empowerment and Equity*. London: Institute for Public Policy Research.

Sampson, F. (1995) 'Killing the Customer?', *Police Journal*, April.

Saulsbury, W., Mott, J. and Newburn, T. (eds) (1996) *Thomas in Contemporary Policing*. London: Policy Studies Institute.

Savage, S. (1998) 'The Shape of the Future' *Criminal Justice Matters*, 32, Summer.

Simpson, P. J. (1994) 'Setting a New Standard for Service Delivery', *Police Journal*, January.

Smith, Sir John (1994), 'Policing into the Future', *Policing Today*, October.

Smith, Sir John (1995) 'A Year in the Life of the Police Service', *Police and Government Security Technology'*, January.

Stephens, M. (1994) 'Care and Control: The Future of British Policing', *Policing and Society*, 4.

Stephens, M. and Becker, S. (1994) (eds) *Police Force, Police Service: Care and Control in Britain*. Basingstoke: Macmillan.

Sutton, C. (1996) 'Performance Measurements for the Police Service', *Intersec*, 6 (9).

Tilley, N. (1995) *Thinking about Crime Prevention Performance Indicators*. London: Home Office, Police Research Group.

Walker, N. (1994) 'Care and Control in the Police Organisation' in Stephens, M. and Becker, S. (eds) *Police Force, Police Service: Care and Control in Britain*. Basingstoke: Macmillan.

Waters, I. (1996) 'Quality of Service: Politics or Paradigm Shift?' in Leishman *et al.*, (1996).

Waters, I. (1998) 'The Pursuit of Quality', *Police Journal*, LXXI (1), January–March.

Waters, I. (1999) 'Quality and the Policing Function: A Management Perspective', *International Journal of Police Science and Management'*, 1 (4).

Weatheritt, M. (1993) 'Measuring Police Performance: Accounting or Accountability?' in Reiner and Spencer (1993).

Wolff, Olins (1988) *A Force for Change: Report on the Corporate Identity of the Metropolitan Police*. London: Metropolitan Police Service.

Woodcock, Sir John (1990) 'Police purpose: Future Issues – Strengths, Weaknesses, Threats', address to the 27th Senior Command Course, Bramshill Police Staff College, April.

Chapter 17

Managing the future: an academic's view

ALAN WRIGHT

Introduction

At the end of the twentieth century, as at the close of the nineteenth, it was fashionable to point to the decadence of some forms of social organisation. Despite the evident pre-millennial tension, the fashion concealed a very real agenda. This is certainly true of the peculiar and complex form of social organisation called 'British policing', which was under considerable strain during the last two decades of the century (Reiner, 1992a). During the early 1980s, the inner-city riots, reviews of police attitudes and the miners' strike provided evidence for those who thought that radical change was overdue (Scarman, 1981: Smith *et al.* 1983; Scraton, 1985). The Police and Criminal Evidence Act 1984 tightened some procedures but miscarriages of justice, including the 'Guildford Four', the 'Birmingham Six' and the Carl Bridgewater murder cases, have increasingly placed the police and the criminal justice system under critical scrutiny. This did not abate during the decade of the 1990s and may well continue well beyond the millennium. Although the Scarman inquiry seemed to defuse (or at least to diffuse) some of the public misgivings about the way in which police were dealing with crime and ethnic minority groups during the 1980s, the problems are now greater than ever. Civil claims against the police for assault and other torts have risen exponentially. The Macpherson Inquiry into the failure of the police investigation into the death of Stephen Lawrence has raised the question of police effectiveness and competence and of whether the police are guilty of institutional or endemic racism.

Police reform has produced its own stresses. The long rearguard action against the Sheehy proposals largely kept the organisational structures of policing intact, although with much discomfort (Sheehy, 1993). Extensive scrutiny of the police by the Audit Commission and the application of new systems for performance management and accountability so far appear to have failed to reassure some sectors of the public as to police effectiveness or legitimacy. Indeed, disclosure of major difficulties may have had precisely the opposite effect. On the economic front, police have increasingly been subject to financial constraints imposed alongside ever more stringent requirements to address the key 'law-and-order' objectives of successive administrations. More than one chief constable has been forced from office by a combination of politics and indiscretion. At the turn of the century, policing (especially police leadership) is on the defensive. As a result, it has become even more highly politicised.

For criminologists, the crisis in policing is not new. The critical consensus has been ongoing during the past two decades and before. For Hall *et al.* it was reflected in the moral panic about mugging and in the conspiratorial nature of the hegemony of power in the relationship between police and state (Hall *et al.*, 1978: 201–17). More recently, David Waddington has defended the long-term critical consensus, in acrimonious claims about public-order policing, against his unrelated namesake (Waddington, P.A.J., 1991, 1994; Waddington D., 1998). There is not the space here for an extensive review of the critical literature. However, it is fair to say that failures of policing (of routine investigation as much as of high-profile cases, of managing public disorder and problems of police culture, organisation and management) have increasingly been challenged by criminologists in ways which are beginning to call into question the very rationale of the public police as an institution. Work by the Association of Chief Police Officers (ACPO), the Home Office, and by what Young (1988) has called 'administrative' criminologists, has not been able to steer the police into calmer waters. On the contrary, the pace and intensity of criticism is increasing, fuelled by an ever-growing catalogue of police malpractice. The implications for the future of police management are immense.

It is within this turbulent environment that the problem of managing the future needs to be considered. This is a difficult field, particularly where projections beyond the short term are required. The future, of course, is not entirely in the hands of senior police officers, the Home Office or politicians, for whom thinking about policing and criminal justice tends to be relatively short term. Generally, policy developments reflect what can reasonably be projected over only one, or at most two, parliaments. Tenure for chief constables is rarely more than five to seven years. In any event, in the longer term, the relationship between police and policy makers is not the most important focus. The key relationship is between policing and the ever-changing political, economic, social and technological environments. The social environment, in particular, seems to have a mind of its own, despite the predilection of some politicians to deny its existence and of others to try to impose central control upon it.

To a greater or lesser extent, British policing in the first two decades of the twenty-first century will be an amalgam of policies reflecting the political, economic, social and technological *milieux* within which it is managed. Whichever way society develops, it is certain that there will be a need for policing to be managed effectively (assuming that public policing will not wither away in any significant sense). How this might be achieved in the midst of extensive social change can only be addressed by projecting the trends forward to develop working scenarios about the police/society relationship. Although it is necessary to resist the temptation to indulge in grand theory, simple explanatory models should not be expected. It is with a profound sense of uncertainty that the relevant questions need to be addressed. Will the disturbed relationship between police and society during the last two decades of the twentieth century continue into the twenty-first? Is the turbulence part of a continuum or is policing in the midst of a paradigm shift that will eventually produce an approach radically different from that which has existed since the development of the new police in the early nineteenth century? What are the implications for police management of the different scenarios that have been identified in 'futures' studies? To get clear about these questions it is necessary to reflect upon the development of policing as a 'modern' phenomenon and to reassess the political, economic, social and technological trajectory of which it is a part.

The crisis of modernity in British policing

From the enlightenment of the eighteenth century, modern thought inherited the idea that reason can operate upon the world in such a way that nature and society can be brought under human control. In the early modern period, the success of capitalism and technology seemed to confirm this central tenet. Despite cyclical fluctuations in economic conditions, growth could be expected. Technological progress was seen as viable through increasing scientific knowledge. The emergence of the 'modern' political state was reflected in the replacement of traditional authority by legal-rational (bureaucratic) models and democratic government (Gerth and Mills, 1970: Held, 1996). At the close of the century, however, global war, an economic system based upon market forces, social fragmentation and problems over controlling the use of technology, have all called into question whether the progress promised by modernity is possible. The role of a 'modern' police in crime control and ensuring order (supposedly based upon the precepts of rational social progress) is now questioned to an unprecedented extent.

Modern organisations, including the police, hospitals and welfare institutions were extensively developed during the nineteenth century. This was the case in Britain and elsewhere. Although police forces in Europe developed in different ways, their development shows common features. This included the idea, even in the notorious *polizeistaat*, that the welfare of citizens would be promoted through law and order measures (Chapman, 1970: 20–32). There are differing views about the development of the new police in Britain. Orthodox historians maintain that the growth of a rational approach to policing was necessary to control the increasing working class in the rapidly developing cities. In contrast, revisionist perspectives emphasise the role of the new police in protecting the assets of the propertied classes (Reiner, 1992). On one hand, for orthodox historians, police are conceived as a means to improve social life, primarily through the prevention of crime. On the other, for the revisionists, police are seen as a means of class repression. In the past two decades, however, the primary role of police as the sole providers of crime prevention and public protection has started to be eroded. The shattered relationship between police and some parts of society has also started to call into question the very status of policing as a 'modern' organisation. There are now many reasons, apart from explanations based upon class conflict, which suggest that the idea of progressive social control cannot remain central to the development of the policing in the next millennium. Several indicators point towards this conclusion.

The emperor's new clothes: the science of the 'new management'

The first indicator of tension is to be found in the difficulties that have been encountered in implementing new approaches to rational management. Despite the application of the 'new management' in the public sector during the last two decades of the century, the police have not been able to stave off the very severe challenges that are now tending to undermine the legitimacy of the institution. The reasons for this are not just matters of will but go to the very heart of the viability of organisational modernity. One key characteristic of modern organisations is their reliance upon rational systems through which 'performance' (understood as outputs and outcomes) is to be attained by the application of resources or 'inputs' (Cooper and Burrell, 1988: 96). Monitoring and audit have sought to ensure that these concepts have become embedded in the routine discourse of public sector management. However, all too often, systematic modernism has substituted instrumental rationality for moral values in its pursuit of measurable ends.

In the management literature, the results-oriented approach first saw light in the work of writers on strategic management such as Drucker (1964) and Ansoff (1965). In policing, modern rational management has been promoted as the method through which an economical, efficient and effective police is to be achieved. Lubans and Edgar's (1979) policing-by-objectives model and Home Office Circular 114/83 both bore the stamp of 'modern' systems thinking. In policing, as in other parts of the public sector, planning was to be geared towards producing measurable results from well-defined goals. During the 1990s, requirements increasingly have been placed upon the police to match local objectives to the goals set centrally by the Home Secretary.

Because of the way in which organisational and personal values have been sidelined by these formal systems, reliance upon extensive audit and performance management has proved to be no guarantee of police legitimacy. Even as means of ensuring effectiveness, the recommended procedures of holistic analysis and action planning have not been an unqualified success. In some police applications they have been little more than presentational strategies (Wright, 1992; Chatterton *et al.*, 1993). Theoretical critiques from March and Simon (1958), Lindblom (1959), Braybrooke and Lindblom (1963), Simon (1976), and more recently Mintzberg (1995), have largely been ignored. Indeed, because they ran counter to the prevailing ideology, it is difficult to see how these critiques could have been accepted, given the political climate of the 1980s and early 1990s.

In practice, convincing evidence linking good policing to formal systems of rational management has also been lacking. Recent downturns in crime, for example, may be attributable as much to a combination of social factors and to good local policing and crime prevention tactics as to systematic strategic planning. Although they rightly suggest that clear objectives are necessary, Stockdale and Gresham (1995) have also highlighted the importance of publicity, intelligence, multi-agency activity and local flexibility as the key to longer-term effective strategies against burglary. Police work remains a matter of managerial skill based upon good information, judgement and co-operation, rather than rigorous conformity to formal-rational systems.

The phenomenon of loose coupling between inputs and outputs has also proved to be a problem in single cases and on a larger scale. Loose coupling can be said to occur when intended outputs or outcomes are confounded by factors beyond the planners' control. This may happen in a single operation. In one case described to the writer, a gang was planning to attack an automatic telling machine (ATM) at a bank using a mechanical excavator. The local crime squad became aware of this through an informant and set up an operation to arrest the suspects as the attack was being carried out. Unfortunately, unknown to the police, the gang aborted the operation just before it was due to start because the only person capable of driving the excavator was taken into hospital suffering from appendicitis. A considerable amount of police resources were deployed on the operation but the circumstances of the 'failure' could not have been reasonably foreseen by the officer running the investigation. Under a system which only rewards achievement, credit could not be given for a well-run operation. On a grander scale, the work of whole units may be affected by 'process' variables that intervene between the planned strategy and the achievement of outputs. These include lack of skills and resources, or poor information systems (Chatterton *et al.*, 1995). Loose coupling can also be brought about by affective factors such as low morale or the existence of racial or other prejudice.

By its over-determined focus upon the instrumental, management-by-objectives and the new management generally has failed to deal with the crucial questions of legitimacy which were already being addressed by criminologists during the 1980s.[1] As proved to be the case with the eighteenth-century thief-taker, Jonathan Wild, who was noted for his interest in 'results' but not for the legitimacy of his methods, results without legitimacy are deeply flawed (Emsley, 1996: 18–19). Although effectiveness is important, because it ultimately depends upon the public providing long-term support for the police, longer-term failures of legitimacy may prove to be the decisive factor in the decline of the public police as an institution.

Policing as social organisation

If modern rational management has failed of itself to provide sufficient grounds to underpin legitimacy, it has been closely followed by a failure to draw upon the lessons to be learned from a range of studies of the culture of workgroups. There is certainly no lack of literature in this field. Scott (1992) points to a range of studies showing how workgroups form powerful social systems. Factors including their functions and structure, in addition to internal and external stimuli, will affect the performance and conduct of such workgroups (Mayo, 1945; Merton, 1957; Parsons, 1960). For Skolnick (1966: 42–70), the working personality of the police officer is affected by relationships inside and outside the police organisation and is particularly influenced by the reality of authority and by the demanding and dangerous nature of the job itself. The currently widespread application of the so-called 'attitude-test' (the way in which a suspect or member of the public initially responds to police as a guide to how police should operate their discretion) provides an example of how workgroup *mores* are more powerful than due process in this respect.

In Britain, the work of sociologists and criminologists including Banton (1964), Holdaway (1979), Chatterton (1983), Fielding (1988), McConville *et al.* (1991), Reiner (1992a, 1992b) and others have variously helped to create a research-based critique illuminating the key factors which affect conduct in police workgroups.[2] Bayley (1994) has also provided a critique of policing sceptical of its widespread 'crime-fighting' ethos. His proposal for a rational police system recommends a new culture of crime prevention where police help to co-ordinate a focused utilisation of community resources. Although Bayley's work retains a reliance upon the idea of rational structures, there are clear departures from earlier understandings of 'modern' rational management. This is a theme to which further reference will be made later in this chapter.

Although this literature should be familiar to policy makers, there is little overt evidence to show that the important lessons of the critical research have been widely recognised. For example, Holdaway's (1991, 1994) work on racism and police recruitment, which was both timely and cautionary, could have provided a compelling platform for understanding and improving attitudes and reducing prejudice. Although training in race awareness was introduced during the early 1980s in the wake of the Scarman inquiry, neither it nor matters of police ethics more generally have previously been accorded a mainstream position in terms of resources or top-level rhetoric. The findings of research into value conflicts in policing (Wright and Irving, 1996), which recommended new methods of training and development, were also largely ignored.

Despite the Statement of Common Purpose (ACPO, 1990), and the fact that some forces have introduced ethical commitments into their public statements, there has been an acute problem of making these effective in the workplace. The abrogation of direction and control has been most evident in the failure of measures for the management of professional conduct. From Scarman onwards, this has often been laid at the door of training rather than supervision and active management of police workgroups. A more important cause of the problems of the management of professional conduct can probably be attributed to organisation factors. An example is to be found in the over-extended use of first-line supervisors (police sergeants) to run custody suites and to supervise the requirements of the Police and Criminal Evidence Act 1984 rather than for intensive operational supervision and guidance. When compared with measures that have sought to promote efficiency and economy, direct management engagement with the problems of professional conduct has often been lightweight. The shortage of highly professional and well-motivated supervisory staff and the absence of strong ethical audit to ensure the health of the police organisation may well be at the root of a variety of problems, including sexual harassment, racism and an increasing number of cases of corruption.

Dinosaurs into chameleons?

Generally speaking, police have been highly skilled in dealing with set-piece events, whether relating to public order or to major disasters. This kind of 'contingency' is well handled by the police. The broader contingencies brought about by political, economic, social and technological change, however, have not been so well handled. Despite measures for public consultation and the preponderance of public surveys aimed at testing public satisfaction with the police, the third crucial failure of the last two decades has been the reluctance seriously to attend to the lessons of the relationship between the police organisation and its working environment. Again, the critical literature has been ahead of the practice.

As long ago as 1967, Lawrence and Lorsch coined the term 'contingency theory' to highlight the symbiotic relationship between an organisation and its environment (Lawrence and Lorsch, 1967). They claimed that organisations should be adaptable to deal with the wide variety of environmental contingencies in order to survive. In police management, however, the more difficult long-term concepts relating to changes in social structure and public attitudes have largely been ignored. The result is that the police increasingly have been strategically unprepared to deal with the most difficult issues, particularly those which concern cultural and ethnic difference. In short, they have not developed the chameleon-like mechanisms for adaptation that will enable them to survive in rapidly changing conditions. The failure to anticipate and to act upon the challenge represented by changing social values is the most compelling indicator of all of the failure of modernity in police management.

Several systematic approaches have been developed for the so-called 'environmental scanning' which is necessary to identify the kinds of contingencies to which organisations should respond (Stoffels, 1994). The importance of these environmental issues has been recognised in academic commentary on policing. For example, Morgan and Newburn (1997: 9–43) include an examination of the changing social context of policing by way of an introduction to their analysis. For policing, the problem is not that information is not available. The difficulty is what is done with it. In fact, a considerable amount of environmental scanning has been carried out by and on behalf of the police. The 1990 Operational Policing Review (Joint Consultative Committee, 1990) included a 'futures' assessment using the PEST model (systematic analysis of the political, economic, social and technological environments). Using a similar approach, the Association of Chief Police Officers (ACPO) has produced an extensive analysis of environmental influences upon the police in England and Wales and their implications at the national level (ACPO, 1996). These documents have tended to remain 'on the shelf', rather than being used in a systematic way to inform practice.

During 1995/6, Staffordshire University facilitated a policing futures forum, providing workshops for researchers and police officers to identify trends affecting the police and to discuss appropriate methodologies (Wright, 1996). This forum was initiated at the behest of middle-ranking practitioners. The programme was discontinued in 1997 at the insistence of ACPO because of possible misunderstandings about its status in the light of their new committee structure. Nothing comparable has yet surfaced to replace it. Many individual police forces (and organisations such as National Police Training) have carried out environmental scanning for their own purposes. A pilot project to provide a long-term database approach to regional scanning was carried out for West Mercia Constabulary during 1996/7 (Kennedy and Wright, 1997). The methodologies for such programmes are well established. What is remarkable about this process, however, is the difficulty which both researchers and police planners have experienced in integrating the products of environmental scanning into planning. This is all the more surprising, given the increasing pace of change and the need for adaptability.

The oracle at Delphi

Recently, the Public Management Foundation has carried out an extensive survey using a Delphi technique[3] to identify factors affecting the future of public services until the year 2008 (Public Management Foundation, 1998). This survey is of relevance to the future of police management. The survey has generated two contrasting scenarios. In the first (more optimistic) scenario entitled 'A Third Way', it is conjectured that the decentralisation of power and economic stability have produced increased prosperity. This has largely been achieved by the shedding of power by central government, the transfer of responsibility to citizens and clearer ideas of partnership and local and regional corporatism.[4]

In the second (more pessimistic) scenario entitled 'Pay as you Go', political power has not effectively been transferred, and there is a great deal of disillusion about politics. Again, the economy is seen as relatively stable, although growth has been modest and there is a widening gap between the rich and the poor. An increase in crime and drug abuse above the level of the 1990s is evident, alongside more family breakdown and truancy. Widespread alienation with the political process has led to protest and Britain has become one of the least cohesive societies in Western Europe.

Table 17.1 paraphrases and compares other aspects of the two scenarios in more detail, showing the distinction between the optimistic and pessimistic extremes.[5]

Table 17.1 Two contrasting scenarios

Area	Scenario 1: 'A Third Way'	Scenario 2: 'Pay as you go'
Government	Confidence retained in political process. Devolution of power to Scottish Parliament and to Assemblies in Wales and the regions. Enabling and monitoring role for central government. Local government retains few core functions: is enabler, not provider. Increased role of 'civil society': not-for-profit organisations provide most services.	Lack of confidence in political process. Haemorrhaging of power has created crisis of English national identity. No proportional representation: no regionalisation in England: state has not 'delivered'. Single-issue campaigns rather than cohesive parties. Local government has shed direct service provision.
Europe	Acceptance that Britain's influence should be exercised through Europe. Lack of resentment of Brussels, Strasbourg and Frankfurt. The euro introduced.	Britain has joined euro. Eastern expansion of EU has hit depressed UK areas. EU directives increasingly affect citizens' lives. Weakening of national government.
The economy	Stability and increased prosperity, much created by information technology. Modest increases in taxation and in public spending. Direct charging for public services. Continued welfare state but through compulsory insurance and pension contributions.	Stable economy, although Britain has fallen behind competitors. Increases in public spending not sustained. Personal taxation as key issue. Long-term unemployment continues. Staff seen as expendable. Continuing squeeze on public services which have rising demands. Rationing and charges in key areas.
Social change	Fall of reported crime: use of 'virtual' incarceration: toleration and marginalisation of racism, homophobia and obsession with family structures. More networking, especially for the elderly.	Widening gap between rich and poor. Social exclusion increased by information technology. Post-industrial malaise. Higher crime, family breakdown, truancy. More people live alone. Large public bodies seen as out of touch.
Employment and education	Labour shortage. Increased self-employment. Gender distinction has withered. Home working and national learning grid are thriving. Increase in educational standards.	Obsession with standards and barrage of critical measurement. Crisis of morale and recruitment. Targeting job creation for low-income families. Education as factory, rather than place of learning.
The environment	Is at centre of public policy. Major cleaner environment projects. Reduction of road transport through disincentives: increase in public transport.	Pressure groups rather than politicians at the forefront. Increasing concern over pollution. Road charging but lack of integrated transport system.

Continued

Area	Scenario 1: 'A Third Way'	Scenario 2: 'Pay as you go'
Citizens	Well informed consumers with greater influence. More active citizens. Rights arguments apply not just to governments but to corporations and public service providers.	Citizens more vocal. Rights still take precedence over responsibilities. Proliferation of small-scale protest. Middle classes protect their homes in siege mentality. Britain one of the least cohesive societies in Europe.

These contrasting scenarios represent a collective 'best estimate' from over 200 opinion-formers drawn from the public services. The panel includes representatives from central and local government, health, education, the police and the judiciary. Both scenarios represent a world quite unlike that of the decades of the 1980s and 1990s. Of course, it is necessary to study and think deeply about the implications of these scenarios, rather than blindly accepting every point. What is striking about them, however, is that despite the fact that one scenario implies versatility, adaptability and responsiveness and the other anxiety and defensiveness, they both accept a trajectory of social and political fragmentation and economic globalisation. In both, the possibility of integrated political, social and economic development has been replaced by pragmatism, pointing to a world that will inevitably become more demanding for what remains of public sector management. Likewise in both, the modern agenda of progress through the application of formal-rational management systems may have to be discarded.

Post-modern police management?

It is clear that much of the scanning and analysis which has been carried out, including that reported above, points to radical change in the political, economic, social and technological environments. Globalisation of commerce and information means that the nation-state itself is under pressure (Rosenau, 1990). Ritzer (1996) has argued that there is an emerging transnational paradigm of consumption, a 'McDonaldisation' of society, which includes the standardisation of products and delivery in ways that ignore local culture and history. Baudrillard (1983) suggests that technology itself can only offer a series of 'models' or 'simulations' which themselves increasingly constitute the reality. Spectacles such as Disneyland become the reality, rather than being separated and distinguished from it. Such claims might be regarded as evidence that the world has moved from a post-industrial to a post-modern phase, although great care must be taken not to indulge in unwarranted labelling of such movements.

Of course, 'post-modernism' is a difficult and controversial term. In one sense it reflects the supposed death of reason and its replacement with a world which questions (or even ignores) modern certainties about meaning, theory and the intellectual capability of the individual 'self'. In this sense, it signifies a deep change in thought patterns and scepticism about the extent to which the world can be controlled by the intellect. Whereas 'modern' constructions seem to suggest that no problem is insurmountable given the right application of science, post-modern thinking is sceptical about such claims. According to Sim (1998: 239), 'One way to define post-modernism is as the end of the enlightenment dream of mastery and definitive improvement to human society, thought, knowledge and technology.' On the surface at least, much of the evidence introduced in this chapter seems to point in this direction.

In a world that may continue to change very rapidly, there is certainly some credible evidence to suggest that policing and police management are changing in ways that challenge their 'modern' status. Organisational certainties are being replaced by new paradigms. As is the case with social change, organisational fragmentation seems to point in the direction of post-modern deconstruction. Initially, there will be a seemingly never-ending imperative for re-organisation, as attempts continue to find workable rational structures. Ultimately, however, there may well be a deconstruction of the old forms of hierarchy. In policing, an early indication of this is the extent to which roles are increasingly being defined by functions rather than by rank. Constables are increasingly taking on jobs which until a few years ago would have been the responsibility of more senior ranks. Interchange between ranks and functions will no longer be found only in specialist fields but also in more general ones such as community safety.

Secondly, for the organisation writ large, there is a seemingly irreversible de-differentiation of roles and functions. Here the term 'de-differentiation' denotes a shift from modern organisations, where the functions of different kinds of organisation are strictly differentiated, to new kinds of organisation where core functions might be shared, diversified or discarded completely (Clegg, 1990). Again, this is becoming increasingly true of the police. Many policing and police management functions will either be transferred to other agencies or out-sourced. The police, for example, already are no longer totally responsible for the enforcement of parking offences which have been taken over by traffic wardens or the local authority. Similarly, the investigation of drugs offences now includes a very substantial (and potentially competing) role for HM Customs and Excise. The Crime and Disorder Act 1998 places increased responsibility upon local authorities for community safety and seeks to involve the private and voluntary sectors in crime prevention. This is the most striking change because of the primacy of the modern police in crime prevention since 1829. The police, in line with many other public-sector institutions, are likely to become enablers for other organisations, rather than the primary providers of particular services.

Thirdly, the notion of risk has been accorded increasing importance. For Beck (1992), contemporary society is obsessed with risk. Douglas (1992) has pointed to the shift from an actuarial understanding of risk based upon statistical probability to risk-perceptions linked to cultural biases. Ericson and Heggarty (1997) have rightly identified the management of risk as a key activity of policing. The police, they argue more controversially, have become 'knowledge workers' in this field, serving a range of other organisations including the insurance and security industries. Policing tasks, including surveillance and identification, increasingly serve this end rather than the ends of criminal justice.

Fourthly, there is a need for the police to respond to the countervailing requirements of different cultures on one hand and the need follow universal principles on the other. One side of this dilemma is represented by the increasing diversity of cultures, communities and life styles with which the police come into contact. Indeed, many 'communities' can no longer be simply defined by geographical location but by *diaspora* or dispersion. Such communities may have cultural expectations which are not represented in the cultural mix of the police service. Bradley (1998) points to the implication of this diversity for police, who may be required to respond differentially to different 'publics'. The other side of this dilemma is represented by the need to develop an ethic of policing which follows the universal principles of human rights. Without considerable effort towards better communication, there will be an ever-widening gap between some communities and police. Without a new reflection upon the purpose of policing, there could be radical conflict between their community-specific and universal responsibilities.

Communication as the key

Organisational fragmentation, functional de-differentiation, risk and cultural diversity all point towards communication as the key management concept in the first decades of the new millennium. This goes far beyond the mere passing of messages or 'marketing'. It implies a move towards shared meaning arrived at through the interpretation of the specific cultural situations of ourselves and others. In various writings, Habermas has argued that communication is the key to the reconstruction of modernity. According to Habermas (1984, 1987), modernity can be reconstructed only by overcoming the systematically distorted communication that is inherent in power relationships. 'Ideal speech situations' provide the possibility of universal truth, in contrast to post-modern relativism and scepticism which is based upon eternal fragmentation.

Similarly, for Reed (1992), theoretical strategies that represent either the possibility of scientific rational management on one hand or the radical relativism of post-modernism on the other are equally flawed. What is required is an improved understanding of modern organisations which live through dialogue and intellectual activity. This reflective dialogue should be characteristic of new ways of organisational thinking.

He says:

> The 1990s seem set to witness a substantial move away from the polarised thinking that has shaped the agenda for and towards a search for intermediation between competing, but nevertheless communicating perspectives, programmes and narratives. (Reed, 1992: 281)

299

This agenda applies to the practice of management as much as to the theoretical understanding of organisations. The phenomenon is continued beyond organisational boundaries.

How does this apply to police management? In discarding the primary reliance upon power relations, police will be moving towards a clearer understanding of the importance of communication. Whereas the old idea of modernity implied human control of society and nature, new understandings will need to include a more symbiotic and discourse-based relationship between police and the policed. This is the sense in which Bayley's 'new rationality' might be interpreted (Bayley, 1994). As such, communication should be the primary concept that configures police management into the new millennium.

In this case, the scenarios set out above can provide a starting point for a new understanding of the enabling and negotiating role of police. This implies a need to develop beyond the crass managerialism which masks power relationships to a more explicit and authentic adoption of the idea of working in and with a diversity of communities. Such a programme implies a diffusion of power. It entails community care rather than surveillance through a new panopticon. It entails the development of skills, knowledge and integrity through lifelong learning (training, education and testing in experience) in working with many cultures. At best, the police become part of these communities at every level, whether of the wider community when working on transnational crime or of specific communities in highly localised surroundings. Inevitably, they will need to look to these communities for support and legitimation.

Over the next 20 years, the policing agenda will no doubt still include issues such as effective performance, future of patrol, equality of service delivery, freedom of information, organised crime and drugs, prevention of terrorism in a liberal democracy, professional integrity and leadership. Although the catalogue of functions[6] discussed in Berry *et al.* (1998) is still appropriate to management in the first two decades of the new millennium, flexibility, adaptability and communication will be the key concepts rather than the formalism which has been characteristic of earlier ideas of 'modern' rational management. A flexible 'portfolio' approach based upon open communication is more likely to ensure survival in the face of rapidly increasing internal and external cultural diversity, than doctrinaire adherence to pre-set plans.

It seems highly likely that we can look forward to a new Police Act or other legislation in 2001 and thereafter, covering many of the things which require immediate legislation. However, what is more difficult (and perhaps impossible to legislate for) is the change in the *ethos* of police management which is concerned with values and a new vision of the future. As might be evident from the above arguments, this will imply a change in mind-set about the very nature of policing. Of course, one might question whether an apparently apathetic and preoccupied public are ready to embrace such a police or whether the police are themselves ready to change: because society may now be so fragmented as to be accurately represented by the sceptical thesis of post-modernity, the task is definitively difficult. The direction of police management will depend on which of the two scenarios described above becomes a reality. A more cautious approach for police management would be to assume and prepare for the more pessimistic of the two. The more constructive approach would be to accept the challenge and to define a new vision of policing which seeks to contribute to the achievement of the positive scenario. Which of these courses of action is adopted will depend upon the quality of police leaders, not just of their own organisations, but as exemplars of civic virtue in the communities they serve.

Notes

1   For an extensive discussion of legitimacy and power that is relevant to the debate upon police legitimacy, see Beetham (1991).
2   This is far from being an exhaustive list of the work of these and other writers in the field.
3   The Delphi technique uses a systematic series of surveys of a continuous panel of well-informed subjects in the relevant field to estimate trends over time.
4   The adoption of the so-called 'third way' in the politics of New Labour in Britain is relevant to this debate and has identifiable theoretical influences (see Giddens, 1994, 1998; Giddens and Pierson, 1998).
5   This paraphrase is no substitute for the document itself. Because of restrictions of space it is inevitably a subjective selection.
6   Managing finance, people, professional conduct, information, managing change and development; managing technology, projects, image.

References

Association of Chief Police Officers (1990) *Strategic Policy Document: Setting the Standards for Policing: Meeting Community Expectation.* London: New Scotland Yard.

Association of Chief Police Officers (1996) *Through the Millennium: The Policing Agenda.* London: ACPO.

Ansoff, H.I. (1965) *Corporate Strategy.* New York: McGraw-Hill.

Banton, M. (1964) *The Policeman in the Community.* London: Tavistock.

Baudrillard, J. (1983) *Simulations.* New York: Semiotext.

Bayley, D.H. (1994) *Police for the Future.* Oxford: Oxford University Press.

Beck, U. (1992) *Risk Society: Towards a New Modernity.* London: Sage.

Beetham, D. (1991) *The Legitimation of Power.* Basingstoke: Macmillan.

Berry, G., Izat, J., Mawby, R.C, Walley, L. and Wright, A. (1998) *Practical Police Management.* 2nd edn. London: Police Review Publishing.

Bradley, R. (1998) *Public Expectations and Perceptions of Policing.* Police Research Series Paper 96. London: Home Office (PRC).

Braybrooke, D. and Lindblom, C.E. (1963) *A Strategy of Decision.* New York: Free Press.

Chapman, B. (1970) *Police State.* Basingstoke: Macmillan.

Chatterton, M.R. (1983) 'Police Work and Assault Charges' in Punch (1983).

Chatterton, M.R., Weatheritt, M. and Wright, A. (1994) *Rational Management in Police Organisations: A Comparative Study in Two Forces.* (Report to ESRC.) Manchester University: Henry Fielding Centre.

Chatterton, M.R., Gibson, G., Gilman, M., Godfrey, C., Sutton, M. and Wright, A. (1995) *Performance Indicators for Local Anti-Drugs Strategies.* Crime Detection and Prevention Series Paper 62. London: Home Office (Police Research Group).

Clegg, S.R. (1990) *Modern Organisations: Organisation Studies in the Post-Modern World.* London: Sage.

Cooper, R. and Burrell, G. (1988) 'Modernism, Post-Modernism and Organisational Analysis: An Introduction', *Organisation Studies*, 9 (1), 91–112.

Douglas, M. (1992) *Risk and Blame.* London: Routledge.

Drucker, P. (1964) *Managing for Results.* London: Heinemann.

Emsley, C. (1996) *The English Police.* 2nd edn. Harlow: Longman.

Ericson, R.V. and Heggarty. K.D. (1997) *Policing the Risk Society.* Oxford: Clarendon.

Fielding, N. (1988) *Joining Forces.* London: Routledge.

Gerth, H.H. and Mills, C.W. (eds) (1970) *From Max Weber.* London: Routledge.

Giddens, A. (1994) *Beyond Left and Right: the Future of Radical Politics.* Cambridge: Polity Press.

Giddens, A. (1998) *The Third Way.* Cambridge: Polity Press.

Giddens, A. and Pierson, C. (1998) *Conversations with Anthony Giddens.* Cambridge: Polity Press.

Habermas, J. (1984) *The Theory of Communicative Action* (Vol. I, Trans. T. McCarthy). London: Heinemann.

Habermas, J. (1987) *The Philosophical Discourse of Modernity.* Oxford: Blackwell.

Hall, S., Critcher, C., Jefferson, T., Clarke, J. and Roberts, B. (1978) *Policing the Crisis: Mugging, the State and Law and Order.* Basingstoke: Macmillan.

Held, D. (1996) *Models of Democracy.* Cambridge: Polity Press.

Holdaway, S. (1979) *The British Police.* London: Edward Arnold.

Holdaway, S. (1991) *Recruiting a Multi-ethnic Police Force.* London: HMSO.

Holdaway, S. (1994) 'Recruitment, Race and the Police Subculture' in Stephens, M. and Becker, S. (eds) *Police Force, Police Service: Care and Control in Britain,* Basingstoke: Macmillan.

Home Office (1983) Circular 114/83. London: Home Office.

Joint Consultative Committee (1990) *Operational Policing Review.* Surbiton: Surrey.

Kennedy, J.A. and Wright, A. (1997) *Environmental Scanning for West Mercia Constabulary: Report on Methodology and Substantive Findings.* Stafford: Staffordshire University Business School (unpublished).

Lawrence, P.R. and Lorsch, J.W. (1967) *Organisation and Environment.* Cambridge, MA: Harvard University Press.

Lindblom, C.E. (1959) 'The Science of Muddling Through', *Public Administration Review,* 19 (Spring), 79–88.

Lubans, V.A. and Edgar, J.M. (1979) *Policing by Objectives.* Hartford, Conn: Social Development Corporation.

McConville, M., Sanders, A. and Leng, R. (1991) *The Case for the Prosecution: Police Suspects and the Construction of Criminality.* London: Routledge.

March, J.G. and Simon, H.A. (1958) *Organisations.* New York: John Wiley.

Mayo, E. (1945) *The Social Problems of an Industrial Civilisation.* Boston: Graduate School of Business Administration, Harvard University.

Merton, R.K. (1957) *Social Theory and Social Structure.* 2nd edn. Glencoe, IL: Free Press.

Mintzberg, H. (1995) *The Rise and Fall of Strategic Planning.* Hemel Hempstead: Prentice Hall.

Morgan, R. and Newburn, T (1997) *The Future of Policing.* Oxford: Clarendon Press.

Parsons, T. (1960) *Structure and Process in Modern Societies.* Glencoe, IL: Free Press.

Public Management Foundation (1998) *The Future for the Public Services: 2008.* London: Public Management Foundation.

Punch, M. (ed.) (1983) *Control in the Police Organisation.* Cambridge, MA: MIT Press.

Reed, M.I. (1992) *The Sociology of Organisations.* Hemel Hempstead: Harvester Wheatsheaf.

Reiner, R. (1992a) '*Fin de Siècle* Blues. The Police Face the Millennium', *Political Quarterly,* 63, 1.

Reiner, R. (1992b) *The Politics of the Police.* Hemel Hempstead: Harvester Wheatsheaf.

Ritzer, G. (1996) '*The McDonaldization of Society*' (revised edn). Thousand Oaks, CA: Pine Forge Press.

Rosenau, J.N. (1990) *Turbulence in World Politics.* London: Harvester Wheatsheaf.

Scarman, Lord (1981) *The Brixton Disorders 10–12 April 1981: Report of an Inquiry by the Rt. Hon the Lord Scarman.* London: HMSO.

Scott, R. (1992) *Organisations: Rational, Natural and Open Systems.* Hemel Hempstead: Prentice Hall.

Scraton, P. (1985) *The State of the Police.* London: Pluto.

Sheehy Report (1993) *Report of the Inquiry into Police Responsibilities and Rewards.* Cm 2280, I, II. London: HMSO.

Sim, S. (ed.) (1998) *Icon Critical Dictionary of Postmodern Thought.* Duxford, Cambs: Icon Books.

Simon, H.A. (1976) *Administrative Behaviour.* 3rd edn. New York: Macmillan.

Smith, D.J., Gray, J. and Small, S. (1983) *Police and People in London.* London: Policy Studies Institute.

Skolnick, J. (1966) *Justice without Trial.* New York: John Wiley.

Stephens, M. and Becker, S. (eds) (1994) *Police Force, Police Service: Care and Control in Britain.* Basingstoke: Macmillan.

Stockdale, J. and Gresham, P.J. (1995) *Combating Burglary: An Evaluation of Three Strategies.* Crime Detection and Prevention Series Paper 59. London: Home Office, Police Research Group.

Stoffels, J.D. (1994) *Strategic Issues Management: A Comprehensive Guide to Environmental Scanning.* Oxford: Pergamon/The Planning Forum.

Waddington, D. (1998) 'Waddington versus Waddington: Public Order Theory on Trial', *Theoretical Criminology,* vol. 2(3), 373–94.

Waddington, P.A.J. (1991) *The Strong Arm of the Law: Armed and Public Order Policing.* Oxford: Oxford University Press.

Waddington, P.A.J. (1994) *Liberty and Order: Public Order Policing in a Capital City.* London: UCL Press.

Wright, A. (1992) 'The Objective-Setting Process: Doomed to Success?'. Paper Presented to Conference on Information Technology and Targeted Police Work, Manchester University, Henry Fielding Centre, September. Unpublished.

Wright, A. (1996) 'Police Research and the Role of the Policing Futures Forum', *Collected Papers from the 3rd National Police Research Conference*. London: Home Office (PRG).

Wright, A. and Irving, B. (1996) 'Value conflicts in Policing. Crisis into Opportunity: Making Critical Use of Experience', *Policing and Society*, 6, 199–211.

Young, J. (1988) 'Radical Criminology in Britain: The Emergence of a Competing Paradigm' *British Journal of Criminology*, 28(2), 289–313.

Chapter 18

Managing the future: a chief constable's view

TONY BUTLER

Introduction

In opposition, the Labour Party proclaimed a policy of being 'tough on crime and tough on the causes of crime'. In the period immediately prior to election they developed a number of themes within their manifesto which took shape rapidly after being elected to government in May 1997. The central plank of this policy has found expression in the Crime and Disorder Act 1998. This major piece of legislation has the potential to change the conceptual framework of crime-reduction strategies and practice. It gives a statutory mandate to a wide range of social agencies to share the responsibility to improve the quality of people's lives by reducing crime and disorder. This long-term approach to solving social problems is particularly evident in the establishment of a provision for national co-ordination of the response to youth offending. However, the process of implementation of this legislation has to be seen in the context of the recent history and change in the police service.

Context

In the first edition of this book, Butler (1996) explored the background to the Conservative government's police reform programme which led to the passing of the Police and Magistrates' Courts Act in 1994, which was subsequently consolidated in the Police Act 1996. The Conservative government's police reform programme provides the context and the contextual framework on which the new Labour government's changes for policing will be based. The most influential changes introduced in April 1995 related to the structure of the police authority and the annual process of performance planning and management. The reduction from in excess of 30 members of the police authority to a maximum of 17 and the introduction of five appointed independent members, has created some interesting changes in police-authority style. There is no doubt that the smaller number of members has led to more opportunities for discussion and dialogue between the senior officers of police forces and their police authority. This dialogue not only takes place in the formal meetings with the authority but increasingly in the context of briefing meetings and seminars where members have an opportunity to study, in depth, specific aspects of policing, the support services, personnel matters and so forth. Consequently, the police authority now have a more knowledgeable base on which to conduct their business. At the time when the Police and Magistrates' Courts Bill was before Parliament, some concerns were raised about the reduction in democratic oversight of policing. Under the previous arrangements two-thirds of the police authority were elected councillors but under the revised arrangements, although they are in the majority, the nine elected members are almost balanced by the five independent and three magistrate members. This change does seem to have reduced some of the party politics in the authority and has generated a more informed debate. In relation to reduced democratic accountability the new authorities have developed close contacts with the community through local consultation arrangements. Overall, the new arrangements appear to be working effectively and have not, apparently, damaged the framework of public accountability.

Another important development in respect of the police authority has been the reorganisation of the representative machinery of local government authorities. The establishment of the Local Government Association in 1997 created one voice for local government. These changes resulted in the demise of the former police authority representative body, CoLPA, which was replaced by the Association of Police Authorities (APA). The formation of the new association provided an opportunity to develop the role of the police authority oversight of policing. The APA has become a more authoritative and knowledgeable voice for the local delivery of police services and this will give added balance to the tripartite structure, particularly in the context of a government which seems to want to become more directive and centralising in its approach to policing.

In respect of performance management and monitoring, the two new elements of key national objectives set by the Home Secretary and local policing plans have provided a useful focus and framework for developing the operational effectiveness of police forces. The key national objectives set by the Conservative administration and their attendant performance indicators were relatively stable during the first three years. This was useful as it allowed the process to bed down and for comparisons to be made year-on-year within police forces. However, there was increasing realisation that the performance indicators were pitched at a tactical level and, since 1998, the Labour administration has moved towards more strategic national objectives now called Ministerial Priorities (Straw, 1998). However, there are still some difficulties with the development of performance indicators which have a high-level strategic focus. The trend is still one of tactical measurement or measures which do not relate directly to performance. This reflects the complexity of the measurement process but also, perhaps, underlines the comfort that ministers may gain from having relatively easy numerical measures on which to base their public comments and gives the illusion of control through demanding increased levels of police performance.

The introduction during August 1998 of the Home Office (1998) Overarching Aims and Objectives adds some interesting dimensions to this process of measurement. The impetus for developing the Overarching Aims and Objectives for the police service was based on the Comprehensive

Spending Review (CSR) (HM Treasury, 1998). The Treasury, apparently, felt uncomfortable in the absence of a framework showing the aims of policing and the underlying objectives. However, accountants and economists have a familiarity with figures which have no disputable definition but they are far more uncomfortable and unfamiliar with the human side of work. They are also unfamiliar with organisational complexity and probably the real world of managing uncertainty. Consequently, their demand for a precisely defined statement of police work in all its areas was only achieved with some compromise for accuracy and the convenient understating of the recognition of the interrelation between social control and organisation structure.

Whilst it is sensible to have a framework of aims and objectives for every public service, the use to which that framework is then committed raises a number of practical and philosophical issues. It would be unrealistic and of potentially little value to attempt to measure every element of policing by means of individual performance indicators. Furthermore, it would be a futile exercise to attempt to place a unit cost on achieving each of these performance indicators. That is not to say that performance in policing should not be linked to the resources deployed, but that it is a far more intellectually challenging exercise than simply reducing policing to a range of performance indicators and a unit cost. The challenge of measuring the resources deployed to policing services and the results achieved will be considered later in the chapter.

Probably the most significant development in respect of performance management was the introduction of the annual policing plan. The potential tension between centrally imposed national objectives and local priorities has been managed to date without too much difficulty. However, that potential still exists and should not be overlooked if there is continuing movement towards central direction by the government. The development of the plan requires a systematic approach to a review of current performance and an assessment of how performance can be developed in the coming year. In those police forces which have suffered reductions in their allocation of funding in the funding-formula arrangements, the planning process has emphasised the need to determine priorities and the financial resources that are required to pursue them. From the perspective of the police authority, they have been involved alongside the police force in seeking the views of the public and they have been parties to the determination of policing priorities and the development of the budget to support them. Through this process police authorities have gained a greater understanding of some of the practical limitations of policing and the police capability and, at the same time, have understood the demands being made on the chief constable and his or her staff to improve productivity and operational performance. The Police Act 1996 contains the seeds of conflict in so far as the Act, in a strict sense, gives the police authority a responsibility to set priorities when it is the chief constable who controls resources to pursue those priorities. Whilst the potential for conflict still exists, since the introduction of policing plans, the spirit of collaboration and joint purpose has ensured that these difficulties have not arisen in practice. Indeed, the process of developing policing plans has acted as a catalyst for bringing the authority and the police force into a shared understanding of the issues and problems.

The annual policing plan has also provided a very useful and objective framework on which the police authority can measure the performance of the police force. All police forces, prior to the introduction of the policing plan, had mechanisms in place for reporting their performance on a regular basis to the police authority, but with the introduction of the policing plan, there is a sense in which the force is making a commitment to targets and the police authority have a means of measuring the extent to which these targets are being met and, where necessary, determine why success has not been achieved. This gives a far more objective framework to the process and can give confidence to the police authority about the extent to which they are meeting their legal mandate on behalf of the community and, furthermore, gives confidence to the chief constable who has a clear framework within which to assess his performance.

The 1990s have seen an accelerating change in police internal structures. Probably the most significant change has been the reduction in senior management ranks; for example, the number of superintendents in the service has declined by some 37 per cent in the last five years. This restructuring has been accompanied by a substantial devolution of responsibilities and management discretion to superintendents and lower ranks. There has also been an introduction of senior civilian professionals at the rank of chief officer. However, of the few Sheehy (1993) proposals that were implemented by the Government, abolition of the rank of deputy chief constable was found to have been accompanied by significant disadvantages, and similar questions were raised about the abolition of the rank of chief superintendent. Both have since been reinstated.

New challenges and opportunities

In a continuing changing world the police service will always be facing new challenges and opportunities. In the medium-term future the Labour government is developing two major policies which will have significant influences on police forces. The first of these policies finds expression in the Crime and Disorder Act 1998, which has the potential to be one of the most significant milestones in developing social control that has been seen for some considerable time. Within the Act the specific provisions for tackling youth crime are a very imaginative combination of dealing with the worst cases of persistent young offenders while, at the same time, making an unequivocal commitment to tackling underlying causes of crime in young people (Home Office, 1998a).

The second policy development reflects the commitment to controlling public expenditure. At first sight, the concepts appear more imaginative than the rather sterile approach taken by the Treasury under the Conservative government. For example, the concept of compulsory competitive tendering has been replaced by the concept of 'best value' (Department of Environment, Transport and Regions, 1998). However, there appears to be the same slavish pursuit by the Treasury of a mechanistic and control mentality to reduce spending on the police service by oversimplifying the realities of police work and its role in the social structure. This is particularly evident in the construction of the 'overarching aims and objectives of policing' which is intended to define in 11 boxes the totality and complexity of policing a modern democratic state at the turn of the millennium (Home Office, 1998).

The major risk to the Labour administration's imaginative developments in terms of crime disorder and youth offending are rooted in the continuing emphasis on public financial constraints. This is not an argument for unlimited funds to develop these initiatives but the crime-reduction policy has two conceptual threads which are complementary to each other. The first is to control current crime and disorder, thereby improving the quality of life for hard-pressed communities. This element of the strategy will consume at least the same amount of resource as at present but there are potentially increased resource demands to respond to the new range of orders and other measures within the Act. The second thread is the imaginative investment in dealing, in a more sophisticated way, with new offenders as they are identified (Home Office, 1998a). There is no doubt that this will require additional resources, not simply for the police but for a range of other agencies such as social services, education, health authorities and so forth. It would be tragic if the Treasury's concern with efficiency savings and cuts in real terms were to prevent an appropriate level of investment in what all the research can confidently predict will be an imaginative way to reduce crime in the future and, in the medium term, substantially reduce the costs of crime to society.

Challenge and opportunity – Crime and Disorder Act 1998

The simultaneous publication of the British Crime Survey (Mirrlees-Black and Allen, 1998) and Annual Home Office Crime Statistics in October 1998 (Povey and Prime, 1998) showed, for the first time, a consistency between crimes recorded by the police and victim surveys. The findings of both reports indicated a decline in the number of crimes being experienced by the public. The police records of crime continued a trend which has extended since 1993. 'Recorded crime has not dropped for five successive years since records began in 1857,' according to the *Guardian* (14 October 1998, p. 21).

There was the inevitable debate as to the underlying causes of these trends. The Conservative government in its later years in office promoted the hypothesis that 'prison works'. The facts would tend to support this notion because over the same period of declining crime rates, the prison population had risen by 50 per cent. However, it is also important to take account of changes to police practice. The most significant change to crime detection has been the development of sophisticated intelligence gathering and analysis which, in turn, has led to targeted operations against specific known offenders. As a result, whereas some years ago an active burglar may have committed well in excess of 100 crimes before being detected, that same offender is now potentially subject to surveillance as he leaves prison and is arrested within days of release if he resumes his criminal activities. Unfortunately, there is growing evidence that habitual burglars and car thieves are driven to sustain a criminal career to finance serious hard-drug addiction. In this sense, prison does work if it enables offenders, who cannot or will not be rehabilitated, to be contained and thus prevented from committing crime.

Although these developments in police tactics have demonstrated significant benefits in reduced crime, they have to be recognised as a short to medium-term solution. The social costs of building more and more prisons are not a sensible or civilised approach to reducing crime. Consequently, the underlying concepts and philosophy of the Crime and Disorder Act have the potential simultaneously to control the current generation of persistent offenders while, at the same time, creating significant opportunities to reduce the potential for the next generation going through the system. The Crime and Disorder Act has two principal components. The first is to engage social agencies and communities in a co-ordinated effort towards eliminating opportunities for crime and assisting the police in dealing more effectively with offenders. The second element is the imaginative co-ordination of what are currently relatively disparate and unco-ordinated responses to young people with behavioural problems and social disadvantage, which start to manifest themselves in crime.

The Act presents some challenges to the police service both practically and financially. The development of crime and disorder plans at district council level introduces a rigorous management framework extending from information gathering to planning through implementation to monitoring and evaluation (Home Office, 1998b). In many police forces, this system of annual planning is well established as part of the force's own management systems. It has been complemented and structured in the context of the annual police authority policing plan which has been mandatory since April 1995. Consequently, the police service is well placed to respond to this planning, implementation and evaluation process.

The challenge for the police service arises in terms of developing relationships with other agencies, the integration of these plans within the overall framework of the broad range of police services and the elements of accountability for performance which will arise from implementing these plans.

In terms of relationships, the chief constable, together with his or her other colleague chief officers in other services, will maintain an accountability for performance of his or her own organisation, but the success of the crime and disorder plans will be highly influenced by the extent to which there is collaboration at operational level. The nature of local government structures will require some variation between and, on occasions, within police forces. Potentially, the simplest structure will be within the metropolitan districts with coterminous boundaries for all the relevant agencies. However, the trend in some forces to subdivide its force into smaller command units raises serious management challenges for the chief constable in co-ordinating a response to a plan which extends beyond an individual command unit. In those police forces based on shire counties, there are added complexities. Where there remains a two-tier structure of county and district councils, there will be a need to co-ordinate services, such as education and social services, delivered on a countywide basis with other services at district level. These complexities become even more potentially problematic in those force areas where there is a mechanism of the two-tier unitary authority structure. Experience will determine how those force models will be managed, but there may be a need for the Home Office to recognise that some police forces may require additional management overheads to deliver the crime and disorder plans because of the complexity of the environment in which they are asked to operate.

The integration of the crime and disorder plans into the police planning process will be influenced by the particular local authority structure. However, there is a more general concern as to the extent to which the police authority annual policing plan can embrace a range of potentially competing demands. The original concept of the policing plan as set out in the Police and Magistrates' Courts Act required a careful balance between the centrally driven national objectives and local priorities and targets but at least the priorities and targets had a degree of consensus across the entire police force. In the future, the annual policing plan will have to acknowledge and include a recognition of a number of other competing and statutory priorities which will be established by the local crime and disorder plan. No doubt these complexities will be managed but, given that plans at all levels are being audited and monitored by the same bodies, it is essential that they do not build conflict into the process. It would be wrong to 'name and shame' a police force for failing to deliver when at a district level the crime and disorder plans were achieving their targets.

These planning complexities also have to take account of limited or declining resources and a greater demand from the Home Office that chief constables should assign a specific proportion of their resources to particular activities, for example the requirement to spend 1 per cent of the police budget on drug referral schemes contained in the Ministerial Priorities (Straw, 1998). Such a demand looks increasingly unhelpful if, in the real world, the chief constable can achieve better results by devolving resources to divisional commanders to enable the local policing objectives to be pursued. There is another issue in relation to resources to the extent that other agencies will be prepared to fund and support their part of the plan. This is particularly relevant to the youth justice provisions of the Crime and Disorder Act.

Crime and disorder plans will be designing out crime through the environment and thereby will be improving the quality of life in neighbourhoods. The approach to youth offending on the other hand is directed towards individual offenders. The approach is to attempt to restrain disorderly and

311

criminal behaviour by direct intervention with the young person and in some circumstances by requiring action by parents. The conceptual strength of the new approach is to require the motivating or causal factors of the offending behaviour to be examined and to integrate action to resolve these issues in the punishment. The legal obligation that will now extend to educational services is a particularly important element of the process. Unfortunately the police service and social services have for too long been left with the difficulties of youth crime with little enthusiasm in many areas for others to become involved. The massive four-fold increase in children excluded from school over the past few years has not been matched with support services for the children and their families. Simply excluding children to commit crime is not a realistic approach to youth offending. There is no doubt that these developments will require additional resources from the police. There may be savings in police time in the future, but in the medium term there will be additional costs without savings elsewhere. However, the extent to which savings are achieved in the future for the police may depend to a very large extent on the willingness of other social agencies to invest resources. The government has said that education is their number one priority. The commitment to raising educational standards for the majority of pupils will have to be matched with funding to help those children who have a range of special educational needs. If the educational system appears not to care for them, we should not be surprised if they take other avenues to achieve status and 'success'.

Challenges and opportunities – 'best value'

During their eighteen-year period in government, the Conservatives consistently portrayed themselves as the party of law and order, but there was apparently growing concern at the end of the 1980s when crime was increasing at an accelerating rate. From 1988 to 1993 there was a very substantial rise year on year in recorded crime in Britain. There is no doubt that this could not simply be explained by changes in police practice, but was a consequence of social and economic change. The continuing relatively high levels of unemployment and the disintegration of many of the social institutions which controlled behaviour were becoming of concern during that period. The Conservative government had two choices, the first to accept responsibility for changes to the social structure which had influenced crime, or else to look around for someone to blame for rising crime. Not surprisingly, the government chose the second option and targeted the police service. Their police reform programme was preceded by a strong media campaign challenging the competence of senior police officers and, in particular, alleging that poor return was being given for the money being invested. The Conservative government promoted a market-forces framework for policing and, at one point, through their 'core and ancillary task' project, saw an opportunity to sell off significant parts of police services to the private sector. Although this turned out to be an ill-fated exercise, it serves to illustrate the extent to which the government believed, as the reform document stated, that 'the main job of the police is catching criminals' (Home Office, 1993), the implication being that everything else is ancillary to that task and not a central concern of the police. This showed a somewhat sterile approach to police work and a substantial lack of understanding of the social dimensions of the role of the police, which had been documented by a significant volume of social research.

The Labour government's approach to gaining value for money from public services is somewhat more sophisticated. Their concept of 'best value' (Department of Environment, Transport and Regions, 1998) does not simply focus on cost but is underpinned with a need to determine, from the community, levels of service and requires the regime to acknowledge the role of quality in public services. However, the danger, once again, lies in the single-mandate approach to cutting social expenditure which may be attractive in the short term but could be potentially very damaging in the medium term. In the last five years, the police service, in collaboration with other agencies, has made a significant cut in recorded crime. In some areas, recorded crime is returning to those levels seen before the relative explosion in crime in the late 1980s. However, this has been achieved at a cost through the investment in the more sophisticated targeting of persistent offenders and controlling them through prison sentences.

The 'best value' (BV) regime was introduced in April 2000. The police service had three pilot sites which were used to test the concepts and process, and was fortunate in that the BV performance management framework mirrors very closely the arrangements for developing the annual policing plan and the methods through which the plan is monitored. The additional dimensions relate to the consequences of failing to achieve targets and the extent to which the government reserves the right to intervene to support or replace local management. It is uncertain as to how this could affect the police, given the operational independence of chief constables and the legal position that they occupy.

Although BV was not implemented across the service until April 2000, the demands for greater efficiencies in policing were implemented from 1 April 1999, with the introduction of what have been called 'Efficiency Plans' (Straw, 1998). When the Comprehensive Spending Review was published in July 1998, the Home Secretary announced that spending on the police would increase by 2.65 per cent in 1999/2000, by 2.8 per cent in 2000/2001, and by 4 per cent in 2001/2002.

In relation to 1999/2000, the figure of 2.65 per cent was clearly well below the expenditure forecasting report which calculated a requirement of 6.1 per cent to cover inflation and new demands on the police service. The settlement was even well short of the 4 per cent increase in salary costs that were agreed for the police in September 1998. Consequently, the Home Secretary had a presentational problem. A major piece of legislation to control crime and disorder which required the unequivocal support of the police service was coming into force at a time when there was a substantial shortfall in the funding of police forces. To bridge this presentational gap, the Home Secretary announced the requirement for the police service to make efficiency savings of 2 per cent a year starting in April 1999, to run for the next three financial years. In making these efficiency savings, the Home Secretary said that the number of staff employed by police forces was not to be reduced. Consequently, there was an implicit assumption that the entire saving was to be achieved from the 15 per cent of the police budget which is spent on costs other than staff, something which, on any analysis, was a challenging and almost impossible target.

It is possible that savings of this magnitude could be made by some police forces, but as the Audit Commission Performance Indicators for Police Services published in January 1998 (Audit Commission, 1998) pointed out, during the previous four years six police forces had had a cut in real terms in their budgets and a further four had no increase at all. In fact, the Audit Commission's approach contains a very significant conceptual flaw. The police funding formula introduced from April 1995 used three elements to calculate the allocation of funding to individual police forces. The cost of police pensions was based on the government actuary's assessment of the anticipated cost of paying existing police pensioners during the coming year. A second element related to the cost of specific security commitments, for example the personal protection of the homes of government ministers and the Royal Family outside of London. These payments were based on a return of the actual cost to individual police forces. Consequently, the costs of paying police pensions and providing security were not capable of being controlled by individual police forces, and this was accepted in the construction of the formula. The third element was a 'needs-based' calculation using a number of social and demographic factors said to be related to demand for police services. By separating these three elements a very different picture of police funding emerges between 1995 and 1998. All but two shire police forces in England and Wales had a reduction in real terms in their needs-based allocation. The apparent increases in funding were entirely consumed by increased costs of pensions and, in some forces, security commitments. In the case of one police force, the real cut in the needs-based element was 8 per cent over the four years. In these circumstances, efficiency savings of the magnitude being required without manpower cuts were likely to be untenable.

To some extent, the police service has become a victim of the complexity of attempting to link resources to results. Unfortunately, there has been a tendency, particularly once again by the Treasury, to grossly under-estimate the complexity of police work as an activity, which is highly integrated into a significant range of social institutions and processes. This rather limited and unimaginative view of the contribution of policing to the social fabric of this country has not been helped by comments from the Audit Commission and HM Inspectorate of Constabulary. One of the main justifications for claiming the ability to achieve two per cent efficiency savings comes from Her Majesty's Inspector of Constabulary's Report, *What Price Policing* (HM

Inspectorate of Constabulary, 1998). There were several important limitations within this report which took generalised concepts and gave them credibility beyond what could be supported by the objective evidence. Unfortunately, there seems to have been an element of finding the facts to fit the theory, the theory being that all police forces are inherently inefficient, and that there is a blanket approach to making them more efficient. This blanket approach is to impose a two per cent efficiency saving on every force irrespective of its current and past performance. The HM Inspectorate report stated that every police force could make savings by reducing sickness absence, reducing medical retirements, reducing the number of management ranks, reducing training costs, improved estate management and improving procurement. The report acknowledged that performance varies between police forces but the 2 per cent saving makes no such differentiation. The unfortunate consequence of this approach is potentially to 'punish' those police forces which had made significant efficiency gains in the recent past because they would not have the same scope for further improvements. For example, what about the police force which, in the face of a real cut in the operational budget of 8 per cent, had reduced the number of superintendents to the lowest in the country, had almost the lowest number of medical retirements, lower than average training costs and lower than the national average sickness absence rates? Where was this police force going to find the 2 per cent saving without reducing staffing numbers?

There was a second significant problem with the HM Inspectorate report. There was a dual assumption that it was possible to develop accurate systems which would enable the cost of police activities to be calculated with a degree of accuracy which would allow for comparisons between police forces. It was argued implicitly that this unit costing approach would in itself bring cost savings. The report described six approaches to the calculation of costs. All these systems were different and used different definitions and costing methods. The approaches were based on the Home Office activity sampling method introduced in 1992 (Home Office, 1992). The question of the accuracy of this method of resource calculation was the subject of a national study co-ordinated by the Home Office. The report (Home Office, 1993) confirms unequivocally that activity sampling could not be used as a reliable and valid method of calculating the costs of specific activities. The problem arises principally by accurately measuring the contribution made by a range of staff to the totality of the delivery of a specific service. There is some possibility of measuring in the broadest sense the resources expended to respond to an incident and the ancillary administration undertaken by the officer responding, but thereafter the measurement becomes extremely problematic. Therefore, the pursuit of the 'unit cost' of a burglary investigation, for example, is impossible to calculate with any degree of accuracy. Consequently, it would be pointless and dangerous to make any comparisons between police forces using these data.

The worst case scenario which could arise from this conceptually limited approach is the enforcement of blanket efficiency demands reinforced by spurious links between resource costs and performance. This approach could easily develop into a 'management-by-atrocity' culture on the part of central government, aided and abetted by the Audit Commission and Her Majesty's Inspectorate of Constabulary. The consequent damage to the services provided by the police and public confidence in the police would be tragic for all concerned.

Responding to the challenges and seizing opportunities

The strength of the Crime and Disorder Act lies in its combination of pragmatism and vision. It is pragmatic in the sense that it relates to the real issues being experienced by people whose lives are damaged by crime and disorder, or the fear of being a victim of crime and disorder. The vision recognises that something can be done to improve the quality of life by tackling the causes of crime and disorder and developing communities that can sustain these improvements into the future. The biggest folly the government can commit is to believe that they can 'order' the delivery of the benefits. They should pause for a moment and reflect on the damage that was inflicted on the image and status of public services by their predecessors. There are very important lessons in the current difficulties which the government has in recruiting teachers and nurses. Salaries may be a factor in encouraging nurses to move from the Philippines to hospitals in England, but all the research into motivation at work demonstrates that wages are a marginal influence on job satisfaction and morale. The need to find an additional billion pounds to attract high-flying graduates into teaching might not have been necessary had the teaching profession not been the victim of a process of almost continuous public denigration over the past few years. There are also some important lessons on the limits which charters and performance indicators have on actually influencing the quality of services (Hall, 1998), and debate still surrounds the annual publication of school-examination league tables (Carvel and Smithers, 1998).

Although charters and performance indicators may have a limited impact on real increases in performance, they can have a range of influences on the behaviour of staff, and some of these influences may be perverse. The police control-room operator will be influenced by the need to respond to emergency calls within a target time, and as a consequence may not take time to elicit all the relevant information. This influence also extends to officers responding to calls. They feel under pressure to deal with incidents as quickly as possible to be available to respond to the next call within the target time. Consequently, achieving the target time may adversely affect victim satisfaction or the potential to detect crimes by inadequate primary investigation. This is not an argument for abandoning performance indicators and targets, but it is a plea for realism and to see them as an aid to improving services rather than an end in themselves, which they can become through the annual publication of league tables (Reiner, 1995). The government should be careful not to be seduced by the attraction of central command and control. Local problems require local action which is not distorted by unrealistic demands.

The government have set out implicitly in the Crime and Disorder Act a vision of what they want to see changed in respect of the quality of life in communities. The financial framework has been defined in the Comprehensive Spending Review and will be monitored through the mechanisms of Best Value. The skill will be to manage the process in such a way to allow the people who can deliver results to get on with the tasks free from overbearing control and scrutiny. The critical success factor in this process will be, in respect of the police service, the men and women responsible for making it happen. Chief constables will have a vital role to play in creating opportunities for these staff to deliver improved services for less cost. Chief constables will also have a responsibility to ensure that their staff do not become alienated by the process.

The potential for staff to feel undervalued will arise from a number of sources. The publication of the inquiry report into the death of Stephen Lawrence has had a profound effect on the public's perception of the fairness of police officers. The apparently conflicting views expressed by senior police officers to the inquiry was not helpful. The critical issue will be to determine how public confidence in the police can be improved generally, and particularly in ethnic minority communities. The wholesale criticism of police officers with blanket claims of racism will not necessarily contribute to this process. There needs to be an objective analysis of the issues to determine the options to improve police relationships. Returning to the comparison with school teachers, the wholesale condemnation of the profession has not been the most successful strategy for attracting and retaining highly committed teachers with a sense of vocation. A similar approach is unlikely to evoke a different response from the police service. That is not to say that there are not important issues to be confronted and solved, but it would be a tragedy if, as a matter of course, all police officers were branded as racist and, as a result, victims of racially motivated crime and harassment became even more reluctant to report those incidents to the police. There is a need to build confidence, not destroy it.

The future funding of the police service represents another potential source to undermine the confidence and motivation of police staff. It is not the absolute spending on the police service that is the issue, it is the misrepresentation of what is happening to funding. The assertion by the Audit Commission (1998) that funding has increased for the majority of police forces, misrepresents the reality of the opportunity for money to be spent on front-line services. It does not help the motivation and morale of staff in those police forces which have suffered significant cut-backs in funding in real terms, but which at the same time have contained increasing workloads and become more effective in reducing crime, to be told to 'shape up' and do better on the basis that they have had more money. Similarly, the production of national league tables of performance covering a limited part of the wide range of policework does not impress officers who ask themselves why other equally important areas of their work are not measured. In reality, local communities and the police authority pay little regard to the national performance indicators. There is more concern with how the police are seen to be contributing to the quality of life in neighbourhoods than globally. The latter may be of interest to the Audit Commission and the government, but not to the people who are receiving the service locally. However, the damage that can be done to the commitment of staff, their self-esteem and morale should not be underestimated.

Looking to the future

The government has set out its medium-term vision to achieve a more effective police service at a significantly lower cost. The measurement of success will apparently be judged on the basis of a suite of performance indicators covering all aspects of the 'Overarching Aims and Objectives'. The achievement of this vision presents some formidable challenges to the government. These challenges arise in the main from the methods it employs to implement the strategies. Commentators point to the government's belief in the ultimate power of being in control of events, processes and people. Unfortunately, this view of the world can lead to the selective use of information. The rhetoric which accompanied the police budget allocation in 1998 had all the hallmarks of seeking to sustain a theory in spite of the facts (Dean, 1998). The assertion that universal capping had been abolished had something of a hollow ring with the actual imposition of penalties for authorities arising from the payment of housing benefit subsidy, if a precept was increased in excess of four and a half per cent.

Further evidence of the command and control culture can be seen in the speeches of government ministers. There is a growing paradox arising from the devolved management regimes employed by police forces being undermined by government directing police tactics. The Prime Minister in his conference speech exhorted police forces to employ 'zero tolerance' methods of policing (White, 1998). The Home Secretary told the Annual Conference of Superintendents that if police forces did not meet tough performance targets, he would send in hit squads to improve the management (Jenkins, 1998). This threat was repeated by the Home Secretary in a report of the APA Conference in November 1998 (*Police Review*, 13 November 1998). Commenting on the implementation of Best Value, Mr Straw is reported as saying '... if local service providers are demonstrated not to be delivering policing to the required standard, they should not be allowed to carry on'. It is not clear how the removal of a police authority could constitutionally change the operational policies of a chief constable.

In addition to this central direction, the policy is now developing to attempt to manage service delivery directly from the Home Office. As part of the defence to real cuts in policing funding, the Home Office is offering limited direct funding for 'crime-reduction' projects. The first was announced by the Home Secretary in October 1998, and was followed by an invitation to bid for money. 'The Crime Reduction Programme: Reducing Burglary' invited bids directly from 'local (police) commanders' supported by their local authority (Boateng, 1998). The bid required signed undertakings, including the requirement to maintain the resources deployed on the project after the Home Office funding had ceased. Further bids were also invited for funding for targeted patrol initiatives. The question here is not whether additional money should be made available for the reduction of crime, the point is the process. The police authority policing plan and the chief constables' management responsibilities are being circumvented. Furthermore, there is the very important question about the legal status of a signed undertaking by a police commander. Can a police commander give an undertaking to maintain resources which are not under his or her ultimate control? Is the government demanding the *de facto* ring fencing of parts of the police authority's budget for purposes that it, the government, defines? That is the implication of these signed agreements.

What are the future implications for accountability for performance? If police forces follow the Prime Minister's direction to adopt 'zero tolerance' policing (White, 1998), and it does not deliver significant improvements in overall police effectiveness, who will be responsible? In this culture, what will be the government's response to dissenting arguments? On the question of the value of zero tolerance, the case is far from clear and furthermore there are some powerfully argued challenges to its value (Pollard, 1997 and Jordan, 1998). Will dissent be seen as simply obstruction, an example of using 'zero imagination', in the words of the Prime Minister, or will any questioning be seen as a response from 'a miserable bunch of sneering cynics', as teachers were allegedly called by the Education and Employment Secretary (White, 1998).

Perhaps the government and particularly the Home Office might wish to consider the advice that the Audit Commission gave to police authorities in the context of clarifying roles (Audit Commission, 1994). Police authorities were urged to limit their direction to chief constables by concentrating on *what* they wanted the police force to achieve. It was a matter for chief constables to decide *how* they would achieve these desired outcomes. This is sound advice because experience demonstrates that the people who are expected to deliver results are more likely to know how to achieve them than some person relatively distanced from the source of the problems.

References

Audit Commission (1994) *Cheques and Balances: A Framework for Improving Police Accountability.* London: Audit Commission.

Audit Commission (1998) *Local Authority Performance Indicators: Police Services.* London: Audit Commission.

Boateng, P. (1998) 'The Crime Reduction Programme: Reducing Burglary', Home Office letter, 10 November.

Butler, A.J.P. (1996) 'Managing the Future: A Chief Constable's View' in Leishman, F.,

Loveday, B. and Savage, S.P. (eds) Core Issues in Policing. 1st edn. Harlow: Longman.

Carvel, J. and Smithers, R. (1998) 'Tables Warp Teaching, Warn Heads', *Guardian*, 1 December, 4.

Dean, J. (1998) 'Counting the Cost', *Policing Today*, September, 12–13.

Department of Environment, Transport and Regions (1998) *Modernising Local Government: Improving Local Services through Best Value*. London: DETR.

Hall, C. (1998) 'The Debate Starts Here, Admits the Charter Author', *Daily Telegraph*, 10 December, 19.

HM Inspectorate of Constabulary (1998) *What Price Policing: A Study of Efficiency and Value for Money in the Police Service*. London: Home Office.

HM Treasury (1998) *Modern Public Services for Britain: Investing in Reform*. Cm 4011. London: The Stationery Office.

Home Office (1992) *Police Activity Sampling: Manual of Guidance on Conducting Activity Sampling Exercises within Police Forces*. London: Home Office.

Home Office (1993) *Police Reform: A Police Service for the Twenty-First Century*, Cm 2281. London: HMSO.

Home Office (1998) 'New Overarching Aims and Objectives Take Police into New Millennium', Home Office Press Office, 5 August.

Home Office (1998a) *Crime and Disorder Act 1998: Youth Justice*. London: Home Office Communications Directorate.

Home Office (1998b) *Guidance on Statutory Crime and Disorder Partnerships: Crime and Disorder Act 1998*. London: Home Office.

Jenkins, C. (1998) 'Squads to Ensure Value Targets are Met', *Police Review*, 25 September, 15.

Jordan, P. (1998) 'Effective Policing Strategies for Reducing Crime' in Nuttal, C., Goldblatt, P. and Lewis, C. (eds) *Reducing Offending: An Assessment of Research Evidence on Ways of Dealing with Offending Behaviour*. London: Home Office Research and Statistics Directorate.

Mirrlees-Black C. and Allen, J. (1998) *Concern about Crime: Findings from the 1998 British Crime Survey*. Research Findings No. 83. London: Home Office Research, Development and Statistics Directorate.

Pollard, C. (1997) 'Zero Tolerance: short-term fix, long-term liability' in *Zero Tolerance: Policing a Free Society*. London: The Institute of Economic Affairs Health and Welfare Unit.

Povey, D. and Prime, J. (1998) *Notifiable Offences in England and Wales, April 1997 to March 1998*. London: Home Office Research, Development and Statistics Directorate.

Reiner, R. (1995) 'Policing by numbers: The feel good fallacy', *Policing Today*, 1 (3), 22–4.

Rutter, M. Giller, H. and Hagell, A. (1998) *Antisocial Behaviour by Young People*. Cambridge: Cambridge University Press.

Sheehy P, (1993) *Inquiry into Police Responsibilities and Rewards*. Cmnd 2280.I. London: HMSO.

Straw, J. (1998) 'Ministerial Priorities, Key Performance Indicators and Efficiency Planning for 1999/2000', Home Office letter, 4 November.

White, M. (1998) 'Blair's Blitz on Crime', *Guardian*, 29 September, 1.